ARCHITECTS
OF
ILLUSION

ARCHITECTS OF ☆ ☆ ☆ ILLUSION

Men and Ideas in American Foreign Policy 1941-1949

BY LLOYD C. GARDNER

CHICAGO
QUADRANGLE BOOKS
1970

For Nancy

 For information, address: Quadrangle Books, Inc., 12 East Delaware Place, Chicago 60611. Manufactured in the United States of America. Published simultaneously in Canada by Burns and MacEachern Ltd., Toronto.

Library of Congress Catalog Card Number: 69-20163

With the discovery of America, West Europe became a province in a gigantic whole. Thenceforward the history of the Western Culture has a *planetary* character.

—Oswald Spengler, *The Decline of the West*

Small islands not capable of protecting themselves are the proper objects for kingdoms to take under their care, but there is something very absurd, in supposing a continent to be perpetually governed by an island. In no instance hath nature made a satellite larger than its primary planet, and as England and America with respect to each other reverses the common order of nature, it is evident they belong to different systems; England to Europe, America to itself.

—Thomas Paine, *Common Sense*

. . . The fact is that Franklin Roosevelt failed to make American democracy work successfully on a narrow, materialistic basis. Our only chance now to make it work is in terms of vital international economy and in terms of an international moral order.

—Henry Luce, *The American Century*

The West has won two "total victories" in this century and it has barely survived them. America, especially, fought the two world wars in the spirit of a righteous crusade. We acted as if we had come to the end of history, as if we had only to destroy our enemies and then the world would enter a golden age of peace and human happiness. Some of the problems that spawned the great wars were in fact solved by our victories; others were simply forgotten. But to our shock and dismay we found after 1945 that history had not come to an end.

—J. William Fulbright, *The Arrogance of Power*

PREFACE

On June 15, 1945, General Dwight Eisenhower held a last news conference in Paris before returning home from his "Crusade in Europe." The atmosphere in the conference room grew tense, a *New York Times* writer observed, when a correspondent said: "There seems to be a large campaign . . . to talk about a Russo-American war. There is nothing in your experience with Russia that leads you to feel we cannot cooperate with them perfectly?" "On my level, none," answered Eisenhower. He had found the individual Russian to be one of the friendliest persons in the world.

Twenty-five years later, on the anniversary of D-Day, another *Times* reporter, C. L. Sulzberger, recalled that when American forces met the advance units of the Red Army deep in Germany, "the latter proved to be a battered, rag-tag outfit, and, Eisenhower said, 'We could have licked the hell out of them.' But he had to stop at the Elbe, which was already far to the east of the political line dividing Germany fixed by the political leaders."

In 1952 Americans called upon Eisenhower to end the Korean War and, less certainly, to reassert America's "moral" leadership. There was a growing feeling in the early 1950's that while Russia was obviously responsible for most of the evil in the world, American mistakes and shortsightedness had brought on the Cold War. Americans were badly divided about whom to blame for these mistakes, and badly divided, too, about their image of Eisenhower. Some quite clearly wanted the man who believed he could get along with the Russians; some just as keenly wished for a man who thought, "We could have licked the hell out of them," but had been restrained by the "politicians." Eisenhower's sponsors in the Republican hierarchy put him forward as a man who could do either.

Even Democratic stalwarts admitted that the Truman-Acheson "containment" policy was constricting American freedom of action as much as or more than it was checking Russian expansion. It made American leaders prisoners of their critics, who were only too happy to exploit every instance where reality failed to conform to their illusions. Under Eisenhower, John Foster Dulles promised to "liberate" the country and the world from the compromising policies pursued by Truman and Acheson, policies which had abandoned 800 million people to Soviet imperialism; in the end, all he did was turn the coin over, leaving the policies intact and the criticisms unanswered. What Dulles proved beyond doubt was that containment had not really met the challenge in Europe and was ludicrous in the "Third World" of uncommitted nations. As the 1950's, then the 1960's passed into history, fewer and fewer policy-makers would admit ever having supported "containment," though the policy went on under a variety of different euphemisms. Despite the pounding it had taken from waves of criticism, each higher than the last, it still stood, though Americans were obviously weary of manning the "ramparts of freedom," and were questioning the need for so many fortresses in far-off places.

The men discussed in this book, the architects of American policy in the years during and after World War II, stood at the juncture of the most fateful confrontation in American history. Behind them lay the fragments of collective security in the 1930's, more than a decade of world depression and disorder, and 150 years of deep suspicion of European diplomacy which had characterized American "liberalism" since 1776. Around them much of Europe was ruined or at least buried under the rubble and debris of war. Great Britain had fallen back against its ramparts, gasping for enough breath to launch a new social policy to save itself from disaster. Asia was aflame with the nationalism released by Japan's defiance and defeat of the white man's colonial myths at Singapore in 1942. The defeated powers were temporarily prostrate, open to whatever military rule the victors might impose upon them—but anxious to be part of whatever new order was to dominate the world. Before American policy-makers lay the task of peacemaking in a world polarized by war and politics, want and plenty, capitalism and socialism.

Each of the architects of American policy tried to make sense of this confrontation of past tradition with contemporary definitions of the national interest and the perplexing challenge of the Soviet Union. They did not really know how the Russians would behave after victory. Some wanted them to behave as partners in the construction of a capitalist world order, in exchange for economic aid in rebuilding the Soviet Union. Others preferred as little contact as possible with them. But none of these men wanted communist doctrine to spread—even into Eastern Europe. When it did, or seemed to be doing so, most American leaders assumed it was a question of ideological warfare, not Russian national interests. The Russians, on the other hand, seemed surprised that Washington made any fuss about Eastern Europe, especially since Stalin after the war had turned his back on the Greek partisans and sent the Chinese Communists home with no encouragement.

If Eastern Europe had been the only issue, however, there probably would have been no Cold War. From the beginning of the war, the most common fear shared by American leaders was their concern about Anglo-Russian "deals" or secret treaties to divide Europe into "spheres of influence," thereby preempting American policy which was based on economic assets. Roosevelt had died without resolving *any* of the crucial issues of the peace, so Eastern Europe became the locus of a broader conflict. While postwar planning, particularly in the economic field, was well advanced at his death, none of the political or economic institutions that had been designed to restore world order could function until these issues were settled, either by Big Three action or by unilateral decision. Only the United States had the power to enforce its decisions world-wide, but using that power in Eastern Europe or in China might involve unacceptable costs and risks. In this complex and contradictory situation, American policy-makers developed a series of rationales, expedients, and explanations which grew into the myths and illusions of the Cold War. And men were later beguiled by their own creations.

The men discussed in this book functioned at a variety of levels in the American policy-making community. They were not equally involved in the decision-making process, and I make no effort to consider them individually except in the context of key issues, where they acted upon or were influenced by ideas. The most traditional of them, William C. Bullitt, was regarded by the administration as something of a nuisance after the war, yet for the purposes of this book he is taken at his word, i.e., he is the "concrete universal" of traditional American attitudes toward Europe. General George C. Marshall, to take another example, found himself in a totally nontraditional situation in China; his foredoomed effort to find a realistic policy compatible with traditional goals was built into a horrible illusion by Bullitt and others who refused to accept the reality of events in that country. The prism through which Americans viewed the postwar world was completed with George Kennan's 1947 article, "The Sources of Soviet Conduct," written for *Foreign Affairs* under the pseudonym of "Mr. X." Instead of breaking down reality into its component elements, this prism refracted them according to the viewers' preconceptions and needs.

What follows is not a history of the Cold War. I make no pretense of offering it as such, nor of examining the "other side's" illusion-makers, except in general terms. The book is premised on the assumption that the United States was more responsible for the *way* in which the Cold War developed, a conclusion which appears even in those books which argue that the United States was merely responding to a Russian challenge. It is a conclusion taken from a simple comparison of the Russian and American situations at the end of the war, a comparison which, on any level or by any index, was favorable to the United States. For example, the American decision to demobilize its conventional forces at the end of the war and rely instead upon the "bomb" for its security profoundly influenced the way in which the Cold War developed. Neither side could fully control events, or even freely respond to them in many instances. But to see the Cold War as a struggle between two scorpions in a bottle reduces history to a cast of witless characters. This book is an effort to establish the major influences on key American policy-makers as the Cold War began and developed to 1949.

Long passages of this book originated in dialogues with friends and professional colleagues. While it is impossible to try to pinpoint the discussions that stimulated the principal themes and ideas, I do want to acknowledge special debts to Barton J. Bernstein of Stanford University, Gaddis Smith of Yale, and Carl Kaysen, director of the Institute for Advanced Study at Princeton, for the opportunity to participate in a seminar on the origins of the Cold War, and to the Graduate Student History Association of the City University of New York for inviting me to participate in a lively debate on this same question with Professors Arthur M. Schlesinger, Jr., and Phillip E. Mosely.

Ivan Dee of Quadrangle Books has been wrestling with each chapter, from first draft to last; his victories will be appreciated by readers. His faith in the book has exceeded the normal obligations of an editor, or a friend. He is the best of both.

The research staffs of all the libraries where I have worked on this book have been of immense help in its completion. My most permanent debts are to Walter LaFeber, Thomas McCormick, Fred Harvey Harrington, David Jennings, and William Appleman Williams. And, finally, I dedicate it to my wife, Nancy, who had to put up with grumpy moods and closed doors while it was being written.

L.C.G.

East Brunswick, New Jersey

CONTENTS

ARCHITECTS OF ILLUSION

ONE ☆☆

William C. Bullitt: Thomas Jefferson in Moscow

"Don't let Churchill get you into any more specific engagements than those in the Atlantic Charter." This warning came to President Roosevelt from the former Ambassador to the Soviet Union, William C. Bullitt, in a handwritten note dated December 5, 1941. "Try to keep him from engaging himself vis-à-vis Russia," Bullitt cautioned the President. "The treaties—if made—will be as difficult for you to handle as the secret treaties were for Wilson."[1]

Bullitt's letter was a concise restatement of traditional American suspicions of European diplomacy, especially British maneuverings. As long ago as 1776, Tom Paine had insisted that it was only "Common Sense" to recognize that America had first to declare its independence from British imperial interests before it could be independent of political entanglements with the rest of Europe. The new nation, Paine had said, could exercise its full influence for political freedom at home and economic liberty abroad only if it managed to steer clear of compromising connections with Old World powers. This advice represented the central meaning of the American Revolution against and away from Europe, its secret alliances and its every mode of thought. It was around Paine's famous pamphlet that American leaders built their traditional foreign policy in succeeding generations.

As Bullitt warned Roosevelt, Woodrow Wilson's ordeal at

Versailles had begun with the confrontation of these traditions and secret Allied war aims. Wilson had some knowledge of the secret treaties but hesitated to denounce the pacts publicly for fear he would lose Allied support for the proposed covenant of a League of Nations. His disgruntled and impatient advisers at Paris demanded he find a way to "handle" the secret treaties, as Bullitt later put it, without abandoning the League. When he could not, they turned their fury upon the besieged President.

Traditional American liberalism was also challenged at Versailles by the newest revolution, the Bolshevik upheaval in Russia. By the time of the European armistice, it threatened to spread into Central Europe and Germany. Wilson had set forth his position on violent revolutions in Europe as a young man in 1889, in an address "On the One Hundredth Anniversary of the Inauguration of George Washington." "For us this is the centennial year of Washington's inauguration," he declared, "but for Europe it is the centennial year of the French Revolution. One hundred years ago we gained, and Europe lost, self-command, self-possession." After agonizing over the Bolshevik Revolution, Wilson still based his policy on that premise. The dramatic events of November 1917 convinced him that the League of Nations was the only way to make the world safe for American democracy, and democracy safe for America. Wilson believed that the solution to both problems—imperialism and social revolution—was not to abandon traditional American policy, which some commentators mistakenly called "isolationism," but to enlarge it into a League of Nations. Put less parodoxically, only after the covenant had been made could the old snarl of entangling alliances be undone and a decent international order woven for the first time. "What we are about to supply," the President said upon his return from Paris, "is an arrangement which will disentangle all the alliances in the world."

The argument he used was a subtle one, not really suited to effective political discourse. Wilson's eloquence notwithstanding, exposure of the secret pacts among the Allies and the vagueness of America's proposed commitments under Article Ten of the League Covenant perturbed a great many of his fellow countrymen who had no wish to be pulled into any future crusades to save British and French investments in the Middle East or protect Japanese "rights" in Shantung.

Despite his continuing public insistence that the only effective way to deal with these problems and those of social revolution was through the League, Wilson himself became increasingly bitter at Allied policies after the victory over the Central Powers and the beginning of the struggle over the spoils of the Ottoman Empire. In the aftermath of the Treaty debate in America, Assistant Secretary of State Norman Davis tried to explain to the British Ambassador how most Americans now felt about Allied policies:

> I told him our withdrawal had not been entirely due to our failure to ratify the Treaty, although this failure had made our official participation more difficult, that we had been impressed with the difficulty of obtaining unselfish cooperation with any of the Allied Powers; England was glad to have our counsel when we happened to take sides against France; France was glad to have us when our views concurred with hers against England, but when we failed to agree with either one of them our presence was not so desirable. I further explained that while the British are no doubt as idealistic as we are, it seems more difficult for them to work in harmony for a common ideal without at the same time attempting to obtain some material advantage, which is probably due to the fact that they have for so many generations been involved in the complicated European diplomacy.[2]

Davis went on to indict Anglo-Japanese conniving over spheres of influence in Siberia and China, secret Anglo-French accords designed to keep American oil interests out of the new League of Nations Middle Eastern mandates, and Allied dealings with the principal anti-Bolshevik leaders, Admiral Kolchak and General Denikin. These leaders' selfish attempts to negotiate exclusive trade agreements with Lenin's opponents had given the communists additional opportunities to attack their patriotism, and had thus helped to insure a Bolshevik victory.

Hitler's attack on the Soviet Union in June 1941 led to American fears that the British would seek to bargain with Lenin's successors over spheres of influence in Europe. Indeed, the "Munich Analogy" had a very real and urgent meaning to official Washington as early as 1941: if Britain and France had appeased Nazi Germany, would they now just as soon concede Eastern Europe to another dictator? Hard-pressed by the Axis, Prime Minister Churchill was in no position to resist Stalin's demands for Russian gains under the 1939 Nazi-Soviet Pact; besides, British imperial interests elsewhere seemed to demand concessions in Central Europe. Either way, the result was bound to be repugnant to American policy-makers.

William Bullitt's experiences in Moscow had brought him to firm convictions about dealing with the Bolsheviks and to serious misgivings about Roosevelt's foreign policies. In part this had resulted from the Ambassador's increasingly unsatisfactory personal relations with the President. In December 1941, however, they were agreed on how to deal with forthcoming Anglo-Russian talks in Moscow, which both Bullitt and Roosevelt feared would compromise American war aims. Even before Bullitt's note arrived in the White House, the President had acted. He had approved a message for transmission to the American Embassy in London, instructing the Ambassador to inform the Foreign Office of the United States' firm opposition to any bilateral decisions on the postwar world. It concluded: "Above all there must be no secret accords."[3]

Bullitt's first mission to Moscow had begun in February 1919 with a secret train ride along the Arctic Circle to meet Lenin's representative. He proposed to offer the Bolsheviks a suspension of counterrevolutionary activity by the Allied Supreme War Council, provided they would suspend their own revolutionary activities.

Far down on the list of Wilson's advisers at Paris, Bullitt had been entrusted with this mission by Colonel House and Secretary of State Robert Lansing, who, in Wilson's temporary absence, had decided to risk such an exploration of the issues between Russia and the West. House had originally helped Bullitt to secure a position in the State Department to provide himself with another listening post there. Jealous of all other advisers, and in need of continuing reliable information, the Colonel was always looking for such men as Bullitt, especially those who enjoyed small intrigues. Large intrigues he usually reserved for himself; in this instance, however, he preferred that the real risks be taken by someone readily expendable.

Bullitt was a lineal and spiritual descendant of Virginia revolutionaries, a young man who found himself completely out of sympathy with his peers among the old upper-class aristocracy of Philadelphia, and disdainful of the *nouveau-riche* atmosphere permeating prewar American society. He had just begun a career on the *Philadelphia Public Ledger* when family connections and Colonel House's patronage secured him his place in the State Department.

Before Versailles, Bullitt's assignment had been to observe closely the events of the Bolshevik Revolution and its spreading influence in Central Europe. His observations quickly convinced him that a decision to join the Allied intervention in July 1918 would be a misconceived response to social revolution. There were, he said in a memorandum written shortly before that decision, three main political categories emerging in the twentieth century: "X"—the imperialists, "Y"—the liberals, and "Z"—the social revolutionaries. "The Social Revolutionary is a frank internationalist," Bullitt explained. "He cares nothing about this war, but only about the class war which is to follow it. His vision of the future contains a world in which national lines are wiped out and the international proletariat rules." This category included not only Bolsheviks but the Avanti group in Italy, the Spartacus party in Germany, and the Industrial Workers of the World in the United States. American policy-makers, he continued, had to enlist the support of the "Y" liberals throughout the world to meet this challenge.[4] From the beginning Bullitt perceived the threat as both an internal and a foreign one, and the appropriate response conversely as an intranational as well as an international one.

So did Wilson. Where they differed was in how to accomplish American aims. As Bullitt saw it, the immediate situation in 1919 was that the Russian Revolution had split liberal opinion badly. While most liberals deplored the Bolsheviks' assumption that violence was the only way to end the rule of the corrupt, the unjust, and the historically backward, they divided sharply over how to meet this challenge. Military intervention was an imperialist idea; if the United States lowered itself to become part of the dark reactionary crusade, the chance to make the world safe for liberal democracy would be lost. America would have failed to fulfill its destiny, and the world would become a battleground on which the fate of man would be determined by the clash of imperialism and social revolution.

Thus, if the initiative for dealing with the social revolutionaries were left to the imperialists, the liberals would eventually be excluded from the world. The 1939 Nazi-Soviet pact proved, to Bullitt's satisfaction at least, that it was possible and even probable for these two sinister forces to join together in the first stages of the destruction of Western civilization.

As Arno Mayer points out, Bullitt advocated a truce with the Bolsheviks in 1919 as the beginning of a "containment" policy, but one opposed to a spheres-of-influence deal, either within Russia or internationally. Returning to Paris with Lenin's signature on his proposal, Bullitt expected a triumphant reception; instead Wilson ignored him. To many younger members of the American delegation, the President's repudiation of the "Bullitt Mission," like his compromises with the imperialists on the questions before the Versailles Conference, seemed vainglorious. They knew that he believed these concessions were necessary for the League of Nations, but they doubted that he or anyone else could do much to correct the wrongs that were being built into the peace structure itself. A great gulf of shattered hopes thus opened between the President and several of his advisers.

At a meeting of these dissidents, Bullitt awarded roses to those who would join him in resigning from the delegation, and contemptuously tossed yellow jonquils to those who held back. Later he put himself at the service of Henry Cabot Lodge and the Republican majority on the Senate Foreign Relations Committee by testifying to the deep internal divisions that Wilson's Versailles policies had created among members of the American delegation.

Wilson's resolve not to talk with the Bolsheviks remained strong even as his hopes for the League collapsed and his health failed. State Department spokesmen, under the guidance of Wilson's third Secretary of State, Bainbridge Colby, put down every congressional demand for a re-examination of the administration's Russian policy. Colby fully shared the President's conviction that the Bosheviks were perverse idealists who must be resisted. Turning Marxist precepts upside down, State Department officers insisted that internal contradictions in the Soviet system would topple it—to the ultimate distress of all those who had sought special advantages from the communists.

"The greatness of a future [non-communist] Russian trade is undisputed," a State Department economist told the House Foreign Affairs Committee,

> and the share obtainable by the United States, from a selfish commercial point of view, depends much upon our future relations with the future Russian Government. Our potentially favorable position can be impaired by an unwise relation with the present authorities. In gratitude for America's friendly attitude toward a future national government, it is to be expected that our opportunities will be unparalleled. The upbuilding of the industries of Russia will not only be a great humanitarian work, but will render a patriotic service to the United States. To foreign investors, Russia will be found a very attractive field. The vast opportunities there will especially grip the imagination of Americans conversant with the development of our own great West; for the physical-geography of many parts of Russia and Siberia bears a striking resemblance to that part of Western America.[5]

In the meantime, according to this view, the United States should do all it could to guarantee the physical integrity of Russia until the time of troubles passed. Closely associated with Colby's Russian policy was the right-wing socialist John Spargo, whose 1920 book, *Russia as an American Problem,* not only gave this thesis its fullest expression but added a powerful geopolitical justification.

Spargo prided himself on being a hardheaded realist, one fully aware of all the pitfalls in the socialist position. If the Bolsheviks succeeded, he thought, they would very likely align themselves with Germany and Japan, America's two major future rivals; the resulting Eurasian monolith would inevitably dominate the world. "There is nothing to be gained," he wrote, "by trying to gloss with sentimental idealization the hard, cold facts of life. We are a capitalist nation, living in a capitalist world in an era of capitalism. Some of us believe that another form of society would be better and give larger happiness to a far greater number of people. In the meantime only visionaries and addle-pated chatterers profess to be indifferent to the success of our capitalist enterprise." The United States, he continued, had a vital stake in the fate of all nations, especially one so large as Russia. "The closing of a great market, interruption of trade communications, or stoppage of the supply of raw materials, means for us closed factories, economic depression, unemployment, hunger, strife, excessive mortality, and increased crime."[6]

Suppose, also, Spargo argued, the communists succeeded in Germany as well. Would not German Marxists come to dominate both nations politically? And would not German machines then soon be converting Russian raw materials into unmatched industrial power? Interestingly enough, Lenin's 1920 analysis was not basically different: "Germany wants revenge and we want revolution. For the moment our aims are the same; but when our ways part, they will be our most ferocious and greatest enemies. Time will tell whether a German hegemony or a Communist federation is to arise out of the ruins of Europe." A temporary alliance with Russia, said Lenin, appealed to many Germans who despised Bolshevism because it had the "possibility of setting in motion gigantic productive forces."

Bullitt insisted that the "Wilsonians" missed Lenin's key point: if Germany and Russia were both excluded from the international community, they would be driven together. While others clung to the policy of isolating Russia, Bullitt lived abroad during the 1920's collecting materials for an indictment of Wilson's foreign policies. During his exile he came to know most of the *philosophes* of the era; in Sigmund Freud he found a perfect sounding board for his ideas. By 1932 they had completed a book on Wilson, but neither wanted it published in the near future.

In fact, Bullitt saw a far better chance immediately to vindicate his views in the presidential candidacy of Franklin Delano Roosevelt. Though Colonel House was unable to secure a personal interview for him with the New York governor, other intermediaries were found; the two met at Albany, New York, on October 5,

1932. This conversation led ultimately to Roosevelt's selection of Bullitt as America's first Ambassador to the Soviet Union in late 1933.

During the campaign itself, Bullitt helped with some of the speechmaking chores. As he explained to Colonel House, he thought the basic problem was that Americans had lost faith not only in Herbert Hoover but in themselves—even in the idea of America itself. He felt that Roosevelt might be able to arouse the country "by the old Jeffersonian appeal of liberty to the individual and service to the nation."[7]

Riding the crest of this new excitement, Bullitt apparently mistook (as did many others) Roosevelt's intentions. The President did like to have around him men who encouraged his own internationalist leanings; but he was not committed to an active involvement in world politics. For the moment, however, Bullitt was pleased to see his approach to the Russian problem gaining in popularity, despite Secretary of State Cordell Hull's prejudice against dealing with state economies.

At the London Economic Conference in the summer of 1933, Bullitt heard Russian Foreign Minister Maxim Litvinov describe the billion-dollar market which awaited the nation that would offer the Soviets satisfactory credit arrangements. Litvinov also spoke of Russia's desire for cooperation in the tasks of preserving peace in Europe and Asia. The forced German-Rusisan entente of the 1920's had come to an abrupt end that summer. Under Hitler's orders, Soviet-German military cooperation had been broken off, and all German army installations in the USSR closed down. It was a key moment in European, and indeed world, history, Bullitt thought.

Meanwhile, American businessmen, eager for new outlets for indigestible surpluses, pursued reluctant State Department officers with newspaper reports of British and German credit offers to the Soviets. The latter insisted somewhat unconvincingly that the Russian market—like all others in the Great Depression—had shrunk for natural reasons and not because rivals had outbid the United States. The economic community nevertheless began agitating for diplomatic recognition of Russia to give the United States more flexibility. Even without recognition, financing for a relatively modest seventy thousand bales of cotton had earlier been achieved by stretching the legal provisions of the Reconstruction Finance Corporation. Stimulated by this success, business then flooded the RFC with more than forty new applications for Russian trade financing. Senator Walter F. George of Georgia, who had visions of clothing the Russian peasants in American cotton, urged Roosevelt to make a serious bid for that market. Anything that could be done to restore the depressed world market for cotton, a loss which now reached more than one million bales annually, had to be done at once, George wrote, or the cotton-growing areas of the country would face ruin.[8]

Bullitt, as much as anyone else, wanted to seize this opportunity. In fact, he told the American Ambassador in Germany, Litvinov had agreed to pay the old Russian war debt to the United States up to $100 million, and to open up large markets not only for cotton but for all kinds of industrial goods. This meant, he confided, that Russia would leave Germany in the lurch.

Settlement of the debt issue became crucial to Bullitt's plans. To begin with, a resolution of this ancient dispute would increase public confidence in the recognition policy. That in turn would better chances for congressional approval of trade credits through some federal agency. But most important in the long run, a satisfactory settlement on these terms would allow Washington to keep close watch over all transactions with the Soviets. As Bullitt pointed out in a speech to the Philadelphia Chamber of Commerce, the United States could no longer risk such "strange financing of foreign sales" as had characterized the 1920's and helped bring on the Great Depression.[9] Bullitt saw recognition of Russia as a policy to promote the nationalization of American capitalism.

Alarmed at the lack of any clear government policy on credits to Russia, Bullitt deplored the way various agencies were all trying to make special deals with the Soviets. They simply added new mistakes to the old. Above all, Bullitt did not want the communists to gain by such speculative dealings, whether public or private. After formal recognition of the Soviet Union in November 1933, trade negotiations produced an ironic situation in which the Russians argued for the classic free marketplace while

Ambassador Bullitt just as stoutly defended state planning! Secretary Hull, who had never been enthusiastic for recognition anyway, distrusted both sides. Hull believed any concession to state monopolies worked against multilateral international trade and restricted the operation of the reciprocal trade agreements program. Bullitt thought Hull was simply being dogmatic and unimaginative.

The administration and the business community still found it hard to work out the best way to finance the Russian trade. Policy-makers and economic leaders used the terms "credits" and "loans" interchangeably, and sometimes quite specifically, as different alternatives.[10] The solution finally appeared in the creation of the first Export-Import Bank, designed to provide credits to exporters to Russia. Yet this matter remained confused for several months, and no doubt had something to do with the way Roosevelt phrased a key agreement during pre-recognition negotiations with Litvinov.

Their Washington talks lasted for several days, and covered three major issues: (1) the loan-credit question, (2) Russia's war debts, and (3) the activities of the Communist International. Without going into detail about the "Gentleman's Agreement" which resulted,[11] it is safe to say that both sides understood that certain necessary ambiguities existed in the final Roosevelt-Litvinov exchange of letters, but it was necessary to have something in writing so as to obtain a favorable reaction in the United States and diplomatic protection in Europe.*

Confident of Roosevelt's support, Bullitt left for Moscow later in November. He was in an especially optimistic mood. "It is

*In 1937 Robert F. Kelley, who headed the Russian Division of the State Department at the time of the Roosevelt-Litvinov talks, explained the Gentleman's Agreement to Secretary of the Treasury Morgenthau. Kelley told Morgenthau: "There was a provision that in return for a loan (that was the word used) by the United States or its Nationals, the Soviet Government would agree to pay, through additional interest on the loan, a sum totaling at least $75,000,000. Then Mr. Litvinov added on to that, further down, that while he thought that was fair, if the President thought that was insufficient he would be willing to recommend $100,-000,000. We, at the time, I think, had been talking $150,000,000." (Morgenthau Diary, May 11, 1937.)

valuable to have the inside track," he wrote the President from Moscow, "but it seems to me not desirable to emphasize the fact to the world."[12] At the Soviets' reception banquet even Stalin dropped in for a few moments. Was there anything the Ambassador particularly desired of the Soviet government? he asked. Bullitt replied that he would very much like a certain site on a bluff above the Moscow River for the American Embassy. He hoped to put a replica of Jefferson's Monticello on that high point overlooking the Soviet capital. "You shall have it," Stalin told him. When Roosevelt read Bullitt's report of this conversation, he passed it on to Secretary Hull with a jovial reference which caught the very essence of their different moods and temperaments: "I like the idea of planting Thomas Jefferson in Moscow."[13]

On February 11, 1934, Roosevelt personally approved a State Department draft which at once dissipated the euphoric aftermath of Bullitt's reception banquets: the Department proposed that Litvinov agree to the highest sum Roosevelt and Litvinov had discussed to cover the Russian war debt principal ($150 million); pledge to pay this amount by additional interest of 10 per cent "on all *credits or loans* to be extended after the date hereof to my Government or any of its agencies by your Government, *its nationals, or any agencies of either*"; and, finally, acknowledge a Soviet obligation to pay 5 per cent interest on the debt principal over a period not to exceed twenty years.[14]

By fusing loans and credits under one category, the State Department had made it plain that it expected to oversee *all* economic relations with the Soviets, and, even more significantly, that it insisted the war debt be paid regardless of whether or not a formal loan was extended to Moscow. Roosevelt's approval indicated that he either accepted this very extreme definition of the Gentleman's Agreement or was not seriously interested in Russian-American relations. In any event, it left Bullitt stranded to face the Russian backlash alone.

In his next conversation with Bullitt, Litvinov exploded that the Gentleman's Agreement referred only to loans, that the surcharge and interest demands would put a tax on Russian trade, and that the Soviet government would never agree to put its trade under the sole jurisdiction of the Export-Import Bank.

If the United States really wanted the war debt paid, the Foreign Minister maintained, it would have to make a cash loan and accept the extra interest from that transaction; otherwise Russia could not make payments to the United States without angering England and France, something it simply could not afford to do, given European conditions in the 1930's. When Bullitt reported this conversation, he was told that FDR was "astonished" that Litvinov had talked of a direct loan.[15]

At first Bullitt thought the Russians were bluffing, that he could still fulfill Roosevelt's changing desires: Stalin needed good relations with Washington because of the Far Eastern situation; therefore, Litvinov would not be allowed to delay things much longer. "If we maintain our position energetically and forcibly we shall be able to arrive at a solution in large measure satisfactory to us," the Ambassador reported to the Department.[16]

Although Litvinov did in fact modify his position in later discussions, President Roosevelt made not the slightest move to interfere with Hull's rigid management of the affair, thus further isolating Bullitt. "I get a lot of chuckles out of the scraps that you and Litvinov have," Roosevelt wrote Bullitt breezily later that spring. "Keep up the good work!"[17] There was never any change in Bullitt's instructions, even by implication, in these letters, nor any serious discussion of Russian-American relations. Bullitt indirectly commented on this situation in a letter he wrote to the President after FDR's unsuccessful fight for the Supreme Court reform bill. The New Deal's efforts to achieve a fairer distribution of America's national income was, said the Ambassador, "our only chance to avoid the clash of classes and eventual crash of all we care about in America." He concluded the letter with this insight: "You will laugh, I know, as you always do, and say 'Aren't human beings awful!' As I am less robust, I do not laugh."[18]

Bullitt clung to the hope that he could maneuver the Soviets into accepting Washington's point of view. When he could not budge Foreign Minister Litvinov, however, he tried to go around him. One time Bullitt suggested to R. Walton Moore, the Counselor of the State Department, that the U.S. use Export-Import Bank credits as a double-edged sword: not only would they be denied to the Russians, the suggestion ran, it might also be hinted that Washington was "inclined to place those or similar facilities at the disposal of the Japanese." Such a "hint" would, Bullitt believed, produce agreeable results."[19]

Another time he reported that he was cultivating good relations with other members of the Soviet hierarchy in the hope of starting a "backfire in the Kremlin" under the Foreign Minister. This dubious intrigue both exposed Bullitt's isolation and dismayed Litvinov, who was one of the few consistent advocates of collective security within the Politburo.[20] Collapse of the debt negotiations at the time that Mussolini was moving into Ethiopia suggested to the Russian Foreign Minister that Roosevelt was not much interested in joint resistance to aggression.

Litvinov's several overtures for a Russian-American détente, on the other hand, had hardly been discussed in deference to the debt question. Even before recognition, in the summer of 1933, he had proposed a nonaggression pact between the two countries. When he later suggested to Bullitt that it might be expanded to include Japan and China, the Ambassador gave him no encouragement at all. To Litvinov's suggestion that Manchukuo be recognized to induce Japan to join such a pact, Bullitt replied that the United States would not recognize Japan's puppet government—"ever."[21]

Once, in the spring of 1934, Roosevelt made a gesture in the direction of détente, but it was abortive in a way which further discouraged Bullitt as well as Litvinov. Roosevelt had originally encouraged the Ambassador to survey Russia and Far Eastern problems and report to him in Hawaii. "I was ganged," he explained to Bullitt when he canceled their conference. The State Department "felt that a gathering of this kind would be almost a Far Eastern Pacific Conference and would create such a stir that there might be real discussion and speculation at a time when they want to avoid just that."[22]

These strains finally began to wear down Bullitt's optimism. He blamed the obvious failure of his mission on Japanese behavior—they had "let us down badly" by not keeping the pressure on in the Far East—or on French courtship of the Soviets. "As they no longer feel that they need our immediate help," he complained of the Soviets, "their underlying hostility to all capitalist countries now shows through the veneer of intimate friendship."[23]

Despite his anger at Litvinov and the rest of the Soviet official family, Bullitt found it possible to talk with Bolshevik intellectuals like Karl Radek and Nikolai Bukharin. In fact, such discussions were one of the few features of life in Moscow he still thought worthwhile. On October 2, 1934, Bullitt sent a long dispatch to Washington containing both his own observations on the Soviet Union and interpretations adopted from discourses with these intellectuals. "No generalization on the Soviet Union," the dispatch began, "can have more than momentary validity. The Russian Revolution is still moving with such rapidity that any picture is certain to be false after the lapse of a few months."

Widespread optimism was the most striking feature of the current scene in Russia, he continued. "Stalin's agricultural policy, however appalling its cost in human suffering, has been successful. The peasants have been starved, shot, and exiled into submission. The new harvest is adequate." Economic successes accounted for this new mood; all together they meant that "state capitalism" was firmly anchored, the dictatorship secure, and the bureaucracy routine.

The Bolshevik intellectual elite were now convinced that the Revolution would succeed; its ability to sustain itself through all past and future trials they attributed to the "potency of the modern machine." Machines developed in England, Germany, and the United States could carry on their backs "all the inefficiency, stupidity, and mistakes implicit in a revolutionary movement."

"In discussing this point," Bullitt noted thoughtfully, "the old Bolsheviks stress the argument that under their system of State capitalism the machine can be allowed to work twenty-four hours a day and produce whatever quantities of goods it is capable of producing without producing at the same time the disasters that overtake private capitalism when the machines produce more than can be sold at a profit."[24] Because of "machines," the Soviets were confident they could achieve economic self-sufficiency within a decade.

When Bullitt mulled over these thoughts late at night in the American Embassy, his private reflections on the state of the world—and America's place in it—left him disquieted and apprehensive. His personal disappointment that things had not worked out the way he planned, his bitter animosity at Foreign Minister Litvinov, and the generally repressive atmosphere of Stalinist Russia, all disturbed him. It was through the dark veil of these concerns that Bullitt viewed the 1935 Moscow meeting of the Third International. While the participation of American Communists violated Washington's interpretation of the Roosevelt-Litvinov agreement on propaganda and agitation, Bullitt's own objections ran much deeper. "The emotions of the Congress," he wrote to Roosevelt, "in deciding to cooperate with the Socialists and bourgeois Democrats in a fight against Fascism are, of course, on all fours with the emotions of the tiger when he went out for that historic ride with the young lady of Niger. The Communists feel sure that they will come back from the ride with the Socialists and Democrats inside."[25]

The Soviets' call for "Popular Fronts" against Germany and Japan now appeared to Bullitt to be a communist maneuver to put the United States at the forefront of a war which would end Western civilization. At the very time the Soviet Union was "postponing" its obligations to world revolution, Bullitt was most worried about "international communism." The reason—in 1935 as in 1945—lay in Bullitt's genuine despair about the future of capitalism, his fear of the "clash of classes and eventual crash of all we care about in America."

In the spring of 1936 Bullitt left Moscow to become Roosevelt's Ambassador to France. Upon his departure he leveled a blast at Russia, but even more at international communism. The time was not far distant, he asserted, when "the Soviet Union will become a dangerous factor in the field of international trade. . . . It is attempting to make itself as self-sufficient as possible and it will use its monopoly of trade ruthlessly to undersell and injure its enemies and to assist its friends. . . . It will . . . try to produce as much chaos as possible in the economies of capitalist countries in the hope that misery may beget communist revotion."

There was but one way to strike a fatal blow to international communism: "The final argument of the believing communist is invariably that all the battle, murder, and sudden death, all the spies, exiles, and firing squads are justified because communist dictatorship is the only method which permits *a modern economic machine to run at full speed and to find always an unsatisfied buying power, whereas the maldistribution of the national income in our system causes inevitably recurrent crises and unemployment.*" Bullitt took this passage almost word for word from his earlier reports on the views of Bolshevik intellectuals, but now added to it his own sober reflection: "The recent conclusions of the Brookings Institution of Washington as to the causes of our crises are, curiously enough, the same."[26]

From the American Embassy in Paris, Bullitt continued to carry on a campaign he had begun even before leaving Russia. "I deviled the Russians," he later boasted. "I did all I could to make things unpleasant."[27] His main goal now was to prevent American involvement in a new war. Germany and Japan had to have "new sources of raw materials and markets," he said in defense of appeasement. The Japanese line was obvious; but Germany might go down the Danube, toward the Balkans, or into the Ukraine.[28] In any event, Russia would be at war with one of them within two years. "I see no way that we can achieve anything by attempting to stop the march of events—horrible as it is—except by our own involvement in war," he wrote Roosevelt, "and I hope that you will turn a very deaf ear to the songs of the sirens who must be keeping you awake nights with their music."[29]

Like most Americans, Bullitt remained sympathetic to China's cause even while urging noninvolvement in Europe, but his sympathy took a most peculiar direction, thought William E. Dodd, the American Ambassador to Germany: "I was surprised to hear Mr. Bullitt say that Russia might well be abandoned, that she had no real right to that peninsula which ends with Vladivostok." "He showed me a little map," Secretary Morgenthau also noted after hearing Bullitt's Far Eastern views, "which shows that Vladivostok is today the center for the Japanese Empire when you include that part of China which is controlled by Japan. He said that the Japanese worry greatly about Russia and that they want the Yellow River as their frontier against Russia."[30]

"I was amazed at this kind of talk from the responsible diplomat who had done much to get Russia recognized in 1933," Ambassador Dodd charged privately. "The President must have known the man's mentality, but if so, how could he have appointed him Ambassador to Soviet Russia?"[31] How, indeed, could this have happened? In part the answer rests in something Bullitt had already come to understand: despite his moral exhortations against Germany and Japan, Roosevelt's foreign policy was cautious and indecisive. But while Bullitt did not wish to be stranded again, his "appeasement" period went beyond personal self-protection. He truly believed that the most serious menace to America was not Germany but the Soviet Union. He thought so not because of power politics or military budgets, but because of a deep sense of foreboding about the social order of the West. In this mood he saw France's pro-Russian policy in the mid-1930's as a dangerous product of misplaced "grandeur." Apprehensive that Paris wished to lay a foundation for an emotional appeal to the United States, he even tried to forestall any settlement of France's war debt to the American Treasury. "I . . . say that, after all, the President is not a god," Bullitt said in explaining how he tried to bring French diplomats to their senses, "and has no godlike power to bend Hitler, Mussolini, and Stalin, to say nothing of the other rulers of Europe, to his will and make them behave. I add that he has but one power, which is the power of the American fleet, the American army, and American economic and financial resources, and that these forces will not, so long as he is in the White House, be placed at the disposal of European peoples by involving the United States in a war."[32]

Should war come in spite of his efforts, Bullitt wrote Cordell Hull privately, "the world communist movement would become a force of the utmost importance . . . in every country." And though diplomatic relations with the Russians were momentarily "distant and unimportant, our relations with the world communist movement can, unfortunately, never be distant or unimportant so long as it continues to exist."[33] Once he had believed that the best way to deal with the Soviets was to confront them in Moscow, but after 1935 he had no interest in any diplomatic initiatives, save those which might delay war. When the first Czechoslovakian crisis occurred in the spring of 1938, Bullitt urged FDR to take the lead in appeasing Nazi Germany. He should call the British, French, German, and Italian Ambassadors to the White House, Bullitt said, and suggest that they convene a peace conference at the Hague. Roosevelt should say to them that they, and the Americans as well, were all children of European civilization, "that as we are grateful for Shakespeare so are we grateful for Beethoven." The President should seek to impress upon the German Ambassador that England and France were indeed willing to fight, but that the best solution was a plebiscite, even though it would probably deliver the Sudetenland to Hitler peacefully. They should all be made to understand that "war in Europe today can end only in the establishment of Bolshevism from one end of the continent to the other, that your proposed conference will leave the Bolsheviks beyond the swamps which divide the Soviet Union from Europe and are Europe's real eastern boundary. I think that even Hitler would accept under such conditions."[34]

But after the September 1938 Munich Crisis, Bullitt did yet another remarkable turnabout, moving abruptly to an extreme interventionist position. And when Germany marched into what was left of Czechoslovakia in March 1939, he pleaded with Roosevelt to demand repeal of the Neutrality Acts.[35] He remained adamantly opposed to any international "Popular Front" with the Soviets, however, and argued vigorously with French officials that they should decline Moscow's overtures for joint military talks. After Russia attacked Finland—striking from behind the shield of the Nazi-Soviet pact—Bullitt hurried to Geneva and began working behind the scenes to have the Soviet Union expelled from the League. As he had long expected, the League had proven a failure; nonetheless there remained the future. Such a moral condemnation had important symbolic consequences for that time to come when United States relations with Russia would demand evidence of Russian perfidy.[36]

When Germany moved east in 1941, most observers thought the Soviets would be doing well to hold out for three months or so. Bullitt reacted in words reminiscent of John Spargo's geopolitical analysis: "We must develop our war production faster than Germany can develop war production in Soviet territory," he warned Roosevelt. While it was proper to take the position that the United States would support "anyone (even a criminal) fighting Hitler," he added, this anomaly must be carefully explained to the American people because they might become confused and somehow reach the conclusion that the "Communists have become the friends of democracy."[37]

Bullitt's misgivings were shared by other American leaders. In June 1941 the National Association of Manufacturers published the results of a recent survey of the members of the American Economic Association on the question, "Can we avoid a post-armament depression?" Eighty per cent of those responding answered: No! Editorializing upon this reaction, the NAM asserted its own belief that lack of postwar planning, labor's growing power, and past New Deal policies made such a depression unavoidable. The profit motive had been so weakened in the depression decade that despite the temporary stimulation of arms spending, the survey concluded, the outlook for free-enterprise capitalism was dim no matter who won the war.[38] In the end, only "statism" of one form or another would win. If Germany should achieve a stalemate, Europe would continue to be divided between economic and political blocs while the United States suffered the increasingly hopeless fate of an old-fashioned general store. If the Soviets should win, and spread their "system" west of Vienna by conquest or subversion, much the same result could be expected. Whichever happened, domestic demands for state socialism would increase, and the New Deal would give way to something much worse.

The most thoughtful and challenging rebuttal to these arguments came from *Life* publisher Henry Luce, in his famous 1941 editorial "The American Century." Later interpretations of this essay suggest that it was simply an overblown celebration of the coming *Pax Americana*. But Luce's opening paragraphs were anything but self-congratulatory: "We Americans are unhappy. We are not happy about America. We are not happy about ourselves in relation to America. We are nervous—or gloomy—or apathetic."[39] According to Luce, extended debate about whether this or that particular diplomatic move would put the United

States into the war was all wasted effort: America was in fact *in* the war.

Reluctance to admit this fact, Luce said, was but another consequence of the nation's failure to solve its problems during the Great Depression. Many Americans were reasonably convinced that when the United States entered the war, constitutional democracy would come to an end. Assaults by demagogic politicians on the already weakened citadels of constitutional freedom, they feared, would yield complete power to the collectivists. After all, the New Deal had already admitted socialist planners and doctrines into the government; both stood ready to help the "new order," whatever it might be.

An older belief that collaboration with Great Britain always ended up with the United States playing the other fellow's game, Luce continued, made others unwilling to admit that the nation was in the war. But of the two apprehensions felt by Americans, this was the easiest one to eliminate. It was now apparent that the British could not stop Hitler without American aid, let alone win any victory. As soon as the United States set forth its war aims, Churchill would accept them outright; in turn, "the entire world including Adolf Hitler would accept them as the gauge of this battle."

In truth, the two problems—democracy at home and collaboration—were not separable, nor was there much choice in dealing with them. Roosevelt *must* succeed where Wilson failed, because now, at the end of a depression decade, the country had proven that it could not make democracy work at home. It was not a question of territorial defense; even if England fell, Luce explained, Hitler probably could not launch a successful military attack on the Western Hemisphere. "No man can say that that picture of America as an impregnable armed camp is false. No man can honestly say that as a pure matter of defense—defense of our homeland—it is necessary to get into or be in this war.

"But the fact is that Franklin Roosevelt failed to make American democracy work successfully on a narrow, materialistic and nationalistic basis. Our only chance now to make it work is in terms of a vital international economy and in terms of an international moral order." It was for America and for America alone to determine whether a system of free economic enterprise—the only economic order compatible with freedom and progress—would prevail in this century.

That was the challenge of the "American Century." Whether or not they shared Luce's gloomy assessment of the New Deal's failures, or if they did, were willing to admit it, most American policy-makers believed that this was the basic justification for America's entrance into the war: world "democracy" was indivisible if Americans were to enjoy liberty and justice. Secretary of the Treasury Henry Morgenthau, for example, had been struck by the way Walter Lippmann seemingly reversed the issue of American recovery yet arrived at the same conclusion: "Recovery in America is in fact indispensable to the defense of law and order in the outer world, to the consolidation of that determination, which is now manifest in every country, to defend the peace against aggression and revolution."[40]

Less confident than Luce that all the Allies would have to accept American war aims, Bullitt issued his warning to Roosevelt against allowing Churchill to take the lead in dealing with the Kremlin. This time Roosevelt had already acted to keep his options open without any special pleading from the former Ambassador to the Soviet Union; but over the next three and a half years he felt it necessary to pursue a more ambiguous line of policy. In FDR's effort to stay on the straight and narrow of traditional American policy toward spheres of influence, he encountered his most frustrating difficulties which ultimately overcame his efforts to secure a lasting peace.

After 1941 Bullitt's career became closely linked with Henry Luce's "American Century" in theory as well as in joint efforts. He was close to American diplomacy through 1949, always representing the concrete universal of traditional American "liberalism" in foreign relations: its demand for open marketplaces for ideas and goods, its determination to oppose violent revolutions except those against European rulers. Highly emotional, always a determined advocate, William C. Bullitt swells a scene or two in textbook histories of American foreign policy. He is usually seen in the reflection of other men's moods or policies, but he comes as close to embodying the traditional spirit of American foreign policy as anyone could. Roosevelt and his successors came to regard him as a nuisance—even an obstacle—but however much they tried to ignore him and his later articles for the Luce publications, they could not disavow the heritage he represented nor his descriptions of the communist menace.

The President's December 5, 1941, telegram to London marked the beginning of "second-front" diplomacy, Roosevelt's plan for checking Soviet territorial demands. Later, at the crisis of that policy, Bullitt would have some remarkable advice to offer, based on his perception of the coming Cold War—a compound of ideological views he had taken to Moscow in 1919, revolutionary predictions he had divined from the thoughts of Bolshevik intellectuals, and deep fears about the "eventual crash of all we care about in America."

TWO ☆☆

Franklin D. Roosevelt: The Perils of Second-Front Diplomacy

"Dear Mr. President: John Sherman said in 1877, 'The only way to resume specie payments is to resume.' Similarly, the only way to get the initiative in this war is to take it."[1] Distrustful of British objections to a large cross-channel invasion of Western Europe in 1942, Secretary of War Stimson urged Roosevelt in this letter to "lean" on those charged with production of "landing gear for the ultimate invasion." He hoped thus to put an end to Churchill's obstructionist claims that such an invasion was logistically impractical for the next twelve months and more. "The rate of construction of a number of landing barges," Stimson counseled, "should not be allowed to lose the crisis of the World War." The "crisis" Stimson wrote about, of course, transcended the war and referred to the shape of the postwar world.

Stimson's letter came at a time when several of the President's advisers were reassessing their decision to postpone territorial and political questions to the end of the war. Cables from London in recent weeks had further revealed England's deep fear that unless Stalin received a countersigned deed from his Allies to much of the Baltic and large parts of Poland he would negotiate a separate peace in the East. The issue before American policy-makers was whether or not it was already necessary to compromise their war aims.

"The Government is widely split," noted a State Department officer, "one group, headed by the State Department, Bill Bullitt, and others, maintaining that if we make a single commitment regarding the peace we have lost the chance of being free agents; that the acid test of our good faith in Russia is whether we deliver the supplies we promise. . . . There is intense bitterness, and meanwhile Stalin in his recent speech tried to hurry matters by throwing out the possibility of a treaty with Germany."[2]

Bullitt had indeed renewed his warning that if Roosevelt should assure an Anglo-Russian victory over Germany without previously obtaining definite written pledges in regard to the political shape of the postwar world, "he would find himself in a far worse situation at the end of the Second World War than that in which Woodrow Wilson had found himself at the close of the first." A Russian victory might well mean "one vast dictatorship extending from the Pacific to Western Europe," imperiling American interests now "covered by our Atlantic Doctrine and our Open Door doctrine."[3]

"Bill, I don't dispute your facts," the President had replied (according to Bullitt), "they are accurate. I don't dispute the logic of your reasoning. I just have a hunch that Stalin is not that kind of man. Harry [Hopkins] says he's not and that he doesn't want anything but security for his country, and I think that if I give him everything I possibly can and ask nothing from him in return, *noblesse oblige*, he won't try to annex anything and will work with me for a world of democracy and peace."

Bullitt first made this exchange public in a 1948 *Life* article. By that time he had already joined Roosevelt's critics who were denouncing the late President's foreign policies and looking especially for his footprints on the path to Pearl Harbor. Bullitt was suggesting that the real clue to the mystery was Roosevelt's naiveté. Some of his readers remained convinced that something more sinister had occurred; meanwhile, the President's defenders explained his wartime policies as a strategy of postponement.

Roosevelt's policy toward his Allies during the war *was* indecisive, but the responsibility for the strategy of postponement cannot be placed upon the President's shoulders alone, nor confined to his personal direction of Big Three conferences during the war.

His ambiguity had broad consequences for the future, as did his reduction of complex issues to matters of personality where he functioned best. But Bullitt's characterization of presidential actions neglects the setting of the war and the problems of alliance warfare. Indeed, it was Roosevelt's effort to get all that Bullitt and other universalists wanted, albeit by a different means, which left crucial issues unsettled at his death.

As Stimson's letter implied, most American policy-makers believed that logistical strength and productive capacity would be America's principal weapons in the diplomatic end game. The War Secretary's own feeling (most of the time) was that the United States should concede parts of Eastern Europe to the Soviets, then strengthen its position in the Far East, where, he felt, Russian-American interests ran along more parallel lines.

Bullitt and Secretary of State Cordell Hull also viewed a second front as a counter to British political aims, but they were more universalist in their approach to the peace. They agreed that America's economic power would not be at its height until the end of the war, but, they argued, that power could never be effective (either abroad or at home) without the opportunity to function in a completely open world—including Eastern Europe. Regionalism, spheres of influence, and bilateral pacts would choke off American potential and plunge the nation back into depression. The main task for wartime diplomacy, therefore, was to prevent such divisions before American economic power could influence England and Russia.

It was up to Roosevelt to find the proper means to accomplish this feat. The President's effort to please both groups and yet secure the postwar peace among the Big Three was an impossible undertaking from the outset. But what sounded naive to Bullitt—"if I give him everything I possibly can and ask nothing from him in return"—was actually Roosevelt's analysis of what he could offer Stalin to accomplish this end that Churchill could not. A little more than two weeks after Stimson's plea that he seize the initiative, Roosevelt wrote Stalin: "I have in mind a very important military proposal involving the utilization of our armed forces in a manner to relieve your critical Western Front. This objective carries great weight with me. Therefore, I wish you would consider sending Mr. Molotov and a General upon whom you rely to Washington in the immediate future. Time is of the essence if we are to help in an important way."[4]

What Roosevelt thought he alone could offer was a military second front, large-scale economic aid for Russian reconstruction, and, finally, security guarantees against a rearmed Germany. Churchill's perception of imperial interests also integrated Russian desires into a postwar system, but one which cut against Roosevelt's policy from the very beginning. Churchill offered Stalin good fences in the Balkans; Roosevelt wanted them both to help him build the town meeting hall.

Within a few days of the German attack on Russia, on June 22, 1941, Roosevelt's second Ambassador to the Soviet Union, Joseph E. Davies, had come to the White House to plead the case for all-out aid to Russia. Aid to Russia, Davies submitted, would preclude a second Nazi-Soviet pact—a separate peace between the two totalitarian powers that would divide Europe once again. After talking with Stalin about Russia's ability to resist the German onslaught, Special Ambassador Averell Harriman reported much the same thing to Roosevelt: "I left feeling that he had been frank with us and if we came through as had been promised and if personal relations were retained with Stalin, the suspicion that had existed between the Soviet Government and our two governments might well be eradicated."[5] From Harriman and others, then, Roosevelt received positive assurances that economic aid and personal diplomacy could bring the two nations together. But trust in such assurances was not the basis of second-front diplomacy. American leaders were determined to redeem their past mistakes. Even if there had been no such suggestion from Stalin, the means they planned to use would not have been altered at all.

That was why Churchill's overtures to Stalin in the summer of 1941 so disturbed the State Department. If the British preempted American policy by coming to terms with the Soviets on a detailed political settlement, economic aid to the Soviets would not produce anything: German hegemony would be replaced by Anglo-Russian dominance. Unhappy rumors about such a settlement were spreading, Roosevelt wrote the Prime Minister. "I am inclined to think that an overall statement on your part would be useful at this time, making it clear that no postwar commitments as to territories, populations or economies have been given."[6] The White House would back up such a statement with one of its own.

This exchange led to an agreement between the two English-speaking powers to discuss this problem off the coast of Newfoundland around the 1st of August. Their meeting ended with an eight-point "Joint Declaration," known thereafter as the Atlantic Charter:

> First, their countries seek no aggrandisement, territorial or other.
>
> Second, they desire to see no territorial changes that do not accord with the freely expressed wishes of the peoples concerned.
>
> Third, they respect the right of all peoples to choose the form of government under which they will live; and they wish to see sovereign rights and self-government restored to those who have been forcibly deprived of them.
>
> Fourth, they will endeavor, with due respect for their existing obligations, to further the enjoyment by all States, great or small, victor or vanquished, of access, on equal terms, to the trade and to the raw materials of the world which are needed for their economic prosperity.
>
> Fifth, they desire to bring about the fullest collaboration between all nations in the economic field, with the object of securing for all improved labor standards, economic advancement and social security.
>
> Sixth, after the final destruction of the Nazi tyranny they hope to see established a peace which will afford to all nations the means of dwelling in safety within their own boundaries, and which will afford assurance that all the men in all the lands may live out their lives in freedom from fear and want.
>
> Seventh, such a peace should enable all men to traverse the high seas and oceans without hindrance.
>
> Eighth, they believe that all the nations of the world, for realistic as well as spiritual reasons, must come to the abandonment of the use of force. Since no future peace can be maintained if land, sea, or air armaments continue to be employed by nations which threaten, or may threaten, aggression outside of their frontiers, they believe, pending the establishment of a wider and permanent system of general security, that the disarmament of such nations is essential. They will likewise aid and encourage all other practicable

measures which will lighten for peace-loving peoples the crushing burden of armaments.

The first three points dealt specifically with the old "secret treaty" problem, though much of the literature on the Atlantic Charter at the time and in later years placed greater stress upon its relevance to colonial questions. At the time London was deeply engaged in Asia with the Congress party's demands for Indian independence. Soon after the Prime Minister returned to England, he found widespread speculation that he had committed the whole Empire to the Charter. The Joint Declaration, he reassured the House of Commons, in no way applied to internal imperial questions.

This caveat was matched two weeks later when the Russian Ambassador to Great Britain, Ivan Maisky, added his signature to the Atlantic Charter, and appended verbally a statement about the "historic peculiarities of particular countries" in Eastern Europe.[7] The whole episode was reminiscent of the way European rulers had replied to John Hay's "Open Door Note" concerning China in 1899. What George F. Kennan wrote of Hay's note was certainly as true of the Atlantic Charter: it amounted to asking everyone in the room who was not a thief to stand up. In each instance American reactions were also remarkably similar. Washington gave these nominal acceptances the widest possible circulation, presuming that a combination of "pitiless publicity" and growing economic power would make good most of the promises in the two documents. At the time of the Atlantic Charter, however, the Open Door policy in China had already led to an increasingly frustrating effort to block Japan's forward movement through such means.[8]

Anglo-Russian negotiations in the summer of 1941 did not produce anything like agreement between the two powers actively engaged in fighting Hitler. This was something of a pleasant surprise to Washington, which accounted for it by the timely issuance of the Atlantic Charter. Churchill still had not yielded to Stalin's demands for Russia's 1941 frontiers even by November, when the Kremlin sent a sharp message to His Majesty's Government through Ambassador Maisky. Stalin began with a complaint that Great Britain had not declared war on Finland, Hungary, and

Rumania, implying that the British had political reasons for not doing so. Then he asserted bluntly that there could be "no mutual trust" until this problem had been resolved and "plans for the post-war organization of the peace" agreed upon. Stalin's diplomatic problems were seriously complicated by the exile governments in London (especially the Polish exiles), whose disposition toward the Soviet Union was less than friendly. Though neither the "Battle of Britain" nor the "Battle of Russia" had been won, or even assured, Stalin was determined to settle postwar matters at once.

Maisky was deeply troubled by Stalin's approach. He regarded all diplomatic and political issues as secondary matters when compared with the urgent need for agreement on a second front in the West. After long thought about how to minimize the impact of the message, he finally took it to the Prime Minister, and said quietly as he handed it over: "I very much ask you, Mr. Churchill, to treat this with the greatest possible calm." As the Prime Minister began reading, his face "immediately went red, and then his left hand began agitatedly closing and opening."[9] When he rose and began pacing the room, Maisky grew fearful that nothing could save the situation. But after his anger subsided, Churchill was persuaded to send Foreign Minister Anthony Eden back to Moscow.

The State Department's warning of December 5—"Above all there must be no secret accords"—went with Eden to Moscow. Maisky went too, to keep Stalin on the matter of a second front; but his apprehensions turned to utter dismay when Stalin demanded that recognition of the 1941 frontier could be put off no longer. Eden replied evasively that Britain had agreed to postpone political decisions, and to seek a peace in conformity with the Atlantic Charter. "As regards your repeated references to the necessity for His Majesty's Government to consult the United States Government," Stalin said angrily, "I must confess that I had overlooked this fact and believed your Government to have more freedom of action in these matters. That is perhaps why it is difficult now to reach an agreement." Then he added: "I thought the Atlantic Charter was directed against those people who were trying to establish world domination. It now looks as if the Charter was directed against the U.S.S.R."[10] Stalin was only half-right: it was also aimed at British imperialism. Germany's defeat was simply assumed in the Charter.

There was no way around this impasse in December 1941. Eden did promise to present the Russian case to the War Cabinet when he returned to London, but the Prime Minister was in serious trouble: if Stalin should make a separate peace with Hitler sometime in 1942, wouldn't everyone be worse off than if the Soviets kept their spoils? At Christmastime Churchill arrived in Washington for the "Arcadia" conference with Roosevelt with these problems very much on his mind. The President was waiting for him with an enlarged version of the Atlantic Charter, a proposed Declaration of the United Nations against the Axis. Once again press coverage and later historical accounts concentrated on American public concern with British colonialism in India. The State Department wanted the Dominion government to sign the document separately so as to demonstrate London's good faith toward colonial peoples. At the time the public did not perceive the relationship of the document to Anglo-Russian negotiations.

"Several times," Churchill confided to Eden, the President "expressed his pleasure to me at the firm line we took at Moscow." The reasoning behind American policy in this matter, he told the Foreign Minister, was as follows:

> No one can foresee how the balance will lie or where the winning armies will stand at the end of the war. It seems probable however that the United States and the British Empire, far from being exhausted, will be the most powerful economic *bloc* the world has ever seen, and that the Soviet Union will need our aid for reconstruction far more than we shall need theirs.[11]

Plans were laid at the Arcadia meeting for a combined British-American expedition to North Africa. But the two months following the conference brought chilling disasters for British arms in the Middle East and Asia. In Europe, meanwhile, the Russians were fighting desperately against the main force of Hitler's armies. In London the exile governments were demanding of the British government that their nationhood be preserved against Russian intruders. "In a deadly struggle," an exasperated Churchill confessed to his personal physician, "it is not right to assume more burdens than those who are fighting for a great cause can bear."[12]

Not long after, Churchill sent a cable to Washington: "The Atlantic Charter ought not to be construed so as to deny to Russia the frontiers which she occupied when Germany attacked." When Roosevelt read it to his cabinet he explained that he had emphatically advised the British not to accede to Stalin's demands—not even to his claims to the Baltic states. Such a concession would lead to ever more demands, FDR thought, eventually including the eastern half of Poland.[13]

At a London diplomatic reception several evenings later, the American Ambassador, John G. Winant, called his Russian colleague aside and confided: "I can give you a pleasant piece of news: President Roosevelt and General Marshall, the Chief of our General Staff, consider Germany, not Japan, enemy No. 1, and think the immediate action by the USA and Britain should be an invasion of Northern France."[14] On April 3, 1942, Roosevelt officially informed Churchill that he was sending Harry Hopkins and General Marshall to London to explain to the British government a proposal that "has my heart and *mind* in it. . . . Your people and mine demand the establishment of a front to draw off pressure on the Russians, and these peoples are wise enough to see that the Russians are today killing more Germans and destroying more equipment than you and I put together. Even if full success is not attained, the *big* objective will be."[15]

Though he had not secured Churchill's final agreement to his plan for a 1942 invasion of northern France, Roosevelt urged Stalin to send Foreign Minister Molotov and some reliable general to Washington. Molotov talked once more with British leaders in London in an effort to solve the political issue in Eastern Europe. The American Ambassador kept close to the talks—to make sure they followed the prescribed adherence to the Atlantic Charter. Molotov arrived in Washington in late May 1942, after he had concluded a short treaty in London which contained no secret protocols about Eastern Europe. The Russian Foreign Minister made it plain to Roosevelt that his government felt it had given up near-vital security arrangements in his talks with Churchill. Roosevelt expressed his understanding of the Russian position and began speaking about the "formation" of a second front in 1942. Military aid, however, was only the preface to an entirely new book on Soviet-American relations, the President suggested. The first chapter of this new book, he continued, had been tentatively titled "The Big Four"—in which the Soviet Union is taken into full partnership with the Anglo-American trust to manage the postwar world. Declaring the League of Nations defunct, Roosevelt then outlined his conception in greater detail, explaining that each member of the big-power trust would be responsible for general obligations in connection with the treatment of the defeated Axis nations, and each would have specific regional obligations as well. One of these last concerned the problem of strategic areas to be put under some kind of international trusteeship. "The President hoped Mr. Molotov would discuss this suggestion with Mr. Stalin."[16]

No Western statesman had ever spoken to a Bolshevik in such fashion. Without doubt it was one of the President's most remarkable performances: a dramatic attempt to strike through Molotov's masklike countenance to the man who sat impatiently in the Kremlin waiting for his emissary's reports. It was also a one-time performance; it is not unfair to say that America reached the height of its wartime diplomatic efforts at this moment. No action at Casablanca, Teheran, or Yalta went so far toward genuine diplomatic adjustment with the Russians. In part this was because Roosevelt was soon put on the defensive by British unwillingness to go ahead with the American plan; in part it resulted from pressures by Roosevelt's advisers against reducing the Big Four to concrete terms. But it was also because FDR had no real faith in the concept, other than as a way of establishing rapport with his Allies. It was the same "pragmatic" style he applied to domestic problems.

Ever since the Roosevelt-Churchill meeting of August 1941, the State Department had been trying to persuade the President to commit himself to an effective international organization to keep the peace after the war. Roosevelt had refused to do it. The last paragraph of the Atlantic Charter, Churchill observed after the war, "was a plain and bold intimation that . . . the United States would join with us in policing the world until the establishment of a better order."[17] Cordell Hull and his aides did not regard the Big Four as a better order at all; in fact, they asserted, it would probably be even worse, and at best hardly more satisfactory than an outright concession of Eastern Europe to Russia.

Stalin considered all this talk about a Big Four no more than algebra; he preferred solid mathematics. Roosevelt's proposal for a Big Four directorate was in fact, as Stalin said, an abstract formula. China, whom Roosevelt proposed as the fourth member, could not be called a big power under any circumstances. Postwar "planning" that depended upon Chiang Kai-shek's government for any kind of international responsibility was speculative beyond all likelihood. In fact, FDR's continuing insistence upon this Big Four rhetoric, even as he undertook to act as China's guardian during Big Three conferences, left his allies puzzled and disturbed. One conclusion they drew was that Roosevelt sought China's "faggot" vote either in support of American anti-colonialism or to increase his influence against Britain and Russia on European questions.

Of more immediate concern to American policy planning and the Allies, however, was Churchill's ultimate refusal to risk an invasion of the European continent in 1942. The only offensive action against German land forces that the British would countenance at all was a modified African campaign, which the American chiefs-of-staff had never liked from the beginning. Roosevelt's political advisers were equally upset by this development, which meant that Churchill would gain a double measure of diplomatic success at America's expense: (1) he would obtain American power in support of his overall strategy for winning the war through the Mediterranean, at least for the time being; and (2) he would retake the immediate diplomatic initiative among the Big Three for his own purposes. He even "volunteered" to carry the news to Moscow. Roosevelt had been trying to achieve a personal meeting with Stalin for several months; now it was to be Churchill who spoke for the West on this crucial question. At Moscow the Prime Minister played the role to the hilt. "Stalin will make a great mistake," Churchill, at his imperial best, warned Molotov, "to treat us roughly when we have come so far." "Stalin," replied the Foreign Minister, "is a very wise man. You may be sure that, however he argues, he understands all."[18]

In all of his explanations of the North African campaign, the Prime Minister insisted that the British and the Americans were "preparing for a very great operation in 1943." Stalin's military advisers could not have been any more skeptical about that claim than the American chiefs-of-staff, who were insisting even as Churchill left for Moscow that the Germany-first strategy be re-examined if the British persisted in their resistance to a cross-channel attack.

Critics later charged that Roosevelt had felt the United States "owed" the Soviet Union a second front, and that he had over-compensated with numerous "concessions" to the Kremlin on a whole series of questions. This is a shortsighted criticism: FDR's central purpose was to realize a second front—when it still mattered to the Russians. The North African campaign not only failed to serve that end, it raised unexpected issues in the so-called "deal" with Vichy French authorities in North Africa which facilitated the Anglo-American landings.

But while American liberals attacked the compromise with Germany's semi-fascist allies as a "separate peace in the West," Stalin's people were more concerned that the West planned a series of holding actions until the tide had turned in Europe, then a rush for Berlin. Roosevelt fully understood this and renewed his efforts to persuade Stalin to come to a Big Three meeting when the North African campaign ended. The site selected was Casablanca, but neither the geographical nor the political climate suited the Russian leader, who decided to stay home to make the most of his role as the injured party. FDR went ahead with the meeting with Churchill alone. To the Prime Minister's complete surprise, Roosevelt then issued his "Unconditional Surrender" ultimatum. The gesture was aimed at convincing the Kremlin that the United States would fight until Germany was crushed—that there would be no separate peace in the West.

Roosevelt's advisers had come to Casablanca in an angry mood. They were irked by Allied political maneuvering and their inability to do very much about it. Determined not to be a fluttering tail on the British kite any longer, they found it difficult to counter British arguments for a full-scale Mediterranean strategy. Had Stalin come to Casablanca, ironically, he would have found Americans grateful for his aid in this matter. The Prime Minister's advisers had brought literally boatloads of documents to bolster their position. Though the British finally "compromised," wrote American Ambassador Robert K. Murphy, their so-called concession still kept Americans "fighting for more than two years in this traditional sphere of British influence. . . . Instead of the quick campaign which Eisenhower had expected to fight in Africa, he had to plan and direct several additional campaigns in Mediterranean islands and in southern Europe. More than a year passed before he could even get back to England to prepare at last for the kind of invasion of Europe which he and other Americans had wanted in the first place."[19]

Murphy's repugnance was more than shared by Roosevelt's military advisers, who had no special sympathy for the Soviets. Several had always thought that America's war was against Japan; others had long believed that Washington's strategic thinking had to be freed from the convoluted designs traced out by British imperial planners. On May 12, 1943, William Bullitt sent Roosevelt a truly remarkable memorandum explaining how the Mediterranean strategy might yet be exploited by the United States without yielding to either British or Russian political ambitions. Now outside Roosevelt's inner circle, the former ambassador was impatiently marking time in an office in the Navy Department, and growing more concerned daily about the political course of the war. Bullitt began by pointing out that the basic theory of American military-political planning for the war and the peace contained two false assumptions: (1) that after Germany's defeat, Great Britain and the Soviet Union would turn their full strength against Japan; and (2) that the war aims of the three powers were identical. Now that the Mediterranean had been cleared of enemy ships, the United States had an opportunity to regain the diplomatic initiative; it could make a credible threat to move from west to east and concentrate its greatest effort against Japan. The British would have to come following after, while the Russians could not afford to stop fighting Hitler.

This strategy, Bullitt wrote, should be substituted for current political planning at once, unless the President received from his two Allies (1) redeemable pledges that they would come into the war against Japan immediately after the defeat of Italy and Germany; and (2) equally binding and redeemable commitments that London and Moscow would agree to a "united democratic Europe."

> Unfortunately, the probability is that, after the defeat of Germany, we shall get no help from the Soviet Union and only conservative assistance from Great Britain in our war against Japan. (When Japan is on her last legs the Soviet Union will probably invade and annex Manchuria.)
>
> Furthermore, it is certain that, if we have a hard war to fight against Japan while the Soviet Union is at peace and Great Britain fighting only conservatively, we shall have no decisive voice in the settlement in Europe. (We shall be asking the Soviet Union for support against Japan, and the whip in all negotiations will be in the hands of Stalin.) Europe will be divided into Soviet and British spheres of influence—according to present Soviet and British plans—and further wars in the near future will be rendered inevitable.[20]

According to Bullitt's plan, once Japan was beaten Washington could renegotiate its entrance into the European war, demanding that its conditions be met. Though it had no chance of being adopted, Bullitt's memorandum underscored the difficulty of achieving American war aims in any other way. Russia's victory at Stalingrad in January and February 1943 was a turning point not only in the military history of World War II but in world history as well. Any assumption that the German Eastern front would hold the Russians until Britain and America were ready to fight in the West had to be abandoned. Bullitt's plan could not prevent the Red Army from moving into Eastern Europe; the question now was where the Allies would meet, and what they would find when they got there, particularly in Italy, France, and Germany.

Roosevelt had already discussed this problem with British Foreign Minister Anthony Eden and Harry Hopkins. The President's close adviser kept a record of what he had contributed to the discussion: "I said I thought there was no understanding between Great Britain, Russia and ourselves as to which armies would be where and what kind of administration should be developed. I said that unless we acted promptly and surely I believed one of two things would happen—either Germany will go Communist or an out and out anarchic state would set in; that, indeed, the same kind of thing might happen in any of the countries in Europe and Italy as well."[21]

In the light of this post-Stalingrad awakening, the "Unconditional Surrender" statement seemed completely outdated, even foolish. Germany could be expected to fight hard against the Russians, but, as many postwar critics pointed out, the unconditional surrender statement weakened the West's bargaining posture. Now that Russia was on the offensive, hard decisions had to be reached quickly. In talks with Eden and Averell Harriman, his newly appointed Ambassador to the Soviet Union, Roosevelt took the position that Churchill had held in 1942: Russia could no longer be denied the Baltic States, a readjustment of the Soviet-Polish frontier up to the so-called Curzon line, and East Prussia as well.[22] But he still counted on Russia's economic dependence on the United States to ameliorate East-West relations on terms favorable to the West. He instructed Bernard M. Baruch to inform Churchill of his continuing belief in the efficacy of economic diplomacy with the Russians. The Prime Minister "was impressed by the argument," reported Baruch, "and even said it was a brilliant idea."[23]

But Roosevelt moved neither to activate this plan nor to prepare the public for diplomatic adjustments. The public face of American wartime diplomacy, the Atlantic Charter, remained unchanged despite the deep lines in Roosevelt's private worries. His indecision about postwar treatment of Germany, for example, may well have been the by-product of the Russian dilemma—or perhaps vice versa. Baruch and Henry Morgenthau, Jr., argued that the "more of Germany that is destroyed, the more the United States becomes the source of rehabilitation in peace as she was the source of materiel, munitions, ships, planes and food in the war."[24] Hull and Stimson countered that this was a shortsighted and foolish position. Roosevelt could not choose between them.

In unofficial private conversations with a wide variety of persons, ranging from liberal journalist and author Edgar Snow to the conservative churchman Cardinal Francis Spellman, Roosevelt tried to indicate how he hoped to resolve European questions in Soviet-American relations. Of course, each of these visitors embellished his record of the conversation with a personal gloss reflecting his own hopes, but their notes are similar enough to offer some idea of how the President was wrestling with the problems. Both Snow and Spellman indicated that Roosevelt had little hope of opposing Russian control in areas where the Red Army had opportunity and power. Spellman received the impression that the President wanted a personal meeting with Stalin in order to agree on the extent of Russian expansion. It is not so certain, however, that FDR also admitted, as Spellman recorded: "The European people will simply have to endure the Russian domination, in the hope that in ten or twenty years they will be able to live well with the Russians."[25] It is unlikely that Roosevelt would have admitted to anyone that he was preparing to make such sweeping concessions to the Soviet Union.

In any event, Spellman was plainly upset by what he heard, of that there can be no doubt. Secretary Stimson was concerned about American policy in August 1943, too, but his was an older worry. The "British theory," he advised Roosevelt, for defeating Germany by a series of attritions in northern Italy, in the eastern Mediterranean, and in the Balkans seemed "terribly dangerous" to him, in light of "the post-war problems which we shall face. . . . None of these methods of pinprick warfare can be counted on by us to fool Stalin into the belief that we have kept that pledge."[26] In the months leading up to the Teheran Conference in November 1943, where Roosevelt would finally confront Stalin face to face, talk of second-front diplomacy shifted to new ground. Now it became a defensive tactic to guarantee the United States enough time to complete its postwar plans before Britain and Russia settled everything between them. Roosevelt in fact told his military advisers at Teheran that he foresaw a race to Berlin, and quite probably the need to put several army divisions into Germany at once to prevent disorder should the surrender take place before American troops managed to fight their way to the

German capital.[27] On the other hand, Herbert Feis comments, Roosevelt planned to appeal more positively at Teheran to the "presumed" Soviet desire for collective security and an "equal" place at the peace conference. "He was also going to try to satisfy Stalin's wish for more direct security by agreeing to join in the sponsorship of such protective measures as the dismemberment of Germany. He hoped that his views could be made more persuasive by offers of American help in repairing war damage in the Soviet Union."[28]

Aside from suggesting that the Big Three consider German dismemberment, and sending Stalin a brief post-Teheran message saying he was sorry he had not been able to take up the matter of economic aid to the Soviet Union personally during their discussions, Roosevelt failed to appeal to the "good side" of Stalin's nature or, as Feis put it, to "presumed" Soviet desires.

Negotiations over a postwar credit to the Soviets did take place in 1944 on Roosevelt's instructions, but as Harriman advised the State Department:

> If aid for Russian reconstruction is to be of real value in our overall relations with the Soviet Government, as a benefit which they can obtain from us if they play the international game with us in accordance with our standards, we must have a well-forged instrument to offer them. Vague promises excite Soviet suspicions, whereas a precise program offered now to them but kept always within our control to suspend will be of extreme value. Stalin must offer his people quick reconstruction to retain supreme leadership. We on the other hand want Russian business quickly during our period of conversion from war production.[29]

But, as in the 1930's, Roosevelt did not intervene when these negotiations became entangled in legalisms and secondary matters.

Searching for an answer to this phase of the strategy of postponement is a frustrating task. Clearly, as Allied momentum toward final victory increased, events foreclosed the President's options; the strategy of postponement strengthened the hand of those advisers who generally shared Bullitt's outlook, if not his ideas on strategic warfare.

British-American attempts to organize a provisional Italian government without close consultation with the Russians, moreover, brought out several facts neither East nor West was exactly happy to acknowledge. Churchill wanted to promote the most conservative pro-monarchy government possible. To most Americans, it looked like North Africa all over again. The Russians at first demanded an equal voice in the Allied Control Commission for Italy, but were granted only a nonparticipatory "advisory" role. Western diplomats realized they were setting a precedent, but a new factor had entered the situation which they simply could not gauge adequately. Until they could do so they were unwilling to test Russian intentions. The swelling power of Italian communism left few doubts that the Russians, if they so chose, could invoke all the dreadful force of revolutionary Marxism against any provisional government. In March 1944 the Russians dropped a bombshell by negotiating an exchange of diplomatic representatives with the Royal Government. When the British raised objections to this independent action, the Russian Foreign Office informed the Ambassador, Sir Archibald Clark Kerr, that its action was intended to strengthen the anti-fascist forces fighting the Germans by unifying the dissidents under the Royal Government's directives. In other words, the bomb had been aimed at Italian Communists.[30]

This impression was confirmed by further conversations in Rome with the Russian "advisory" representatives to the Allied Control Commission. There was no doubt, concluded a British aide, that the "Russians intend to take a strong line with the Parties of the Left in Italy and that they intend to ensure that these Parties do nothing to upset the war effort by actions which might dislocate the administration." At the same time, this reporter cautioned London, the Russian diplomat gave him "the impression of a Penitent Cobra being matey."[31]

Despite Stalin's dissolution of the Comintern in 1943, Russian intervention in Italy demonstrated that the political power of the Soviet Union would be far greater after the war than it had ever been before, and that Great Britain and the United States would either have to tolerate such interference or face the likelihood of Moscow-inspired disruptions. No matter what the Russians said, their power to do all sorts of unpleasant things in Western Europe after the war was all the more disturbing because it could not be calculated. As the Russian representative in Rome explained to Sir Noel Mason-MacFarlane, if Moscow had wanted to do any "abnormal" business in Italy, it would not have been "so stupid as to exchange representatives. They had quite different and much more effective ways of doing that sort of thing."[32]

On April 1, 1944, the Soviet Ambassador in Washington frankly informed Secretary Hull that Russian penetration into Rumania "was the beginning of a full re-establishment of the border delineated in 1940," but he gave assurances that no further extensions were planned. Stalin's behavior since the Anglo-Russian talks in 1941 had been consistent in this regard, and calculated to discourage those in the West who warned that Russia had not given up its revolutionary aims. But the louder he talked of Soviet honor, the faster the State Department counted its spoons. This paradox arose (as in Italy) from a situation that neither Russia nor the West could control.

In an article for *Life,* written from Rome, William C. Bullitt, now a major in Charles de Gaulle's Free French army, expanded his original 1918 memorandum once again with heavy emphasis on the current situation in Italy. The picture from that ancient capital, he began, was "an old picture which has been familiar to the Romans since the time of the Caesars—a picture of western Europe and Western Civilization threatened by hordes of invaders from the East." The "Romans" thought that America had made a grave mistake in not securing redeemable pledges from Russia in 1941; the "Romans" thought the "deepest moral issue of the modern world—the issue of man as a son of God with an immortal soul, an end in himself, against man as a chemical compound, the tool of an omnipotent state, an end in itself—may thus be fought out in Italy."[33] Though the article drew heavy fire from American liberals, Bullitt's theme of a barbarian invasion was sounded almost continually from this time forward.

During the war political polarization in Europe had actually intensified. The most dynamic resistance groups were communist or militant left-partisan forces in northern Italy, France, Yugoslavia, and Greece. Barbara Ward suggested what larger ramifications this would have in a 1946 *Foreign Affairs* article: the Russian Revolution had been followed by the rise of Italian fascism and then

German National Socialism. This had created a Left-Right division throughout Europe long before the war itself, "with the issue of nationalization at the center of the resulting tension." Political leaders in the postwar period, even those on the moderate right, would espouse some form of socialism (at least temporarily) to contain the growing demands of militant socialists and communists.[34] Fascism might well be replaced in many countries by communism.

Realizing the possibility of such developments, Churchill and Stalin tried to settle their affairs before postwar politics overwhelmed them both. The Prime Minister wanted to secure British interests in Greece and the Eastern Mediterranean; Stalin wanted security in the Balkans. FDR reluctantly agreed that Churchill might try to reach a temporary *modus operandi* with Stalin, but he warned the latter that in a global war there was "literally no question, military or political, in which the United States is not interested." Any decisions they might reach on Eastern Europe must be regarded as only preliminary to a second Big Three meeting some time after the American elections in 1944. And to Ambassador Harriman he wrote that the United States must retain complete freedom of action when the conference ended.[35]

Despite Stalin's "surprise" at this message—he had assumed Churchill was coming as the result of an Anglo-American understanding—the two settled their business in no more time than it took for Churchill to scrawl some figures across a half-sheet of paper and pass it to Stalin, who took a blue pencil, made a large tick upon the paper, and passed it back. After this brief exchange there was a long silence broken finally by Churchill's suggestion that they burn the paper, lest they be thought "rather cynical" for having disposed of these issues, "so fateful to millions of people, in such an offhand manner." "No, you keep it," said Stalin.[36]

Churchill's figures called for 90 per cent Russian "predominance" in Rumania and 90 per cent British-American interest in Greece. Yugoslavia and Hungary were to be divided equally, and Russia was to have 75 per cent influence in Bulgaria. In the wake of the retreating German army, Churchill directed British forces to restore order—and the monarchy—in Greece. American reactions to British policy pointed up Roosevelt's dilemma and the pressures upon him to do something to head off the division of Europe in spheres of influence. The dreaded "secret treaty" had in fact been signed; now Roosevelt was left with Wilson's predicament in full.

Even worse, though Russian military observers had joined the British and their Greek clients in the effort to persuade partisan leaders to lay down their arms, that solution did not stick. The partisans had been led to believe that all other groups contending for power in Athens and the countryside would also be required to put aside their weapons. When this renunciation did not occur, the partisans called for a protest march in Athens on December 3, 1944. British authorities first granted permission for the parade, then grew fearful and revoked the permit at three in the morning; but by that time—even if they had been willing to do so—it was too late for the partisan leaders to call it off. As the crowd neared the Grande Bretagne Hotel, the royalists opened fire on the unarmed marchers, killing or wounding nearly two hundred people. From the point of view of local communists, this panicky act successfully completed the polarization of Greek politics. As in Italy and France, communists occupied key positions in the movement, but its popular support stretched across nearly the whole Greek political spectrum, except for an inch or so at the end controlled by British-supported royalists and conservatives.[37] "Do not . . . hesitate to act as if you were in a conquered city where a local rebellion is in progress," Churchill instructed the British commander. "We have to hold and dominate Athens."[38]

Not since the Indian question in 1942 had the American press reacted so violently as it did to this blatant display of British imperial policy. It was a perfect editorial subject to illustrate—and condemn—American acquiescence in Russian and British "spheres of influence." Only the Soviet Union, busy with its own share of the Balkans, kept silent—a stance gratefully acknowledged by Churchill during parliamentary debates on Greece. "Naturally I felt the sudden way in which very large sections of the American press which has hitherto appreciated my ceaseless efforts to keep our two countries in harmony turned upon me over the Greek affair," the Prime Minister wrote an American friend at the height of the controversy. "How stultified they must feel today when, after infinite toils and many hazards, every ideal in the Atlantic Charter is being secured for Greece, and when the gratitude of her people for their deliverance from a dictatorship of a Communist gang is expressed on every side."[39]

As reports of daily events in Greece and Eastern Europe came in to the American press during December 1944 and January 1945, the new Secretary of State, Edward R. Stettinius, put a worried notation in his private memoranda: "United States military people were going so far as to say that we ought to withdraw from Europe and 'go to the Pacific now and win the war there.' "[40] A political columnist flatly told Stettinius that "we are letting the British and Russians ride roughshod over us." The Secretary asked him to be patient yet a while.

Business Week, usually well informed on such questions, suggested (and probably hoped) that the President would finally use his economic leverage to secure reasonable terms from Stalin not only on Poland but on other questions as well.[41] Though no more than a surmise, it was still a logical one; during those weeks the press was filled with suggestions for dealing with the imperialists and social revolutionaries. The problem they all perceived so well was how to convert economic power into political advantage, how to save the United Nations from the spheres of influence agreements—the secret treaties of World War II.

As Ambassador Harriman explained it to Stimson, it would be practically impossible for the United States to convince the Russians to eliminate the secret police from the areas where the Red Army penetrated. Therefore the administration had to find a way to keep the Russians from introducing the OGPU and communism into Hungary and other Eastern European countries.[42] Harriman was still convinced that the answer was economic diplomacy. On January 3, 1945, Foreign Minister Molotov made a formal request for a $6 billion credit for postwar purchases in the United States. The way he made the request irritated Harriman—a gratuitous offer to save capitalism from serious surplus crises in the transition period—but the Ambassador remained convinced that the Russians really needed American aid and would make political concessions to get it.

Almost at the same time, Henry Morgenthau proposed a different use of American economic power: he argued that the United States should extend an even bigger credit, $10 billion, without such obvious strings as Harriman's crude "Dollar Diplomacy" plan, though with other less visible ties and obligations to the American postwar economic system then being formulated. "If we were to come forward now and present to the Russians a concrete plan to aid them in the reconstruction period [as had already been promised the British]," contended Roosevelt's old friend and adviser, "it would contribute a great deal towards ironing out many of the difficulties we have been having with respect to their problems and policies."[43]

No one appreciated the President's dilemma more fully than Reinhold Niebuhr, who commented pessimistically in the *Nation*:

> . . . the world is wondering just how we will use the tremendous preponderance of economic power which we undoubtedly have. It must be observed furthermore that we are, naturally enough, more inclined to throw our weight around in the economic sphere because we lack the political points of contact to do so in the political sphere. *The very sense of frustration of a nation which has preponderant military power in the hour of crisis and preponderant economic power after the crisis but none of the political pawns used by other nations is a hazard to America's continuing responsibility in the community of nations. For it produces that nice mixture of nationalistic and idealistic isolationism which the other nations fear. . . .*
>
> The fear of our isolationism and of the unilateral expression of American economic power drives European powers into unilateral policies of security, which in turn makes our isolationism more probable.[44]

Harriman and the State Department succeeded in forestalling serious consideration of Morgenthau's proposal, and in convincing Roosevelt that he must keep foremost in mind the "tactical point of view." It would be "harmful for us to offer such a large credit at this time and thus lose what appears to be the only concrete bargaining lever" America had.[45] FDR told Harriman he had a "keen interest" in taking up the subject at Yalta; consequently, it should "not be pressed" until he had a chance to talk with Stalin personally. But once again, as at Teheran, Roosevelt did not broach the subject at Yalta.

The State Department had also been urging Roosevelt to confront his Allies in another way, through the creation of a European High Commission to enforce the Atlantic Charter throughout liberated Europe.[46] The Department wanted the President to introduce a Declaration on Liberated Europe at Yalta, and insist upon the creation of a commission to see that it was in fact carried out. Quite obviously something had to be done—and soon. On January 1, 1945, the Soviet Union had extended formal diplomatic recognition to the so-called Lublin Government in Warsaw, its own creation. As these pressures mounted, Roosevelt's temper flared up at Ambassador-designate to Poland Arthur Bliss Lane, who told him to get tough with the Russians. "Do you want me to go to war with Russia?" FDR snapped.[47]

The Polish question brought a loud protest from Senator Arthur Vandenberg of Michigan, the most important convert to "internationalism" the war had made. But wrapped inside the Senator's denunciation of Anglo-Russian secret diplomacy on the floor of Congress was a concrete plan for testing Allied intentions—if only the President could find some way to use it. After demanding a peace with justice for all the small nations, Vandenberg suddenly shifted to a consideration of the legitimate "security" problem posed by postwar Germany: "I know of no reason why a hard-and-fast treaty between the major allies should not be signed today to achieve this dependable end. We need not await the determination of our other postwar relationships. This problem—this menace—stands apart by itself."

The American response to Vandenberg's speech was tremendous. "I wish somebody would psychoanalyze that speech," the Senator confided to his wife. "I can't understand why it has been such an appalling sensation."[48] Walter Lippmann called it one of the few speeches ever to affect the course of events: "The immense importance of Senator Vandenberg's proposal is that it would end the policy of postponement and thus restore American influence in the settlement of Europe."[49]

Another of Vandenberg's listeners was equally struck: Secretary of War Henry L. Stimson wrote Stettinius that the speech had caused him to reconsider what had happened at the end of the last war. He now recalled that President Wilson had tried to create a League of Nations without a strong security foundation first. Wilson had belatedly recognized this failure in his offer of a security treaty to France "as the pillar of western Europe" against a new German menace, but it had been too late. Stimson urged Stettinius to present this point of view to the President before he reached any Big Three decisions at Yalta.[50]

Life devoted an editorial to the Senator's speech and press reaction to it, observing that while incorrigibly isolationist papers and journals like the *New York Daily News* and the *Chicago Tribune* considered the speech a mortal blow to the Republican party and their cause, sound thinkers like John Foster Dulles had praised it: "Having made such a treaty—and only after having made it—America would then have the 'duty and right' to demand that political and boundary questions in Europe be kept open and subject to postwar review. Thus we might stop the present series of unilateral acts. If we do not stop it we are heading for trouble."[51]

Vandenberg noted in his personal diary that Roosevelt had in fact asked for several copies of the speech to take with him to the Crimea. But as far as one can tell from the published records of the Yalta Conference, FDR made no use of them. Deeply concerned about the coming "isolationist" reaction to the United Nations, Roosevelt may well have decided that Wilson's greatest mistake had been to divide his supporters by demanding *two* kinds of internationalism at once—a League of Nations *and* a security treaty with France. At any rate, Stimson heard indirectly that the President was not much interested in his suggestion for settling the German question by an Allied treaty before tackling other problems at Yalta.[52]

Since 1941 Roosevelt's principal advisers had been steering him away from Big Four trusteeship and toward a new League of Nations. By the time of the Teheran conference he was moving rapidly in that direction. How that affected his consideration of a proposal for a Big Four treaty over Germany is problematical, but this much is clear: Roosevelt had allowed his alarm at Anglo-Russian secret diplomacy (and the politics of American reaction to it) to inhibit his genuine desire for good postwar relations with the Soviet Union. His concern about spreading communism also inhibited necessary decision-making. Responsibility for the public face of American diplomacy was not his alone, but when opportunities arose for direct use of economic diplomacy or political initiative, the President retreated into a protective ambivalence, waiting for something to turn up.

Plans were well advanced for the new United Nations when the Allies sat down at the first plenary session of the Yalta Conference. Despite all his efforts to prevent history from repeating itself, FDR found himself where Wilson had sat before him. Churchill and Stalin had seen to their security and their ambitions outside the framework of the new collective-security organization, and Roosevelt was left with the task of reversing an accelerating course of events. A few days before leaving Washington, Roosevelt had himself outlined the situation in his 1945 State of the Union message:

> During the interim period we and our Allies have a duty, which we cannot ignore, to use our influence to the end that no temporary or provisional authorities in the liberated countries block the eventual exercise of the peoples' right freely to choose the government and institutions under which, as free men, they are to live.

But at Yalta Roosevelt demurred when the State Department offered him the Declaration of Liberated Europe to accomplish this end, extracting from it the mechanism which Secretary Stettinius and his aides had put behind the rhetoric to see that something would come of it. Why the President acted in this fashion has never been satisfactorily explained,[53] but Churchill's behavior at Yalta was perhaps as much responsible for the lack of effective action on Eastern Europe as Roosevelt's, and it illustrated how complex the President's problems were. After exploding at one session that he would never allow fifty or more nations to put their interfering fingers into imperial affairs, the Prime Minister made a bad slip when the American Secretary of State read the proposed Declaration on Liberated Europe. Obviously worried about American postwar policy toward the Empire, Churchill remarked, to the dismay of American policy-makers, that he did not dissent from the President's declaration "so long as it was clearly understood that the reference to the Atlantic Charter did not apply to the British Empire." He added that he had long ago informed Wendell Willkie, then on his famous "One World" tour, that the Empire was excepted from all that kind of talk. Roosevelt inquired in mock seriousness if that was what had killed Mr. Willkie.[54]

Stalin, however, kept his silence. He had seen that the Prime Minister had overlooked the fact that the American proposal referred only to the former German satellites in Eastern Europe. While FDR did insist at this plenary session that there be free elections as soon as possible in Poland, the final protocol of the Yalta Conference stated only that the new Polish provisional government should be a "reorganization" of the Lublin government. This was to be accomplished by consultations with "other Polish democratic leaders from within Poland and from abroad." Admiral William D. Leahy, Roosevelt's military aide, saw the document and threw up his hands. "Mr. President," he said, "this is so elastic that the Russians can stretch it all the way from Yalta to Washington without ever technically breaking it." "I know, Bill—I know it," FDR replied. "But it's the best I can do for Poland at this time."[55]

On board ship during the return voyage from Yalta, reporters asked the President if Churchill's stubborn attitude on colonial issues did not negate the Atlantic Charter. Roosevelt answered simply: "The Atlantic Charter is a beautiful idea."[56] Although he explained a bit, the report of this interview set off another public discussion of Russian and British imperialism. Against these charges, Roosevelt's appeal for the United Nations sounded like an unhappy echo from an earlier day. His report to Congress on the Big Three conference ended with a dangerously overoptimistic assessment of the future. Yalta, he declared, spelled the end "of the system of unilateral action and exclusive alliances and spheres of influence and balances of power and all the other expedients which have been tried for centuries—and have failed."

Roosevelt put all his failing strength into the fight for an international organization; unlike Wilson, he had the votes in the Senate to complete the task. Yet the only way to make this new

League work was to have reached prior agreement on issues left by the war itself, and hope that postwar questions could be handled as they arose. But the President had not been able to make decisions on any of the really crucial problems, issues that were fundamental to the peace. The United Nations was designed to be a peacekeeping device; but it could not be made into a peacemaking device without dividing the Big Three. Stalin's demand for three votes in the United Nations was primarily his way of calling attention to this fact. America could build up numerical majorities with its allies and the Latin American nations, but the Russians would regard the result as meaningless because it was based upon the assumption that there was a genuine consensus in the world when such a thing did not exist. Roosevelt did not tell the American people this—or even the Vice-President.

Even those informed persons who recognized this unhappy predicament had little inclination to face up to its implications. Besides, American goals as set forth in the "American Century" and the Atlantic Charter still might be achieved by ignoring the legitimacy—or even the existence—of everything else. Henry Luce sounded the call to reassert these goals in the May 1945 issue of *Fortune.* "If our hardboiled school of liberals acquiesces in the destruction of Poland for the sake of Big Three unity," he charged, "will it also acquiesce in the partition of China for the same reason? If so, how should China be divided? What is to be the fate of Germany in a Europe divided between a Russian and a British sphere? Who is to have the Middle East?"[57]

It was almost completely a false issue: no one was acquiescing in these developments after Roosevelt's death. During the war he had held out the belief that America's traditional goals might yet be reached, even after he himself had come to doubt it. Harry S. Truman once implied that he and Roosevelt had agreed upon what was almost an ideological justification for the containment policy more than two years before it became doctrine. It sounded very much like Bullitt's description of the world from Rome in 1944. Truman wrote:

> We did on occasion talk about some of the history of the past, the War between the States and the Napoleonic Era. I recall we once talked about the Islamite approach to the conquest of Europe, and

> how Charles Martel turned them back at Tours. We discussed such episodes in history as the turning back of the Turks at Vienna, and how Genghis Khan was stopped before he could reach Austria. These were the things we talked about when we were through with our business. Roosevelt was just as interested as I was in history, and knew more about certain phases of it than I did.[58]

If Truman was playing tricks on the dead, it was because he needed a strong ideological foundation for his foreign policy, and Roosevelt's ambivalence had not provided it. FDR's attempt to make reality conform to the Atlantic Charter, even after the complete failure of second-front diplomacy, was a vain hope. The measure of his ability to project this illusion was soon evidenced in Harry Truman's mystification that things were not what he, and much of the rest of the country, supposed.

This illusion was born of a deeper pessimism—the pessimism Luce had tried to dispel in the "American Century," the pessimism Niebuhr feared would lead Americans to perform the very acts most likely to drive their allies to unilateral measures. "Despite military victories," the OSS chief in Berne, Allen Dulles, wrote, "I feel apprehensive as to what we will find in Europe for years to come. We are moving towards the dramatic finale which will leave a large part of Central Europe in chaos. If Hitler succeeds in nothing else, like Samson, he may pull down the pillars of the temple and leave a long and hard road of reconstruction." At Roosevelt's death Dulles was engaged in secret negotiations to minimize the impact of these falling pillars. He later wrote that it was important to achieve a German surrender in northern Italy in order to prevent unnecessary destruction in that area where leftist partisans were strongest, and to permit British and American troops to get to Trieste before "either Soviet troops coming across Hungary or Tito's followers reaching up out of Yugoslavia, supported by the pro-Communist partisans," could reach that city "and possibly west of there before we arrived."[59] Truman proposed measures at Potsdam designed to rebuild the temple according to American plans.

THREE ☆☆

Harry S. Truman: From San Francisco to Potsdam

"I would convey to you most earnestly," Acting Secretary of State Joseph Grew wrote to Representative John Coffee and several other "liberal" congressmen, "my own conviction that editorial comment characterizing President Roosevelt as playing a mediator role in European areas is doing an injustice to our late President, since he pursued in those areas a policy looking towards the concrete attainment of the objectives for which we fought, rather than a policy of the disinterested mediator."[1]

Disturbed by Truman's strong policy in Eastern and Central Europe, Coffee and his colleagues had sent to the State Department Walter Lippmann's discouraging account of Russian-American conflicts over Poland at the San Francisco Conference on the Organization of the United Nations. Lippmann had written: "At San Francisco we allowed ourselves to become involved in the Polish matter in exactly that sort of Anglo-American 'front' against Russia which Mr. Roosevelt had consistently striven to avoid; and compounded the mistake by also getting involved in what appeared to be a Western Hemisphere 'front' directed both against Russia and against the idea of an effective general security organization."[2] Grew's efforts to dispel these liberal doubts about Truman's foreign policies were largely successful, because Roosevelt had never resolved the conflict between his rhetoric and the complicated strategy of postponement, between his defense of traditional American objectives and the requirements of an effective coalition in peacetime as well as in war.

Early Cold War critics soon all but disappeared because Acting Secretary Grew was right: American foreign policy *was* directed at specific positive objectives—traditional American liberal objectives—and not at perpetuating a big-power oligarchy. Truman's discovery that he must resolve these contradictions is summed up in this paragraph from his *Memoirs*:

> President Roosevelt had built up the idea that China was a great power because he looked to the future and wanted to encourage the Chinese people. In reality it would be only with the greatest difficulty that Chiang Kai-shek could even reoccupy South China.[3]

What was true of Roosevelt's China policy was just as true of other issues; the late President had looked to the future for solutions to all the difficult issues left by the war. With Roosevelt gone, Secretary Stimson thought the impetus for a strong policy toward the Soviets would now come from Churchill, and he advised General Marshall that they "ought to be alert now that a new man was at the helm in the Presidency to see that he was advised as to the background of the past differences between Britain and America on these matters."[4]

Truman's other advisers kept him fully informed on past Anglo-American differences—and on current ones. But they really were no longer the issue. "It was clear that the Russian foreign policy," Truman wrote in his *Memoirs*, "was based on the conclusion that we were heading for a major depression, and they were already planning to take advantage of our setback."[5] He had reached this conclusion, he says, after two weeks of Big Three meetings at Potsdam, where American proposals had been sidetracked by Old World diplomatic maneuvering. To Truman, Stalin's tactics meant only one thing: "The Russians were planning world conquest." There was only one way to deal with the threat: "Force is the only thing the Russians understand." By the time Truman wrote these impressions of his meeting with Stalin at Potsdam, the Cold War had become a hot war in Korea, and Truman may have been anxious to demonstrate how tough he had been in containing the Russians even in 1945. Nonetheless, the talk about the Kremlin's expectation of an American depression was very much on Truman's mind in 1945. He meant to disabuse the Soviets of any such notion as soon as possible, for he thought it was influencing their tactics in Eastern Europe as well. In assuming that Stalin refused to talk about internationalizing key waterways in Eastern Europe and facilitating East-West trade in other ways because he anticipated a depression in the United States, Truman also projected American economic concern onto Russian minds.

State Department briefing papers drawn up for the Potsdam Conference made frequent references to America's "strong interest in the preservation of conditions in the countries of Eastern Europe which will permit the continued operation of . . . multilateral trade, and accordingly . . . a necessity for maintaining not only its own trading interests and positions in those countries, but also the trading interests and positions of other countries which were importers to, and exporters from, Eastern Europe before the war." America's direct interests in Eastern Europe were far less important than the rebuilding of an effective European and world economic system; but the only way to promote such reconstruction was for America (the only nation powerful enough to do it) to take the lead in keeping the door open in Eastern Europe. This fact and not simple economic motives alone prompted Washington's strong efforts to enforce equal economic opportunity there. Had he lived, Roosevelt would have been faced with the same situation. Truman clearly saw it not only as an international question but as a domestic one. Without a functioning world system, depression was inevitable. The belief that Russia was counting on an American downturn to further its own goals was the natural result of such a preoccupation, and of the assumption that abstract Marxism moved Stalin's hand in world affairs.

In January 1945, *Fortune* magazine's survey of American opinion revealed that 68.2 per cent of those queried believed that unemployment would be the most important issue after the war; 48.9 per cent also believed there would be a serious depression within ten years. After the Potsdam Conference, 58.9 per cent still felt that unemployment was the most important domestic question, but 55.6 per cent now thought Russia was an even larger problem.[6] The more Washington pressed the Soviets, the more adamant they became about maintaining their sphere of influence in Eastern Europe, and the bigger the problem looked to the public.

Only with Russia "playing her part," said *Fortune*, was there hope for the future of an open economic order. More than a year before, the magazine's editors continued, Stalin had jokingly told Eric Johnston of the United States Chamber of Commerce that the United States would have to give the Soviet Union credits to avoid a depression. Much had changed since that time. "Until profound political differences are resolved," *Fortune* said, "Russian credits should remain in abeyance."[7]

Truman's effort from the time of the San Francisco Conference through the Potsdam meeting was twofold: he wanted to teach the Russians that they had to play their part in the new order, and he wanted to do it by making it clear that America did not need Russian markets. If Stalin had closed Eastern Europe in order to increase economic pressures in the United States, he would have to be made to face the consequences of such a miscalculation at once. On the way back from Potsdam, Truman informed the officers' mess on board the *USS Augusta* that it did not matter if the Russians had been obstinate, "because the United States now had developed an entirely new weapon of such force and nature that we did not need the Russians—or any other nation."[8]

Ambassador Averell Harriman rushed home after Franklin Roosevelt's death just as soon as he had completed arrangements for a meeting between Foreign Minister Molotov and the new President. It was essential, Harriman thought, that the two meet before Molotov went on to San Francisco for the opening of the United Nations organization conference. Harriman wanted to make sure that the Russian leader learned "from the very highest source that we would not stand for any pushing around on the

Polish question." To his relief he found that Truman's "mind didn't need any making up from me on that point."[9]

Despite his continuing irritation at the gratuitous Soviet offer to relieve American surpluses by accepting a credit, Harriman wanted to assure Truman, as he had assured Roosevelt before him, that the Soviet government "placed high importance on a large postwar credit as a basis for the development of 'Soviet-American relations.' "[10] It was true, however, Harriman said, that "there were some quarters in Moscow that believed it was a matter of life and death to American business to increase our exports to Russia." This Marxist fantasy complicated the issue, the Ambassador suggested, and had to be dispelled at once. Only then would these statements be revealed for what they were—cryptic admissions that "the Russians needed us more than we needed them."[11]

There was a good deal of guesswork in Harriman's analysis, both about Moscow's thinking and even to a certain extent about Washington's plans. No doubt he had taken Roosevelt's failure to broach the subject at Yalta, for example, as agreement with his position on economic aid to Russia. How else to interpret FDR's inaction, given the rejection of Morgenthau's proposal for aid to Russia? Roosevelt himself had never decided what he would do with American economic power in response to the Russian occupation of Eastern Europe, except to tell Grew after a cabinet meeting on March 2, 1945, that the allocation of certain warships to the Soviet Union "might be used as a *quid pro quo* in persuading Russia to let down the bars for American businessmen to enter Rumania."[12]

Truman's first formal news conference, held while Harriman was en route to Washington, suggested the mood the Ambassador would find in Washington. A reporter for *Time* magazine wrote a public "memorandum" of the crucial part of that dialogue, one which fully briefed the magazine's readers on what to expect from now on:

> The day's most provocative question came innocently enough: "Do you expect to see Foreign Commissar Molotov before the conference?"

> Harry Truman said he did. Firmly he said that the Soviet official would stop by and pay his respects to the President of the United States. The President of the United States added: he should. It had been a long time since White House reporters had cheered a President's answer, but they clapped and laughed and cheered for a full minute.[13]

After explaining his views on Russian thinking about economic aid from the United States, Ambassador Harriman warned Truman "that in effect what we were faced with was a 'barbarian invasion of Europe,' that Soviet control over any foreign country did not mean merely influence on their foreign relations but the extension of the Soviet system with secret police, extinction of freedom of speech, etc., and that we had to decide what should be our attitude in the face of these unpleasant facts."[14] Truman emphasized that he planned to be firm with the Russians and make no concessions which would weaken in any way American principles. He did not expect to get "100 per cent of what we wanted but that on important matters he felt that we should be able to get 85 per cent."

The Ambassador explained that while he was not pessimistic about ultimately achieving working relations with the Russians, that achievement would require facing up to the reality that the Soviets would not voluntarily cooperate with the United States in the construction of the postwar order. "Stalin [has] discovered from the Lublin Poles that an honest execution of the Crimean decision would mean the end of Soviet-backed Lublin control over Poland," Harriman explained to prove his case, "since any real democratic leader . . . would serve as a rallying point for 80 or 90 per cent of the Polish people against the Lublin Communists."[15] The rationale for continued nonrecognition of other Russian-sponsored governments in Eastern Europe was similar: so long as there was a rallying point for opposition to the Soviets, there was a chance that their governments might not endure.

As Harriman said later, Truman's mind didn't need any making up on this point. At 2 P.M. on the afternoon of April 23, 1945, the President asked Harriman to join the Secretaries of State, War, and Navy, as well as the Joint Chiefs and Admiral

Leahy, to discuss the Polish matter with him before he saw Molotov later that day. Stimson noted in his diary that Truman went around the circle of his advisers until he found support for a firm policy over Poland. On the other hand, General Marshall fully agreed with Stimson's contention that the Russians "perhaps were being more realistic than we were in regard to their own security." And Admiral Leahy admitted that the Yalta agreement was unclear.[16]

Harriman tried to reassure Stimson and Marshall that proper handling of the situation could avert a break with the Russians. When Molotov entered the President's office a few hours later, Truman immediately demanded not merely a reorganization of the Lublin government but a "new" provisional government to be made up of "genuinely representative" democratic elements from within Poland and abroad. Then he tested Harriman's analysis. "Legislative appropriation [is] required for any economic measures in the foreign field," the President said, measuring each word carefully, "and . . . [I can] not hope to get these measures through Congress unless there [is] public support for them." He hoped the Foreign Minister would keep this factor well in mind as negotiations over the Polish question continued at San Francisco.[17]

Two days later Harriman met with the American delegation to the United Nations Conference, already assembled in San Francisco. He began with a simple statement that, since Yalta, relations with the Soviets had taken a different turn. In part this was normal because wartime relations always changed under peacetime conditions, but all "men who have dealt with Russia know of the Russian attempt to chisel, by bluff, pressure, and other unscrupulous methods, to get what they wish. . . . While we cannot go to war with Russia, we must do everything we can to maintain our position as strongly as possible in Eastern Europe." There was no need to elaborate on the levers available to the President; they were apparent to the delegates. But Representative Sol Bloom, somewhat concerned by Harriman's sharp description of Russian policies, finally asked if the Yalta agreements were in fact quite so explicit as all that—and was it all that obvious that the Russians were violating them? Harriman cut him off at once. "All decent people could understand it," he said.[18]

"Now we are getting somewhere!" exulted Senator Vandenberg, a member of the delegation. Secretary Stettinius had also brought a "thrilling message" to San Francisco, Vandenberg wrote in his diary. FDR's appeasement was over. "The new President . . . has declined to even wink at a surrender to Stalin on his demand for representation here for the Lublin Poles."[19] Both Vandenberg and Harriman had resolved their own doubts about Russia's behavior and about America's proper response. Vandenberg, for example, all but forgot at San Francisco that he had warned against pushing the Russians until a security treaty over Germany had been signed, and Harriman forgot that weeks before he had advised Washington that Russia was likely to be suspicious of the new United Nations for some time to come. "The court, they believe, is packed against them." Despite their new world-power status, Harriman noted, the Soviets believed that most nations remained hostile to them. They therefore regarded the new organization as a means of protecting the Soviet Union against invaders, but they opposed its use to mediate disputes between the Soviet Union and other nations. This accounted for the Kremlin's adamant position on the veto, even on subjects to come before the Security Council for general debate, for fear that free discussion might lead eventually "to an appearance of disagreement between the great powers." Truman also noted this consistent Russian attitude, and he tried to discourage it. Stalin was always talking about the Big Three, the President complained. "I felt very strongly that participation of all nations, small and large, was just as important to world peace as that of the Big Three."[20]

Stalin had put Russian fears as forcefully as he could at Yalta:

> MARSHAL STALIN said that his colleagues in Moscow could not forget the events of December 1939 during the Finnish war when at the instigation of England and France the League of Nations expelled the Soviet Union from the League *and mobilized world opinion* against the Soviet Union, even going so far as to speak of a crusade.[21]

Bullitt had correctly anticipated the value of his activity in Geneva after all! Molotov's opening speech at San Francisco was a further demonstration of these deep-seated fears. Denouncing any attempt to limit the Security Council veto, he charged that the opponents of "effective" international organization had never ceased their activities, even though they now hid behind the most virtuous of pretenses: "For this purpose they frequently use ostensibly the most democratic watchwords and arguments, including the professed protection of the interests of small nations or the principles of the equity and equality of nations."[22]

It was inherently a difficult position to take before a conference called at the end of a life-and-death struggle against fascist powers which had crushed the rights of small nations and launched the Second World War. In private the Soviets had complained to the United States and Great Britain that while the Lublin government was being excluded on the grounds of nonrecognition by Washington and London, invitations had been sent to India, not even an independent nation yet, and to small countries like Haiti, Liberia, and Paraguay—and this in spite of the fact that the Soviet Union had no relations with these countries.[23]

Throughout the conference sessions the line between spheres of influence and "collective security" was drawn again and again—on both substantive and symbolic issues. The American delegation, nominally led by Stettinius, was often in fact guided by Senator Vandenberg in alliance with Harold Stassen and John Foster Dulles. These men reinforced the demand for majority decisions on all issues, as if the kind of *de facto* consensus on fundamentals which existed on Capitol Hill could be assumed in San Francisco as well. For example, Russia wanted a rotating chairmanship among the Big Four to emphasize the continuation of the Grand Alliance and its veto power; the United States contended that the chairmanship belonged only to the host country, thus depriving the office of any symbolic meaning and further emphasizing the changed conditions since Yalta.

But it was the debate over Poland and Argentina which dominated the early sessions of the conference—and determined what kind of organization would emerge from San Francisco. On the day after the Russian Foreign Minister's harsh speech against those who opposed an "effective" international organization, Jan Masaryk rose to speak on the Polish question for the Czechoslovakian delegation. At the time he still envisioned a mediating role for his country between East and West. Chastened by the Munich experience and their futile reliance upon the West for help against Germany, he and his countrymen had a strong premonition of disaster for Central Europe if disagreement over Poland continued. Consequently, Masaryk urged the admission of the Lublin government to the United Nations.

Before Masaryk could finish, Vandenberg leaned forward and whispered harshly in Stettinius' ear, "This move must be killed at once and in the open." He wrote out a short statement for Stettinuis even as Stettinius was asking for the floor. Taking Vandenberg's note, the Secretary declared that the United States was waiting for Russia to carry out the Yalta agreements on Poland. Truman had said this privately; now it was a public matter.[24]

In making the matter public, the American delegation also opened the way for press criticism of Russian behavior throughout Eastern Europe. Some newspaper reports even speculated that the conference would break up over the issue. Molotov countered the introduction of the Polish question with recriminations on the proposed admission of Argentina. At a specially called press conference he read a series of damning quotations from Cordell Hull and Roosevelt on the fascist regime in Buenos Aires. Having made his point, Molotov put the papers aside and hinted at Russian willingness to strike a bargain. "Perhaps it is necessary to forget the sins of Argentina," he said. Then he repeated the word "perhaps" twice more, very slowly. "But why is it necessary to forget all about Poland? Why should not Poland be represented if Argentina is?"[25]

Stettinius responded through his own press conference, announcing the Russian arrest of several Poles who had supposedly gone to Moscow under the impression they had been invited to discuss the composition of the new provisional government. At the next session of the conference, the American delegation supported a motion for immediate Argentine membership. When Molotov asked for a delay in the vote, several Latin American delegations demanded at once that the conference accept the decision of the recent Mexico City Conference where Buenos Aires had been accepted back into the Western Hemisphere community. Particularly emboldened by the Soviet-American split, the Peruvian delegate asked what right the conference had to inquire into the nature of the Argentine government now that it was recognized by its neighbors.[26]

Ironically, the American delegation had itself previously been split over the Argentine question. Those who favored the motion, however, could now cite two reasons for their position: (1) the need to maintain Washington's leadership in the hemisphere, against both outsiders and insiders; and (2) a growing conviction that the United States would sooner or later need Latin American votes against the Russians. But the delegation did not consider what majority votes would be worth if the Soviets should conclude that their security interests would receive no consideration in an American-led United Nations.[27]

It was Senator Vandenberg who pushed for a regional security agreement under the U.N. Charter, which would protect American leadership in the hemisphere at the same time it would avoid regional blocs (especially in Europe). A compromise was finally reached whereby regional security organizations against enemy states in the Second World War would be permitted under Article 51 of the new Charter until such time as the United Nations could be charged with the full responsibility for preventing further aggression by those states. "I do not object to this exemption," Vandenberg wrote Stettinius, "and I am quite willing to continue it for the very good reason that we can't expect our allies to depend upon an untried Peace League for their defense against a resurgent Axis until it has demonstrated its adequate capacity to serve this defense function." But despite this brief restatement of his January position, Vandenberg could not see any connection between his own insight and Soviet policy on Poland.[28]

At San Francisco the United States thus protected its prerogatives in Latin America while only half-recognizing other nations' "rights" to regional security measures, and continued to force the issue in Poland and Eastern Europe in spite of Article 51. Even Stimson rationalized the American position as almost equitable: Russia was "not such an overwhelmingly gigantic power from the ones which she's probably going to make a row about as we are here, and on the other hand our fussing around among those little fellows there doesn't upset any balance in Europe at all. That's the main answer."[29] To a great extent, of course, how one received that answer depended upon where he lived.

Having secured Article 51, however, the United States immediately moved to secure another of its desiderata by insisting upon a trusteeship which allowed it to retain unilateral control over the former Japanese mandated islands. It also supported a system that kept the European empires fully intact but denied support to a Russian request for a trusteeship over a former Italian colony in Africa. Roosevelt himself had suggested to Molotov in 1942 that Stalin should consider expanding his international responsibilities in this fashion, but at Yalta, when the Soviets had raised this question in specific terms, Stettinius had agreed only that they should be "eligible" for such a trusteeship. American control over the Japanese mandated islands was quickly and efficiently accomplished by inserting a provision in the U.N. Charter providing that the trusteeship terms be negotiated in each case and evolved by the states directly concerned, then submitted to the United Nations for general approval. Under the specifications of the American trusteeship, the United States reserved the right to establish naval, military, and air bases on the islands, to make use of local volunteers to protect those bases, and to exclude all other members of the U.N. from using those facilities—a most favorable "trusteeship" indeed.[30] The Russians accepted this plan when it came to a vote in the Trusteeship Council in late 1946 because it was a frank recognition of a sphere of influence. But the United States did not reciprocate the favor, as we shall see.

Immediately after the German surrender in May, Truman curtailed Lend-Lease to the Soviet Union. He later disclaimed personal responsibility for the abrupt way the cutback was accomplished—so dramatically, in fact, that ships on the high seas were ordered to turn back to the United States. But at the time he carefully allowed newsmen a hint of the idea: the administration would handle future aid to the Soviet Union "in a way which we think will be all right for the peace of the world."[31]

The *Nation* thought the obvious hitch in this line of reasoning had somehow been overlooked: that it would strengthen economic ties between Russian and Germany.

> Russia . . . can be counted on to make a good recovery even if left to its own—and Germany's resources. Without help from us it will still be able to adopt the policy of self-sufficiency, more or less isolated from the world economy, which it followed with some success during the 1920's and 1930's.[32]

In San Francisco one of Molotov's aides told John Foster Dulles much the same thing. "He said," Dulles later reported to Stettinius, "that the failure of the U.S. to grant large Soviet credits was construed by him and others as a measure of class warfare against the Soviets, designed to coerce them in . . . their legitimate field of political activity. He said the Soviets would not be coerced; that they could, if necessary, get along without U.S. credits and would do it rather than surrender their independence of action." Dulles had earlier replied to Molotov's aide that he knew nothing about current policy on the matter, but that there was a general impression in the United States that the Russians had not carried out their agreements, an impression which always made for bad relations and public pressure on government.[33]

Truman made one more effort before the Potsdam Conference to use "carrot" diplomacy on the Kremlin: he approved a new statement on American reparations policy in regard to Germany. It remained fundamental to United States policy, said the pronouncement, that German war potential must be destroyed to the extent of leaving no possibility for its future reconstruction. The United States therefore opposed "any reparation plan based on the assumption that . . . [it] or any other country will finance directly or indirectly any reconstruction in Germany or reparation by Germany."[34]

In the context of Russian-American disputes over Poland and Eastern Europe during May and June, the pronouncement's change in emphasis hinted that the United States was preparing to take a tough stand on all reparations not directly related to the narrowly defined destruction of German war potential. By denying Russia economic aid, first from United States sources, then from German resources, Truman might be able to undo the hitch in economic diplomacy at the same time he kept Germany and Russia apart.

On June 26, 1945, the sixty-third day of the San Francisco Conference, the President delivered a benediction to the assembled delegations. Molotov was not there; he had long since gone home. After the Polish debate and Molotov's departure, the Russian delegation had raised few additional objections. When Truman finished the benediction, Stettinius stepped forward, and with a single rap of his gavel declared the meeting adjourned. "The band played the Star Spangled Banner," Stettinius wrote in his diary, "and then it seemed as if school was over and everybody was going home for vacation."[35]

Truman, with his new Secretary of State, James F. Byrnes, was preparing for the trip to the Potsdam Conference. Despite Churchill's anxiety about getting at German and other problems before British and American troops withdrew from advanced positions, Truman had postponed the conference and ordered General Eisenhower to proceed with the zonal occupation agreements. The President had assured Stimson that he had postponed the Big Three meeting in order to have his "master card," the atomic bomb, in hand when he left for Potsdam.[36] But the first test of the new weapon did not occur until after the conference began, and it was still difficult to tell how important it would be in the diplomatic equation. In the aftermath of San Francisco, America's principal lever was still economic—and it did not appear to be strong enough to pry the Russians out of Eastern Europe. As Truman pondered this situation, his attitude toward Soviet obstinacy—that was all he could conceive it to be—hardened, his impatience grew, and his willingness to listen to Russian complaints about the abandonment of Big Three diplomacy completely disappeared. It all added up to a new sense of urgency that something be done to prevent Anglo-Russian division of the world.

Nor could the United States' domestic situation be separated from Anglo-Russian developments. As Robert Wagner said in opening hearings on the administration's full-employment bill at the time of the Potsdam Conference:

> Mass unemployment would drive us toward both economic isolationism and economic imperialism; economic isolationism in the vain hope of providing jobs in America by excluding the products of other nations; economic imperialism in the vain hope of creating markets abroad for American products at the threat of the sword.[37]

Somewhat later in the hearings on this proposed measure, which many argued was the capstone to the whole New Deal effort, Chicago Mayor Edward J. Kelly dramatically introduced former Senator Harry S. Truman's own report as chairman of the War Contracts Subcommittee of the Military Affairs Committee. Truman's committee had concluded that:

> Unless an economic substitute is found for war contracts, mass unemployment will become a serious threat, and the number of unemployed men and women in this country could easily surpass anything that was dreamed of during the last depression.
>
> The fight for full employment is a twofold battle. On the one hand, the Government must do everything in its power to stimulate increased opportunities for employment in private enterprise. This is the major front. On the other hand, to the extent that private enterprise cannot by itself assure full employment, the Government must take such measures as may be necessary to fill the gap.[38]

Although Secretary of State James F. Byrnes could not appear before Wagner's committee before leaving for the Berlin Conference, he did send the Senator a message explaining the interdependence of American foreign and domestic policies:

> The United States is today a bastion of democracy and private enterprise. In many countries throughout the world, our political and economic creed is in conflict with ideologies which reject both of these principles. To the extent that we are able to manage our domestic affairs successfully, we shall win converts to our creed in every land. . . . It would thus contribute to the establishment of a liberal trading system and the attainment of an expanding world economy.[39]

The demand for a full-employment bill in the United States, where homage to the shibboleths of free enterprise was still greater than anywhere else in the industrial world, was the American reflection of a world-wide movement against laissez-faire capitalism, and fear of a new depression. Articles and advertisements in business journals constantly reminded economic leaders of industrial strife, sit-down strikes, and the general turmoil of the depression. An ad placed by the state of Georgia, urging businessmen to locate in that state, appeared in several business periodicals:

> Here are a people bred in the American tradition—99% native-born—who believe in business enterprise, who welcome new industry, who are friendly, intelligent and cooperative.[40]

Georgia and other Southern states yearned for "foreign" capital after the war; their governments held out promises of stability, tax advantages, and nonunionized labor. The goal as American leaders saw it in 1945 was to bring that kind of stability to the whole world. To the extent they succeeded, the demand for state intervention at home would decline. The problem was to induce the British and the Russians to stop building blocs against the American system.

These problems were truly reciprocal: a renewed labor-capital struggle in the United States was almost a certainty, Truman had said in his subcommittee report, unless some substitute for war contracts could be found. Policy-makers feared that those in the country most concerned about this problem would turn inward and demand a super New Deal to ward off disaster. This internalization would bring into being a coalition of extreme New Deal liberals and various vote-supplying blocs, probably including the more radical labor unions, which would then quickly gain the upper hand in the transition period. A postwar "popular front" would set a direction for the government which could not be easily reversed.

At the center of these concerns stood Henry Wallace, now Secretary of Commerce, but always a potential leader of such a coalition. Already there was some feeling that Truman was a usurper in the White House. Roosevelt's true heir was Wallace, said many liberals, and they waited for the chance to answer his call for a new domestic crusade. Henry Wallace was never quite what these liberals supposed, nor was he what his enemies asserted. But his appointment as Secretary of Commerce in January 1945 focused political tensions on a single individual. Wallace's insistence—or persistence—in proclaiming himself a production-oriented Commerce Secretary, one wrapped in "one-world" rhetoric and "soft" policies toward Soviet Russia, heightened these tensions.

Addressing a forum under the auspices of the *New Republic* on January 29, 1945, Wallace had declared: "The nation must not be subject to an economic Munich or Dunkerque. To have 10,000,000 men unemployed is as dangerous to the nation as it was for the British to have 250,000 men on the beaches at Dunkerque. Kaiser, Higgin and a multitude of industrialists like them know the answer and it is . . . full production, full use of all resources. We must give these production-minded men a chance. They must not be ruined by financiers, seeking control through scarcity."[41]

A powerful appeal—and a dangerous one—many thought. What if the production-minded men failed? The choice seemed obvious to Wallace's critics. "Wouldn't it be strange if we were to adopt State Socialism for ourselves," said a prominent financier, John M. Hancock, to the San Francisco Commonwealth Club, "while we have been fighting the war to destroy it elsewhere in the world?" His choice of words—"state socialism" instead of fascism or Nazism, or even National Socialism—seemed to confirm the belief that nationalization was at the heart not only of European political tensions but (along with Wallace) of American tensions as well. "Though we all recognize," Hancock continued, that "a strongly centralized federal government is helpful in fighting a war, don't we also recognize that the idea is contrary to the entire history of our nation and the philosophy of life of our people?"[42]

Memories of the first New Deal with its "intranationalistic" NRA and AAA, of the mid-1930's when the world seemed to be closing into hard-bitten political-military blocs, now swirled into a dark and unclear picture of the immediate future. Several prominent Americans believed that the United States might be forced to adopt some form of state socialism simply to meet the challenge from nationalized economies in the world market. Herbert Hoover, for example, who had early recognized this challenge as well as others in the Russian Revolution, pointed out that Soviet expansion meant not only the spread of an ideology alien to the West, not only a denial of Eastern Europe to American exports and investments, but also (and most significantly) a foreign trade by those nations that "will be conducted through government agencies and thus American exporters will need to deal, in effect, with a single-front, gigantic monopoly. These monopolies will compete with us in other markets."[43]

Another echo from the 1930's, Alfred M. Landon, warned that the British Labour party's victory would mean "a big barrier to the American program of removing obstacles to world trade. It definitely increases the trend towards bilateral trade treaties."[44] "It would be hard to conceive a plan more directly designed to divide the United Nations," Eugene Rostow, a student of the Russian political-economic system and future State Department planner wrote in *Fortune*, "than to translate all trade among them from the commercial to the political and governmental plane."[45]

As these comments make clear, the real issue was not preservation of Eastern European markets but the preservation and extension of a trade system among all nations (if possible) which would enable the United States to keep government intervention to a minimum. If Russia was not aiming at world revolution, most American leaders reasoned, it should be willing to participate in such a system, or at least not obstruct those nations in its "security zone" from participating in the reconstruction of the world economy. But even if Stalin was himself a "conservative," i.e., nonideological, his use of foreign communist parties to further Russian national aims would inevitably bring the Soviet Union and the United States into conflict.

In other words, the expansion of the Soviet state-socialist system, even if limited to countries geographically close to Russia, was a potential threat to the next "tier" of states in Central Europe. Therefore, American interests were endangered both politically and economically. The more states Russia fenced in behind the "Iron Curtain," the more likely it would be that the American economy would be forced to the left. Some American leaders also saw the leftward trend in Britain and France as communist-inspired, though most regarded this development simply as an unhappy consequence of the war. Nevertheless, it was a "leftist" movement and, as such, part of the overall threat to American interests.

"If the English nationalize their cotton industry," wrote Bernard Baruch to Senator Albert Gore, "does that not mean that there will be only one buyer of raw cotton in this country? And if France nationalizes her industry, will we not finally have to put all the cotton growers into some nationalization? The totalization or nationalization of industry keeps moving towards Statism and towards the destruction of the system which has made this country great."[46] "I am waiting to see whether the Big Three meeting in Berlin will have the effect of increasing this tendency or stopping it," he added in a note to Congressman Wright Patman of Texas.[47]

When Truman arrived in Berlin for the TERMINAL Conference, as it was code-named, he was ready to make a number of proposals to reverse that tendency, and to insure the peace as well. He thought, for example, that the whole Balkan area might be neutralized. As he wrote in his *Memoirs:*

> I told Stimson of the talks I used to have with my friend Senator Elbert Thomas of Utah. I would point to a map of Europe and trace its breadbasket, with Hungary a cattle country and Rumania and the Ukraine as the wheat area. Up to the northwest lay Western Germany, Northern France, Belgium, and Britain with their coal, iron, and big industries.
>
> The problem, as Senator Thomas and I talked about it, was to help unify Europe by linking up the breadbasket with the industrial centers through a free flow of trade. To facilitate this flow, the Rhine and Danube could be linked with a vast network of canals which would provide a passage all the way from the North Sea to the Black Sea and the Mediterranean. This would constitute free waterways for trade, while each country bordering on the waterways would have the riparian rights it should have. In addition, it would be possible to extend the free waterways of the world by linking the Rhine-Danube waterways with the Black Sea straits and making the Suez, Kiel, and Panama Canals free waterways for merchant ships.[48]

Truman's idea for "revolutionizing" the Balkans began with

this plan and went on to even grander things, including a TVA for Central Europe. A strikingly similar analysis of the postwar potential of the area, and the way Soviet expansion darkened this bright vision, appeared about the time of the Potsdam meeting in *Business Week:*

> In an age of light metals, a TVA for the Danube and the harnessing of the area's hydroelectric power to an aluminum industry based on rich local bauxite deposits (in Yugoslavia and Hungary) could revolutionize the Balkans.
>
> But already the trade of the area is being turned eastward. This week [June 9, 1945] Rumania signed a trade agreement with the U.S.S.R. calling for the exchange of Soviet machinery for Rumanian oil, foodstuffs, and metals.
>
> If the eastern area is virtually closed to the exports of western Europe, a new "ruble bloc" may emerge on the Eurasian continent.[49]

The issue was in Truman's hands at Potsdam.

Opening exchanges at Potsdam were not encouraging for American plans. Reparations negotiations which had been going on at lower levels since Yalta, and which both sides knew were now deeply involved in the Polish question, were at a standstill. Washington had recently advanced the "first charge" principle governing exports from current German production. Though the Yalta formula had stipulated that reparations could be taken from German production on a daily basis, i.e., from current production, American delegates to the reparations commission now contended that the first charge against German exports must go to pay for needed imports and other necessities.

In answer to a newsman's direct query on this point, the President had previously denied any connection between this position and broader questions involving Poland and other countries. Nevertheless, the climax of the issue at Potsdam came in a sharp exchange with Stalin over the Soviet Union's unilateral assignment to the Polish Provisional Government of German territory up to the so-called Oder-Neisse Line. At Yalta it had been agreed that Poland should be compensated in the west for its forced cession of territory to Russia. Great Britain and the United States had since refused to draw a specific boundary, insisting that such things could be decided only at the final peace conference. There were several reasons for this attitude, but most relevant was the Western belief that boundary lines should not be conceded lightly without obtaining important concessions from the other side, especially since the new boundary by itself would go a long way toward making both Poland and eastern Germany client states of the Soviet Union.

Truman asserted at Potsdam that Stalin had actually assigned Poland a zone of occupation in Germany. Very well, Stalin replied, the Big Three should go head and settle that matter at once by deciding the permanent boundary:

> THE PRESIDENT stated that he had no objection to an expression of opinion regarding the western frontiers, however, he wanted it distinctly understood that the [German] zones of occupation will be as established. Any other course will make reparations very difficult, particularly if part of the German territory is gone before agreement is reached on what reparations should be.
>
> STALIN replied that the Soviet Union was not afraid of the reparations question and would if necessary renounce them.[50]

This confrontation had been building since Truman first advised Molotov to think over what he had said about economic cooperation. After things cooled a bit, both sides re-examined their position on the reparations question. The President and Secretary of State James F. Byrnes finally decided, reluctantly, that if they could not reverse Russian actions in Poland and Germany through economic diplomacy, they could at least prevent further incursions into western Germany by temporarily abandoning the eastern zone to what Henry L. Stimson called the Red Army's "oriental" reparations and war-booty policy. One redeeming element in this unhappy situation was that the Russians could not extract anything like their previous reparations demands without impoverishing East Germany, thereby making it difficult for them to maintain order and nearly impossible to integrate even that part of Germany into a permanent Soviet bloc economy.

Still, such stand-offs only increased Truman's frustration at Potsdam. He found that he was really alone in wanting to settle things quickly. Though the debates began as an exchange of opinions among the Big Three, they very often ended in long harangues between Stalin and Churchill, and later Stalin and Attlee. Truman soon became aware of how easily Roosevelt had been trapped in the mediator's role after the failure of second-front diplomacy in 1942. That year it had been Churchill who had carried the word to Moscow that the Yanks were not coming, at least not then; and it had been Churchill who had taken the lead in the 1944 Anglo-Russian talks about the Balkans. Truman determined to pull himself out of that hole as soon as possible.

After just two days of old world diplomacy, the President later complained, "I was beginning to grow impatient for more action and fewer words."[51] Near the end of the conference, after a particularly frustrating exchange with Stalin, Truman turned to Byrnes and exclaimed: "Jimmy, do you realize that we have been here seventeen whole days? Why, in seventeen days you can decide anything!"[52] British and Russian diplomats seemed more than willing to put off, re-examine, debate, and in general elongate the diplomatic process whenever agreement was not easily attained. Truman had come prepared to act decisively on all issues. When the President leveled a general indictment against Soviet-sponsored governments in Rumania, Hungary, and Bulgaria, Stalin promptly placed similar charges against the British-installed regimes in Greece and Italy. At once the British Prime Minister and the Soviet dictator began trading charges, while Truman watched from the sidelines.

The British replied to Stalin's attacks on the Greek government with a new paper on Yugoslavia. This was met by a second paper from the Russians on Greece. Finally, Foreign Minister Ernest Bevin asked that all three be dropped. "Stalin quickly replied 'Yes, welcome.' It was a good demonstration," Byrnes noted sarcastically, "of the seriousness with which some of the charges and countercharges were made."[53] From the American delegation's point of view, such maneuvering left the real issues unresolved and even raised serious doubts about Washington's purposes in advancing the questions in the first place. Unlike Churchill and Attlee, Truman was not seeking to exchange anything. As much as anything else, it was this constant diversion of

American proposals into Anglo-Russian debates that annoyed Truman and his aides.

American experience with previous Anglo-Russian maneuvering had led to the drafting of three major proposals in Washington for presentation at Berlin. The first of these was for a permanent Council of Foreign Ministers. "It is to be expected that the British will 'hedge' against a possible unsuccessful outcome of international collaboration," read the State Department paper, "and will attempt at the same time to strengthen their position by the old power politics system." The United States, therefore, had to make good at once on its intention to establish a functioning collective-security organization. It could not afford to wait until the United Nations itself was actually functioning, even if that took only a few months. The first step should be the creation of a Council of Foreign Ministers so that work could begin at once on European peace treaties. The key to turning the council into a collective-security organ, instead of a stand-in body for the Big Three, was the inclusion of France and China. As we have seen, Truman wrote later in his *Memoirs* that Roosevelt's China policy was no more than a hope: "We in America always think of China as a nation," he said. "But the truth is that in 1945 China was only a geographical expression."[54]

Yet by including China as an equal on the Council of Foreign Ministers, the China "hope" could be converted into something "realistic," even if the real Chinese situation remained unchanged. The council would be genuinely representative of the new security organization, or at least of the five permanent Security Council members who enjoyed the veto power: "Such a Council would tend to reduce the possibilities of unilateral action by either the Russians or the British and would serve as a useful *interim* means through which the United States could work for the liquidation of spheres of influence."[55]

When Truman presented the proposal on July 17, 1945, both Stalin and Churchill raised objections to China's presence on the council as an equal. Something of a compromise was reached whereby China's participation in the European peace treaty-making procedure was severely limited. Although the American delegation was not really satisfied with the agreement, it was gratified that the principle had been established.[56]

Truman's second proposal called for the implementation of the Declaration on Liberated Europe through free and unfettered elections in Rumania, Bulgaria, and Greece. Stalin replied with a promise of minor concessions to democratic rule, but the British proposed that the first step should be to create the proper conditions for democratic rule by the conclusion of peace treaties with these countries. In other words, the British said, not much could be accomplished in this direction until spheres of influence were recognized by the Big Powers. The State Department reaction was just what could be expected: "We think that only after some change in the composition of the governments in Rumania and Bulgaria should we proceed to normalizing relations."[57]

The third proposal was one that Truman had been thinking about for several years—free and unrestricted navigation on inland waterways. And he regarded it as the best test of Soviet intentions—of whether they were concerned only with their own security or were aiming at something much bigger. Truman did not raise the issue until Stalin asked about a revision of the 1936 Montreux Convention governing access to and from the Black Sea. Russia had long wanted a complete revision of that convention, Stalin said. At present his country still had less say on that question than Japan, a defeated power, and before defeat a non-Mediterranean power. Moreover, Russia wanted the return of lost territories, Kars and Ardahan, which Turkey had taken at the time of the Bolshevik Revolution. Finally, Russia wanted the right to protect its interests in the Black Sea Straits with military bases. "A small state supported by Great Britain held a great state by the throat and gave it no outlet," Stalin concluded. What a "commotion there would be in England if a similar regime existed in Gibraltar or in the Suez Canal, or what a commotion there would be in the United States if such a regime existed with regard to the Panama Canal."[58]

Before Stalin and Churchill could begin arguing over this issue, Truman moved to direct the discussion toward his planned proposal, even though he had to ad lib some major changes in it. First he agreed that the Montreux Convention should be revised. As far as the territorial questions were concerned, that was something for the Russians and the Turks to work out between them. The key problem was to insure free passage in the Straits. Truman "had come to the conclusion after a long study of history that all the wars of the last two hundred years had originated in the area from the Black Sea to the Baltic and from the eastern frontier of France to the western frontier of Russia."[59]

Having thus secured his opening, the President read his paper on the free and unrestricted navigation of inland waterways. In his *Memoirs,* Truman described the conversation and the purpose of his paper as follows:

> I was offering as a solution of the straits problem the suggestion that the Kiel Canal in Germany, the Rhine-Danube waterway from the North Sea to the Black Sea Straits, the Suez Canal, and the Panama Canal be made free waterways for the passage of freight and passengers of all countries, except for the fees for their necessary operation and maintenance.[60]

As later printed in the State Department edition of the Potsdam Papers, however, Truman's paper limited the experiment initially to the creation of navigation agencies for the Danube and the Rhine. Membership in these agencies was to include the Big Four (China again) and the sovereign riparian states "recognized by these Governments." In the preamble, moreover, was a third point which was at odds with Truman's claim that he was thinking of Suez and Panama as well as the Black Sea Straits. The preamble to the American proposal said: "The United States Government proposes that there be free and unrestricted navigation of such *inland waterways as border on two or more states* . . ."[61] This language excluded by definition the Suez and Panama canals.

No doubt the President had gotten himself into a bit of trouble by trying to interject his prepared proposal into a debate over the Montreux Convention. But his later explanation of what he had hoped to do by way of expanding the inland waterways navigation plan does not provide an accurate account of what happened at Potsdam, nor is it really helpful in understanding the Russian response.

After a sharp exchange over Russian policy in Eastern Europe at the eighth plenary meeting the next day, Truman asked if the others had studied his paper on inland waterways. Stalin answered briefly that the American proposal did not deal with the Black Sea Straits, only with the Danube and the Rhine. The Soviet delegation, he said, would like a reply to its Montreux Convention proposals first. Truman suggested considering them together.

The Soviet Premier then remarked that since they so obviously differed, the question had better be postponed. But Churchill seized upon this statement to press forward against the most difficult of the Russian demands, the right to establish military fortifications in the Straits, saying that his delegation agreed that freedom in the Black Sea area should indeed be guaranteed by all the Big Three. American participation in such an enterprise was a "remarkable and important fact." And with this attempt to pull Truman back into British Mediterranean diplomacy, the Prime Minister and Russian Foreign Minister Molotov squared off for another round of one-upmanship:

> CHURCHILL said that the guarantee they [the United States and Great Britain] proposed would be more than a substitute for the fortification of the Straits.
>
> MOLOTOV inquired if the Suez Canal were under the same principle.
>
> CHURCHILL rejoined that it was open in war and peace to all.
>
> MOLOTOV inquired if it were under the same international control as was proposed for the Black Sea Straits.
>
> CHURCHILL said that this question had not been raised.
>
> MOLOTOV said that he was asking. If it was such a good rule why not apply it to the Suez.[62]

When Truman finally got back into the conversation, he said he wanted to make it clear that his idea of an international guarantee for the Straits did not contemplate "any fortification of any kind." For all practical purposes, this clarification ended the discussion for the duration of the conference. At the final session, when the Big Three were about to approve the protocol, the President asked that his proposal on inland waterways be made a part of the formal document, but only as a personal favor to him so that he could discuss it with Congress. According to Ambassador Robert Murphy, the conversation went this way:

> Stalin listened closely to the President's statement, which was addressed directly to him, and apparently the Soviet dictator understood most of the English words. Before the translation into Russian was finished, he broke in abruptly with the familiar Russian negative, "Nyet." Then, very deliberately, he repeated in English, "No. I say no!" That was the only time I heard Stalin speak English at the Conference. Truman could not mistake the rebuff. His face flushed and he turned to the American delegation and exclaimed, "I cannot understand that man."[63]

The formal minutes taken down by a State Department reporter do not suggest any such finality in Stalin's reply. In fact, at one point he is recorded as saying that while he did not want the matter included in the protocol, they should not be in a hurry to dispose of it.[64] Truman's reaction, however, picked up where Murphy's record leaves off:

> The persistent way in which Stalin blocked one of the war-preventative measures I had proposed showed how his mind worked and what he was after. I had proposed the internationalization of all the principal waterways. Stalin did not want this. What Stalin wanted was control of the Black Sea Straits and the Danube. *The Russians were planning world conquest.*[65]

Personal memoirs are often postdictive; in this case it would seem that Truman regarded Stalin's attitude at Potsdam as indicative of how Truman himself would have responded to such a proposal if *he* had been planning world revolution. To begin with, the paper Truman had presented at Potsdam was not really a proposal on "internationalization of all the principal waterways." Second, even his limited experiment could not begin until there were "recognized" governments in the Danubian states—recognized, that is, according to American standards: the Atlantic Charter and the Declaration of Liberated Europe. Third, the regime Truman offered for the Danube and the Rhine would have extended Anglo-American power into Central Europe (and with China, majority power at that) without any equivalent concessions. In fact, when the Russians suggested Suez as a countertest, Churchill flatly refused to consider the idea, nor did Truman intervene to correct his interpretation of the plan. Yet on the basis of this test Truman decided he knew full well what the Kremlin was after—nothing short of world revolution.

Hence Truman felt justified in turning his thoughts from economic diplomacy to S-1, the atomic bomb. When informed of the bomb's successful test in New Mexico early in the conference, he was, according to Stimson who had brought the news, "tremendously pepped up by it . . . and said that it gave him an entirely new feeling of confidence."[66] Truman had previously decided not to make any full revelation of the discovery to the Russians until at least one bomb had been "laid on" Japan.

This decision had been debated before the opening of the conference. Stimson had, he said, "advised the President to watch the atmosphere at the meeting. If mutual frankness on other questions was found to be real and satisfactory, then the President might say that work was being done on the development of atomic fission for war purposes; that good progress had been made; and that an attempt to use a weapon would be made shortly, though it was not certain that it would succeed." If Stalin pressed for details, Stimson had gone on to advise, the President should say he was not prepared to take the matter further at the present time.[67]

After several talks with Churchill and his own advisers at Potsdam, however, Truman decided that all he wanted to do was tell Stalin enough to invalidate any future reproach that military information had been kept from him.[68] He carried out this decision on July 24, 1945. Churchill, who had previously been informed, stood no more than five yards away, eagerly watching Stalin's face to see what would happen to his usually impassive expression. Nothing happened. Stalin merely said that he hoped the United States would make good use of any new discovery against Japan.[69]

"Truman's statement," wrote Herbert Feis, "did not seem to

either the American or the British observers to influence the Russian attitude toward the situations that were being talked about at the conference."[70] Truman could not be sure that Stalin even knew precisely what he was talking about; that was what he had wanted, but it did not allow him any real satisfaction during the conference. On the other hand, according to Marshal G. K. Zhukov's newly available account of the incident, Stalin called him and Foreign Minister Molotov aside after the conversation with Truman and declared: "They simply want to raise the price. We've got to work on [Dr. Igor V.] Kurchatov and hurry things up."[71]

But when Truman reported to the nation on the results of the Potsdam Conference, his new confidence remained high; he asserted unequivocally that Rumania, Bulgaria, and Hungary were not going to be "spheres of influence of any one power."[72] He followed this up on Navy Day, October 27, 1945, when he christened the new carrier *USS Franklin D. Roosevelt* with the promise that when demobilization was complete, the United States would still be the greatest naval power on earth. He went on to explain that such power was still needed to fulfill the objectives of American foreign policy. These objectives included refusal to recognize any government imposed upon any nation by a foreign power; the establishment not only of freedom of the seas but of equal rights to the navigation of boundary rivers and waterways passing through more than one country; the protection of the Western Hemisphere states from outside interference; and the cooperation of all states, great and small, in the restoration of the world economy.[73]

For the next year and a half these tasks fell principally to Secretary of State Byrnes, who agreed solemnly: "There must be one world for all of us or there will be no world for any of us."

FOUR ☆☆

James F. Byrnes: Collective Security Through Public Diplomacy

President Roosevelt once offered James F. Byrnes the position of High Commissioner for postwar Germany. Byrnes turned it down, suggesting that he would be more useful in persuading his former colleagues in the Senate to ratify the peace arrangements after the war: "One difficulty I anticipate is the ratification of a treaty providing machinery for the preservation of peace. I was interested in that cause in 1919 and am still interested."[1]

A traditional Southern "internationalist," Byrnes represented South Carolina in the House and later in the Senate, where his major concerns were to promote foreign trade and build up the Navy. In 1941 Roosevelt chose him to lead the floor fight for the Lend-Lease Bill. Byrnes never "led" his colleagues by lengthy speeches or oratorical fireworks. Patient and persistent, he used timely facts and bits of logic to persuade. As wartime Director of Economic Stabilization, a title which Roosevelt dreamed up for him, Byrnes set himself the task of regulating American capitalism so that when the war ended, the nation's productive powers could be released to the immense task of restoring the world economy. He approached his tasks as Secretary of State in the same frame of mind. Any time a nation engaged in state planning, Byrnes believed, traditional freedoms were seriously endangered.

"If anything like inflation happened," he said in his first public speech as Stabilization Director, "our people would not be ready to take the part which we are pledged to take to organize the world for peace. There could be no greater tragedy. After a while, by drastic national action and radical social planning we would recover, but there would have passed the time when our leadership must be asserted if peace and order are to be established in a prostrate world."[2]

In 1944 Byrnes was the leading candidate of the Democratic party's conservative wing to replace Henry A. Wallace as Vice-President on the national ticket. "As you know," the President wrote him, "you are indespensable on the handling and the actual settling of scores of problems which are constantly arising. You have been called 'The Assistant President' and the appellation comes close to the truth."

Perhaps because he was grooming Byrnes to replace Cordell Hull as Secretary of State after Stettinius' interim appointment, Roosevelt asked Byrnes to accompany him to Yalta. There Byrnes kept for the President a separate shorthand record of the meetings and decisions. As the conference neared its end, FDR asked Byrnes to fly home ahead of the main party to explain what had been achieved and what Congress now had to do. This was an assignment Byrnes had requested, and he carried it out loyally; yet he could not conceal his discomfiture that the Russians were not serious about the United Nations. "Jimmy Byrnes intimated to us very clearly that while Stalin was going along with Dumbarton Oaks," one of Roosevelt's isolationist critics wrote to a friend, "he did not have much faith in machinery of this kind. He kept repeating, so Byrnes says, 'If the three of us stick together, we can maintain the peace of the world.' By sticking together, of course, he meant we would have to agree with him, and he had his way at the Yalta Conference."[3]

Whatever his doubts, Byrnes did not believe that Stalin had had everything his way at Yalta; nonetheless, he *was* concerned about the future of Woodrow Wilson's dream when, following the San Francisco Conference, Truman appointed him Secretary of State. Truman's reasons for thinking he needed Byrnes in the Cabinet had mostly to do with matters other than foreign policy, but ironically Truman soon came to resent the way Byrnes managed that policy—often with only the briefest consultations. He especially resented being left in the dark when criticism arose in the Senate or in the press. After Byrnes's resignation in 1947, the public debate between the two obscured more fundamental questions about Byrnes's concept of "collective security" and public diplomacy.

Professional diplomats in the Foreign Service also had serious criticisms of the new Secretary. Observing his behavior at the Moscow Foreign Ministers' meeting in December 1945, George F. Kennan wrote: "His main purpose is to achieve some sort of an agreement, he doesn't much care what."[4] Yet no one had found the way to transform the "spheres of influence" turbulence into clear-cut collective security when Byrnes became Secretary of State after the San Francisco Conference. Byrnes knew full well how deep the problem went, because he had heard Roosevelt assure his allies at Yalta that "the peace should be written by the Three Powers represented at this table."[5] To clear up the situation, the Secretary planned to use a basic formula that consisted, at the outset, of the beguiling illusion Roosevelt had cast with his China policy—and little more. At Potsdam Truman and Byrnes had secured tentative agreement to a Big Four or Big Five Foreign Ministers' Council, as the State Department said, to serve as an interim means of preventing the solidification of Anglo-Russian spheres of influence.

The first meeting of that council was scheduled for London in September 1945. It was to be the first step in negotiating treaties with Italy and the former German satellites controlled by Russian military and political authorities. Much to the surprise of some of Byrnes's detractors, the treaties that finally resulted from the Secretary's efforts offered a fair chance to "bridge the gap" had other disagreements and disturbances not occurred in Russian-American relations. "Before you leave," Senator Vandenberg, the chairman of the Senate Foreign Relations Committee and one of Byrnes's former critics, declared at the hearings on the treaties in 1947, "I want to say once more, as I want to say it on every occasion I have, that I think you are one of the Secretaries of State in the very great American tradition."[6] But even as these hearings continued, the President's speech announcing the Truman

Doctrine interrupted another Moscow Foreign Ministers' Conference in March 1947, and the gap between East and West widened beyond all bridge-building.

When an aide first showed Secretary Byrnes the original Russian request for a multi-billion-dollar credit, he had it placed, he recalled in 1958, "in the 'Forgotten File.' "[7] Simple economic pressure on the Russians was not going to force them out of Eastern Europe. What was needed, Byrnes felt, was some combination of levers and policies which would reverse the general trend on all fronts.

After a series of consultations in Moscow during mid-June of 1945, Ambassador Harriman had recommended recognition of the Provisional Government of Poland. Although he was not entirely satisfied with the consultations, he advised Washington that the stage was "set as well as can be done at the present time. . . . If we continue to take a sympathetic interest in Polish affairs and are reasonably generous in our economic relations there is a fair chance that things will work out satisfactorily from our standpoint."[8] But Ambassador Arthur Bliss Lane's attempts to use Warsaw's desire for American credits as a means of securing fulfillment of the Yalta and Potsdam pledges—at least as the State Department interpreted them—and of demanding equality of opportunity "for us in trade, investment and access to sources of information," ran into Russian-Polish obstructionism almost at once.[9]

Elsewhere in Eastern Europe the situation remained static after Potsdam. On August 19, 1945, for example, the State Department *Bulletin* announced that Washington would not consider forthcoming elections in Bulgaria free and unfettered, and that the negotiation of a Bulgarian peace treaty could not therefore take place until Sofia had a genuinely representative government. In Rumania, American nonrecognition policy had apparently encouraged King Michael to resist the Russian-installed Petru Groza regime. But the stalemate had to be ended soon. The essential precondition for a functioning economic diplomacy—or any other kind of policy—was assured access to the whole area. It was unlikely that this could be accomplished without a large peace conference. The problem was how to get Russia to the table. Once that was accomplished—if it could be—Byrnes was optimistic that the Russians could be "forced by world opinion to co-operate." That proved not to be the fact, but probably not for the reasons Byrnes's critics have put forth.[10]

The first step in getting the Russians to Paris was to make the best possible use of the nonrecognition policy. Mark Ethridge, the liberal owner and editor of the *Louisville Courier-Journal* who was close to Byrnes during this period, later wrote of the situation:

> It is true that for about a year after the defeat of Germany the United States and the United Kingdom continued to exert a considerable influence on Balkan affairs. . . .
>
> Even after V-J Day, when the rapid demobilization of American armed forces and the abrupt discontinuance of Lend-Lease marked the end of the principal sources of United States bargaining power, a number of possibilities remained for the exertion of some influence on Soviet policy in the Balkans. The Soviet Union desired to obtain recognition for its clients, as well as agreement on the peace terms for the former Axis satellites, and the withholding of its accord on these matters remained an important American instrument of pressure.[11]

Byrnes had chaired the original committee which President Truman had appointed to determine whether and, if so, how the atomic bomb should be used against Japan. Several of Byrnes's associates, particularly the scientists, were worried about his outspoken comment that the bomb might make the Russians more "manageable" in Eastern and Central Europe. One atomic scientist said later that he was "dismayed" when he learned that Byrnes was to be Secretary of State.[12] "I was completely flabbergasted by the assumption that rattling the bomb might make Russia more manageable," Leo Szilard wrote of his first encounters with Byrnes. "Well, you come from Hungary," the Secretary had replied to his objections, "[and] you would not want Russia to stay in Hungary indefinitely." As compared to an atomic arms race, Szilard said, he "was *not* disposed at this point to worry about what would happen to Hungary."[13]

At Potsdam, Secretary of War Stimson had also urged upon Truman the importance of basing a firm policy toward the Soviets on America's atomic monopoly; but Stimson already had doubts about the "new" post-Roosevelt policy in Central Europe. In the weeks following the Berlin Big Three meeting, he began a process of rethinking the problem which eventually led him to the opposite conclusion. On September 4, 1945, Stimson talked with his cabinet colleague about the dangers of atomic diplomacy; he came away from the conversation deeply discouraged:

> I found that Byrnes was very much against any attempt to cooperate with Russia. His mind is full of his problems with the coming meeting of the foreign ministers and he looks to having the presence of the bomb in his pocket, so to speak, as a great weapon to get through the thing he has. He also told me of a number of acts of perfidy, so to speak, of Stalin, which they had encountered at Potsdam and felt in the light of those that we could not rely upon anything in the way of promises from them.[14]

As the meeting of the Foreign Ministers opened in London in September 1945, British Foreign Secretary Ernest Bevin was also concerned about Washington's determination to challenge Russian domination of Bulgaria and Rumania. He was prepared to assert British interests in the Mediterranean just as aggressively as any Tory had ever done, but he was also willing to follow Churchill's 1944 bargain with Stalin a while longer. Foreign Minister Molotov did not recognize these differences between the British and Americans at London, or, if he was fully informed, chose not to act upon his knowledge. At the first plenary session, he brought forward a memorandum on "the political situation in Greece." Complete with demands for reorganization of that government before "free elections" could be held, the memorandum was a mirror image of the various documents on Hungary, Bulgaria, and Rumania which had been published that summer in the State Department *Bulletin*.[15]

The Russian tactic angered Bevin, who was presiding at the session, and Molotov failed to get the Greek situation placed on the agenda. He also failed in a later attempt to call American policy in Japan before the Council. As in San Francisco, the basic

Russian strategy was directed toward territorial *quid pro quos.* But since neither Greece nor Japan was formally placed on the agenda, the Russians found themselves at a decided disadvantage from the beginning of the London Conference.

The only significant decision at the first plenary session—and it was to prove highly significant for Byrnes's diplomacy—was a verbal agreement that France and China should have the right to participate in the discussions on the former German satellite peace treaties. Byrnes had tried to get more—recognition for France and China as voting members of the Council on the treaties—but Molotov successfully resisted the move by citing the Potsdam protocol which supported the Russian position in limiting French and Chinese participation.

On the second day of the conference, Molotov submitted proposals for treaties with Finland, Rumania, Bulgaria, Hungary, and Italy. In all save the case of Italy, the proposals would simply have confirmed existing armistice agreements—ones signed originally by the Big Three, but in fact dictated almost exclusively by the Soviet Union. "The acceptance of anything along these lines," commented one of Byrnes's aides, "would have the effect of confirming the present situation under which these countries are under effective Soviet domination and would mean the abandonment of the opportunity for establishing democratic governments in these countries. . . . Treaties of this type would constitute an abandonment of the agreement reached in principle at Potsdam for equality of economic opportunity in these countries." On the other hand, the American plan for treaties with the former German satellites spelled out in great detail economic and commercial provisions for preserving unconditional most-favored-nation treatment to all members of the United Nations.[16]

The real problem, of course, was that the State Department felt that no Soviet-sponsored or -controlled regime would be willing to carry out such provisions faithfully. Already several of the Balkan countries had signed "crushing" economic pacts with the Russians. These would have to be repudiated, at least in part, if the State Department's draft treaties were adopted. In each instance the American drafts contained a specific clause that the Soviet-sponsored regimes would not maintain governmental trade monopolies or allow foreign trade on any but strictly commercial principles. (Such clauses were in line with American policy toward the British Labour government as well.) In any event, the State Department thought it unreasonable to assume that any of the Balkan governments would be able or inclined to accept that clause. The American representative in Bucharest, Burton Y. Berry, put the solution in a private letter to Byrnes at London. The Groza government, he said, would have to be "retired" before any Rumanian treaty could be negotiated.[17]

When Molotov came to Byrnes's London rooms to discuss the satellite treaties in private, the Secretary did not go quite so far. For the present, he said, the inclusion of several noncommunist leaders in Rumania, for example, would make it possible to hold free elections and fulfill the Yalta Declaration on Liberated Europe. Molotov, who at first seemed to be in a particularly angry mood, charged bitterly that "the only reason that he could find for our attitude was that the present government was friendly to the Soviet Union, and the United States did not want that." Byrnes replied "emphatically" that this was not the case, that the United States was opposed only to the way in which the Groza government had been established—Mr. Vyshinksy had given the King two and a half hours to install Groza—and that there had been no change in the American attitude since shortly after Yalta. Despite his outward aggressiveness, Molotov pressed the Secretary to disclose how far the United States wanted to go in this direction, or, better put, what parties or men Washington wanted in the government.[18] A compromise was clearly implied.

The next day Molotov called a press conference to explain Russian policy in Rumania. The previous government, he said, which had had anti-Russian elements in it, could not have insured internal order. Now Prime Minister Groza was simply trying to live up to the terms of the armistice. "You, as well as I myself, know well that not everybody is pleased with the existing governments in Rumania or Bulgaria, but I don't think that there are any Governments with which everybody is pleased." Elections were already scheduled in those countries which, Molotov asserted, would be free and secret on the basis of universal suffrage. Could the authorities in Greece say the same?[19]

Prevented from formally discussing Greece and Japan in the Council itself, Molotov took full advantage of Byrnes's desire for as much "public diplomacy" as possible to restate the Russian position. By this time the London Conference had already fallen into the San Francisco pattern of rival press conferences. Secretary Byrnes could regard Molotov's public and private attacks on British policy in Greece with some degree of tolerance—and realistically so because of similar American press attacks—and with perhaps even a measure of secret satisfaction because they forced Bevin to rely even more heavily, both then and later, on official American good will. But the Secretary of State was still worried about Russian attacks on American occupation policy in Japan. "I thought it was just an element in [Molotov's] campaign of counterattack," he wrote afterward. "Nevertheless, we were placed in an embarrassing position."[20] Although President Truman's decision not to allow the Soviets a significant role in the Japanese occupation could not be reconsidered, Byrnes remained concerned about public reaction to the charge that Washington had shut the Russians out.

The situation in Rumania had become particularly dangerous by the time of the London Conference: King Michael was using his power to boycott the Russian-supported government. Molotov's initial efforts at achieving recognition for that government, even his statements to press conferences, left compromise possibilities open. Sensing the weakness of the Russian demands, Byrnes met them in two ways: first, he stepped up the pressure in the Foreign Ministers' Council by insisting upon a formal declaration—which he knew would be leaked to the press—stating that the United States would negotiate no treaty at all until Bucharest had a government "broadly representative of all democratic elements in the population."[21] Second, he offered Molotov postwar "second-front" diplomacy; i.e., he proposed to trade a four-power security treaty against German remilitarization for a Russian withdrawal from Eastern Europe.

The other members of the American delegation, especially John Foster Dulles and Charles Bohlen, had some doubts about the first part of Byrnes's plan. They felt the United States should not make recognition of Rumania the key question in any way which would force the Soviets into a public defense of the Groza government. That would only harden attitudes, they said. Byrnes answered these doubts with the comment that he had been rereading the Yalta decisions during one of the Council's sessions; he had decided that it would be a good idea to use the very language from the Yalta Declaration on Liberated Europe: the United States would recognize only "broadly representative" governments. Dulles protested that the real issue was access for American newsmen and other American representatives. A long-range nonrecognition policy toward Rumania was likely to be as barren as nonrecognition of the Soviet Union had been.[22] Despite Dulles' own later criticisms of Byrnes, therefore, the major responsibility for a no-compromise policy on Rumania was the Secretary's more than the delegation's.

Nor did Byrnes really consult with the delegation about his plan to approach Molotov with the security treaty proposal. As Molotov knew, Byrnes told him in a private conversation, the United States had always been reluctant to enter into political treaties with foreign governments; however, Byrnes said, he had been mulling over for some time a statement Marshal Stalin had made at Yalta about the still-present danger of some future invasion of Russia through Poland. He wished to ask, therefore, if the Soviet Union would be interested in a four-power treaty to insure Germany's demilitarization for at least twenty to twenty-five years. The Secretary added that when he had discussed it with Truman before leaving Washington, the President had reacted favorably.[23]

Unfortunately, this proposal came more than eight months after Vandenberg had first offered it—essentially as a way out of spheres of influence—to the Roosevelt administration. As American policy-makers were eager to point out in discussions with their Soviet counterparts, the world had changed since that time. Most recently it had entered the atomic era—but even before that, the Potsdam Conference had divided Europe into reparations and occupation zones. While Byrnes had played a key role in those decisions, he was now trying to reverse them on both fronts, first by pressing the Russians over Eastern Europe, then by calling for a Big Four security treaty over Germany.

The Soviet Union was already concluding a series of bilateral treaties with France, Poland, and the Eastern European countries against German resurgence. World revolution certainly took second place to that aim; thus Truman might better have used the original Vandenberg proposal as a test of Soviet intentions at Potsdam. In fact, he had thought briefly about doing just that. On June 9, 1945, he had written Acting Secretary Grew to inquire about the Department's attitude toward an attempt to begin negotiations for such a treaty at Potsdam: "a 25-year treaty between the three or four principal powers to demilitarize Germany, to keep her demilitarized by force if necessary, somewhat along the lines suggested by Senator Vandenberg in his speech in the Senate last winter." The State Department replied that such a treaty was still being considered; pending a final decision, however, it was being left off the American agenda.[24] News of the successful atomic test in New Mexico had pushed the proposal even further into the background. "The German menace should not be exaggerated," Truman told General Charles de Gaulle after Potsdam, "for the United States possessed a new weapon, the atomic bomb, which could defeat any aggressor."[25]

At London, Molotov responded cautiously to Byrnes's sudden suggestion of this all-but-forgotten plan: it was a very interesting idea, he said, but why had the Secretary found it necessary to put such a statement on Rumania in writing? An oral statement that the United States did not regard its taking part in the drafting of a Rumanian peace treaty as an act of diplomatic recognition would at least have made it possible to go on with the work of the Foreign Ministers' Council. When Byrnes refused to withdraw the statement, his conversation with Molotov ended in mutual warnings and recriminations.

After two days of unproductive exchanges in the plenary sessions, Molotov telephoned Byrnes on the morning of September 22 to say that he was not calling a meeting for that day. He insisted that a mistake had been made on the opening day of the conference; the Potsdam decisions on the Foreign Ministers' Council and the agreed-upon procedure for drafting peace treaties were both being violated. Every member of the American delegation knew that if Byrnes withdrew his Rumanian caveat this procedural obstruction would disappear.

Byrnes could have simply denounced the proposed "deal" as beneath American dignity. But he chose not to do that because Molotov had provided him with a much better argument, one that would readily appeal to public opinion in the United States. The Russian Foreign Minister had declared that the mistake in procedure lay in allowing France and China to have any part at all in the discussions on Balkan peace treaties. Seeing that Molotov was demanding a return to Big Three diplomacy, Byrnes used the opening thus provided to argue the case for the rights of all small nations: "Our attitude was a shock to them. . . . Our fight to have France and China remain in the Council was generally applauded, and our fight for the peace conference and for the right of the smaller states to participate in the peace won for us the good opinion of those states. And it forced the Soviets to begin to re-orient their policy."[26]

By centering attention on Russia's desire for secret diplomacy, Byrnes's response relieved pressure on the American delegation over the Greek and Japanese problems and permitted him to characterize as imperialistic Molotov's renewed demand for one of Italy's former African colonies. Since the Potsdam Conference, State Department planners had been trying to decide what reply to make when Molotov finally decided to press seriously for an African trusteeship under the United Nations. In England the demand sent shudders down Foreign Minister Ernest Bevin's broad back: "A great power was cutting across the throat of the British Empire," he told the House of Commons after the break-up of the London meeting.[27] Stalin's blunt insistence that Russia be granted military bases in the Dardanelles, his demand that Trieste be turned over to Yugoslavia, and his request for an African trusteeship—all foretold the undoing of a century of British foreign policy.

While the African trusteeship was not quite so serious a matter for the United States, no one really wanted to see the Russians south of Suez. Moreover, there was a growing feeling in the State Department that Italy should be allowed to retain its pre-fascist holdings in Africa. One State Department memorandum asserted that Italy had been a more responsible colonizer than either France or Great Britain; even more important, it was the one sure place where Anglo-American policy would prevail.[28] Though the matter had not been fully decided when Byrnes left Washington, Molotov's assertive statements about Russian expectations in the Mediterranean made up his mind for him. Said Molotov:

> The Soviet Union should take the place that is due it, and therefore should have bases in the Mediterranean for its merchant fleet. We do not propose to introduce the Soviet system into this territory apart from the democratic order that is desired by the people.
>
> This will not be done along the lines that have been used in Greece.[29]

Stettinius had said at Yalta that Russia would be "eligible" for a trusteeship, but Byrnes now denied that this statement was in any way binding upon the United States. Instead he offered the Soviets an advisory role equal only to Washington's in the administration of the Italian colonies! Here was a perfect example of the philosophy of Article 51 at work: American hegemony in the Western Hemisphere and the Pacific, and strong influence everywhere else.*

The United States had also reconsidered its efforts to extend the inland waterways proposal to the Dardanelles in the three months since Potsdam. At London Byrnes presented it as it had originally been intended. Molotov queried him on this point, asking what significance should be drawn from the absence of any reference to the Black Sea. Byrnes admitted candidly that the U.S. delegation had come to the conclusion that the definition of an international inland waterway could not be agreed upon without prolonged discussion. This admission, of course, makes Truman's account of the Potsdam discussions in his *Memoirs* still more doubtful. But the Russians were not at all interested in the original proposal anyway. Near the end of the London Conference, Byrnes said he was "sorely disappointed" that no progress had been made

*Over the next eighteen months, the Russians gradually retreated from most of these territorial claims in the Mediterranean. Molotov later complained that the West had not responded to this "concession." Stalin may have regarded these questions, except for the Dardanelles, as bargaining counters. In any event, at the time of the Truman Doctrine, Soviet foreign policy in the area was no longer on the offensive.

on that question, which remained a major goal of American diplomats throughout the next two years.

On the 26th of September, Byrnes suggested a way of getting around the procedural tangle in London through a two-step plan for negotiating the satellite peace treaties. In the plan's first stage, only the members of the Foreign Ministers' Council which had signed the armistice agreements with Italy, Rumania, Bulgaria, Hungary, and Finland would draft the treaties. In the second stage, a conference would be held at which all members of the United Nations who had been at war with these countries would deliberate the peace treaties, using the Foreign Ministers' Council drafts as the "basis" for their deliberations.

Molotov came back the next day with a counter-offer: while his first stage was the same as the American proposal, his second stated that the conference would consist only of the states "chiefly interested" in the various peace treaties. Averell Harriman warned Byrnes that this stage was a ploy to create a situation whereby the United States would be forced into accepting the governments of those countries. At such a conference of "chiefly interested" nations, Molotov would also be in a much stronger position than in the Council of Foreign Ministers, where the vote was usually 4 to 1 against him. The issue of substance, Harriman insisted, was always the governments of Rumania and Bulgaria, not the peace treaties, which could be negotiated with anyone.[30]

"The seriousness of what happened in London cannot be underestimated," *Izvestia* stated on October 5, 1945. "If the American and British Governments will in the future insist upon their position, which in no way can be brought into accord with loyalty to the already concluded tripartite agreements, then this will shake the very basis of collaboration among the three powers." Byrnes's public statement on the outcome of the London Foreign Ministers' Conference was not so pessimistic. It could not be denied that the meeting had ended in a stalemate, he admitted, but that should not remove a second and better chance to get on with the peacemaking procedure.

Presuming that he would continue to have a fairly free hand in managing the peace, Byrnes shifted tactics without really explaining to the President or the British what he was about to do.

Like Roosevelt, he felt it was important to get to Stalin directly, rather than deal with him through Molotov. Thus he would propose to Stalin both the security treaty over Germany and a plan for control of atomic energy through the United Nations. By means of these inducements he hoped to bring Russia to accept the large peace conference. Though he would be speaking privately to Stalin, the conversations would not represent a return to Big Three diplomacy.

Byrnes did not fully explain his plans to Truman. By that time, *Time* magazine had also commented on the London Conference: "at the . . . Conference, U.S. diplomats had been reluctant to talk about the bomb. When the subject came up in private conversation, they would say something like: 'Of course, the world knows that the U.S. would never. . . .' Such sentences usually trailed off into inaudible mumbles."[31] Despite the failure of atomic diplomacy at London—or perhaps, as Byrnes now appeared to believe, the failure to *use* atomic diplomacy properly—he continued to think that peace was just a matter of mixing various policies. When John Foster Dulles submitted a draft of his planned radio address on the London Conference, Byrnes requested that he delete one sentence: "They want to know what our attitude will be in dealing with the atomic bomb."[32] Byrnes still could not decide what to do with atomic diplomacy.

Then, on November 7, 1945, Molotov delivered a major speech which, by confirming Dulles's analysis, convinced Byrnes that he must abandon his public pretense that atomic bombs were the furthest thing from anyone's mind at these diplomatic conferences. Reporting on the failure of the London Conference, Molotov told a Moscow audience that the atomic bomb, even the secrets of technical "know-how," could not be kept private for long: "the discovery of atomic energy should not encourage either a propensity to exploit the discovery in the play of forces in international policy or an attitude of complacency as regards the future of the peace-loving nations." In other words, the postwar situation in Eastern Europe could not be changed by direct threats—or by those left unmade.[33]

Earlier, on November 1, the State Department had announced plans for an International Conference on Trade and Employment to be held the following spring. If the peace treaties were not settled by then, Byrnes thought, there was a very real danger that war-shattered economic trade patterns would mend in the wrong way. He did not want to have to rebreak them in order to save the world economy. Time was short indeed: the two specialized economic agencies of the United Nations, the International Bank for Reconstruction and Development and the International Monetary Fund, were both shortly to begin functioning; thus it was important that any "freely elected governments in the Balkans" be able to take advantage of the financial assistance offered by these agencies.[34]

As of November 1945, there was at least one "freely elected government" in Eastern Europe. Under American pressure the Russians had postponed scheduled elections in Hungary; but even while the London Conference was still in session, Byrnes had promised that diplomatic recognition would be granted Hungary. In fact it was extended two days before the election. The results of this gamble were more than gratifying to the State Department: a noncommunist government was swept into office in Budapest, the only democratically elected one in that nation's history.

"We are going ahead with plans to make available cotton, vehicles, construction machinery, etc. to Hungary and any other ex-satellite regime which has been able to hold free elections," the head of the State Department's Eastern European desk wrote to Ambassador Lane in Poland at the end of November. In addition, President Truman had personally promised the noncommunist Vice-Premier of Poland, Stanislaw Mikolajczyk, limited credits as a further inducement to that country to cooperate with the United States—even though, as Truman said, "it would be difficult for us to give credits to a regime whose foreign economic policy was so contrary to ours."[35]

These Hungarian and Polish examples, Byrnes apparently thought, justified an equally well-calculated gamble with Rumania and Bulgaria. Adding the possible recognition of those less-than-perfect governments to his offers of a security treaty over Germany and atomic controls, Byrnes then initiated a new Big Three meeting without consulting the British. They were, however, later invited to come along for the ride to Moscow.

At first Stalin was not much taken with Byrnes's suggestion for a Big Three meeting to consider the composition of the large peace conference: "What ha[s] Puerto Rico to do with Rumania?" he complained to Ambassador Harriman, who had presented the list of nations which the United States felt should be invited. "It ha[s] not sent one soldier abroad. Greece and Yugoslavia . . . fought against the Italians. The Chinese ha[ve] not." To Harriman's explanation that China was a permanent member of the United Nations Security Council, Stalin merely replied that the peace treaties should be settled now; the Security Council's work lay in the future.[36]

When Byrnes greeted Ernest Bevin at Moscow—to make it clear that the British had been invited to a Russian-American conference—he said he was there to talk serious business, not procedure, and that the United States "was in favor of discussing any and all matters informally" in the hope that such discussions might lead to a "better understanding" among all three governments.[37] Byrnes had placed atomic energy control at the top of his agenda to ease the conference into other subjects, but the Russians promptly asked that it be placed at the end of the list, after other questions had been settled. Byrnes later wrote that this was Molotov's "way of informing me that he regarded the subject as one of little importance." More likely, the Russian Foreign Minister was informing him that this new brand of atomic diplomacy would not work either. Without the bomb, the Russians had little interest in abstract plans for its control, and certainly none unless their political situation in Europe was fully secure. If the Americans wanted to talk about atomic controls, the Russians reasoned, they must create the political atmosphere in which such problems could be discussed.

For three days Molotov held out against inviting all those on the original "American list" of nations for a large peace conference. While they sparred on this question, Byrnes brought forward a report on conditions in Bulgaria and Rumania prepared by Mark Ethridge. Not surprisingly, Ethridge had concluded that the United States should refuse to extend diplomatic recognition to those two governments. Molotov took one or two swipes at Byrnes's insistence that Ethridge was truly impartial, but aside from these, he was not as pugnacious as he had been at London.

When he finally got to see Stalin, Byrnes commented that he had been having trouble with Molotov over the Balkans. Stalin "smiled broadly" and said that that was unexpected news. But Byrnes continued directly to the point of the meeting: "It is terribly important to settle this matter and to proceed with the peace treaties so that we can be in a position to render them effective economic assistance." If they were not now able to agree, Byrnes continued, he would be compelled to publish the Ethridge report. Stalin still maintained a half-serious, basically aloof attitude. If the Secretary did that, he remarked, then he would have to ask Ilya Ehrenburg, also an impartial observer of recent events in the Balkans, to publish *his* views. In Hungary, Stalin continued, the Soviet occupation forces could easily have dictated the result; nevertheless, the elections had resulted in a noncommunist government. In practical terms, the Soviet Union could—as Molotov had said at London—offer to include one or two noncommunists in Bulgaria and Rumania. Stalin then asked that Byrnes discuss this solution with Bevin. "The Secretary agreed and jokingly said that although they were supposed to have a bloc with England, he had even neglected to inform Mr. Bevin soon enough about the proposed meeting in Moscow. Stalin replied that this was obviously only a cloak to hide the reality of the bloc."[38]

The next evening, Christmas Eve, Stalin entertained Byrnes at dinner in the Kremlin. The Soviet Union had by this time also agreed to the large peace conference; debate therefore shifted to the conference's authority to make changes in the draft treaties. After dinner Stalin and his guest moved off to a private drawing room for coffee, accompanied only by a single interpreter. The Secretary led the conversation away from pleasantries with the remark that he had been disappointed not to have heard further from Molotov about his plan for a German security treaty. Carefully re-explaining the plan, Byrnes ended with a new "punch line." Perhaps, he said, such a treaty would relieve Soviet fears and "influence your actions in the Balkan states." According to Byrnes's account, which is the only one we have, Stalin responded warmly: "If you decide to fight for such a treaty you can rely on my support."[39]

A reasonable translation of this exchange would go as follows:

Byrnes: Are you willing to trade your sphere of influence for an assurance of protection against German resurgence and participation in the American system?

Stalin: When the assurances are spelled out, we may talk again about this matter. In the meantime, the Soviet Union will reserve its position.

During the next few days, Byrnes and Molotov took up the problem of the peace conference's powers. The Secretary had two proposals on this question, but neither one was acceptable to the Soviets, who still wanted to limit the functions of the conference to ratification of the previous drafts. In Washington, President Truman, after reading summaries of these sessions, could not make out what Byrnes had agreed to. Were the decisions of the large peace conference to be binding on the treaties, or merely advisory? Byrnes answered this query in a brief cable which explained very little: "While signatories of the armistice would not be bound by the recommendations of the conference, we could, if we thought it proper, refuse to give final approval to any treaty which unwarrantably disregarded recommendations."[40]

This vague reply presumed much on Byrnes's part—too much, Truman thought. Congressional opinion was lining up against the apparent retreat from London, the resumption of secret Big Three diplomacy, and the Secretary's decision to talk about atomic energy with Russia before dealing with Great Britain. The announcement that Byrnes had further agreed to recognize broadened governments in Rumania and Bulgaria brought on even more criticism of the administration. "I still have the final say on what we will do in those two countries," Truman remarked curtly at his next press conference. American recognition of Yugoslavia, he said, was "conditional"—just as any recognition of Rumania and Bulgaria would be. Although Truman and Byrnes differ in their memoirs over what happened when the Secretary returned from Moscow, there can be no doubt that the President was angry at being left in a vulnerable position by Byrnes's change of tactics.

In 1952, while he was still in the White House, Truman permitted the publication of a letter which he had supposedly given Byrnes during a confrontation in the Oval Room of the White

House on January 5, 1946. Byrnes then replied in a magazine article that the incident never took place. However that may be, the "letter" provided strong evidence that the President had opposed all private conferences with the Russians, except those on the San Francisco or London pattern. Truman began the "letter" by venting his anger at the Secretary's lack of communication with the White House during the Moscow Conference. Compromises at the earlier conferences, he continued, had first been personally approved by himself. But he had learned of the Moscow compromises only when he saw the protocol and the public communiqué.

Then he turned to the Ethridge report, which he said he had read only that morning. It revealed many facts about Rumania and Bulgaria that he had not known before; thus he would not recognize those governments until American conditions had been met to the letter.

After all this, the President listed every grievance the United States had against the Kremlin since the end of the war, including disorders in northern Iran, Russian demands on the Black Sea Straits, and, of course, the turn-down on the Rhine-Danube waterways plan. The more he wrote, the more he seemed to be carried away by the spirit of the moment:

> There isn't a doubt in my mind that Russia intends an invasion of Turkey and the seizure of the Black Sea Straits to the Mediterranean. Unless Russia is faced with an iron fist and strong language another war is in the making. . . .
>
> We should maintain complete control of Japan and the Pacific. We should rehabilitate China and create a strong central government there. We should do the same for Korea.
>
> Then we should insist on the return of our ships from Russia and force a settlement of the Lend-Lease debt of Russia.
>
> I'm tired of babying the Soviets.[41]

A likely explanation of the mystery of this "letter" is that Truman originally made notes for his talk with Byrnes, then later embellished them with justifications for his Cold War policy. In 1947, Byrnes wrote that he had been surprised at press criticisms which charged him with appeasing the Russians. In any event, the steady barrage of criticism during January and February of 1946 certainly forced Byrnes out into the open, but his critics probably aided the Soviets as much as or more than anyone else. Knowing where the United States stood on the ultimate disposition of the treaty issue may have satisfied Vandenberg, but it did not improve chances for the success of American policy. In fact it lessened them. On February 28, 1946, Byrnes delivered a "tough" speech on Russian-American problems. In it he assured his domestic critics that private conferences between the Big Three or, as in Moscow, the Big Two with guests, were occasionally useful, but that the United States would "do nothing to break the world into exclusive blocs or spheres of influence." "In this atomic age," he said, the United States could not find security unless the world was "one and indivisible."[42]

Inevitably Byrnes's speech was linked to Winston Churchill's famous "Iron Curtain" speech at Fulton, Missouri, eight days later. The former Prime Minister's denunciation of Soviet policy in Eastern and Central Europe has rightly been looked upon as one of the milestones in the early Cold War, but it has gone largely unnoticed as an appeal for an Anglo-American military alliance. Fully committed to "public diplomacy" and collective security, neither Byrnes nor Truman was interested in such an alliance. Churchill's speech helped to shape "world" opinion properly, but its usefulness ended there.

As the special train carrying Churchill left Washington for the Midwest, British aides passed out to press representatives advance copies of the speech and suggested that a good lead would be: "Churchill proposes Anglo-American alliance as Russian shadow darkens over the world."[43] American reporters covering the trip abruptly stopped playing cards, recalled one of those present, and moved from compartment to compartment talking of what would happen when Churchill finished. The answer was not quite what they expected. The next day Truman introduced his guest with the pregnant comment, "I know he will have something constructive to say." But then he sat down and played bemusedly with the tassel on his mortarboard, while Churchill described all the horrors of Russian expansion. Ten days later Secretary Byrnes assured the Sons of St. Patrick (a more perfect occasion could not have been found) that the United States was not interested in an alliance with the Soviet Union against Great Britain, *or* in an alliance with the British against the Russians.

Churchill had been pressing for a military alliance since before Potsdam. The American reaction to these overtures should make it clear that the "Cold War" then developing was not simply a Russian-American conflict. The struggle was one involving differing conceptions of world order; in addition, Americans believed that where they had inherited Great Britain's role as arbiter of world affairs, they had not inherited its methods.

The 1946 peace conference lasted in all its phases from April to October, with a grand finale in New York the following month when the Foreign Ministers met to discuss the results. Even without any major disagreements the process would have taken nearly that long because of the complicated procedure finally adopted at Moscow. It had been decided that the nations which had signed the armistices should prepare the drafts; these would then be considered by the large conference and finally ratified by the members of the Council of Foreign Ministers.

Walter Lippmann noted at the conclusion of this long, often frustrating process that Byrnes, before tackling the German and Japanese treaties, had chosen to clear away the underbrush in the one area where the Russians were most certain to be "brutal, stubborn, faithless, and aggressive." And when this proved to be the case, Byrnes still dealt with the peace conference as if he were marshaling votes in the United States Senate. The trouble with this attempt to impress Molotov with the opinions of mankind, concluded Lippmann sadly, was that it equated domestic checkers with international chess.[44] Even Byrnes admitted that the conference opened in an atmosphere charged by his speech, Churchill's Iron Curtain oratory, and Stalin's so-called "election" speech, which some prominent Americans believed was tantamount to an undated declaration of World War III. As the Secretary of State noted: "It was not surprising, therefore, that Mr. Molotov regarded the American proposals to guarantee equality of opportunity in economic affairs and free navigation on the Danube simply as additional efforts at imperialist expansion and capitalist domination."[45]

Despite this strained beginning, the first Foreign Ministers' meetings in April and June produced some important concessions from the Soviets, including the relinquishment of nearly all their territorial demands in the Mediterranean. They gave up the quest for a trusteeship over an Italian colony and their "suspicious" proposal that the Dodecanese Islands not be returned to Greece. And though the Trieste question remained deadlocked for many more months, it was now apparent that the Kremlin would not press the West to a danger point on behalf of Marshal Tito's claims. All these concessions, Foreign Minister Molotov complained with some justice, did not meet with "due appreciation or fair recognition."[46]

Encouraged by these developments, Byrnes pressed on toward all his goals. The strictly political clauses of the satellite treaties were negotiated by the Foreign Ministers without undue difficulty. When the expected confrontation appeared in discussions on the economic clauses, Byrnes threatened to call the large conference into session at once, or even to take the whole matter to the United Nations General Assembly, despite the vehement Russian protest that the Moscow agreement had stipulated the drafting must be completed prior to the convening of the large conference.

Byrnes's increasingly tough "public diplomacy" reassured Senator Vandenberg, whom he had brought along with other members of the Senate as part of the American delegation. Indeed, Senators Scott Lucas and Tom Connally were actually a bit worried that the Paris Conference was turning out to be just a little too much like what happened in San Francisco. Interviewed on the radio, both men somewhat surprisingly stressed the need for compromise, not majority votes. Tom Connally was especially emphatic on this point, recalling that the original job of the United Nations (of which he was one of several godfathers) "was not to *make* peace, but to preserve and extend peace after it has been re-established. But this is a rather artificial division of labor," the Senator decided in the next sentence, "and it has already broken down to some extent." Lucas cited Russian retrenchment in the Mediterranean, and added, "At the last meeting it seems to me that Mr. Molotov met us at least halfway."[47]

Vandenberg and Byrnes were untroubled by such doubts. The former was perfectly sure that the world's moral leadership belonged to the United States; if there was to be any serious regeneration in Europe it was up to the American delegation to bring it about. In January 1945 Vandenberg had warned that a peace treaty guaranteeing four-power control over Germany should be signed before the United States asserted moral leadership in Central and Eastern Europe. Although he had had some doubts at San Francisco, he now saw no need to wait.

Vandenberg also justified his position by the fact that the Soviets now seemed totally uninterested in any kind of security treaty over Germany. Byrnes had submitted a draft of a four-power treaty to keep Germany demilitarized for twenty-five years in February, but the "Iron Curtain" speech had taken all the headlines, not only in Washington but in London and in Moscow. Stalin gave an interview to a *Pravda* "reporter" which made it plain that he regarded Churchill's "call to war with the Soviet Union" as far more important than any long-term treaties to take effect at some future time. Protesting Churchill's denunciation of Soviet policy in Eastern Europe, Stalin said he could not forget that the Germans had attacked the USSR through those countries, and were able to do so because these countries had governments inimical to the Soviet Union.[48]

During the Paris Conference, when Byrnes pressed the Russians to accept the treaty over Germany, the official Soviet news agency, Tass, suggested that "sometimes new agreements for any more or less long period are proposed by those who are doing everything possible to break existing treaties."[49] And Molotov told the conference that the future disarmament of Germany was less important than its present disarmament. There was evidence, the *Nation* asserted, that both Britain and the Soviets were beginning to think of a resurgent Germany as a potential ally in a future struggle for Europe:

> Walter Lippmann, whose political philosophy centers about the indestructible unity of Britain and the United States and who therefore can scarcely be accused of Anglophobia, returns from Europe with the alarming comment that "there is . . . a German army, a large and good one, which surrendered to the British. . . . The

> story of what happened to that German army after the surrender is still hidden behind a silken curtain."
>
> Mr. Lippmann further hints darkly that the German officers captured at Stalingrad may still have their uses. He suggests that just as the British may be returning to the Chamberlain doctrine of turning a revived Germany against Russia, the Soviets, in turn, "are reverting toward the basic conception which produced the Molotov-Ribbentrop pact of 1939: that Germany can be turned away from Russia against the West."[50]

Molotov also objected that the security treaty would not take effect until after a German *peace* treaty had been signed. And since there were no special provisions for reparations deliveries in Byrnes's draft, Molotov apparently suspected that the proposal was some kind of ploy either to repudiate Big Three decisions providing for the shipment of German reparations from the western zones into the Soviet zone of occupation, or to get the Soviet Union to give up the demand for four-power control of the Ruhr. Very few reparations deliveries to the East had been made when General Lucius D. Clay, the American zone commander, tried to pressure the Russians into four-power economic agreements by suspending further deliveries in May 1946. Molotov referred to this "unlawful" act when he finally turned down Byrnes's offer. The Secretary of State replied only that the question of reparations was "irrelevant" to the disarmament treaty. Unhappily, all these other questions were indeed relevant, and blocked one of the most important anti–Cold War measures proposed by either side.

Undaunted by the Russian reaction to his proposal for a security treaty, Byrnes once more stepped up pressure on Russian policy in Eastern Europe. As early as April, at the first phase of the Foreign Ministers' drafting session before the large peace conference, Byrnes had asked for open meetings; as William Hardy McNeill wrote, "the pivot of international relations shifted from the conference tables to the actions of rival pro-consuls in Germany. . . . By degrees, too, the United States emerged in Britain's place as the Soviet Union's main opponent."[51]

Later the newly elected noncommunist Premier of Hungary visited Washington during one of the "recess" periods and suggested that he was interested in talking about the American plan for international control of the Danube. He even repeated this statement in public appearances. Delighted by this show of "independence," Byrnes ordered the return of American-captured gold belonging to Budapest. In Moscow, meanwhile, Molotov declared that the Danube question was "primarily the affair of the Danube states themselves, and it cannot be settled in peace treaties with individual Danube states." This speech sounded a double warning, directed both to the peace conference and to the Hungarians, who were straying dangerously close to the "imperialist" camp.[52]

The State Department met Molotov's blast with one of the toughest notes it had yet directed to the Kremlin, on Soviet economic policy in Hungary and elsewhere in Eastern Europe. Filled with references to the Yalta Declaration on Eastern Europe, it accused the Red Army, according to "reliable information," of removing more than four million tons of grain from Hungary alone. If that country's total economic disintegration were now to be prevented, the Big Three would have to agree at Paris to cooperate with other nations to "provide a framework within which the rehabilitation of that country, and its early reintegration with the general economy of Europe, will be possible."[53]

Russian Deputy Foreign Minister Andrei Vyshinsky opened the reconvened peace negotiations with a denunciation of "hand-out" diplomacy, and was applauded by two Czech delegates seated just in front of Secretary Byrnes. The Secretary was informed that the Czechs were about to receive an American credit of $50 million for the purchase of surplus property. Consistent with his Hungarian policy, Byrnes ordered the credit cut off.[54]

The full clash on economic clauses in the treaties came on October 10, 1946, when both Vandenberg and Molotov addressed the conference. Striking a familiar theme in American diplomacy, Vandenberg asked why neighboring states should demand any special privileges from one another in the name of economic reconstruction:

> It seems to us obvious that in the very nature of things neighboring states enjoy a preferential position in each other's trade as a result of their geographical propinquity and the advantages it con-

> fers with regard to cheapness of transport costs, speed of communications and other similar factors. . . . We call on the Conference to endorse the economic provisions of the Atlantic Charter, to which we have all subscribed.[55]

But why propose equality only for the Rhine-Danube? retorted Molotov. Why not also Suez or Panama?

> It is surely not so difficult to understand that if American capital were given a free hand in the small states ruined and enfeebled by the war, as the advocates of the principle of "equal opportunity" desire, American capital would buy up the local industries, appropriate the more attractive Rumanian, Yugoslav and all other enterprises, and would become the master in these small states. . . . Was this what we fought for when we battled the fascist invaders, the Hitlerite and Japanese imperialists?[56]

Molotov's crude Marxism and his hypocritical concern for the economic welfare of Eastern Europe swayed few votes at the Paris Peace Conference. But even if he had been sincere, or if the countries of Eastern Europe had experienced genuine socialist revolutions, would the attitude of the United States have been any different? In all, some fifty-three recommendations were adopted by a two-thirds majority and an additional forty-one others by a simple majority. Putting these recommendations into the original Big Three or Big Four treaty drafts was a more difficult problem. At the opening of the New York meeting in November 1946, Molotov refused to accept any of the recommendations; but when Byrnes made it plain that he was prepared to end the discussions without the treaties' being completed, and therefore without a chance for stability in East-West relations, Molotov yielded. At New York it was agreed that for eighteen months each of the former satellites would grant equal trade privileges to all members of the United Nations. The year before, at London, the United States had sought five years of nondiscrimination, but as the official State Department report on the New York Foreign Ministers' meeting said, even the shorter period of time was sufficient to determine "whether international trade throughout the world will follow the liberal principles outlined in the American proposals for the expansion of world trade or whether various countries themselves will revert to discriminatory and restrictive trade regulation."[57]

Byrnes had even gotten a two-thirds majority in favor of a clause for freedom of commerce on the Rhine and Danube, as well as similar rights for American civil aviation. He hoped to force these issues at the New York meeting. When the treaties came before the Senate Foreign Relations Committee in March 1947, Byrnes testified:

> Another important provision directed to the maintenance of the open door in the Balkans is the treaty clause on the Danube and the related agreement by the Council of Foreign Ministers to summon a conference to establish a new Danube regime.
>
> These arrangements were a compromise, and I think a reasonable one, between the desire of the Soviet Union that arrangements respecting the Danube should be left solely in the hands of the riparian states, and the view of the other three powers which participated in drafting the peace treaties that the Danube question concerns all countries and that its settlement should involve appropriate participation by non-Danubian states.[58]

One of the Senators asked:

> Yesterday the *New York Times* issued a very dramatic series of reports from its correspondents all over the world. These reports pointed out the fact that state-controlled economies have appeared everywhere, and that only here in the United States and in Canada, actually, are we still devoted to a belief in so-called private enterprise.
>
> I should like to ask the Secretary if any of these treaties give us reason to believe that they lay the present foundation for the defense of individual enterprise in a world in which state-controlled economy has become so dominant.

Byrnes replied:

> The answer to your question is, "Yes." The treaties do envisage the right of each of the United Nations to negotiate with any of the ex-enemy states as to the restoration of commercial relations between the two countries.[59]

"If we follow the United States in all its chivalrous adventures," wrote the British diplomat-historian Harold Nicolson skeptically in a *Foreign Affairs* article in January 1947, "if we allow the missionary spirit of the Americans to lead us into arduous paths, what happens if a wave of isolationism returns? We have slight faith in the continuity of American policy, knowing full well the sudden tides of popular emotion by which it can be deflected. It is not only righteous, it is even profitable, to maintain the open door in Central and Eastern Europe; but supposing that America becomes bored by the open door?"

Boredom was not a factor in Washington's failure to follow up these promising efforts in Eastern Europe. Instead it was an inevitable result of America's response to the British petition for support in salvaging the Mediterranean situation in Greece and Turkey. The enunciation of the Truman Doctrine in March 1947 finally divided Europe in two. In addition to the Greek and Turkish situations, the spreading fear of political instability in Western Europe helped to force the decision to abandon (temporarily) Eastern Europe to the ideological requirements of anti-communism.

Before the Truman Doctrine, William L. Clayton, Assistant Secretary of State for Economic Affairs, claimed the satellite treaties would bridge the gap until these nations could be integrated into the United Nations and the American-led economic system. Though Byrnes's diplomacy had not quite shocked the Russians into going the way he had wanted them to go at London in September 1945, his diplomacy had been at least partially successful by January 1947. The Russians seemed uncertain and on the defensive throughout much of the debate at Paris.

But by March 1947 higher priorities had developed in other places; it was even more important to make sure that Great Britain was firmly locked into the American international system. Will Clayton's main responsibility since V-J Day had been to see that there would be no turning back by the Labour government to the closed-empire policies of the 1930's, no retreat into prewar imperial preferences, no political deviation toward the Soviet Union, no neo-mercantilist Keynesian state monopolism. For Clayton, that responsibility was to be a continuing and a continually important one.

FIVE ☆☆

Will Clayton, the British Loan, and the Political Economy of Cold War

British economist John Maynard Keynes, representing the Exchequer, arrived in Washington in the summer of 1941 to work out details of the Lend-Lease agreement. His visit offered State Department officials the first real opportunity to talk with the British about the world to come after the defeat of the Axis powers. Before leaving England, Keynes had sent ahead a memorandum which disturbed American planners. Designed to counteract German economic propaganda, to the State Department it also suggested a perpetuation of British "closed-empire" policies of the 1930's. Though Great Britain had made an attempt to return to its pre–World War I "free-trade" policies after Versailles, the world depression had forced London to adopt a militant, nationalistic, imperial preference policy which discriminated against all outsiders. This system was formally adopted at the conclusion of a full Commonwealth meeting at Ottawa, Canada, in 1932.

From an American point of view, the British "Ottawa Preference System" belonged to the abnormal world of the 1930's, characterized by such aberrations as German autarchy in Central Europe, Japan's so-called "Co-Prosperity Sphere" in Asia, Italian fascism in the Mediterranean, and the Soviet Union's state trading system. Of course, the British Empire had not gone the same political route as those totalitarian regimes, but in closing down a greater number of the world's important marketplaces, the "Ottawa Preference System" was ultimately more significant to long-range American planning. After all, two-fifths of the world's prewar trade had moved through English and Dominion ports.

In the United States the brief New Deal experiment with intranationalism, the National Recovery Act, was gradually replaced by an effort to reestablish internationalism after the 1934 passage of the Reciprocal Trade Agreements Act. Secretary of State Cordell Hull was at the forefront of this effort, and his main goal from the outset had been to put a lever under the British imperial system. With the aid of the German threat, he achieved the first step in 1938 with the signing of an Anglo-American trade agreement. When the war began in September 1939, American negotiators intensifed their efforts to conclude trade pacts with individual dominions. The American Minister to Canada, J. Pierrepont Moffat, told Assistant Secretary of State Adolf Berle, for example, that there was "increasing evidence" in 1940 that the British were "planning a huge trading orbit within the pound-franc area designed to exclude us."[1]

While American leaders did not wish to strip Great Britain of all its assets in return for Lend-Lease aid, neither did they intend to pass up a marvelous opportunity to commit the whole British Empire to a postwar multilateral trade system. Among all wartime goals, this effort took precedence because it was the key to the political economy of the postwar world. Shortly after the 1941 talks began, therefore, Keynes was handed a preliminary draft of the Lend-Lease agreement which contained an article stating that the two nations "shall provide against discrimination in either the United States of America or the United Kingdom against the importation of any product originating in either country; and they shall provide for the formulation of measures for the achievement of these ends." When he came to this provision, Keynes objected "wildly" (according to State Department minutes of the conversation) to this attempt to break down the imperial preference system through Lend-Lease. The American plan, he said, would fix the moribund hand of nineteenth-century "liberalism"—now the main shibboleth of reaction—upon efforts to construct a decent postwar society.[2] Like several other British economic thinkers, Keynes was intrigued at the time with the notion of converting the Empire into a socialist commonwealth of nations. Far to his right were other critics of nineteenth-century "liberalism" who saw the Empire's postwar salvation and independence in terms of continued preferences and discrimination. Some months later, however, Keynes opted for participation in an American-led economic system rather than risk such uncertain eventualities—and then spent the rest of his life fighting to maintain some British independence within its confines.

At the Atlantic Conference between Roosevelt and Churchill, Sumner Welles and Harry Hopkins urged the President to extract formal commitments from the Prime Minister before Keynes's ideas set too firmly. Article IV of the original American draft of the Atlantic Charter had been carefully phrased so as to achieve open markets in a very few words. When Churchill raised his expected objections, Welles systematically recounted American efforts to reduce world trade barriers. The Prime Minister obligingly remarked that he had never especially liked the Ottawa System; but, after all, he said, the British had tried to follow a free-trade policy for seventy-five years in the face of steadily rising American tariffs. "Of course," Roosevelt replied (according to his son Elliott's notes), "after the war, one of the preconditions of any lasting peace will have to be the greatest possible freedom of trade. . . . Those Empire trade agreements are a case in point. It's because of them that the peoples of India and Africa, of all the colonial Near East and Far East, are still as backward as they are." The Prime Minister could restrain himself no longer: "Mr. President, England does not propose for a moment to lose its favored position among the British Dominions. The trade that has made England great shall continue, and under conditions prescribed by England's ministers." While Roosevelt was not interested in a lengthy argument at such a crucial moment, he did want to make sure that he was understood: "You see . . . it is along in here somewhere that there is likely to be some disagreement between you, Winston, and me."[3]

Churchill and Keynes thus found (or were forced onto) common ground in defending the Empire's freedom of action—and "under conditions prescribed by England's ministers." On the American side, Harry Hopkins and former "Liberty Leaguer" Will Clayton also found a common ground exactly opposite the British salient. They stood together to promote American postwar economic plans against every attempt to divert them from their main goal of an open world.

Offshoot of a Virginia family which had taken up cotton growing in Mississippi, Will Clayton first backtrailed to New York City in the late 1890's to serve as clerk and secretary for the American Cotton Company. In New York Clayton soon observed that the United States was gradually accumulating enough capital to break the pattern of foreign dominance over its international trade. This dominance, and the costs of reconstruction after the Civil War, had been largely responsible, he felt, for the retarded growth of the South. With barely $9,000 in capital, he and two partners established Anderson, Clayton and Company in Oklahoma City in 1904—still Indian territory at the time.

The partners took a chance that times were right for a bold effort to assert domestic control of the marketing of American cotton. They guessed right: by 1944 the company had sales of $272 million annually and was the largest cotton exporting firm in the world. It had expanded over the globe in related industries. Discouraged by early New Deal AAA restrictions, Clayton had nevertheless realized that the remedy was not to be found in the rantings of the Liberty League against "that man!" Instead, his company moved abroad where it could do business unhindered by national acreage restrictions. It built fourteen cotton oil mills and seventy-five cotton gins in Brazil, Mexico, Argentina, Peru, Paraguay, and Egypt.[4]

When Edward R. Stettinius became Secretary of State upon Hull's retirement in 1944, he asked Clayton to join him as Assistant Secretary for Economic Affairs. Clayton at once plunged into the complicated negotiations with American Treasury officials and British planners over the economic shape of the postwar world. Since 1942 the British had been insisting that American economic planning was merely self-serving, and unless modified in favor of state intervention in national economies—indeed, to facilitate that intervention—it would push the rest of the world with the United States into a new depression.

Shortly after he came into the State Department, Clayton attended a meeting in November 1944 where a prominent American economist suggested that strong federal measures in the United States could sustain domestic employment—without abnormally high export levels. Startled by the implications of what he had heard, Clayton at once wrote Hopkins: "Does he face with equanimity the possibility of a reconversion in our export industries from the present level of 15 billion dollars annually to the prewar level of 3 billion dollars?" The only way to achieve full employment without such exports was to adopt the Russian system, or at least something close to it. Unless the country was ready to do that, Clayton continued, the United States would have to emulate Great Britain's policy after the Napoleonic Wars: manage the vast credit resources at its disposal to further its own export trade *and* furnish sufficient capital for general world recovery and world trade. Hopkins readily assented: "I just cannot understand what is going through the minds of those fellows who wash up foreign trade in such cavalier manner. It seems to me they are quite unrealistic about what makes the wheels go round."[5] In fact, Hopkins had already written in a magazine article: "It must be further agreed that money lent by this Government to other nations must be spent for purchases in this country. . . . And it is highly important that business and government have an early meeting of minds as to general policy governing private investments abroad."[6]

This exchange between Clayton and Hopkins illustrated a broad-based agreement in the United States, and it was matched, as we have just seen, by an understanding between Churchill and Keynes. When Clayton informed Keynes that Congress would no doubt tie loans from the proposed "world bank" to purchases in the United States, Keynes replied glumly that the American plan would guarantee American exports, then, but little else.[7] The answer to such complaints, wrote Lamar Fleming, Clayton's former associate in Anderson, Clayton and Company, was that Britain's very salvation against the threat of Russia's overwhelming land power lay in promoting American well-being: the "British empire and British international influence is a myth already."[8] While Clayton thought Fleming made a lot of sense, and advised his State Department colleagues to read his letters with some care, he certainly did not regard Empire trade as mythical, nor did he assume that the sterling area could be opened up successfully without careful planning. "If you succeed in doing away with the Empire preference," General Robert E. Wood, the former head of the America Firsters, wrote Clayton, "and opening up the Empire to United States commerce, it may well be that we can afford to pay a couple of billion dollars for the privilege."[9]

Wood was referring to a proposed loan to Great Britain negotiated in the months immediately following the end of the Second World War. This "British Loan Agreement" was sold to doubters in the United States on the basis that it would complete what had been started in the Lend-Lease negotiations in 1941. Clayton and his colleagues argued that the "loan" was the final knot needed to tie together the American postwar system. A few critics argued that the loan would be regarded by the Russians as an Anglo-American alliance, but by the time it came to a final vote in Congress a vast majority regarded it as a counter to the Russian threat. Its place in the development of Cold War policy is therefore somewhat unclear; but this much is certain: without it the United States would have found it much more difficult to align its economic system properly and pursue goals which the Russians were opposing. The loan entered into the Cold War debate in various other ways as well, because it was at the heart of American determination to restore a completely open world, and because it suggested what could be done with economic power. In that sense, it was a turning point.

Churchill's refusal in August 1941 to guarantee equal access to world markets and raw materials forced the compromise language finally written into Point Four of the Atlantic Charter:

"Fourth, they will endeavor, *with due respect for their existing obligations,* to further the enjoyment by all States, great or small, victor or vanquished, of access, on equal terms, to the trade and to the raw materials of the world which are needed for their economic prosperity." Returning to Washington, Welles and other State Department planners immediately began work on a new draft of Article VII for the master Lend-Lease agreement. When the British signed that agreement, they were obliged, the State Department said, to confer with the United States on the ways to eliminate all forms of discriminatory treatment in world trade. For its part, the United States promised only to seek tariff reductions from Congress. It soon occurred to British officials that while they were being called upon to turn over a whole new leaf in imperial policy, the United States was pledged to do no more than erase some tariff schedules.

Wary of this wide discrepancy, Keynes met American planners halfway in 1942. He had already modified his earlier "left" nationalism, in large part because he had come to realize what it would mean to oppose the United States so completely after the war, but also because he had had some second thoughts about the political implications of an entirely closed economy—even one so big and diverse as the British Commonwealth. With significant reservations, therefore, British officials were ready to approve U.S. Treasury plans for an International Monetary Fund—to replace the obsolete "gold standard"—and an International Bank for Reconstruction and Development. American negotiators listened to the British explain their remaining reservations and discussed their differences, but, when necessary, ended by pointing out that such-and-such was the way it was going to be.[10]

Between logic and leverage the Anglo-American drafts for these postwar financial instruments were thus completed; then the rest of the "United Nations" were asked to take part in a final polishing session at Bretton Woods, New Hampshire. The so-called Bretton Woods system which emerged from these talks in the summer of 1944 leaned much farther to the right and international "free-enterprise" laissez faire than Keynes had hoped would be the case. He was frankly worried how a "socialist" government in England could adjust to it. "We in the United

States," said a candid Treasury Department memorandum on Bretton Woods, "believe that the greatest possible freedom should be given to our own businessmen engaged in international trade. But we know that this freedom will be meaningless unless other countries accord an equal measure of freedom to their businessmen."[11]

The Soviet Union's place in such a scheme of things was even more uncertain than the most extreme Keynesian system; nevertheless, the United States had urged the Russians to send delegates to the 1944 conference. To a few diplomatic "realists," this invitation no doubt seemed nothing but wasted energy and further evidence of how little Washington understood the Soviet system. But the economic advisers argued that it was useful to find out what the Russians thought about the Bretton Woods system, how they were planning to adjust to it, and whether there was any way to integrate state planning systems into that new economic order.

Actually the Russians were fairly straightforward at Bretton Woods in urging that special treatment be granted through loans and credits to nations that had been overrun by the enemy. They also asked how far the International Monetary Fund would reach into its members' internal affairs. The answer was quite extensively. IMF regulations were being deliberately designed to encourage other countries to accord "an equal measure of freedom to their businessmen," so essential to sustaining freedom in America. After the talks, the Russians told an American official in London that they suspected the "real object of the advanced industrial countries in advocating freer trade was to hold the markets for manufactured goods in the less developed countries and to check their industrialization." But this was less a reference to Asian and African "colonial exploitation" as to something much nearer home. "Protection," they argued, "was necessary for the industrialization of Eastern European countries, and their industrialization was necessary to free them from economic domination by the capitalist countries. Their doctrines seemed to be a compound of those of Lenin and List."[12]

Back in England, Keynes faced a crossfire from a left-right alliance which charged that he had sold out to American demands. While Tories were outraged by Keynes's seeming willingness to sacrifice the imperial preference system, the Labour party's victory in July 1945 turned attention to several other problems related to the Bretton Woods agreement. In the first place, London had not yet ratified that agreement at the time of the election; since the Atlantic Conference Churchill's strategy in this matter had continued to be one of delay. The resulting uncertainty of British action gave rise to three separate but closely related fears in Washington. First—and easiest to dispel—was the fear of those who confused Ernest Bevin with Aneurin Bevan—that is, the fear that Labourite foreign policy might sympathize with the Soviet Union.

The second and more serious fear inhered in the example set by the election of a socialist government committed to national planning on a far more extensive scale than anything contemplated by either Roosevelt or Truman. If Commonwealth nations tied to the sterling bloc followed a Labour government's lead away from multilateralism—even if they did not themselves elect socialist governments—American postwar policies would be placed in great jeopardy. In 1955 British left-wing economist Thomas Balogh wrote that the growth of a closely knit sterling bloc during the war had offered the Labour party a unique opportunity to construct a true socialist commonwealth of nations. It was rejected, Balogh said, in favor of the easier course—acceptance of American economic aid. This done, the encouragement of "self-determination" within the Empire was little more than a hypocritical way of shedding unpleasant responsibilities. "Hostility to new responsbilities, which are in fact inescapable for a Socialist . . . [were] politically better clothed in terms of the well-worn phrases of anti-imperialism."[13]

Even though the Labour government did turn its back on socialist responsibilities to the Commonwealth—to the great relief of American planners—in 1945 it was yet capable of influencing Western European thinking toward the left. To take the most critical possibility, would the British attempt to socialize their zone of occupation in Germany, a zone which included the Ruhr coal and steel industry? German socialists were more militant, and if they were given the slightest encouragement, what would be the result for Germany and Central Europe? And if that happened, wouldn't it bring Britain closer to the Soviets—even though Labour's foreign policy might not openly sympathize with them? Since Germany was the key to European recovery, wouldn't the entire American plan thus be preempted before it even had a chance to operate? So the argument came full circle.

The third and least obvious fear raised by Labour's victory can be discussed only in generalities. In part, it centered vaguely on memories of pre–Adam Smith economic theory and its practice in England and on the continent. More recent memories of the proposed Allied economic alliance during World War I for "the war after the war" also suggested that Labour might well attempt to emulate such a program of subsidies, state corporations, state-financed exports, and all the other methods of economic warfare. If the Labour government should in fact make that effort, so this line of reasoning went, competition for world markets between socialist-mercantilist states and capitalist economies would become a serious problem indeed.

Partially counterbalancing these grim possibilities was the Russian threat. As Clayton's thoughtful partner Fleming had said, Britain's salvation lay with America. Already apparent in July 1945, this fact limited Labour's maneuverability: economic planning like that favored by the neo-mercantilists on Keynes's right, or by the ultra-socialists on his far left, could not be introduced in such an unsafe atmosphere. Thus if war promoted state planning, cold war reduced the chance that it would lead to socialism —at least in Britain. But the stakes were too high to run any risk. The United States, Clayton told a congressional committee on March 11, 1945, "is exporting over $14,000,000,000 worth of goods a year. We simply can't afford after this war to let our trade drop off to the two or three billion figure it hit in 1932. . . . Some of our best economists estimate that we will probably have to sell $10 billion worth of goods a year abroad if we want to have relatively high-level employment and a national income in the neighborhood of $150 billion. In other words, we've got to export three times as much as we exported just before the war if we want to keep our industry running at somewhere near capacity."[14]

To another committee Clayton repeated what he had told Hopkins the year before in respect to postwar long-term foreign investment: "I don't know whether we'll ever want to take the principal back. We'll probably leave it there increasing our creditor position. I hope we'll do it and take our interest and dividends on these loans in goods and services."[15] Charles P. Taft, Senator Bob's "internationalist" better half, joined the State Department campaign: "Free enterprise cannot be confined within even our wide borders and continue to exist. The destruction of free enterprise abroad like the destruction of democracy abroad is a threat to free enterprise and democracy at home." At that moment, he continued, the world was perilously balanced between those who favored state controls on international trade and those who wanted to restore international trade liberalism: "That balance will be tipped one way or another in the next twelve months."[16] Clayton himself summed up all the arguments in one sentence of a speech delivered to the Detroit Economic Club: "Nations which act as enemies in the marketplace cannot long be friends at the council table."[17]

When, on August 21, 1945, the United States cut off Lend-Lease to Great Britain, the Labour government was put on notice that there would be no further aid until it made the long-awaited specific commitments to the Bretton Woods system. As Washington had planned, the British were floored. "We weren't in a position to bargain," wrote former Prime Minister Clement Attlee. "When the end of the war brought the end of Lend Lease it was made as black as it could possibly be. We'd used up all our resources. We'd allowed the Americans to have all kinds of export trades that we used to have. We'd emptied the till of our foreign investments. . . . We had to get our exports going. When they cut off Lend Lease we were given a body blow."[18] It was Lord Keynes who had to answer the bell for the new round of Washington negotiations. Keynes hoped somehow to persuade the Americans that it would be best for them and for the world economy if they would make the United Kingdom a multi-billion-dollar grant with no strings or promises of repayment.

The atmosphere in Washington that fall was anything but congenial to such a request. Navy Secretary Forrestal, for instance, warned Secretary of State Byrnes that the British would come fully prepared. American negotiators had better know exactly what the issues were and what their country should demand in return for a loan:

> What is to be our policy as regards British loans to South American countries? Will the British make them privately or as a government (and I am sure we should not permit this)? To what extent shall we permit the British to finance the Argentine, Brazil and Chile in an effort to re-establish the dominance of the Pound Sterling in the South American market? . . . We should be able to say that we have received considerations for what we have done above and beyond the broad, general abstraction that we get the benefits accruing from order, stability and prosperity in the rest of the world.[19]

American officials had long been concerned about the British use of Lend-Lease, especially in South America and the Middle East, to further imperial goals related not to the war effort but to the postwar effort.

The only hope of British negotiators in the 1945 talks rested on a presentation skillful enough to provoke just the right response from Americans concerned about the new Labour government's policies. One of the Keynes's aides, R. H. Brand, made this attempt in a letter to Bernard Baruch:

> If you cannot help us, or if you can only help us on terms which we feel certain we cannot fulfill and, therefore, which we must decline, we shall be left, of course, with an immensely difficult problem which will necessitate immediately extreme austerity on the part of our population and our being compelled at once to enter into all sorts of trading and financial arrangements with other countries, which are bound to be most distasteful to the United States. We must cease to buy anything from you if we can possibly help it, and we must look to all other countries in the world to help us over the stile. For the time being the only alternatives before us would be to borrow or starve. Thus we

> should be forced inevitably to enter on a path of special agreement, bilateral arrangements, and so on, with other countries, simply in order to exist. That course we could not then avoid. But you would regard it as "ganging up" against you. . . . Like Russia after the last war, we might have to disappear for the time being, in order to devote all our efforts towards making our own livelihood. Who can tell what might be the consequences in the next few years if events were to develop in this direction?[20]

"Nonsense!" Baruch scrawled angrily across Brand's letter. Of all the opponents of a large British loan, Baruch was perhaps the most effective. He thought the United States should have encouraged Great Britain to seize those markets left vacant by the elimination of German and Japanese economic power. Now the British delegation was trying to frighten Americans into an unwise loan, he wrote Churchill in December 1945. The Labour government only wanted the loan, Baruch asserted publicly and privately, to help it survive the transition from capitalism to socialism, to nationalization of its industries and the totalization of its economy. "I told our people they should be careful in lending money, to see exactly what it was to be used for. Nationalization of one country will finally end up by the whole world being nationalized and the greatest economic warfare will then be upon us."[21]

Clayton's central problem, on the other hand, was to find just "what the traffic would bear" so far as conditions and restrictions on the British loan were concerned. "I don't know of anything that we could or should do to prevent England or other countries from socializing certain of their industries if that is the policy they wish to follow," Clayton finally wrote Baruch in response to the latter's persistent criticism. "To attempt to force such countries to adopt policies with respect to their domestic economies contrary to their wishes would, in my opinion, be an unwarranted interference in their domestic affairs."[22] While Clayton never could convince Baruch that many of the nationalized industries would eventually be returned to private control, the key point, he thought, was that any loan would tie the British to the Bretton Woods system, and therefore impose limits on how far the Labour government might go toward socialism in the first place. Equally important—if not more so—several provisions in the Anglo-American financial agreement made it impossible for the British to lead the rest of the Empire back into a closed system.

The agreement was signed in December 1945. Its major provision was a $3.75 billion credit at 2 per cent interest, but both sides recognized that over the long haul that provision was probably the least significant. The United States "forgave" the British Lend-Lease debt and other war debts, except for a nominal $650 million which was to be repaid upon the same basis as the $3.75 billion credit. These special advantages in regard to Lend-Lease were granted to no other "debtor," a point often neglected by those who argue that the original legal provisions of Lend-Lease deterred favorable credit negotiations with the Soviet Union. The real difference was that forgiveness in the British case could help the Bretton Woods system get started at the same time it might yet serve as a diplomatic weapon in the conflict with the Soviets.

Other provisions of the loan agreement required the British to spend the proceeds in the United States and to eliminate their most onerous exchange restrictions and import controls by mid-1947. In other words, the agreement required the rapid extinction of the so-called "dollar pool" (to save critical dollars during the war, the dominions had pooled their dollar credits in London) and ultimately the complete elimination of Empire preferences. It also required that Britain accept no loans or credits on more favorable terms, even from the dominions. So long as the "dollar pool" continued to be dammed up by convertibility restrictions, permission for the dominions to purchase American goods had to come from His Majesty's government in London. But if this sterling bloc could be eliminated, American access to new markets in Egypt and India, as well as the rest of the Empire, would be assured.

"With the aid of this credit," Clayton told a press conference after the formal signing, "Britain is enabled to abolish the sterling area dollar pool within one year from the effective date of the agreement, so that whatever sterling is earned in Britain . . . can be used for buying in any country in the world."[23] The two key phrases here are "is enabled" and "any country," and their translations are obvious. However, their meaning specifically in regard to India perhaps best illustrates what the British loan was all about, and how the political economy of the Cold War took shape in this one area.

India had built up a tremendous surplus of dollar credits by the end of the war. More than ever before she was the jewel in the crown of the Empire, but her demand for immediate independence had put London on the defensive. Roosevelt had kept his silence after one direct attempt in 1942 to persuade Churchill to promise Indian independence after the war; nonetheless the whole thrust of American foreign policy from the Atlantic Charter on challenged London's colonial prerogatives. State Department officers continued to agitate the question privately, while Treasury officials regularly pointed out to the British that according to Lend-Lease regulations London's dollar balances had to be held under a prescribed figure. Both State and Treasury made it plain in these conversations that, after the German surrender, the United States would seek an immediate end to the "dollar pool." If this were not done, asserted one of Washington's "special observers" in India, British exporters were sure to preempt the Indian market.[24]

"Having done business in India for many years," Clayton wrote James Forrestal, "having visited the country and knowing a little something about it, I certainly agree . . . there are enormous possibilities there for American capital and American brains."[25] The Commerce Department's *Foreign Commerce Weekly* devoted one whole issue to the Indian market—actual and potential. Though full of warnings against dreams of India as a new great China market, its articles were generally optimistic. The basic problem was still how to convert temporary Lend-Lease foreign trade into permanent postwar commercial sales. Before the war American exports to India had comprised only 1 per cent of the nation's foreign sales, and only 6 per cent of India's imports. But by 1944 the United States was sending 5 per cent of its exports to India, or 17 per cent of the Dominion's total imports. "However small a percentage of the Indian people can buy manufactured goods," said *Foreign Commerce Weekly*, "however low the purchasing power of the country, India is not a negligible market, with or without possible stimulation for its projected industrialization program."[26]

"Once India gets rid of Imperial Preference," declared a Dominion spokesman to the 1946 National Foreign Trade Convention, "you might as well supplant Britain as our principal supplier. We want capital goods and technological assistance from the United States." The representative of the National Foreign Trade Council who chaired this session responded enthusiastically on behalf of the American audience: "India has spoken, and I think you will agree with me that she has spoken very well indeed."[27]

From Moscow came a strikingly similar analysis by the somewhat "unorthodox" Soviet economist Eugene Varga. Varga asserted that Anglo-American rivalry over India was at the heart of postwar issues within the capitalist world:

> Historical development is unquestionably driving towards the disintegration of the British colonial empire. Even the most astute maneuvering of British colonial politicians cannot delay India's liberation much longer. And, as Curzon once said, without India there is no British Empire. . . . Should American policy succeed in breaking down the system of imperial preferences and the sterling bloc, and, consequently, severing the special economic ties binding the Dominions to Great Britain, the latter will be reduced to a second-rate power with a population of 48,000,000. The United States will then remain the only capitalist Great Power.[28]

Russian views of the British loan were of interest to many Americans. When the Anglo-American financial agreement was presented to Congress, several legislators were confused by charges that the loan was really an Anglo-American economic alliance against Russia. Many more, however, ultimately voted for the loan on the basis of its insurance that Britain would not look toward Moscow for help—political or economic. Having largely abandoned hope that direct economic pressure would sway the Kremlin from its course of action in Eastern Europe, American policy-makers were not inclined to grant large sums of aid unless they promoted multilateralism; a loan to the Soviets would hardly advance that end. On the other hand, if a credit were denied to the Soviet Union, trouble could be expected in Congress from liberal New Dealers and their allies. At Bretton Woods, provisions had been made for state-trading economies to participate in the IMF and the International Bank on the basis of pledges that they would conduct their trade in conformity with basic capitalist commercial standards. Russia had not yet joined these agencies and seemed unlikely to under any circumstances. Unless there was something else to be gained—such as a Russian withdrawal from Eastern Europe—the United States saw little reason to set a precedent by making a loan to a state-trading nation which offered no special political reasons for doing so.

Thus the conflux of these several issues worked to prevent large credits to the Soviet Union. Truman's evasiveness whenever he was confronted with direct questions about a Russian loan pointed up the shift in American diplomacy since Harriman's early advocacy of a new-style Dollar Diplomacy in dealing with the Russians. Did the United States now plan to begin negotiations on the old Russian request for a $6 billion credit? a newsman asked the President. Truman replied that such a request had "never been officially given to me. They never asked me for a $6 billion loan, since I have been President."[29]

While Truman's reply was literally true, of course, it was not really an "answer" to the reporter's question. Continued evasiveness by the administration provoked conservatives and liberals alike to challenge the proposed loan. Increasingly disturbed by the deterioration in Russian-American relations, Eleanor Roosevelt wrote Truman that the United States should make roughly equal loans if it hoped to preserve world cooperation. The President replied that the British loan took precedence because the restoration of the world economy depended on it; but what the United States did for Great Britain, "we also hope to do eventually for Russia and our other Allies."[30]

At least one other ally, France, did receive a large loan from the United States in the next few months, but it was a corollary to the British loan, and was made under conditions which the United States could never exact from the Soviet Union. "What is contemplated," explained Clayton, "is a line of credit by the Eximbank [Export-Import Bank] on the basis of the submission by the French, from time to time, of itemized lists of materials and equipment. . . . There is no thought of making a lump sum loan to the French Government to spend as they please."[31] Supposedly the Export-Import Bank was "reserving" a billion-dollar credit for the Russians, but Congress had great difficulty obtaining details about it from administration spokesmen. Suspicions arose that this "reservation" was being held for the Russians only so long as necessary to quiet liberals during debates on the British loan. Truman's mysterious behavior in press conferences added to these misgivings. On February 21, 1946, he was asked again if he had any plans to ask Congress for a Russian loan. The answer was: "No."

Did that then mean he had excluded all possibility of such a loan? "No, it does not."[32]

Under pressure to clear up the "mystery," the State Department announced on March 1 that it would be willing to discuss a second Russian request for a $1 billion credit, provided the Soviets agreed to a Lend-Lease settlement (after Russian and American economic experts examined the Russian economic situation, including Russian relations with Eastern Europe) and promised to join the IMF and the World Bank and abide by their rules and the principle of nondiscrimination in international commerce. The *New York Herald Tribune* was more puzzled than ever by the administration's explanations. "A strange story emerges from Washington," the paper said on March 3.

> A Russian request for a billion-dollar loan—surely an item of first importance in relations between the United States and the U.S.S.R.—somehow managed to get itself lost in the files of the Foreign Economic Administrator. It stayed lost for six months, while Administration officials denied that it had ever been received, while public protests mounted against the Russian delays in participating in various international economic agencies and the like. . . . Doubtless they considered that they were being met with an example of their own inscrutability and proceeded on their course with redoubled zeal. The fact remains that an inexcusable blunder has placed American protests to Russia on very much the same plane as condescending remarks from the pot to the kettle—a relatively small pot, but still a pot.[33]

While Clayton refused to be drawn into the dispute before the

House Banking and Currency Committee, his attempts to avoid it led to the following double-take worthy of W. C. Fields:

MR. BUFFETT. Now, on the subject of peace I see by the papers that some of our noted columnists are saying that there has been no stability established in Europe between the line of Russian imperialism and British imperialism. Would you agree with that?

MR. CLAYTON. I just do not feel myself competent to discuss that. I really do not. I have devoted all my time to these economic matters, and it does not give me any time to think very much about the political situation in the world.

MR. BUFFETT. Does not this loan tie right in with the political situation?

MR. CLAYTON. Yes; it does.

Since Clayton did not offer to explain his contradiction, the Congressman pursued his question from a slightly different angle:

MR. BUFFETT. . . . In 1941 we made a lend-lease agreement with Great Britain, which was stated at that time to contemplate only financial assistance, and I believe to give us certain trade advantages at some time in the future. Is that right . . . ?

MR. CLAYTON. Not that I know of. Trade advantages to Britain?

MR. BUFFETT. To us.

MR. CLAYTON. Oh, to us? I do not know, Mr. Buffett. Perhaps I am not entirely familiar with provisions of the lend-lease agreement, but I do not know of any trade advantages to us.

MR. BUFFETT. Well, in the investigation . . . by the Senate, they announced that the United Kingdom had promised, in the master lend-lease agreement, to participate in an international conference to consider ways and means of eliminating obstacles to trade between the nations.

MR. CLAYTON. Oh, yes; that is Article 7. I did not know you referred to that. That is correct.[34]

Clayton's desire to avoid talking European "politics" and his profession of ignorance about Article VII had two sources: he wanted to keep out of the area of Russian-American conflict, but he also wanted to convince the legislators that the British loan actually replaced Anglo-American economic "bloc-ism": "If the agreement is ratified," Clayton said, "we will have multilateral trade, and no bloc in that part of the world comprising

83 per cent of the area, 87 per cent of the population, and 95 per cent of the world trade."

This posture also supported the argument against Baruch's criticism that the British would discourage free enterprise in favor of socialism. "Our agreement with the British," he told Baruch,

> if ratified by Congress, will help to slow up or prevent further nationalization of industry and commerce by Britain. If Britain doesn't get the loan from us, she will be compelled to adopt all sorts of restrictive measures in order to make 'buckle and tongue' meet, and complete nationalization of her foreign trade will be inevitable. Under our agreement this will be avoided, because Britain will go on a multilateral basis. . . .
>
> The only way Britain can convert her foreign trade to a multilateral basis is through the assistance that she will get in this financial agreement in order to help her over the next three or four years of reconversion from war to peace.

Clayton also tied the effort to the problem of making the United Nations work: "Our task in restoring the world to a multilateral trade basis is an extremely difficult one, and we don't expect immediate success, but we are convinced that we must succeed if UNO is to have a fair chance of preserving the peace."

"I believe firmly and strongly," he continued in testimony before a Senate committee, "that if we force Britain into a bilateral system in her relations with the rest of the world, we shall have these three great economic blocs, and that will force us into the complete regimentation of our external trade; and I just raise the question as to how long we could keep our domestic trade and our domestic economy free if our external economy was regimented."[35]

"The British loan is a tough conundrum for me and my Republican colleagues," Senator Vandenberg wrote after listening to the testimony.

> Of course, I . . . agree that we must face the over-all program and know precisely what we are going to do with other "customers." . . . That tremendously disturbs me. I very much doubt whether a majority of this Congress would vote a postwar loan to Russia—at least not until the "iron curtain" reels up for keeps. Yet it seems that if we grant a loan to England and then deny

one to Russia . . . we have thereby made further cooperation among the Big Three practically impossible.[36]

Despite these doubts Congress finally voted in favor of the British loan. House Speaker Sam Rayburn said that the issue was really quite simple: "I do not want Western Europe, England, and all the rest pushed towards an ideology that I despise."[37]

As it turned out, the favorable vote on the British loan amounted to a favorable vote on other administration plans for restoring a multilateral world trade. The State Department had previously issued a call for an international economic conference to discuss an American draft charter for a new international trade organization; the British loan was the key piece to these plans as well. Russian opposition to the draft was thus minimized—and kept localized. Article 31 of the State Department's proposed constitution for world trade provided that no member could become party to any agreement with a nonmember from which the nonmember might benefit. Members could not even grant tariff reductions to nonmembers without the consent of the proposed organization. These clauses made it impossible for Eastern European countries to join the organization unless the Soviet Union was already a fully participating member—or, of course, unless those countries were willing and able to defy the Kremlin.

In respect to these provisions, former State Department economic adviser Herbert Feis criticized his successors' strong emphasis upon rigid formulas, noting with some concern that Washington had seldom pushed its views so vigorously as it had done in protesting Soviet trade agreements with the satellite countries. Although he suggested that this forceful display made it all the more unlikely that these nations would ever adhere to the Bretton Woods system, Feis did feel that there might still be room for reasonable compromise. But if each side continued to insist upon total victory for its trading system, there could be no agreement. After all, he pointed out, United States practice in Latin America could hardly be defined as free-enterprise capitalism. Often controlled by giant monopolies, the American trading system in Latin America was fully as monolithic as any communist state-trading organization.

Yet, Feis added: "In this matter the United States cannot

compromise happily or too far. For it is not striving merely to obtain a few extra million dollars of trade or profit. It is seeking to assure that these small countries have a genuine chance to follow their independent judgment in economic and political spheres. And it is seeking to protect American trade relations throughout the world against a possible assault of a combined bloc of countries under the leadership of the U.S.S.R."[38] If, as now seemed likely, no compromise were found, what would happen if the Soviets tried to negotiate major bilateral agreements with nations in Western Europe or possibly even in the Americas? Feis did not go into that problem, but while such agreements would not have the same obnoxious political content as those with Rumania or Hungary, they would just as surely challenge the U.S.-led multilateral, liberal capitalist economy.

Without the British loan, of course, the United States might never have felt able to take the chances it did in 1946 and 1947 to stop any such attempt. An August 1946 Swedish-Russian trade agreement, completed only a month after the loan agreement with Britain had passed in Congress, brought a sharp protest from the United States. The protest went unheeded. In fact, Sweden audaciously made several additional, long-term bilateral trade agreements that year which finally totaled more than $1 billion. *Business Week* observed that official Washington was disquieted by both this trend and Swedish neutralism in early Cold War clashes between East and West.[39] Consequently, in 1947, when the United States prepared to take its formal ITO proposals to Geneva for a final international conference with eighteen other nations, Sweden was put in the same pigeonhole with the Soviet Union and much of Eastern Europe and was not invited to attend. "An economic bloc means the regimentation of international commerce," Clayton insisted. "Lincoln said, 'This nation cannot exist half slave and half free.' This applies to commerce as well as to human beings. If we have regimentation in our foreign trade, how long do you think free enterprise can continue in our domestic commerce?"[40]

In 1940 Henry L. Stimson had used the same allusion to describe the Axis threat. Now Will Clayton was using it once again to explain the political economy of America's postwar policies. By 1949 he had reached the further conclusion that it was necessary to form a political and military union of the world's democracies. He had reached this conclusion, he said, not long after British failure to sustain currency convertibility in 1947, as per requirements of the financial agreement. When London tried to make pounds sterling freely convertible into dollars that summer, the dollars flowed out of England like water through a break in the dike. All the precious time supposedly gained by the huge credit was lost, spilled out wastefully to no constructive end. "It would not be so bad if we had had goods and services from it," declared a Member of Parliament, "but it is estimated that a good half or more of it vanished in a few days when the convertibility clause came in."[41]

"Not many people in this country believe the Communist thesis," declared the London *Economist*,

> that it is the deliberate and conscious aim of American policy to ruin Britain and everything that Britain stands for in the world. But the evidence can certainly be read that way. And if every time that aid is extended, conditions are attached which make it impossible for Britain ever to escape the necessity of going back for still more aid, to be obtained with still more self-abasement and on still more crippling terms, then the result will certainly be what the Communists predict.[42]

"Our loan to Great Britain is a good example of how not to proceed," charged John Foster Dulles in testimony before the Senate Foreign Relations Committee. "The grant of these three and three-quarters billion dollars solved nothing because it created nothing."[43] Currency controls were quickly re-established to last for ten more years.

England's salvation came only with the Marshall Plan. Clayton's last important work as Assistant Secretary of State was concerned with formulating that aid program. Both Clayton and Dulles believed that the Marshall Plan would be a fresh start, toward not only economic recovery but Western European political unity. It was more and more apparent, Clayton and Dulles thought, that no plan would succeed without such unity. In fact, Clayton wanted to condition Marshall Plan aid on a lowering of trade barriers, with periodic checks to make sure the recipients were really carrying out their promises. "We will hold in our hands the powerful weapon of discontinuance of aid if contrary to our expectations any country fails to live up to our expectations."[44]

After leaving the State Department, Clayton became vice-president of the Atlantic Union Committee; in that capacity he testified once more before Congress, on the North Atlantic Treaty Organization in 1949. The chief obstacle to freer world trade was still currency inconvertibility, Clayton said, not only in Great Britain but throughout the European area. Even the Marshall Plan was proving unable to change that situation. To meet the communist challenge, which he said was directed at keeping Western Europe in so much turmoil that capitalism's normal recovery was held in check, he advocated complete elimination of all trade barriers. Since this could not be accomplished without political unification, he also proposed a Federal Union of Democracies. This new European political order would exert such a pull on the satellite countries that Russia would finally be unable to hold them; thus there would be no World War III. Instead of chronic dollar crises in England and Western Europe, these nations' debts would be consolidated at one stroke by the Federal Union. "You remember Alexander Hamilton was a great exponent of the idea that the new Union should not only assume the debts of the Confederacy that preceded it but also assume the debts of each individual state of the 13 states."[45]

Instead of meeting the Soviet bloc inefficiently with outdated national remedies, Clayton's proposed Federal Union would ease the financial and military burden for all. His ultimate rationale for it was therefore much the same as it had been for the Anglo-American financial agreement in 1945:

> If western Europe is overrun by communism, I think the situation which we would face in this country would be a very grave one, even if we faced no great military danger—and we would. The economic consequences of such a disaster would be very, very great to us. We would have to reorder and readjust our whole economy in this country if we lost the whole European market.[46]

Clayton's ideas, while admittedly too extreme for most Americans, even for those who favored NATO, put a new light on

American encouragement of the European Common Market movement during the next two decades. Not yet ideologically rearmed for the Cold War, Reinhold Niebuhr put his pen on the central point in the American attitude toward Great Britain at the beginning of that conflict:

> The more our economic power grows the more we are inclined to assume that political power, being more overt, is less ethical than the more covert economic power. This illusion is generally shared by American liberalism and is one of the most fruitful sources of friction between the two nations, which are enacting on an international scale the old tension between the landed aristocrats and the rising bourgeoisie. The British own more castles than we; we, increasingly, own the mortgages to these castles. We do not quite know whether we ought to resent the fact that we do not live in the castle or rejoice that we have the mortgage. In this moral predicament we resolve our difficulty by calling attention to the fact that the owner of the castle has not liquidated serfdom on his estate, but we do not mention that the owner is in danger of becoming our serf.[47]

"When we set up the European Economic Community," a Belgian economist said in the mid-1960's, "we did something useful, but limited and still incomplete. So far its major result has been to increase our economic prosperity by creating the most favorable climate for a growing invasion of American industries. They and they alone have acted upon the logic of the Common Market."[48] "The Common Market," added Jean-Jacques Servan-Schreiber, "has become a new Far West for American businessmen. Their investments do not so much involve a transfer of capital as an actual seizure of power within the European economy."[49]

Clayton had first developed this vision twenty-five years earlier; in fact, he and Harry Hopkins had shared it in 1944. Two years later Clayton and William C. Bullitt came to the same definition of the principal threat to American plans. It was, as Bullitt described it in *The Great Globe Itself*:

> The United Kingdom and the Empire are by far the greatest customers of the United States. If their peoples should be unable

> to purchase in the United States because they were forbidden to exchange their pounds sterling for dollars, the reduction of American exports might make the difference between prosperity and hard times in America. The area to which it is possible to make exports normally from the United States has already been reduced by the Soviet monopoly of foreign trade. . . . Every time the Soviet Union extends its power over another area or state, the United States and Great Britain lose another normal market.[50]

Clayton and Bullitt agreed fully on another key point: that the "loss" of China, imminent by the time of the NATO hearings, would put terrific pressure on new American "frontiers" in both Europe and Asia. "If the mainland of Asia falls to the Communists," Clayton warned in his testimony, "we will maintain that frontier with a great deal of expense."

Bullitt despaired even more. He felt certain that Europe could not be held alone; and he was convinced that Secretary of State George C. Marshall had failed in China. On March 23, 1948, he advised an old friend: "Marshall still remains in frozen opposition and is blocking any genuine cooperation between the American and Chinese Governments. I am afraid we shall have to take him apart."[51]

Once more Bullitt symbolized a large segment of American opinion, this time one which would soon blame Marshall for the "loss" of China. Marshall's "error," his illusion, lay in trying to enslave the future to the present. But then, even Stalin had a mistaken idea about postwar China.

SIX ☆☆

George C. Marshall: Traditional Policy in Post-Traditional China

On November 27, 1945, the mantle of America's China policy fell to General George C. Marshall. Since the last decade of the nineteenth century the United States had been involved in China's affairs, particularly those concerning Manchuria. The routes from that province back to China proper were filled with political traps for the unwary, and led into mazes which perplexed the best-intentioned statesmen. Several times in the twentieth century American diplomats had sought to "neutralize" the whole area; this was still Washington's approach when Marshall went to China at the end of the Pacific war.

Half a century before, in the dangerous aftermath of the Boxer Rebellion when tsarist Russia occupied Manchuria, the American Ambassador had urged the dying Manchu rulers to modernize their foreign office and accept American help in reforming the tariff. But he could not promise what the Chinese really wanted: enough military aid to drive the Russians out of the province. In 1903 the State Department sent an economic missionary, Professor Jeremiah Jenks, on the first of several unsuccessful efforts to persuade the Manchus and then their "Republican" successors to turn China's financial affairs over to a board of foreign advisers headed by an American. President William Howard Taft once poked the Chinese Ambassador in the ribs after dinner one evening and asked him to trust Secretary of State Philander Knox's attempt to "neutralize" Manchurian railways—a suggestion General Marshall would make again in 1946. At Versailles, and again at the 1921 Washington Naval Conference, American diplomats assumed responsibility for Chinese interests without being asked. Even at the 1937 Brussels Nine-Power Conference, the United States delegates told China's emissaries not to interfere while they tried to cajole and coerce the Japanese out of North China and Manchuria.

"President Roosevelt's policy," General Marshall once commented with the proper emphases, "was to *treat* China *as* a great power."[1] During the war Roosevelt and his advisers hoped the myth might father something real, that China might somehow replace Japan as the principal stabilizer in the Pacific. By 1944 many Americans had abandoned that long-time dream, but most were still enslaved to past attitudes toward Chinese politics and international relations. A State Department officer briefing Vice-President Henry A. Wallace before Wallace left on a special mission to China still stressed "the rivalries for power under personal leadership which began with the overthrow of the Manchus" as the most important characteristic of Chinese internal affairs. "Warlordism" and the "so-called communists" were, according to this view, roughly equal factors in the Chinese situation.

The original identification of Mao Tse-tung's supporters as "so-called communists" or "agrarian liberals" was first made not by confused or naive liberals but by the Department's tough-minded Far Eastern advisers in the decade before the war.[2] Thus American policy from the Moscow Foreign Ministers' Conference in late 1943 through the Marshall mission was predicated upon the erroneous assumption that the only way "communism" could come to China was through Moscow. The answer was therefore to build a wall between the Soviet Union and the Chinese Communists. If Nationalist China and Russia were signatories to the same pact (or series of agreements), then, it was thought, Moscow's cooperation in the rehabilitation of Asia might be secured.

More important, the "so-called" Chinese Communists would be isolated and eventually absorbed into a reformed and strengthened Nationalist government. Henry Wallace's report to Roosevelt summed up the limitations of the traditional American view of China, and how they constricted policy-makers:

> At this time, there seems to be no alternative to support of Chiang. There is no Chinese leader or group now apparent of sufficient strength to take over the government. We can, however, while supporting Chiang, influence him in every possible way to adopt policies with the guidance of progressive Chinese which will inspire popular support and instill new vitality into China's war effort.[3]

Perhaps the most dramatic proposal for keeping the Soviet Union and the Chinese Communists isolated from one another came from those who argued for working with Mao and abandoning Chiang to his fate. This radical alternative really came from the heart of America's traditional China policy. Though the men who argued for it may well have been deceived about the nature of Mao's movement, to work with him was certainly no less realistic than presuming that Chiang could be forced to accept "American" solutions for his problems while holding onto the "Mandate of Heaven" to rule China. As in the past, the American dilemma was best illustrated by the Manchurian situation in 1945. At Yalta Roosevelt had bargained with Stalin over the Far East, dispensing to the Soviets rights and concessions in Manchuria in exchange for Stalin's promise to support Chiang's government in China proper. Some of these "rights" had belonged to the Tsar before the Russo-Japanese War, and Stalin would undoubtedly have the power to take much of what he wanted at the end of the war anyway. The terms of the bargain also weakened Chiang's stature with his people and undercut his claim to national leadership. Neither Roosevelt nor Stalin fully grasped the situation. Both were too deeply absorbed in the problems of the likely Russian-American confrontation in the Far East at war's end.

"We in America always think of China as a nation," Truman

wrote ruefully in introducing the "Marshall Mission" in his *Memoirs*. "But the truth is that in 1945 China was only a geographical expression."[4] In the first few weeks after V-J Day, General Albert Wedemeyer, the American commander in the China Theater, rushed Chinese troops north and east to accept the surrender of the Japanese armies in Manchuria. "A struggle for positions of strength," he wrote later, "was already in progress between America and the Soviet Union in Manchuria and North China." Wedemeyer asked for seven divisions of American soldiers to "create a barrier through North China and Manchuria against Soviet Russia." He was granted two Marine divisions which were sent to Tientsin and then dispersed throughout North China from Peking to the sea. Stalin answered this move by refusing to allow Chiang's troops to disembark from American ships in Manchuria, and by turning Japanese arms over to Mao's forces. General Marshall arrived in China, then, faced with the imminent collapse of the Yalta Far Eastern agreement.

Two important points emerge from a review of Marshall's legacy. First, despite their often expressed wish for a genuine "nationalist" government in China, American leaders had generally despaired of Chinese democracy and supported strong men, from Yuan Shih-kai to Chiang Kai-shek—but in ways that actually weakened the leadership of these men. In fact, Washington automatically opposed nationalist movements that endangered American interests, usually without even bothering to try to understand them. Second, and largely as a result, American policy debates over how China could best be aided had always been bitter and divisive, even before the communist issue appeared. From William Howard Taft's time to the height of the McCarthy era, critics of established policy readily seized upon Chinese complaints to attack their domestic political opponents. Of course their charges were equally unrealistic, short of changing traditional policy. Thus in 1909 Secretary of State Knox attempted to "neutralize" Manchuria; in 1945 General Wedemeyer suggested to Chiang that the Chinese government propose a temporary five-power guardianship over Manchuria by the United States, Great Britain, France, China, and the Soviet Union. Wedemeyer realized that the United

States would not give Chiang sufficient military aid to take over Manchuria, and that the Chinese government would not be able to govern both North China and Manchuria if it attempted to reoccupy Manchuria unaided.[5]

Wedemeyer recognized—even if he did not fully assess—the factors which made it difficult for Chiang to accept this advice, including the Generalissimo's reliance on "men without scruples" who were primarily interested in self-aggrandizement, and the dangerous weaknesses of the Kuomintang in North China. In a shortsighted effort to overcome these handicaps, Chiang had appointed his Southern Chinese supporters to key posts throughout the North. "It seems apparent," Wedemeyer wrote, "that he has no confidence in the Northern Chinese. The people of the North have been embittered by these appointments, and the political, economic, and military stability of North China has thus further been retarded."

Until the 1943 Cairo and Teheran conferences, the Chinese Nationalists had assumed that a massive American campaign against the Japanese in North China and Manchuria would eliminate the Communists and secure the Kuomintang occupation behind the aegis of United States military power. When such action failed to materialize, Chiang's bitterness was never assuaged; he threw it up to Americans in various ways for a long time afterward. With the other factors we have noted, it helps to explain why he was unwilling to accept General Wedemeyer's proposal for neutralizing Manchuria. Instead the Chinese leader requested ever larger doses of direct financial aid, but it was not forthcoming for several reasons, including the growing fear that right-wing Kuomintang groups would push the Chinese toward anti-Western fascism unless the United States made good use of its economic diplomacy. The publication in 1943 of Chiang's ghost-written *China's Destiny* further increased this American concern. "The book shows a definite Fascistic tendency in ideology," commented the American Embassy in Chungking. "It is another reflection of the phases of mordant and morbid nationalism which are being currently experienced by the Kuomintang. If this kind of nationalism is persisted in and encouraged, it will not be very conducive to China's wholehearted cooperation in the period following the war."[6] On December 9, 1943, Ambassador Clarence Gauss had added:

> Referring now to the Chinese tendency toward a closed post-war economy, I recommend strongly that without further delay we should quietly put China on notice as to what we expect before policies are adopted by China which later for reasons of oriental face she may not be willing to change, by opening negotiations for our commercial treaty, advancing our proposals in respect of the treatment of American commerce and American financial and industrial interests, emphasizing that mutual consideration and mutual benefit are necessary and insisting that rights and privileges comparable to those which Chinese enjoy in the United States should be enjoyed by all Americans and American interests in China.[7]

In the summer of 1944 Roosevelt sent Donald M. Nelson with Vice-President Wallace to China in order to have someone on the top level of American industry directly advise Chiang to turn his back on those who had led him to believe that there would be large credits or loans forthcoming to help the Chinese nationalize their industries. Nelson recommended that while some industries, primarily transportation and power projects, might be developed by state aid, most industries—textiles for example—ought to be developed entirely by private enterprise. "This could be done, Nelson urged, "by the setting up of Sino-American corporations—e.g. from five to ten in the textile industry—in which the major investment and control would initially be American." "For the United States," Nelson reported to FDR, industrial development of the Yangtze Valley "would mean large exports, the stimulation of key industries and many jobs for workers. Several agencies of our government, and members of the House and Senate, are actively interested, as are a number of private industrial and engineering concerns."[8]

General Wedemeyer also pointed out very clearly to Chiang that foreign advisers were necessary to China's recovery, and that these men could not be effective if his government placed restrictions on foreign business interests. There simply were not enough Chinese technicians and managers to operate those industrial establishments, utilities, and lines of communications which had been built before the war by foreign interests. But Nelson and Wedemeyer neglected to note that if Chiang were unable to prove his nationalism through economic policy reforms, he was even more likely to turn to "foreign" expansion—Manchuria.

Nelson and Wallace had urged the Kuomintang leader to make a political effort to come to terms with the Soviet Union. He would find himself without breathing space to resolve internal political questions, they said, unless a Sino-Russian accommodation kept Moscow interested in supporting the Nationalist government. Wallace "expressed the opinion" in his first conversation with the Generalissimo that there should be no question left pending "which might result in conflict between China and the U.S.S.R."[9] The Vice-President also said that Roosevelt might be willing to mediate the internal political question inasmuch as the Kuomintang and the Communists, both being Chinese, "were basically friends."

Chiang responded that while he would like to have Roosevelt mediate Russo-Chinese differences, he had no desire or intention to involve the President in Chinese national politics—except as a gun-runner to the Nationalist forces. "The best assistance that the United States could give in this matter," he told the Vice-President, "would be to display 'aloofness' to the Communists." Then, he concluded, they would have to settle with the Kuomintang—but on its own terms. Ever since General Stilwell had insisted on training Mao's men, and the State Department had established so-called listening posts in Yenan, Chiang had expected something like Wallace's proposals; now he wanted to set Roosevelt's emissary straight about the matter once and for all.

Despite a strong disclaimer that Roosevelt would not mediate Sino-Russian affairs, Wallace did probe China's likely reactions to Russian claims on Dairen in southern Manchuria. The Generalissimo's reply indicated that he had already approved such a claim, but with the provision that Moscow cooperate with Nationalist China and not seek to impair its territorial sovereignty elsewhere. Chiang concluded this part of the discussion by repeating his desire that Roosevelt sponsor a Pacific "Big Three" conference. As Wallace implied, however, the President preferred to keep to himself the problem of building China internationally; besides, Wallace said, the Soviet Union was not yet at war with Japan. In the end, the President's concern that Russia enlist against Japan, and his desire to settle the seemingly less complicated political issues in the Far East, led to the Yalta Far Eastern agreement—and to the later charge that pledges to China made at Cairo had been abandoned.

At Yalta Roosevelt and Stalin agreed upon the following conditions for the Far East:

> 1. The status quo in Outer-Mongolia (The Mongolian People's Republic) shall be preserved.
>
> 2. The former rights of Russia violated by the treacherous attack of Japan in 1904 shall be restored, viz:
>
> (a) The southern part of Sakhalin as well as all the islands adjacent to it shall be returned to the Soviet Union.
>
> (b) The commercial port of Dairen shall be internationalized, the preeminent interests of the Soviet Union in this port being safeguarded and the lease of Port Arthur as a naval base of the USSR restored.
>
> (c) The Chinese-Eastern Railroad and the South-Manchurian Railroad which provides an outlet to Dairen shall be jointly operated by the establishment of a joint Soviet-Chinese company, it being understood that the preeminent interests of the Soviet Union shall be safeguarded and that China shall retain full sovereignty in Manchuria.
>
> 3. The Kurile Islands shall be handed over to the Soviet Union.
>
> It is understood, that the agreement concerning Outer-Mongolia and the ports and railroads referred to above will require concurrence of Generalissimo Chiang Kai-shek. The President will take measures in order to obtain this concurrence on advice from Marshal Stalin.
>
> The Heads of the three Great Powers have agreed that these claims of the Soviet Union shall be unquestionably fulfilled after Japan has been defeated.

In exchange for these "concessions," Stalin pledged: "For its part the Soviet Union expresses its readiness to conclude with the National Government of China a pact of friendship and alliance between the USSR and China in order to render assistance to China with its armed forces for the purpose of liberating China from the Japanese yoke."

After Roosevelt's death the Yalta agreement was reconsidered, but while Stimson asserted that it was the Polish question all over again, and Byrnes hoped to get the war over before the Russians got into Dairen and Port Arthur, Truman's advisers finally concluded that there was little that could be done to keep the Russians out of the war if they chose to come in at the last minute.[10] Consequently, these advisers thought Roosevelt's bargain with Stalin remained the lesser evil. Some hoped for an apocalyptic solution, but the dropping of the atomic bomb only complicated the Far Eastern crisis, for it left intact a large Japanese army in North China and Manchuria, and gave the Soviets an excuse for extended occupation of those areas.

In 1946 Bullitt summed up the status of the traditional Far Eastern problem. "The present situation in Manchuria," he wrote,

> which is now the richest province in China and contains approximately seventy per cent of her industries, resembles in many respects the situation after the Boxer Rebellion. The Soviet Union has promised to withdraw her troops from Manchuria and to restore the province to China. But such Soviet troops as have been withdrawn, have been replaced by Soviet-armed units of the Chinese Red Army. It was Japan, backed by the friendly neutrality of Great Britain and the United States, which drove the Russians from Manchuria in 1904. At the present time only the United States has the physical power to force the Russians to withdraw.[11]

After Nelson and Wallace, Roosevelt's third and last special "missionary" to China had been Brigadier General Patrick J. Hurley, who resigned with a flurry of charges and accusations directed at State Department officials. He charged they were helping the "imperialists" and the "communists" rather than America. "We finished the war in the Far East," he wrote Truman, "furnishing lend-lease supplies and using all our reputation to undermine democracy and bolster imperialism and Communism."[12] Hurley's letter, so strongly reminiscent of Bullitt's thesis, became a key document in the China "lobby" brief during the McCarthy era. It charged Roosevelt and his successors with failing to carry out the Atlantic Charter, a theme which would swell in coming years to drown out the voices of reason and entice others to adopt a strident Cold War line, if only in self-defense against such attacks. "There is a third world war in the making," Hurley continued ominously. "We are permitting ourselves to be sucked into a power bloc on the side of colonial imperialism against Communist imperialism. I am opposed to both. I still favor democracy and free enterprise."

Although the former Ambassador's letter wandered—and even argued against itself—the members of Truman's cabinet recognized at once its political potential. Agriculture Secretary Clinton P. Anderson suggested that General Marshall's appointment, if it could be done quickly, would divert newspaper headlines from the accusatory letter. When Forrestal seconded the idea, Truman called Marshall the same day that Hurley's letter appeared. Thus the mission which had frustrated American diplomats since the turn of the century at last fell to the chief architect of America's military victories in World War II. But the central problem which Marshall faced had always been beyond military solution: how to make China strong enough to resist aggressive foreign powers, and how to modernize its government and economy against internal disruptions and revolutionary nationalism.

Secretary Byrnes explained to Marshall that the State Department wanted to put sufficient political and economic weapons at his disposal to induce the Nationalists and Communists to get together. What if Chiang refused? Marshall asked. Would Marshall then have to deal with Mao? Byrnes replied that he would, at least so far as the pressing business of disarming the Japanese army in Manchuria was concerned. For the rest, Byrnes could make no clear answer; the final draft of the State Department's instructions to Marshall simply hammered on the need for unity. Military aid, economic credits, technical assistance—all depended on a "realistic" situation in China; they could not be offered to a country "disunited and torn by civil strife." After these instructions had been so phrased, Truman directed all government departments and agencies with Chinese business pending to suspend their discussions with that country's officials at once. Now, Truman ordered, all negotiations with China were to be coordinated through General Marshall as special emissary: he was to have complete control of America's China policy.[13]

In a last meeting with Truman, Byrnes, and Admiral Leahy, Marshall defined the basic unreality of his mission: if the United States precipitately abandoned the Nationalist government "there would follow the tragic consequences of a divided China and of a probable Russian resumption of power in Manchuria, the combined effect of this . . . [would result] in the defeat or loss of the major purpose of our war in the Pacific."[14] Thus Marshall was bound to a definition of the issues that put the Chinese problem squarely within the framework of past experience with Russo-Japanese rivalry over Manchuria. It left out of account the Chinese themselves.

Chiang, however, still hoped to use America's "traditional" interest in Manchuria to further his own ends and to overcome the Yalta agreement. If he could force the issue over reoccupation of Manchuria, his original plan for a final solution of the Communist problem might yet be realized. Chiang's estimate of America's position was only partially correct, not enough to do him any ultimate good. Marshall's concern about Russian power in Manchuria did lead initially to two military decisions favorable to the Nationalists. First, despite the growing public clamor that the troops be brought home, American Marine divisions were to be left in North China until the situation was clarified. At peak strength these forces never totaled more than 113,000. Even so, American military advisers in China felt they offered a crucial stabilizing force, protecting vital communications lines from Communist guerilla raids throughout the winter of 1945–1946, and thus keeping open roads from China into Manchuria.[15] The second decision was to finish moving Chiang's forces into North China and Manchuria. Once this dual mission was completed, more than 400,000 Chinese Nationalist soldiers had been moved into battle positions and helped across the straits into Formosa. Americans were shocked, however, at the attitude of Kuomintang generals who looked upon this aid as an opportunity to satisfy their own greed. As the State Department's 1949 "White Paper" put it concerning Formosa: "The new Governor arrived with an imposing retinue who proceeded with great efficiency to exploit

Formosa. In addition the local population was ruthlessly excluded from any important role in public life and was made to feel that it was again under the rule of a conqueror."[16]

The situation was much the same in Manchuria, where Chiang's viceroys completed the pillage begun by retreating Soviet armies. But while such awakenings embittered Americans who had been sent to China to help rehabilitate the country—and even drove some to Mao's side—Marshall still hoped to mold the Kuomintang and the Communists into a coalition to rule China. The Communists would be dissolved as an independent political force, but they would give the new government a reform flavor. Their appeal would become indistinguishable to the great majority of Chinese who, while they disliked and feared the Kuomintang, had not yet been won to Mao.

Byrnes's off-the-record comments to newsmen explained how this was to be done:

> I think that some of our arrangements made with Soong [T. V. Soong, sometime Chinese Ambassador to the United States and a member of Chiang's inner circle] (who is a very able fellow) have made for difficulties. I can just imagine Soong dropping in on Chiang after one of his trips to Washington and saying, "Well, I have just got another 500 million. . . ." And I can see Chiang saying, "The hell you say. . . ." and then calling in the Communists and telling them that there was no need to talk any further; that they would have to come to terms or else. There's a lot of human nature in the Chinese.[17]

In preparing Marshall's instructions, said John Carter Vincent, head of the Department's China Desk in 1945, the plan was to draw the Communists into the central government in a minority position; then "we could eventually strengthen the Chinese Government to eliminate the Communists."[18] To work with any degree of success, the plan required a great leap of faith on Chiang's part. He was being asked to commit himself, once again, almost totally to the good intentions of the United States. China's past experiences with American advice hardly provided the kind of foundation needed for this new blueprint, but the new American Ambassador, John Leighton Stuart, a seventy-year-old former president of the missionary-sponsored Yenching University, explained in his memoirs why the United States could in all good conscience ask the Generalissimo to put himself in such hands. "It happens that we Americans have at this crucial period of human history a fortunate combination of enormous natural resources, new technological inventions and the human capacities for utilizing these, stimulated and improved in military affairs by the exigencies of the last war. . . . For reasons such as these it was in no sense derogatory to the Chinese nor supercilious on our part to emphasize their need of the kind of advice we were fortunately able by force of circumstances to give them."[19]

While Marshall's approach did not envisage military aid, he was plainly worried about the too rapid demobilization of American forces at the end of the war. Nonetheless, before American soldiers went home they had created in Asia a new military line extending from Japan to Formosa, including all of South Korea. American military men on the leading edge of that line spoke confidently of their purpose, assured that behind them was the most powerful weapon in history, even if it remained unused. Major General A. V. Arnold, for example, first military governor in South Korea, told a reporter, "It is our job to see that the Koreans get the American type of democracy and not communism; call it the rule of enlightened dictatorship."[20] General Douglas MacArthur could not have stated his own aims in Japan more clearly. "The conqueror of Japan became her savior," wrote Anthony Kubek, one of Marshall's severest critics. "There was no one to save China."[21] Stripped of its suggestions of betrayal in high places, this "conservative" interpretation is surprisingly similar to claims that American good intentions were not supported by military power equal to the noble task. The answer to both interpretations is that the problem was not military.

At home, Under Secretary of the Army William H. Draper, Jr., reassured the 1948 National Foreign Trade Convention that American demobilization did not mean disarmament or disengagement. Draper was one of the architects of the successful occupation policy in Germany—a policy which had not relied on massive ground forces. Demobilization, he admitted, had invited unwanted interference in the nation's peace efforts, but the United States remained a "bulwark of peace." "The American flag,"

Draper declared, "now flies not only in Tokyo, in Osaka, in Yokohama, but in Seoul, the capital of Korea, in Vienna, in Frankfurt, and in Berlin. Our flag gives assurance in today's uneasy world to freedom-loving peoples everywhere that America is staying on the job until security and peace have been achieved."[22]

Secretary Byrnes had hoped to reduce Russian-American tensions in Asia by suggesting at Moscow in December 1945 that American forces were in North China only to disarm the Japanese, and by submitting new proposals for a Far Eastern Commission and Allied Council for Japan. But Stalin himself probably had two objects in mind at the Moscow meeting. First, he still wanted recognition of the East European governments, and was willing to do some trading over Japan to get it. Second, he wanted a government in China that could buffer Soviet-American conflicts in Asia. Shortly after the war in the Far East ended, the Russian premier had summoned the Chinese "comrades" to Moscow, and (adhering to his pledges under the Yalta Agreement and the Sino-Russian Treaty of August 14, 1945) "told them bluntly that we considered the development of the uprising in China had no prospect, and that the Chinese comrades should seek a *modus vivendi* with Chiang Kai-shek."[23]

A month later at London, however, Molotov had attacked American occupation policies in Japan. While Byrnes had thought the Russians were merely trying to cloud the issues, when Ambassador Harriman next spoke with Stalin the Russian leader made it quite clear that he was indeed concerned about United States military plans in Japan. The Soviets had been arguing for some time that Russian forces should be used in occupying one of the northern islands, Hokkaido. Instead of seeing this request as an effort to protect Russian Far Eastern interests, however, MacArthur believed it was aimed at communizing Japan. Still, he felt that he could not flatly refuse that request without offering something else; he therefore suggested a Russian occupation zone in heavily bombed central Honshu, one flanked on both sides by American zones. The Russians then dropped their demand, but Byrnes suspected that Stalin was holding up disembarkation of Nationalist Chinese troops into Manchuria partly to bring pressure on the Japanese matter.

In October Stalin had suggested the creation of a control commission for Japan similar to the one in Rumania in that its chairman, General MacArthur, should have the final voice in most matters—in fact, just as he wanted the Soviet commander to have the final voice in Eastern European countries.[24] Not willing to make a quid pro quo on Rumania, Byrnes had to come up with a scheme that would leave American occupation policies largely untouched, yet satisfy Stalin's concern about a rearmed Japan. When Byrnes and Stalin dined together on December 23, the Secretary of State explained that General Marshall's first aim was to establish a truce in China so that the Japanese troops could be disarmed. Stalin's reply further established both the Soviet Union's attitude toward the Chinese Communists and his own personal conservatism:

> STALIN said that if the Chinese people became convinced that Chiang Kai-shek was depending on foreign troops, he would lose his influence. Chiang Kai-shek apparently does not understand this, but the three Governments should understand it for him. It would be much better for Chiang Kai-shek to rely on his own forces, but if we desired to help Chiang Kai-shek we should not give him help in such a manner as to destroy his authority with the Chinese people.[25]

In 1964 a former Foreign Service officer who had suffered for his views on China during the McCarthy period, John Paton Davies, suggested that the full Soviet view must have been something like the following: Aware that U.S. forces were stationed in China, Korea, and Japan on at least a semi-permanent basis, the Soviets had moved to counter that advance by occupying southern Sakhalin, the Kuriles, North Korea, and Manchuria, "thereby forestalling American contact with the hypersensitive Soviet frontier." But even this occupation was not enough to quiet the "Russian neurosis over security." Since the Americans would still be uncomfortably close, something had to be done to keep them busy. "And what could be more distracting for them than to undertake to unify China under Stalin's old protégé Chiang Kai-shek? So Stalin's plea to American statesmen that their government back the Nationalists was sincere, as sincere as the exhortations of a Charles Addams character urging an innocent to explore a swamp at midnight."[26]

Having stripped the province of key Japanese industrial assets in the same crude fashion that it had exacted reparations in Europe, and having held up occupation by the Chinese Nationalists, Moscow switched its tactics in 1947 and formally asked Chiang's government to take over the civil administration of Dairen and Port Arthur, as well as the joint administration of the railroad to Changchun. "Just what this caper means is less than clear," noted John Melby, another Foreign Service officer in China at the time. But, he added, such switches were really to be expected, "because Sino-Soviet relations in practical terms are a by-product of the broader struggle of Soviet-American relations." The Russians could afford a complaisant attitude because if Chiang dropped the "Mandate of Heaven" to rule China, their "cohorts" would simply pick it up. On the other hand:

> Too much we tend to look on this as a struggle for power; it is indeed that, but we overlook the third major participant, the people of China, who might just have a few ideas of their own as to what they would like to see happen in their country. In the long run it is they who will decide. We alone maintain the illusion of Nanking as a major power and insist it go through the motions of acting like one, when in fact it can be little more than our third withered arm. China can never be more than that until someone manages to attract the real sources of Chinese power and put them together.[27]

On January 10, 1946, within a fortnight of his arrival in China, Marshall had succeeded in obtaining a truce between the two sides, specifying that the Nationalist forces would be allowed to move into Manchuria and take it over from the Russians. Meanwhile, Stalin had invited Chiang's son, Chiang Ching-kuo, who had been designated by his father to oversee the Manchurian occupation, to meet with him in Moscow. They talked twice, and each time Stalin stressed the need for cooperation between China and Russia, and between the Kuomintang and the Communists. Stalin also said he wanted cooperation with the United States in Asia, but that he would oppose American military presence in Manchuria. Urging the Chinese Nationalists to adopt an independent stance, he asked Chiang Ching-kuo to arrange a meeting for him with his father, either in Moscow or at some mutually suitable place on the Sino-Russian border.

Soviet Defense Minister Rodion Malinovsky delivered a sharper message: "It is hoped that the question of economic cooperation in Manchuria can be quickly settled. Soviet Russia does not wish to have any third party come in. She is particularly opposed to Manchuria being turned into an anti-Soviet base." Besides Stalin's political appeals, Moscow had sought economic cooperation with Chiang through the establishment of joint Russian-Chinese commercial enterprises in Manchuria. The State Department protested such undertakings in a note to Moscow and Chungking on February 9, 1946, reasserting the old Open Door policy and warning against the creation of Sino-Russian monopolies which might discriminate against American commercial interests. But at Yalta it had been decided that the Chinese Eastern Railroad and the South Manchurian Railroad should be operated by a "joint Soviet-Chinese company," with an additional understanding that the "preeminent" interests of the Soviet Union should be protected—a provision left open to different interpretations. Chiang recalls in his memoirs that he could satisfy Russian demands only by violating his government's long commitment to the open-door principle, and his own policy of inviting foreign capital to aid in the development of Manchuria.[28] Whatever Chiang planned for Manchuria, he did not intend to allow Russia or the United States to dictate his policy. But the situation was further complicated when Washington made known to the world the terms of the Yalta agreement. Under its terms, Chiang had been expected (indeed ordered) to reach economic agreements with the Russians in Manchuria—because the Americans had committed him to do so. Now, by their note of February 9, the Americans had warned him *not* to do so. It was an impossible situation.

Chiang finally asked Marshall what he thought of the idea of his meeting with Stalin. He recalled that Marshall replied: "Anything that can help relations between China and Russia, I am for it." Other sources suggest an even more positive response by Marshall. Leighton Stuart's close adviser, Phillip Fugh, recalls that Marshall actually had three meetings with Chiang to try to persuade him to accept Stalin's invitation. Putting aside the complications of the Yalta agreement and Washington's protest note of February 9, Marshall argued that a meeting between Chiang and Stalin would warn the Chinese Communists that they could expect little or no aid from Moscow. Madame Chiang argued against the plan, however, insisting that her husband's personal destiny and the "Mandate of Heaven" could be fulfilled only by the independent Manchurian policy he had already begun. The Russian Ambassador attempted to bypass Madame Chiang through T. V. Soong; the American Embassy in turn tried to assure the Russians that, while they welcomed the proposed meeting, nothing could dissuade Madame Chiang or persuade her husband.[29] Madame Chiang may have been the determining factor, but the Generalissimo's choices were also circumscribed by the contradictions in American policy and the demands of the Kuomintang.

Marshall was anxious at this time that Chiang not upset the delicate workings of either the January truce or the Political Consultative Conference, the mechanism he had created to convert the cease-fire into a reformed central government. During the last three weeks of January 1946 the PCC managed to pass five resolutions anticipating a political settlement throughout China. By this settlement the Communists would have gained several advantages in a proposed national legislature as well as in local governing bodies in the provinces. These would have been balanced by a pro-Nationalist military agreement establishing a five-to-one Kuomintang manpower superiority in the new Chinese army. This agreement would also have finally sealed off the Communists from any Russian aid. Late January 1946 was therefore the high point of the Marshall mission; he seemed very close to pulling the marble cake out of the oven.

But it fell flat. Already bitter about the likely outcome of the Marshall mission, Kuomintang "reactionaries" joined Madame Chiang in discouraging Chiang from accepting Stalin's invitation. This was only one evidence of their opposition (and their power). But the "reactionaries" also warned that such a conference would make it seem that the Nationalist government had accepted as inevitable "cooperation between the Kuomintang and the Chinese Communist Party." Chiang also explains in his memoirs that he was convinced the Russians were behind the Communists; therefore, the invitation amounted to an invitation to his own humiliation—a banquet where the Russians planned to feast upon Chinese independence.[30]

At this inopportune moment, Washington decided to release the text of the Yalta Far Eastern agreement. Its publication further undermined Chiang's position with important uncommitted groups. It happened in the following manner: At his January 31 press conference, President Truman was subjected to heavy questioning about the Yalta Pact. Asked if he could recall exactly when he learned about the cession of the Kurile Islands to Russia, Truman said it had been sometime prior to Potsdam. Then came this question:

> Mr. President, are we going to have any more of these agreements brought out later?
>
> I can't answer that, I can't answer that.

Truman went on quickly to explain that such agreements had to be made for America's own advantage during the war. "That is what this Yalta agreement was."[31] His answer was obviously insufficient; shortly thereafter the administration made the full text public.

In an unsuccessful attempt to regain prestige, the Kuomintang announced that China would not be bound by the terms of the Yalta agreement. Ironically enough, Ambassador Stuart shortly found himself in an embarrassing dinner discussion with Mao on the Yalta agreement. The Communist leader's objections, which were no less strenuous than those voiced by Chiang, once again illustrated how differently from the Russians and Americans the Chinese on both sides viewed the situation. Hinting that Yalta was merely a wartime agreement, Stuart even implied vaguely that it might somehow be adjusted or even renegotiated.[32] The imbroglio grew ever more dense.

In Chungking the Kuomintang Central Executive Committee adjourned a special session without accepting the PCC resolutions, relieved that events had provided an excuse for rejecting the compromises. For their part, the Communists insisted upon immediate acceptance of the resolutions. Behind this political façade, both sides clearly felt impelled to risk a military showdown in Manchuria.[33] Chiang told Marshall he could not accept anything less than complete sovereignty over Manchuria. Mao's assessment was essentially the same: the Communist party should make war against the American imperialists who backed Chiang Kai-shek. "Sometimes Marshall reacts," John Melby observed, "as though he were slowly coming to the reluctant and rather sickening conclusion there is only one answer left and that is to pull the props and turn the country over to civil war."[34]

The Manchurian situation appeared one way to the non-Chinese powers, but quite a different way to Chiang and Mao, who saw that the epic battle for China would begin there. Driven by the dynamic of the Kuomintang (which, as Barrington Moore has suggested, was like that of European fascist governments in that it had to resolve its internal problems through military force and expansion), Chiang ignored Wedemeyer's and Marshall's advice. He seemed confident that the United States would have to support him because of its "traditional" interests. Yet this allowed Mao to take advantage of Chinese nationalism by condemning Chiang's reliance upon Americans, and in June 1946 he renamed his army the "Army of National Liberation" with the announced purpose of driving the American imperialists out of China.

Marshall left China for five weeks in this critical period to speed up economic and technical aid to the new coalition government he thought would emerge from the PCC resolutions. Three days before his return, on April 18, 1946, the Communists attacked the Manchurian city of Changchun, evacuated by the Russians only a few days earlier. This attack climaxed a series of feints and provocations by both sides which went back to the actual signing of the truce on January 10. Even then, neither side had wanted to extend the cease-fire into Manchuria.

On December 25, 1947, Mao presented a report to the Central Committee of the Communist party entitled "The Present Situation and Our Tasks." It described Chiang's "counterrevolutionary" war as having begun in July 1946, but it was quite accurate as a description of what had prompted the earlier Communist strike at Changchun. At the end of the Second World War, Mao stated, the United States stepped at once into the shoes of German and Japanese imperialism, "against the national movements in the colonies and semi-colonies and against the liberation of the Chinese people."

> At such a time the Chinese reactionaries headed by Chiang Kai-shek acted as the running dog for U.S. imperialism. . . . At such a time, if we had shown weakness or given ground and had not dared to rise resolutely to oppose counter-revolutionary war, China would have become a world of darkness and the future of our nation would have been forfeited.[35]

But a string of military successes in July and August 1946 encouraged Chiang to think he had been right all along in disregarding American advice, in undercutting Marshall's efforts whenever possible, and, most importantly, in believing he could draw the United States ever more deeply into the struggle. As Wedemeyer and Marshall had feared, Chiang's forces were weak; eventually they crumbled under pressure from the Communists. But for the moment the Generalissimo was exuberant in discussing the situation with Marshall. "Given time," he boasted, "the ripe apple will fall into our laps." Most Americans in China remained skeptical. On August 10, 1946, President Truman sent Chiang a combined warning against such optimism and against assuming unlimited American support for this adventurist military policy. A growing school of thought in the United States, Truman said, demanded a re-examination of the nation's China policy. The Kuomintang's reliance upon "military or secret police rather than democratic processes to settle major social issues" had reduced its standing in the United States. Truman then attacked supposed "extremist" elements in both the Kuomintang and the Chinese Communist party, and implied that the United States was really seeking a disinterested or neutral position. In his careful reply to Truman, Chiang insisted that it was up to the Communists to come to terms with his government, and that he relied "on your continued support in the realization of *our* goal."[36]

Chiang wagered that Washington could not really play a neutral role in China. Despite his warnings to the Nationalists, Marshall did approve new sales of surplus material to Chungking. When Chou En-lai, the chief Communist negotiator, asked about the sales, Marshall replied that they did not include combat weapons. Someone was certainly confused here: *New York Times* reports called attention to the inclusion of old bombers among the supplies.

Stalin, meanwhile, also warned the Generalissimo about his actions, suggesting that both countries should be more concerned with America's unilateral policies in Japan. The Soviet dictator asked once more for a Sino-Soviet summit meeting, prophesying that it could be the beginning of a new era of Sino-Russian cooperation against Japan, such as Trotsky had proposed in the 1920's.[37]

Chiang's Manchurian offensive had already passed its zenith when Henry Luce arrived in Nanking, bringing with him the first of several new *Time-Life* "experts" who were to tell the American people about that epic struggle between good and evil. "The conversation was incredibly unreal," Melby noted grimly after an official government dinner for Luce:

> The remarks of the *Time-Life* people nearly convince me that I have been right as to what the new line will be—the problem has been solved, there are only scattered groups of bandits left, and they don't amount to much. *It is, I think, the beginning of the blackout.*[38]

While Luce and his aides listened uncritically to Kuomintang leaders tell of their magnificent victories, Marshall despaired of bringing about a peaceful settlement. A new truce would take months to negotiate. "And I can't go through it again. I am just too old and too tired for that." Chiang was boasting that the Communist issue would be eliminated within six to ten months, certainly within the next year. The Generalissimo wanted Ambassador Stuart to persuade Marshall to stay on as his chief of staff; Marshall wanted only to get out as soon as possible. Whatever aid the United States now gave to the Kuomintang, the special emissary said, would mean the triumph of the reactionary cliques. And Ambassador Stuart specifically warned Chiang that the United States would be unable to give him assistance in a civil war.[39]

Marshall's only suggestion for a new beginning was similar to the one proposed by Secretary of State Philander C. Knox nearly thirty years before: neutralization of China's railroads. The unreality of that alternative became apparent when the 1943 Sino-American Commercial Treaty was finally published on November 4, 1946. The Communists immediately seized upon its publication as yet another opportunity to attack the Kuomintang's subservience to the imperialists. The treaty's "reciprocal" provisions for protection of foreign investments provided the main target. Nonexistent Chinese investments in the United States were assured protection from government action, in return for a reciprocal assurance from China. After publication of the treaty, "Anti-American Movement Committees" sprang up in several cities, followed by forums, parades, and violent demonstrations. Chinese who were not willing to attack their own government were "educated" into that position through anti-American rallies.

Although the treaty was primarily intended as a defense against Chinese right-wing nationalism, it was evidence that American postwar policy was of a whole. Even if the great dream of a China market had never come true, Washington feared the results of such a large country's adoption of an alien economic policy. Addressing the 1946 National Foreign Trade Convention, John Carter Vincent traced American involvement in Chinese politics back to economic roots, and then brought his listeners up to date: "Our enunciation of the Open Door and our insistence on non-discriminatory and most-favored-nation treatment were motivated largely by a desire to promote American business and expand international trade relations." That motive still lay behind American policy, Vincent insisted. While some people had regarded the Marshall mission as solely political, the State Department looked upon China as a "nuclear" country in the establishment of the proposed international trade organization. Therefore the recent Sino-American Commerial Treaty had been more carefully worked out than other commercial pacts: "Chinese economy is in a vicious circle. General Marshall is fully aware of this state of affairs and it has been his purpose to encourage the Chinese to break the vicious circle by reaching a political settlement that would result in a cessation of civil strife and make possible a revival of economic activity."[40]

There is little point in documenting this concern to excess, but Truman's own extemporaneous remarks to McGraw-Hill editors and executives in July 1946 revealed that the full-blown vision once conjured up by John Hay and Brooks Adams still had a firm place in the American image of the world:

> The difficulties in China are still very, very bad, but we appointed a new Ambassador the other day, which will be very helpful to General Marshall, and we hope in the long run that peace will come out of the Chinese situation; in which case there is an unusual chance for a development in the Far East which I think will be exceedingly helpful to us from a trade standpoint.
>
> *Our future, I think, lies in the Pacific, from a foreign trade standpoint, if we can get peace in the Pacific—and I think we will eventually get it.*[41]

After Marshall returned from China and assumed the office of Secretary of State, one of the first recommendations he received concerning the Chinese situation came from Forrestal. His idea was to turn China over to American businessmen. They could make it plain that we still wanted to help, "but not as a source of charity which turns to booty for the particular piratical group that you found leaching the economic health and prosperity of China." Forrestal had felt for several months, ever since his own personal observation trip to the Far East, that the great need was to allow business and international trade to generate world recovery: "There is a vast amount of trade in the Far East which is now lying dormant.[42]

Forrestal's *bête noire,* Henry A. Wallace, pretty much agreed with this estimate. His statements before a congressional committee in 1951 revealed at once the chronological and ideological span of America's China policy. Within its wide boundaries, Forrestal and Wallace could agree upon goals even if they divided sharply on methods. "You see," Wallace explained, "I have had the view for many years, ever since 1909, in fact, that eventually the west coast would have as great a significance for this Nation as the east coast." The basis for this development, Wallace added, was calculated upon "the mounting percentage of our imports coming from the Far East and the possibility of our exports to the Far East mounting through the west coast ports." In 1944 he wanted the nation to realize that only the United States could furnish the capital exports to "get this area of the world really clicking in a way it should click."[43] A few years later Wallace publicly blamed Chiang Kai-shek for blocking the development of the great China market.

Marshall left China in January 1947 in no mood to become further embroiled in the Chinese civil war, even from a distance of several thousand miles. But Henry Luce and Bullitt would not let the dream go, though others now said it was a nightmare, and even though they themselves had seen the nightmare first hand. Luce sent Bullitt to China in the summer of 1947 to find out why the struggle was not going the way it was supposed to. Bullitt was appalled by what he saw in the Nationalist capital of Nanking. "Someone," he kept muttering to those around him, "someone has not been telling the truth."[44] But when, back in the United States, he wrote his article for Luce, "Report to the American People on China," he insisted that the threat was purely an external one—the Soviet Union's ambition to dominate Manchuria. Of course this was Luce's only hope to enlist the nation in his crusade to save the American dream in China: the Chinese Communists were only Stalin's agents. Then Bullitt hit upon the real weak spot of Roosevelt's China policy, which would become the major theme of its critics. The late President had "betrayed" his own commitment to China to restore all its lost territories, freely given at the Cairo Conference in 1943, by his clandestine bargain with Stalin at Yalta. "We handed to Stalin a deadly instrument for the domination of China and thereby paved the way for war in the Far East." When war came in 1950, American leaders and the nation believed for the most part that the Kremlin was behind the North Korean invasion. But Bullitt was convinced in 1947 that it was not too late to save China from Stalin's dark minions. He put forward a great display of statistics supposedly demonstrating that military and economic aid could turn back the red tide. The total cost of such aid, Bullitt concluded, would not exceed $450 million a year over a three-year period. While he admitted the necessity for radical reforms, he concluded, as Wallace had in 1944, that there was no alternative to Chiang Kai-shek. Thus Truman should send Chiang the one man who could most aid him, Douglas MacArthur, a general of supreme stature; together as "two comrades in a front-line trench" they could work out a plan to prevent China's subjugation by the Soviet Union:

> The cause is a common cause. If China falls into the hands of Stalin, all Asia, including Japan, sooner or later will fall into his hands. The manpower and resources of Asia will be mobilized against us. The independence of the U.S. will not live a generation longer than the independence of China.[45]

But MacArthur still had problems of his own in Japan in 1947. He was deeply concerned about underground agitation, and he believed Moscow was directing the Japanese Communists and their liberal sympathizers in efforts to discredit his policies. Instead of accepting Bullitt's proposal for shifting MacArthur to China, most American leaders preferred to shift America's Far Eastern policy to Japan. MacArthur's conservative occupation policies had thus far kept this option open, but if Japan were to be rebuilt properly, foreign markets would have to be developed and Japan reintegrated into the community of nations at the earliest moment. At first this shift in American policy was signaled only in negative terms—statements that Japan could become a "vacuum of power into which influences other than ours are bound to be attracted as much by the internal suctions as by external pressures." By November 1947 the discussion was of the need to restore the balance of power in both Europe and Asia. As Forrestal then asserted in Cabinet meetings, such considerations surely called for a review of the limits on industrial reconstruction in all the defeated Axis nations.[46]

But the more it became apparent in China that American policy looked to Japan, the easier it was for the Chinese Communists to recruit the powerful forces of peasant nationalism, then ally them with student unrest. Chinese intellectuals who had once looked to the United States now decided that no matter how well intentioned America had been, the Chinese revolution had to come from within—it could not be imported from the United States. At a meeting of the Kuomintang Central Executive Committee in September 1947, Chiang's Prime Minister tried to halt these defections by affirming that Chinese policy toward Japan generally coincided with that of the Soviet Union "and was opposed to American policy . . . therefore China would be obliged to strengthen its relations with Russia while at the same time preserving its traditional tie of friendship with the United States." This speech simply revealed how desperate the Kuomintang had become. But the opportunity for working with Stalin had passed.[47]

On June 24, 1948, Ambassador Stuart lectured anti-American demonstrators in China as if he were still holding forth in a Yenching University classroom:

> If those of you who agitate or who participate in the agitation against the United States on the question of Japan disagree with what I have said, then you must be prepared to face the consequences of your actions. . . . I hardly need protest my affection for Chinese student groups. If my life has not proven that, then it has been a total failure. I trust then that you will take the harsh words I have felt compelled to speak in the spirit in which they are intended.[48]

In his private reports to Washington, however, the Ambassador spoke far less patronizingly about the student situation. They were dispirited, he said, and "with no proper outlet for their patriotic urgings." Moreover, another group, "the crassly capitalist interests," also opposed American policy toward Japan because, none too efficient, they feared Tokyo's future competition in Chinese and Southeast Asian markets.

No matter what happened in China, restoration and expansion of Japan's prewar markets to the Japanese was the only alternative now, argued several American policy-makers. The only fully industrialized nation in the Far East, Japan had to be kept on the right side in the Cold War. In addition, this task was far more congenial to most State Department officers. It was not at all surprising that the principal "realist" critique of America's traditional China policy should have later emerged from among those Foreign Service officers who were now in the ascendant. Rebuilding Japan's economic empire, while certainly difficult, was largely a technical problem. If the State Department's Europe-firsters understood sympathetically any Far Eastern question, it was the key role Japan had played in the old alliance system. The Anglo-Japanese alliance had long been an elementary fact of life in European diplomacy, a fact which they had learned well at their first diplomatic posts or perhaps even earlier in their training. Now it had to be replaced with an American-Japanese alliance.

The President began cutting the last threads of Marshall's China policy at a press conference on March 11, 1948. Asked about the origins of the Marshall mission and the General's supposed plan for bringing the Communists into the central government, Truman denied that there had ever been any such intention. "I don't think General Marshall intended to take any Communists into the Chinese Government. We don't want a Communist government in China, *or anywhere else,* if we can help it."

One alert newman tried to ease the President out of a likely predicament by suggesting that perhaps there were different definitions of the word "communist." Truman seized on that defense for a moment, but just as alertly a less friendly reporter pushed him off: "Well, Mr. President, could you tell us what sense you are using it in?"

Now another newsman came to the rescue: Didn't broadening the base in China mean taking in Communists *or* at least Chinese liberals? Now Truman was home: Why, yes, in fact he had been talking to a Chinese "liberal" "just the day before yesterday. . . . They are the people in whom we are interested principally." Then Truman locked the door behind the Marshall mission and his responsibility for it:

> Q. Mr. President, the distinction between liberals and Communists would also apply in this country too?
>
> THE PRESIDENT. Yes. That is a very good definition. Same difference exactly.[49]

More than a year later, Truman admitted to David Lilienthal that Marshall's plan had called for a reorganization of the Chinese government with two-thirds Nationalists and one-third "so-called Communists." The President explained that Stalin had told him that the people of northern China would never be true communists, "and he's about right, at that." Nothing could be done about China until things settled down. "The dragon is going to run over and after that perhaps some advances can be made out of it."[50] It was an amazing conclusion to the Marshall mission; Truman citing Stalin on the Chinese Communists—and both were already proven wrong.

"Marshall flubbed China and Asia," Henry Luce insisted, clinging to his "American Century." It would be a tremendous thing to recover the ground that Marshall had lost by new "missions." He even proposed that Lilienthal undertake one:

> It would be a world sensation, and do great good. . . . The trustee for the world of this new scientific marvel, atomic energy, the builder of TVA, goes to India, Burma, and China. He is accompanied by half a dozen news correspondents from this country, and we send along our best man—I know just who he would be right now. You visit Hangkow, etc., and at each place you visit the university, talk to the students. You are the exponent of the third of Sun Yat-sen's three points—for TVA is the American example of that. The Chinese recover face—the atom chief comes across the sea to sit down and talk with them. Marshall flubbed China and Asia; this is a bold way to recover that.[51]

Two months later Luce's dream was shattered with the publication of the State Department's "China White Paper" in August 1949. Much of its documentation was so recent as to be indiscreet by traditional diplomatic standards. What to do next in Asia was discussed at Harvard University during the summer of 1949 by John King Fairbank, Edwin O. Reischauer, Harlan Cleveland, and William L. Holland. China scholar Fairbank said that the lesson of the American defeat in China was that it had let its policy become more anti-Russian than pro-Chinese. In the future the United States would have to come to terms with Asian nationalism, and even to align itself with its positive purposes and aspirations. "We must revive the pioneer revolutionary spirit in our approach to Asia." Private capital and technical skill would have to be used effectively, and the development of Asia would have to become an integral part of American business, education, and administration. But it could not depend "solely on the profit motive for its inspiration."

Harlan Cleveland, then with the Economic Cooperation Administration, the administrator and manager of Marshall Plan funds, tried to put the problem in its broadest perspective. "There is a natural and growing disposition . . . to start looking toward the Far East once again primarily for available raw materials and potential market outlets." There was a great danger that this need would be exploited by communist movements in both Europe and Asia to attack the United States and its allies for being exploiters and imperialists. It was therefore necessary to make sure that trade with Asian countries helped to balance and diversify their economies. But it still remained accurate to say that the basic task would have to be accomplished by private capital, albeit with government aid. To encourage capital to go into troubled areas, the federal government would have to offer guarantees to the investor, negotiate special treaties with the nations concerned in order to improve the "climate" for private investment, and grant tax-relief measures to its entrepreneurs.

William Holland concluded that with the collapse of "our historic position of influence in China," the American government would have to find "a relatively stable and secure Far Eastern nation where it can have friends who have some appreciation for our ideals of political democracy, private enterprise, and equality before the law." Japan was not yet a free agent, so Holland nominated India.[52]

A few weeks later, at a State Department round table on Asia, Harold Stassen nominated Thailand. National sensitivities in India, so recently freed from British imperialism, threatened any attempt to move the headquarters of our Asian policy to New Delhi, Stassen argued. Besides, the United States might become involved in the yet unsettled religious wars there, which could turn out to be every bit as bad as the Chinese civil war. America still had a more favorable position in Asia than either the British or the French; we must not become tied too closely to the policies of those static powers. Independent Thailand was the best answer all the way around.

The opening speaker at the conference had been George Frost Kennan. He began with a brief lesson in geopolitics, as it had been traditionally understood among the European trained, drawing a mental picture for his listeners of the Central European–Russian land masses set against the two island bastions England and Japan. Though a Communist victory in China was worrisome to the West and its allies, Kennan said, the Russians were less threatening in Asia than in Europe. It seemed unlikely to him that they could combine with the Chinese Communists to produce anything "which in a physical sense would be dangerous to us." China lacked plentiful resources of the kind which we regard as the "guts of industrial power." It had other significant weaknesses as well. "I do think," he noted in response to a question, "the possibilities are greater in India than they are in China and if India, which is almost a blank check to us today, can create the prerequisites to be a world trading power . . . I believe then you could get certainly a fifth world industrial center of great importance."

But the "terrific problem" before the United States in 1949 was still how the Japanese "are going to get along unless they again reopen some sort of empire toward the south. Clearly we have got, if we are going to retain any hope of having healthy, stable civilization in Japan in this coming period, to achieve opening up of trade possibilities, commercial possibilities for Japan on a scale very far greater than anything Japan knew before."[53]

Though not sure that even a restoration of Southeast Asian markets would be enough, Special Ambassador John Foster Dulles began with a similar assumption when he agreed to negotiate a peace treaty with Japan. Defending the treaty before a somewhat doubtful Senate Foreign Relations Committee, Dulles kept repeating that the situation on the Chinese mainland could not be regarded as permanent: "We must and can assume that there will be a change from the present China situation which now compels the free nations temporarily to restrict closely their economic relations with the mainland of China." The best-informed Japanese, he asserted, were also confident that this change must come. To quiet fears that Japan would resume its economic policies of the 1930's toward China, Dulles had previously secured a letter from the Japanese Prime Minister which set forth assurances that his country would not reopen strategic trade with Communist China.

"To me," said Dulles,

> the most important single thing that the United States can do and the thing which is indispensable to hold a free world position, not only in Japan but in Korea, Formosa, and Indochina, and to spread it, is that we must adopt . . . positive policies and get away from the idea that this overrunning of China by Soviet Communism is a final last word as to what is going to happen to China. There have never been those final last words as regards China in the past, and I do not think it is so now.[54]

If one includes military aid to China, both in strategic movement of troops and billions of dollars of supplies, the United States has been fighting almost without pause in Asia since 1941, in large part to prove that "those final words" on our traditional policy would not be pronounced.

On August 21, 1946, General Marshall replied to a letter from Bernard Baruch about American atomic policy. The turbulent situation in China made it difficult for him to think seriously about this other problem, he said, but he was led by that situation itself and its tragic consequences for more than 500 million people to see "the urgency in this period of our civilization for finding a development without further delay of a positive means to put a stop to the probability of wars.

"My own experience here," Marshall continued, "has led me to a few conclusions which of themselves might seem rather small factors. It grows more clearly evident to me every day out here that suspicion of the other fellow's motives, lack of understanding of his conception of your motive, are the greatest stumbling blocks to peaceful adjustments. When trade factors and the pursuit of the dollar are added to the plot the problem grows even more complicated in time of peace."[55]

Marshall had assumed there was some basis for compromise in China if he could just get hold of the thing; he was mistaken. Baruch assumed there was no basis for compromise on atomic energy; whether he was also mistaken is still an open question.

SEVEN ☆☆

Bernard M. Baruch: Atoms for Peace

President Truman's announcement to the American people on August 6, 1945, that the first atomic bomb had been dropped on Hiroshima deliberately misled the world about the extent of America's military superiority and capabilities in the near future. As a wartime statement there was of course some justification for its exaggeration, if only to hasten Japan's surrender; but it had the effect of establishing the first in a series of assumptions about American possession of the bomb which profoundly influenced American foreign policy and world history. Truman said:

> We are now prepared to obliterate more rapidly and completely every productive enterprise the Japanese have above ground in any city. We shall destroy their docks, their factories, and their communications. Let there be no mistake; we shall completely destroy Japan's power to make war. . . . If they do not now accept our terms they may expect a rain of ruin from the air, the like of which has never been seen on this earth.

The terms Truman demanded were unconditional surrender; the political terms of American proposals in the United Nations for control of atomic energy in 1946 were essentially the same. Under any circumstances it was almost inconceivable that the Soviet Union would agree to atomic disarmament until it had its own weapons of terror. The development of American proposals can therefore be considered as an effort to convert its discovery into that famous lever Archimedes had once asserted could move the world. The ancient Greek's allegorical prediction of man's ultimate mastery of the physical universe had come true; yet that truth had come in a way which threatened man's destruction. Hence there was safety for the owner of these "levers" only so long as he enjoyed the monopoly; political settlements had to be achieved quickly while technological superiority was improved. Americans consequently behaved more like Zeus than Archimedes, jealously boasting of their ability to bring a "rain of ruin from the air," placing Zeus's symbolic thunder and lightning on Air Force service caps, and finally creating the Strategic Air Command with its *1984* motto, "Peace Is Our Profession."

In his "Iron Curtain" speech, Churchill confidently asserted that it had been divinely ordained that America, rather than a fascist or communist state, should develop the bomb. It was, to be sure, a weapon well suited to a struggle between moral absolutes. American policy-makers did not expect to threaten atomic attack to force the Russians out of Eastern Europe or Manchuria, although a few military leaders later developed a sterilized version of preventive war—preemptive action against an aggressor who was known to be building his forces. What Truman and his advisers did intend was to use the bomb to back the full range of peaceful pressures—economic and moral ones as well as standard military displays—to create the world they wanted. The dividing line between the two policies wavered and constantly imperiled the so-called balance of terror which finally became the dominant characteristic of the atomic era.

Truman's public claim to a near-ultimate weapon revealed the way he envisioned America's use of the weapon after the war. He told Charles de Gaulle, as we have already noted, that "The German menace should not be exaggerated" as a future threat because "the United States possessed a new weapon, the atomic bomb, which would defeat any aggressor."[1] On board the *USS Augusta* on the way back from Potsdam, Truman declared spontaneously upon hearing the first report of the bombing of Hiroshima, "This is the greatest thing in history." The night before the President had been entertained at the officers' mess. "What did you think of old Joe Stalin, sir?" asked the ship's doctor. Truman thought a moment, then replied, "I thought he was an S.O.B." An awful silence followed, which the President broke with a grin. "But of course, I guess he thinks I'm one too." Table talk turned to speculations about the war and the peace to follow. The President assured the men that no new deals had been made at Potsdam. "If the Russians had been somewhat difficult at Potsdam," he said, enlarging on a related theme, "it did not matter so far as the war against Japan was concerned, because the United States now had developed an entirely new weapon of such force and nature that we did not need the Rusians—*or any other nation.*"[2]

As James V. Forrestal, the first Secretary of Defense (a title to match SAC's motto), said in a letter to a friend in 1947: "As long as we can outproduce the world, can control the sea and can strike inland with the atomic bomb, we can assume certain risks otherwise unacceptable in an effort to restore world trade, to restore the balance of power—military power—and to eliminate some of the conditions which breed war."[3] But to argue therefore that Americans never made political atomic threats like those later hurled by Khrushchev during the 1956 Suez crisis is to miss the point. As an example of American policy, Truman's language in his August 6, 1945, announcement assured the bomb a seat at subsequent Foreign Ministers' conferences; even political cartoonists understood this point and often drew the bomb at the head of the table. In fact, Truman's advisers had long been saying much the same thing as Forrestal. "The present advantage held by the English-speaking world through possession of atomic bombs," Admiral Leahy wrote in June 1946, "should be advantageous in negotiating with our former enemies [sic] treaties that are designed to preserve world peace."[4] However, there was no need to flaunt that monopoly in order to use it effectively. "We should increase production of fissionable material," argued one of Bernard Baruch's associates in a letter to Secretary of State Byrnes, "speed up the program for bases and B-36 planes, and in effect give notice that *we* are the future police force of the Security Council."[5]

The contention that the United States never used the bomb

politically misses the point in a second way as well: it assumes a much too narrow base for atomic policy. In part this is the result of sensational attempts to make Harry Truman the villain in the drama of "atomic diplomacy." More fundamentally, however, it stems from a misunderstanding of the famous "Baruch Plan" for international control of atomic energy, rejected by the Russians at the United Nations in 1946.

Misunderstanding of the Baruch Plan went so far so fast that in 1954 the Atomic Energy Commission charged the former scientific head of the Manhattan Project, J. Robert Oppenheimer, with indiscreet political behavior on several counts; in this regard they were indirectly criticizing his role in drafting the first version of the Baruch Plan. Frustration pervaded the atmosphere of that famous hearing: with all its supposed technical and industrial superiority, with unlimited resources at its command, the United States had not only lost its atomic monopoly but had failed to maintain a clear lead over the Soviets in the development of new weapons of terror. With that failure—sometimes charged off to espionage and betrayal—it became evident also that the Baruch Plan had failed.

At heart, the Baruch Plan was part of a broad effort to use America's atomic monopoly, through the United Nations, to get "collective security" on American terms. Baruch and his aides did not really expect the Russians to accept the plan right away. But they hoped, for a variety of reasons, that it would be useful in shaping discussions that promoted general goals, regardless of immediate practical results. Thus, anticipating a Russian refusal, they were concerned in the short run that the American people believe every effort had been made to secure an early agreement. The Baruch Plan assumed that America's technological lead would be maintained, and that eventually the Russians would have to meet America's terms. Like other language of this new era, confusion and misunderstanding were built into the plan. Oppenheimer himself suggested this as early as 1948 in a *Foreign Affairs* article, but few were inclined to probe further into its meaning. "The prevalent view," Oppenheimer wrote,

> saw in the problems of atomic energy not an opportunity to allow the leaders of the Soviet State to carry out a policy of international

> cooperation, of openness, candor and renunciation of violence to which they were already committed; rather, it saw an opportunity to cause a decisive change in the whole trend of Soviet policy, without which the prospects of an assured peace were indeed gloomy, and which might well be, if accomplished, the turning point in the pattern of international relations.

In 1954 Oppenheimer added:

> I think that any attempt at that time to establish control along these lines [the Baruch Plan] would, if accepted by the Soviets, have so altered their whole system and so altered their whole relations with the Western World that the threat which has been building up year after year since could not have existed. I think that no one at that time could with much confidence believe that they would accept these proposals. I think it was important to put them forward, and it was also important not to express too much doubt that they might be accepted. . . . It would have meant that the Russian Government gave up control over things going on involving their citizens on their territory. It would have permitted free intercourse between Russian nationals and people of the rest of the world. It would have meant that there could be no iron curtain.[6]

Characteristically obtuse, these statements nevertheless make it clear that the prevalent view held that the Baruch Plan was a one-time opportunity to achieve some lasting result while the United States could still use its possession of the weapon with impunity. Technological superiority, according to this view, made older diplomatic means outdated and assured a clear-cut victory for the "right." Repulsed by the triumph of expediency which had governed the first atomic bombings, many liberals—and most scientists—found themselves in a terrible bind: if the United States, a democratically governed people, could—despite the "textbook" checks and balances system—develop a weapon so completely outside the control of that people, and if the President could then order that weapon's use without taking any other branch of government into his confidence, what would happen when a powerful dictator like Stalin finally caught up technologically? Fear of Russian atomic blackmail soon brought together the Baruch "team" and those liberal groups originally critical of policy-making elites. When the Soviet Union turned down the Baruch Plan, these groups saw evidence that the Kremlin was planning world conquest—and this despite their previous contention that the Soviets would turn it down for legitimate reasons! In fact, as in Oppenheimer's case at the height of the Cold War, adherence to the Baruch Plan sometimes became a serious charge. On the other hand, and provided one used proper discretion, a diplomat could refer to it during later United Nations disarmament debates as "proof" that the United States had wanted atomic disarmament. Thus, by convenient hindsight, the Baruch Plan had always represented America's original "Atoms for Peace" offer, and the Russians could be blamed forever for the ensuing arms race.

To begin the story of atomic policy in 1945 is to start out *in media res*. The story properly begins early in World War II when the Soviet Union was still allied to Nazi Germany. It was at that time that serious work began on nuclear fission with the combination of American and British efforts in the Manhattan Project. Churchill and Roosevelt had no advantageous opportunity to tell Stalin of the project until August 1942 when Churchill arrived in Moscow to inform Russian leaders that the second front was not possible within the next year. In the aftermath of that announcement, the Anglo-Russian conversations were understandably bitter and filled with mutual suspicion. Stalin's mood seemed to change somewhat at the end of one of the sessions, and he proposed exchanging information on military inventions. Churchill quickly agreed, as one historian put it, "with only slight reservations."[7] But it takes a good deal of stretching to make that phrase cover the Manhattan Project.

Churchill might then have suggested to Roosevelt that the Russians be asked to join in the effort to produce an atomic bomb. Such an invitation, if made soon after the Moscow conversations, might have helped sweep away the growing accumulation of mutual suspicion. On the other hand, of course, it could have made the postwar situation even worse for the Western powers. The important point here is that atomic policy was always a gamble, both politically and militarily. When Stimson learned of Soviet-

British negotiations on weapons development, he cautioned Roosevelt that they might create a "very serious situation" in regard to American sharing of atomic information with the British. Actually, there was little reason for concern. Churchill had not even informed Clement Attlee about S-1, the atomic project, and he personally reassured American officials that he looked forward hopefully to the bomb to protect British independence against any "international blackmail that the Russians might eventually be able to employ."[8]

According to General Leslie Groves, the military chief of the Manhattan Project, security precautions during the war were directed primarily against communist and Russian espionage. Ironically, this emphasis prompted several atomic scientists to seek a change in Anglo-American policy while there was still time to head off an arms race. Basing their arguments on a realistic assumption that Russia would catch up much sooner than was supposed regardless of security precautions, they sought to reach President Roosevelt. One scientist, Niels Bohr, finally succeeded in obtaining an appointment with the President in July 1944. Bohr came away from the conversation with an impression that Roosevelt would inform Stalin of the weapon before it was used. But when he tried to see Roosevelt and Churchill at Hyde Park that September, he was completely unsuccessful; indeed, he later learned that instructions had been issued to have him watched closely by security agents.[9]

Two other scientists, Vannevar Bush and James Conant, sent Secretary of War Stimson memoranda on the problem at the end of September. Both emphasized that America's atomic monopoly would not last long. Any attempt, they said, to preserve and extend American national security by continuing military secrecy into the postwar period was a simplistic and potentially disastrous response to the most challenging problem man had yet confronted on this earth. It was not at all improbable that a research accident might put another country (the standard euphemism for Russia) ahead at some future date. Finally, attempts to preclude an arms race by extending the American monopoly to include all the world's known resources of uranium and thorium outside Russia were equally shortsighted: once a breakthrough was made to hydrogen weapons, such a monopoly would be useless, for supplies of heavy hydrogen were virtually unlimited.

Bush and Conant proposed to start in another direction: an exchange of atomic information through an international office, deriving its power from the expected new league of nations. The exchange should begin as soon as the first atomic bomb had been demonstrated. The technical staff of this office should then be granted unimpeded access to scientific laboratories, industrial plants, and military establishments throughout the world. During this period, however, the U.S. should not disclose its manufacturing and military details. Although impressed with their reasoning, Stimson still needed time, a very long time, to work it out in his own mind.[10]

He next spoke to Roosevelt about atomic energy on December 30, 1944, and again the following day. On the second day the President seemed especially concerned about relations with Russia, bringing up his allies' constant efforts to surround themselves with "friendly nations." Stimson agreed that it was a serious problem, remarking upon reports he had received from General John Deane in Moscow which warned that nothing toward this end could be gained by making concessions to the Russians. Stimson continues:

> And in this connection I told him of my thoughts as to the future of S-1 in connection with Russia; that I knew they were spying on our work but that they had not yet gotten any real knowledge of it and that, while I was troubled about the possible effect of keeping from them even now that work, I believed that it was essential not to take them into our confidence until we were sure to get a real quid pro quo from our frankness. I said I had no illusions as to the possibility of keeping permanently such a secret but that I did think it was not yet time to share it with Russia. He said he thought he agreed with me.[11]

Stimson's record of this conversation marks the beginning of a reassessment of atomic weapons and international relations which he did not complete until after the war. He was still convinced in December 1944 of the need for secrecy, but he was obviously troubled about the likely outcome of developing the bomb without informing the Russians. On February 15, 1945, he spoke again with Vannevar Bush about his pre-Yalta advice to the President, repeating once more that it would be best not to offer the Soviets information without first obtaining political advantages. And he disputed the idea that the United States would gain much from an exchange on purely scientific grounds. A month later he saw Roosevelt for the last time on atomic energy. He wrote of this meeting in his diary that he had gone over the two schools of thought—continued military secrecy versus an open exchange of information—without recommending either of them. Instead, he pressed Roosevelt to decide: "I told him that those things must be settled before the first projectile is used and that he must be ready with a statement to come out to the people on it just as soon as that is done. He agreed to do that."[12]

Stimson's desire to avoid responsibility for the decision was frustrated a few weeks later by Roosevelt's death. Forced back to the center of the decision-making process, the Secretary of War suggested to the new President that an interim committee be appointed to consider whether the bomb should be used—and how—and its secret revealed to other nations. Truman responded by appointing him chairman of the committee. At first Stimson reacted to this new responsibility with exactly the narrow gesture that Bush and Conant had warned against, asking the committee to consider how the bomb could be used to get "less barbarous" relations with the Soviets. Counter-pressures were forming, meanwhile, among the scientists who wanted to be heard on all the issues. And the War Department was engaged in two top-secret projects, Operation HARBORAGE and Operation ALSOS, aimed at keeping atomic secrets and scientists in France and Germany from falling into Russian hands. In yet another direction, the British-American Combined Policy Committee was moving to secure as many options as possible on Brazilian and Belgian Congolese uranium and thorium deposits.[13] Time was short. Stimson could no longer assume that the Russians were unaware of these specific operations or their general meaning. On May 12, 1945, the State Department asked him if he still thought Russia was needed to end the Pacific War. Stimson's mind turned at once to S-1.

Ever since Roosevelt's death, Stimson had been increasingly

alarmed about advice coming to Truman from various sources who advocated a stronger Central European policy. He was still undecided about which course to follow in atomic policy, but in general, he told the new President, it was unwise to "get into unnecessary quarrels by talking too much." "I told him this was a place where we really held all the cards. I call it a royal straight flush and we musn't be a fool about the way we play it."[14] While it might be necessary ultimately "to have it out with Russia on her relations to Manchuria and Port Arthur," Stimson did not want to go into new Big Three negotiations without this "master card" in hand.

On May 18, James F. Byrnes firmly took the initiative in the interim committee. Stimson had originally suggested to Truman that he appoint someone to be his special representative on that body; Byrnes was Truman's choice. The Secretary of State–designate began that day's discussion by remarking that he had now had time to read the Bush-Conant memorandum of September 30, 1944. Like Stimson, he had been impressed with its assertion that the atomic monopoly would not last more than three or four years. That was an important consideration, he admitted, in determining whether or not to tell the Russians about the weapon immediately after it was first tested. (At the time the committee thought the test would take place in July.) General Groves quickly spoke to dispute the Bush-Conant estimates: it would take the Russians more like twenty years to make an atomic bomb. Conant unsuccessfully tried to refute the General; and a pattern for atomic policy was already well on its way to being established. Whenever Byrnes had a choice between the scientists and General Groves—between technical and military-political opinion—he invariably chose the latter. On another occasion Leo Szilard urged Byrnes not to take the longer estimates for granted, and was met with the dogmatic reply: "General Groves tells me there is no uranium in Russia." The scientist then tried to explain the differences between high-grade ore, relatively scarce in Europe, and more plentiful low-grade ore, undoubtedly available somewhere inside the Soviet Union's borders.[15] His attempt went unheeded.

Where Stimson only hoped there might be some way to get "less barbarous" relations with Stalin, Byrnes seemed convinced of it. In fact, he went further in private conversations with the President, stating that the bomb "might well put us in a position to dictate our own terms at the end of the war."[16] At the May 31 meeting of the committee, the vexatious matter of whether or not the Russians should be told about S-1 intruded into its deliberations one final time. Byrnes put forth his position so authoritatively that the question was settled—and for months to come. General Marshall had just suggested inviting one or two Soviet scientists to view the test at Alamogordo, New Mexico. Byrnes responded that even if the Russians were informed only generally of American progress on such a weapon, they would ask to become full partners at once. The United States' best policy was to push production and research so as to make certain of staying out ahead.

Following this lead, the committee easily resolved the problem of whether to inform the Russians: no revelation of any kind should be made until the "first bomb had been successfully laid on Japan." Stimson also reported to Truman that the committee had looked briefly at the problem of postwar control. If the Soviets proved unwilling to accept a plan for international control, like that suggested in the Bush-Conant memorandum, the Secretary of War said, "we were far enough ahead of the game to be able to accumulate enough material to serve as insurance against being caught helpless." Putting aside the committee's specific recommendations, Stimson suggested several political questions which should be settled prior to "our taking them into partnership." "[Truman] said he had been thinking of that," Stimson noted in his diary, "and mentioned the same things that I was thinking of, namely the settlement of the Polish, Rumanian, Yugoslavian, and Manchurian problems."[17]

"We thought," Oppenheimer later said in a further explanation of the committee's secret deliberations, "the two overriding considerations were the saving of lives in the war and the effect of our actions on the stability, on our strength [sic] and the stability of the postwar world. We did say we did not think exploding one of these things as a firecracker over a desert was likely to be very impressive."[18] Oppenheimer's precise meaning cannot be determined from this statement alone, but his belief that there were two questions at issue is clear. From conversations with other scientists, Leo Szilard, for example, it also becomes clear that Oppenheimer, like Byrnes, opposed a demonstration of the weapon for *anyone* before it had been used militarily. Oppenheimer told Szilard that the best policy would be to advise the Russians of our intention to use the bomb on Japanese cities, then to go ahead and do so. Szilard demurred. "Well," Oppenheimer insisted, "don't you think if we tell the Russians what we intend to do and then use the bomb in Japan, the Russians will understand it?" Szilard replied grimly, "They'll understand it only too well."[19]

Unaware that the committee had reached a decision on June 1, several atomic scientists signed Szilard's petition opposing the bomb's use against Japanese targets. Looking ahead to the postwar world, the petition stated: "It may be very difficult to persuade the world that a nation which was capable of secretly preparing and suddenly releasing a new weapon, as indiscriminate as the rocket bomb and a thousand times more destructive, is to be trusted in its proclaimed desire of having such weapons abolished by international agreement."[20]

At Potsdam, Stimson still seemed to be juggling politics with the atomic bomb, though he may well have been trying simply to divert attention from Eastern European questions. Probably he was doing both; in any event, he advised Truman to exclude Kyoto from the list of targets for the bomb. An attack of this kind against Kyoto, with its religious and cultural treasures, Stimson said, would be a "wanton act." It might very well create such bitterness in Japan that proposed reconstruction policies would fail: "It might thus, I pointed out, be the means of preventing what our policy demanded, namely a sympathetic Japan to the United States in case there should be any aggression by Russia in Manchuria."[21]

But the actual bombing of Hiroshima and Nagasaki jolted Stimson out of the geopolitical era. Retreating into seclusion with his closest adviser, John J. McCloy, he attempted to retrace his steps to the time he had informed Roosevelt of the two alternatives for dealing with this vast new power. Though he had once cautioned FDR to decide *before* the weapon had even been demonstrated, since that time he himself had occupied a position much closer to Byrnes's attitude. But the bombings of the two Japanese cities had changed his mind once again, and about many things. For example, since 1942 Stimson had opposed sharing the bomb's secret with a totalitarian police state such as Soviet Russia; now he felt this was a much less important consideration. Consequently, the memorandum Stimson and McCloy worked out on international control of atomic energy began with a new premise: a blunt statement that in some quarters the atomic bomb was already being viewed as the offsetting force to Russian influence in Europe. We could be certain, the paper continued, that the Soviets were aware of this feeling, and that their leaders would be strongly tempted to put aside everything in an attempt to develop their own super-weapons in the shortest possible time. The bomb had therefore come to dominate international relations, and it would be difficult, if not impossible, to make progress on other issues until the questions that it raised had been settled.

To head off this nascent arms race, Stimson proposed a direct approach to the Kremlin. If the Russians accepted, the first step should be that

> we would stop work on the further improvement in, or manufacture of, the bomb as a military weapon, provided the Russians and British would agree to do likewise. It might also provide that we would be willing to impound what bombs we now have in the United States provided the Russians and the British would agree with us that in no event will they or we use a bomb as an instrument of war unless all three Governments agree to that use. We might also consider including in the arrangement a covenant with the U.K. and the Soviets providing for the exchange of benefits of future developments whereby atomic energy may be applied on a mutually satisfactory basis for commercial or humanitarian purposes.

As to the possibility of initiating discussions in the new United Nations, Stimson said:

> Action of any international group of nations, including many small nations who have not demonstrated their potential power or responsibility in this war, would not, in my opinion, be taken seriously by the Soviets. The loose debates which would surround such a proposal, if put before a conference of nations, would provoke but scant favor from the Soviets.[22]

When Stimson read this memorandum to Truman on September 11, 1945, he paused several times for comments or questions. Since the President only nodded his agreement, Stimson thought he had convinced him. But the underlying assumptions of the memorandum were at variance with those generally shared by Truman's other advisers. In fact, Stimson was one of a small minority which still supposed that the Big Three, acting together, would continue to be the main guardians of the peace, and that the United Nations would assume that role for itself alone only after a long period of big-power trusteeship. In January, for example, Stimson had proposed that FDR offer a security treaty over Germany to the Soviets *before* the United Nations was formally organized; in April he had cautioned Truman about threatening to withhold credits over the Polish issue; and now he was arguing a similar position in regard to the atomic bomb. But even those liberal skeptics who opposed Truman's "get-tough" policy with the Soviets often confused Byrnes's public diplomacy and "collective security" policies with the "internationalization" of the New Deal.

In contrast to Stimson, Truman's other advisers were opposed to ending bomb production and impounding existing weapons as a first step: since the United States was the only nation producing bombs, they argued, it would be a unilateral step based on "hope." How could the United States be assured that any covenant for doing away with atomic bombs would be faithfully adhered to by all sides? This argument was the main support for those who maintained, for whatever reasons, that the United States must remain sole trustee of the bomb until a foolproof inspection and control system could be worked out and put into force.

Stimson's memorandum was debated in the Cabinet on September 21, 1945. The next day a *New York Times* story claimed that the proposal had split the Cabinet, and that during the secret discussions Henry Wallace—purely as an act of good faith—had suggested sharing atomic secrets with the Soviet Union. Such reports obviously hurt Stimson's case, for Wallace was already becoming known as a "softie"—and a mystic. Moreover, cables from the London Foreign Ministers' Conference, where the United States and the Soviet Union had clashed over the satellite peace treaties, were also appearing in the press. Molotov's puzzling attitude toward France and China angered those who believed in "collective security" and public diplomacy. The Cabinet press leak undoubtedly sprang from the office of an official who had opposed the Stimson plan—Forrestal perhaps, Clinton Anderson, or Fred Vinson. In any event, the plan became associated with the left-liberal wing of the Democratic party.

Truman, however, had uncharacteristically left the issue unresolved, requesting papers from each participant so that he might study the alternatives further. Under Secretary of State Dean Acheson, who was sitting in for the absent Byrnes, and Stimson's successor, Robert Patterson, complied almost at once. Patterson's short memo simply agreed with Stimson's arguments, adding only that the scientists who had originally advised the War Department on the construction of the bombs had now warned that their use in a future war "may well mean the end of civilization." Acheson's paper stressed the need to approach the Soviets on the same basis as our partnership with Great Britain as soon as possible. "For us to declare ourselves trustee of the development for the benefit of the world will mean nothing more to the Russian mind than an outright policy of exclusion."

This statement was directed at Navy Secretary Forrestal, who had argued for such a position in the Cabinet discussion. Though Acheson wanted more than Russian promises of good faith to control production of atomic energy, like Stimson he put the creation of a United Nations authority last. As he saw it, a plan should be "worked out to extend these principles to other countries in due course, probably through the mechanism of the United Nations."[23] This was, of course, a very different view from that of his superior, Secretary Byrnes.

The President also received a third "memo" on atomic energy about this time—a long letter from British Prime Minister Clement Attlee. "Am I to plan for a peaceful or a warlike world?" asked the head of the Labour party. "If the latter, I ought to direct all our people to live like troglodytes underground as being the only hope of survival, and that by no means certain."[24] Attlee wanted an early decision so that some plan could be initiated for the control of this awful new weapon.

In response to these papers, Truman issued an ambiguous public statement on October 3. He declared that the atomic bomb could not wait for the United Nations to become fully established, and he proposed immediate discussions with Great Britain and Canada, to be followed by talks with "other nations." Five days after this statement, the President held an informal press conference at a fishing resort near Tiptonville, Tennessee, at which he in effect flatly rejected the Stimson proposal. A reporter began the conference by asking if it was the President's position that the atomic secret would not be shared unless and until we had positive assurance that the world had progressed to a point where individual nations put the common welfare above national gain. No, Truman replied, it would not be correct to say that, because scientific knowledge needed for producing the bomb was already world-wide. "It is only the know-how of putting that knowledge practically to work that is our secret; just the same as know-how in the construction of the B-29, *and the plane soon to follow the B-29,* the greatest long-distance bomber in the world, and the mass production of automobiles. So far as the scientific knowledge is concerned, all the scientists know the answer, but how to put it to work—that is our secret."

Understandably confused by this answer, the reporter asked specifically if the United States was willing to let other nations in on the know-how.

"Well, I don't think it would do any good to let them in on the know-how, because I don't think they could do it anyway. . . . If they catch up with us on that, they will have to do it on their own hook, just as we did."

Then, pursued the reporter, we will not share that knowledge with our allies? After yet another clarification of this already direct question, Truman finally replied: "Not the know-how of putting it together, let's put it that way."

Truman's account of this remarkable press interview in his *Memoirs* ends with that sentence. In the official report published several years later, the episode ends much more dramatically. Press Secretary Charles Ross interrupted to ask if the President was speaking on or off the record. This precautionary device was occasionally used in the pre-television age to soften the impact of presidential statements and to warn the President he might be committing himself to a policy. Turning to Ross, Truman tossed aside all admonitions and even emphasized his point. In fact he made the policy then and there: "I am talking *on* the record, Charlie." Though Ross issued the usual stricture against direct quotation, Truman's meaning came through loud and clear.[25]

The President's August 6 announcement and the transcript of this press conference suggest an additional problem about international atomic policy. It has been argued that the Soviet Union was not much alarmed about the American bombings of Hiroshima and Nagasaki, and only later accused the United States of "atomic diplomacy" in their use of the weapons. Presuming that the Russians were not at first overly impressed with the bomb, the problem of how they viewed America's attitude toward its new weapon remains unresolved. Truman's boast of a "rain of ruin from the air," and his statement about the B-29 and its successor soon to come, whatever the Russians thought about the bomb's actual usefulness, must have caused them to base their policy in part upon what they thought America believed about its new weapon.

Though Secretary of War Patterson pointed out in his memorandum that Stimson had not meant to propose immediate revelation of secret ordnance procedures, whatever Stimson had intended was less important than the way he wished to approach the Russians. The tone of the President's statements seemed to foreclose the possibility that any proposal would ever be discussed reasonably with the Russians. Truman had ignored—or perhaps did not consider significant—a key point Acheson had made in his memorandum relating to American public opinion. The Under Secretary had insisted that the nation's opinion should be "given an opportunity to mature at the same time that action is taken to prevent Russian fear and suspicion from increasing and crystallizing." Truman's informal declarations amounted to a quick-step march in the opposite direction. If Truman's public statements were intended to calm American fears about Soviet development of a counterweapon, on the other hand, this interpretation would further characterize his policy as opposed to international control.

On October 10, 1945, Secretary Byrnes, just back from London, told his colleagues in the War and Navy departments that he had begged Stimson not even to recommend discussion of international consultation. He was, he said, in agreement with General Groves that not enough was yet known either about atomic energy or about the future world situation to allow a profitable discussion with the Russians on atomic energy. Even the vague promises of British-Canadian-American talks would no doubt give him trouble at future international conferences, Byrnes thought. Molotov would cite these promises and demand to take part in discussions on controlling the bomb.[26] At a later meeting with Patterson and Forrestal, Byrnes added that he thought too much attention had already been paid to the views of scientists when it came to estimating how long it would take Russia to catch up. Their information about Soviet industrial capabilities was no better than his. When a plan was developed it would have to include free access to industrial plants in all countries. "He said," according to the State Department minutes of this meeting, "that we can't get into Rumania and Bulgaria much less Russia and that it is childish to think that the Russians would let us see what they are doing." The principal reason Russia wanted one of the former Italian colonies, Byrnes concluded dramatically, was to secure a base close to the sources of uranium in the Belgian Congo![27]

Byrnes's determination to use atomic policy to speed up collective security led him to such unsupported statements, and to equally surprising tactical changes. On the other hand, Stimson's proposal was predicated upon the antithetical assumption that debating satellite treaties and other issues with the atomic bomb "rather ostentatiously on our hip" could only slow down the work of making peace, if in fact it did not touch off a dangerous arms race. Clement Attlee wrote Truman on October 16, 1945, that the atomic bomb had completely overshadowed the London Foreign Ministers' Conference. Dissident members of his own party were demanding to know when Great Britain and the United States were going to initiate the international discussions Truman had talked about so vaguely, and when some approach would be made to the Soviets. Both Attlee and Canadian Prime Minister Mackenzie King felt that a meeting was now an urgent necessity. Attlee's not-so-gentle reminders did not change American policy

—at least not in the direction the British wanted to go. The United States, despite what the British and Canadians had done to develop atomic energy during the war in cooperation with the Manhattan Project, now refused to share its "know-how" even with those two nations; in the end the British had to build an atomic bomb solely on their own.

Truman's famous Navy Day speech of October 27, 1945, was much like Forrestal's original answer to the Stimson proposal. The United States could act as trustee of this new weapon for the world, the President said, because of its well-known love of peace. All thoughtful people knew that America would never violate such a trust and that it would be faithfully executed always. One dissenter from this "prevalent view" was future Secretary of State John Foster Dulles. During this period of difficult negotiation, he said on November 15, 1945, the United States must not give the impression that it wanted to preserve its atomic monopoly "long enough to increase our bargaining power." Other nations would not follow the country's lead in such a policy, and the Russian Foreign Minister had been "quite right" to insist that atomic energy not be thus exploited in international politics.[28]

When such staunchly conservative voices as Dulles' suggested it was time for a more realistic approach to break the deadlock at London, it was clear that they were right. Truman had finally met with the British and Canadians on November 6, 1945, and issued a tripartite statement setting forth a several-stage plan for exchange of atomic information. From Moscow the British Ambassador, Sir Archibald Clark Kerr, advised Foreign Minister Bevin, who relayed the cable to Washington for the State Department's information, that the Russians had been shocked into a deep sense of insecurity by the dropping of the atomic bomb. Despite Molotov's bold assertion that atomic threats would not work, the Russian victory over Nazi Germany and the seemingly matchless power of three hundred divisions had suddenly been reduced to nothing by the bomb. Moreover, the Kremlin was disappointed and humiliated that the Western powers had so far refused to take the Soviets into their confidence. "If my interpretation of the state of mind of the Russians is anything like right," Kerr warned, "we may I think expect them to approach the proposal to discuss Atomic Energy in the first instance in the open forum of the General Assembly with all the prickliness of which they are capable."[29]

Stimson, Dulles, and now the British Ambassador in Moscow—all had issued approximately the same warning. Despite their concern, however, Byrnes went ahead at Moscow with just the proposal they had warned against. In 1947 he said that Molotov's seeming lack of interest in the proposal—the Russian Foreign Minister wanted it placed last on the agenda—had been his way of telling the Americans that the Soviet Union considered the whole subject of little importance. But in 1958 Byrnes recalled that at dinner on Christmas Eve of 1945, Molotov had proposed a toast to James Conant, who had accompanied Byrnes to the conference, with the jocular statement that he had been assured that the scientist did not have an atomic bomb hidden in his pocket. Later Stalin rose and remarked that he thought his Foreign Minister was wrong in "speaking so lightly about the American scientist." Stalin himself was no scientist, he said, and he had no knowledge of physics; but he thought Conant and his associates "deserved the plaudits of all peoples."[30]

Molotov adopted a tactical position at Moscow not much different from Stimson's, and based upon exactly the same assumption of the need for Big Three diplomacy. Stimson had said the bomb would soon dominate all international relations; Molotov seemed to deny this, but the proposal Byrnes had brought with him was precisely the one which Stimson had said would not be well regarded by the Russians. Molotov's only effective answer was to insist that if America wanted these negotiations in an open forum, then there must be a Big Three political settlement of other issues simultaneously, and not lengthy United Nations peacemaking. Molotov was trying to use American concern about Russian development of atomic weapons—the reverse of what is usually called atomic diplomacy—to stimulate concessions from Byrnes on Eastern Europe. Minimal compromises by Byrnes brought minimal Russian agreement to begin discussions of international control of atomic energy through a special United Nations Atomic Energy Commission.

After the Moscow Conference Truman appointed a special committee, led by Dean Acheson and David Lilienthal, to prepare American proposals. They worked in an atmosphere which was from the beginning clouded by renewed Soviet-American disputes at the first meeting of the United Nations General Assembly at London, prompting some committee members to urge the possibility of altering Russian society through the atomic proposals. While the chairman quickly put this suggestion down, there was a consensus that so long as the world situation remained as it was, any plan must allow the United States to continue producing atomic bombs in the interim period before verifiable controls came into effect.[31] While the committee deliberated on the details of the American proposal, Washington cut off sales to the Soviet Union of all products potentially useful for the construction of atomic plants, thus bringing pressure to bear in a very obvious fashion.[32]

The Acheson-Lilienthal plan which finally emerged from these discussions was premised on the realistic assumption that there were no known adequate countermeasures against atomic warfare; therefore, the momentary advantage the United States held was only that and no more. In fact, the situation could be reversed very quickly in the future. A second premise was that any known form of international inspection not only would be inadequate, but would inevitably raise additional problems and suspicions. Reliance upon international inspection and control therefore had to be minimized.

This was not such a great obstruction in the way of real international agreement as it appeared, argued the committee report, because while uranium and thorium deposits were relatively abundant in different areas of the world, they occurred in high concentration only where special geological conditions obtained. "This would seem to mean that the areas which need to be surveyed, to which access must be had, and which ultimately have to be brought under control, are relatively limited."[33] The plan also featured the staged process of internationalization common to most American thoughts in past months. Only at the end of the several steps would the monopoly be surrendered. "Should the worst happen and, during the transition period, the entire effort collapse, the United States will at all times be in a favorable position with regard to atomic weapons."

Acheson and Lilienthal were furious when they learned that Byrnes had given their plan to Bernard M. Baruch for presentation to the U.N. commission. They knew that Baruch and his cronies could secretly mutilate it into a patched-up proposal, so they determined to publish it before that happened. Though Lilienthal was later reconciled with Baruch, he never changed his mind about the latter's insistence upon introducing "condign punishment" into the plan, and upon making elimination of the veto power in the proposed U.N. atomic development authority the key issue. Lilienthal thought these conditions were not only unnecessary but provocative as well. America was sufficiently protected, he thought, by the main element in the Acheson-Lilienthal report, the principle of step-by-step internationalization. In the March 31, 1946, issue of the *Nation,* liberal columnist I. F. Stone argued that America was already expecting too much from even that principle. The step-by-step process would take several years; meanwhile, "other nations would be asked to hand over control of uranium deposits and presumably to end their own atomic-bomb work at the beginning of the process in return for a promise that at its end we would make the bomb know-how available. But what if at that time we changed our mind?"

As soon as Byrnes asked him to undertake the U.N. mission, Baruch assembled his own private "team" to assist him. It included banker John M. Hancock, mining engineer Fred Searls, historian Denna Frank Fleming, publicist Herbert Bayard Swope, and industrial consultant Ferdinand Eberstadt. Then Acheson and Lilienthal released their report for publication, and it was Baruch's turn to be infuriated. He was fuming when he went to see the Under Secretary of State: Was the report intended to be the final American proposal? he asked. Acheson replied affirmatively. Then Baruch really exploded: "I told him that Western Union doesn't take messenger boys at 76—he would have to get some other messenger boy." Baruch went at once to Truman and asked who was going to write the policy. The President answered, "Why, hell, you are."[34]

The first thing Baruch wanted written into the policy was the elimination of the big-power veto from the projected international atomic energy authority. The key to understanding the "Baruch Plan" can therefore be found in his original letter of acceptance to Secretary Byrnes of March 13, 1946. "Unless we get a better working UNO," he wrote, "which is the only hope of the world, we will be unable to discuss the elimination of the atomic bomb from armaments because we will be the only ones who will have them."[35] Baruch thought that eliminating the veto in the U.N. Atomic Energy Commission would unlock one of the doors to collective security. Less well known, however, is that the American plan contained its own special veto power. No time limit was put on each of the so-called stages of the American plan, and all members of the international authority had to agree that a stage had been successfully completed. This gave the United States an extra measure of security *and* a veto over the workings of the plan.

Baruch objected to two other features of the Acheson-Lilienthal draft: it had no provision for punishment of violations by member nations; and its provision for international ownership of raw materials would, he insisted, be opposed by capitalist nations. He preferred to rely upon extensive and thorough international inspections, even though the authors of the earlier plan had carefully detailed the reasons why this was less feasible as a safeguard and more provocative to the Soviet Union. If Baruch and his team thought the Russians were bound to reject the plan anyway (Oppenheimer complained to Lilienthal that they "talk about preparing the American people for a refusal by Russia"), then it was logical to oppose the introduction of international ownership as a precedent not only for disarmament plans but for other United Nations operations in general. However that may be, the contracts which General Groves had already negotiated for American atomic energy facilities were decidedly advantageous to both United States capitalists and foreign entrepreneurs. A Belgian mineowner, sent to Baruch by Groves, told the new head of the American delegation that his mine put out 300,000 tons of ore a year and was under contract to the United States for ten years. "He feared the international authority [as proposed in the Acheson-Lilienthal plan] would upset wages, dissatisfy people, and have tremendous difficulties of operation on account of the different nationals involved."[36] High officials of Union Carbide told the Baruch group that they were "violently opposed to the Acheson Report in its emphasis on the ownership of raw materials in the ground."[37]

At a meeting between Acheson and Lilienthal and Baruch's private team, Hancock asserted that international ownership of these resources "would be too great an interference with private enterprise." Baruch told Byrnes privately that taking control of mining operations would seriously limit private enterprise in several countries:

> I refer to the need of purchasing the entire Rand mines and taking over control of a large part of the international mining activities, thus destroying or seriously limiting private enterprise in the capitalistic countries. I believe that America, Canada, Britain, Belgium (probably), the Belgian Congo, the Union of South Africa would certainly object to the Acheson plan. The plan would seem to all men in the capitalistic economy as the first start to an international socialized state. Even if the Acheson plan of ownership were to gain the approval of Russia, *in preference to my plan of inspection,* I think the capitalistic nations would check off that aspect of the plan as being thoroughly distasteful.[38]

Lilienthal felt that the Baruch people had in mind something else than international control of atomic energy as their first priority. At a May 17, 1946, meeting of the combined groups, Hancock proposed that at the first meeting of the U.N. commission Baruch should sponsor a resolution that, prior to any agreement on a plan, the U.N. would organize a world survey of raw materials and send fifty two-man teams all over the world. This way it would be possible to find out what was going on in Russia. "And if the Russians refused to accept this proposal, then we would know that they would not go along on any international scheme, and . . . he didn't finish the statement, but his eyes indicated what he thought should then be recommended, and it was anything but pleasant."[39]

On June 7, 1946, Baruch saw Byrnes and Truman about the other matters of eliminating the veto and inserting a provision for the condign punishment of violations. He went over both questions carefully with the President, pointing out specifically that the only punishment that would mean anything would have to be a declaration of war. In that case the United States would come up against the big-power veto. Consequently, it was obvious that there could be no veto allowed over the punishment, and therefore over the rules and regulations of the development authority. The President should understand that this would also mean an "inroad on the general theory of the veto power."

Some people, Baruch continued, thought it was bad to put that in right at the start because it might end the negotiations. But of what use was a treaty if there was no way to enforce it? Truman replied at once, "I quite agree with you." Then the President said he thought the original veto power had been a mistake. "He said that if Harry Stimson had been backed up in Manchuria there would have been no war."[40]

The first Russian response to the Baruch proposals was made by Andrei Gromyko, who disputed the step-by-step process with the argument that the political situation in the summer of 1946 precluded normal scientific cooperation between the world's major powers. "At the very basis of the present situation, which is characterized by the absence of any limitation in regard to the production and employment of atomic weapons, there are reasons which can only increase the suspicion of some countries in regard to others and give rise to political instability." Gromyko then proposed an immediate end to production of atomic weapons. His proposal was similar to Stimson's 1945 memorandum in that the international development agency would come into being only after completion of a covenant among the big powers calling for the elimination of atomic bombs. He offered no details as to how this covenant would be enforced. When pressed on this point, he answered simply that the Soviet Union relied upon the normal operations of the Security Council. With the veto power intact, that meant big-power oligarchy over the world—a situation most favorable to the Russians. Gromyko did acknowledge that such a treaty would eventually require an elaborate system of controls and sanctions. And by the end of the year the Soviets were ready to make some concessions toward implementation of these controls. On October 28 Premier Stalin declared in a rare press interview that "strong international control of atomic energy" was necessary. This was followed by Gromyko's statement in the U.N. commission that the Russians would allow the international agency to carry on necessary functions of inspection and investigation by majority decision. But he would not yield the veto right on questions of punishment or sanctions.

As Baruch had originally informed Truman, it all came back in the end to the problem of the big-power veto, for, as the Russian proposal developed, it was not incompatible with the original Acheson-Lilienthal plan. Of course, Gromyko might have raised other difficulties later if he thought an agreement were really possible. But his proposal caused some wavering in the American delegation. As early as June 20, the delegation held a meeting in which Oppenheimer and Admiral Richmond K. Turner opposed trying to abolish the veto on sanctions. Others pointed out that probably nothing less than full world government could ever provide adequate control measures.[41] Moreover, what was at issue here was whether the Baruch plan was a proposal for control of atomic energy or not. It can be conceded that no plan had much chance of success until something near a "balance of terror" had been reached.

Baruch reported to Truman about two weeks later that the Russians had asked the United States to agree not to use atomic weapons, to cease all production, and to destroy existing stockpiles—in advance of adequate measures of control. The President resolved any divisions in the American delegation with his brief reply that Baruch should stand pat. "I am of the opinion that we should not under any circumstances throw away our gun until we are sure the rest of the world can't arm against us."

"I think we understand each other on this subject," Truman ended.[42]

Even if the United States had gone all the way to accept the Gromyko proposal, what would it have lost in *immediate* atomic security? Gromyko's proposal called for a ban on atomic weapons —like other international conventions of the past—and then an effort to negotiate a proper inspection and control procedure. The United States had built its lead during the war, in secret. The most pessimistic estimate was that the lead was good for three to five years. Without inspection, the U.S. had no way of finding out what the Soviets were doing, but then, neither did the Russians presumably—and America was ahead. Though it might be argued that the United States was far more open to espionage, surely the Gromyko proposal was a gamble for the Soviets as well.

On the other hand, if the Russians failed to follow through within a reasonable time on Stalin's public statement that controls and sanctions would be necessary, the United States could have resumed its production. Though Baruch's technical experts did not give the U.S. a twenty-year lead, as Groves insisted, they did believe a three- to five-year margin was a safe bet.

A more serious argument against the Gromyko plan was that it would have left the Soviets with their armed might in conventional weapons massed against a rapidly disintegrating American land and sea force. Quite clearly, then, if the United States had been serious about atomic disarmament, it would have had to maintain much stronger conventional forces. Domestic pressures—not all of them so obvious as might be thought—prevented that alternative. In early 1947 the Soviets offered an across-the-board reduction of conventional forces by one-third. Unilateral American demobilization probably made it impossible to accept this overture—even to test its sincerity—but it might also be remarked that the Soviets nevertheless unilaterally demobilized. They reduced their army from 11.5 million to less than 3 million. Adam B. Ulam views this development another way. "The American monopoly of the atomic bomb," he writes,

> played a perversely ironic role, frustrating American intentions and undercutting the United Nations' potential role on the disarmament question. Had the dread weapon not existed, it is possible that America's demobilization in the wake of the war would not have been so rapid or thorough. . . . There would have been, then, a considerable incentive for the Russians to engage in serious negotiations about disarmament. . . .

Again, the abolition of the veto on *any* issue deemed vital to the Soviet Union would, in their view, put their country at the mercy of an agency in which she was bound to be in a minority. To give the Soviets their due, one may note that in 1946, three years before the first Russian atomic tests, it would have been in their interests to temporize, to feign agreement on the principle of atomic disarmament, and to delay the final convention in the usual diplomatic way for as long as possible. But though there are traces of such a technique being used in subsequent proposals, the Soviets refused to budge on the principal issue, that of abandoning the veto on punitive decisions by the International Authority.[43]

With the Gromyko proposal, administration leaders began to be concerned that the Soviet bid for atomic disarmament in the United Nations would create "irresistible public pressure to adopt such a plan forthwith, regardless of world conditions which for some time will require existence of force to accomplish stability." These were Forrestal's words, but the thought was shared by Truman's advisers.[44] Upon his return from the Bikini tests, the commander of the *USS Burleson* stated tersely in the Washington Navy Yard, "These tests are one form of being prepared for war."[45] American military policy, then, presented a puzzling Janus-like appearance to the rest of the world. On the one side there was rapid demobilization of conventional forces; on the other, vivid demonstrations of America's awesome new weapons. "You'd never convince a Russian factory worker," Senator Scott Lucas asserted in a radio interview, "that the Bikini experiment was made in the interest of world peace. He undoubtedly considers it a saber-rattling demonstration."[46]

Russian policy in turning down Baruch's proposal was undoubtedly based on a political estimate of American intentions, backed by scientific estimates that the United States would not have sufficient atomic strength to compensate for its other weaknesses after the war. American estimates were calculated not only on the risks of a Russian turn-down but on political goals which could be gained by insistence on bringing the Baruch Plan to a vote in the United Nations, rather than settling for a stalemate. In fact, Baruch moved for a showdown vote at the same time Byrnes was driving for a similar finale at the Paris Peace Conference. "Baruch's report . . . is far more important to the peace of the world than anything that happens here," Senator Vandenberg asserted in his diary. "It is *the* 'showdown' with Moscow. Russia's first response presents us with the *reality* (if she persists) that this will be two worlds instead of *one*."[47] There were two reasons for pushing for an immediate vote on the Baruch Plan. The first was to complete the "showdown" with Moscow, as Vandenberg put it, in Paris and in New York; the second was to retake from the Gromyko proposal the initiative for an immediate covenant outlawing the atomic bomb and ending its production. The Russian proposal, Walter Lippmann said to Forrestal, was "one of the most astute and formidable things that we have had to deal with yet." The Soviets were aiming at a preponderance of power in the general settlement of the issues left by the war. "And that's why we cannot dare get into that trap." Forrestal fully agreed, adding that the only balance America had for abundant manpower was abundant technology.[48] It was Truman's Tiptonville statement rephrased.

In mid-September Baruch asked Truman to support his decision to press for an immediate vote in the commission before its membership changed on January 1, 1947. He wrote again in late October, this time more insistently: "Time is running out against us. Now we have 10 votes to 2. Three fellows we are sure of are going to leave us. We will lose 3 sure votes."[49] When the vote was taken, the Baruch plan carried ten to nothing, with Russia and Poland abstaining. Secretary Byrnes was delighted with the outcome. "It was a great victory for Baruch and his associates."[50]

Baruch's associate, banker John M. Hancock, explained American tactics to the students at the National War College on December 5, 1946. There were still a few people, Hancock began, who had the impression that the Baruch plan was a giveaway of America's atomic monopoly. The abolition of the veto in the field of atomic energy had broad implications. Five nations had the veto privilege; if it were not eliminated in that area, then each of these big powers could try to gather satellites around it with the assurance, "Boys, you play with me and you can go as far as you like on atomic energy, and I'll see that you are not punished because I will use my veto to save you from punishment." If the veto in the Security Council increased the likelihood of such satellite empires, by removing the veto in the U.N. Atomic Energy Commission the United States could decrease that likelihood by destroying a good part of the satellites' *raison d'être*. The Russians said that the Baruch plan would split the U.N., Hancock concluded, but the American position was that it would build up the world organization.[51]

"America can get what she wants if she insists on it," Baruch assured a dubious Lilienthal after the vote was taken. "After all, we've got it and they haven't and won't have for a long time to come." Even when the Russians conceded that the veto should be eliminated in daily operations of the proposed international authority, Baruch maintained his all-or-nothing philosophy. If they were willing to do away with it in that instance, Baruch wrote James Conant, why shouldn't the world be willing to take the only step that would make for a sure peace, "by agreeing that no nation who threatens to break the peace can escape its violation of an agreement or treaty by the use of a veto, or the veto of a friendly nation, once a treaty has been agreed upon?"[52] The only reason Baruch could adduce for the Russian refusal to take that step was that they were seeking "the whole control of the world." Their proposal for a convention to outlaw the bomb was only part of that plan, for by destroying American power the Soviets could really get moving with economic and ideological penetration.

Baruch resigned in early 1947, still fully convinced that the Russians would eventually come around. Both sides knew that what had been at stake was the general organization of the peace. The Russians quite obviously preferred an atomic arms race to giving up their position in that debate: on this latter point there is nearly unanimous agreement, even though the Baruch Plan is seldom put into its proper context as part of the American postwar effort. Having decided to deal with atomic energy as part of the "peacemaking" effort of the United Nations, Truman and Baruch also insisted that the American monopoly of atomic weapons would insure that peace. But there was nothing in the Baruch Plan politically or militarily to induce the Russians to negotiate. "How can we," asked Harold Ickes in September 1946, "in good conscience, complain that Russia, for instance, is maintaining a tremendous land army while we flaunt our stockpile of atomic bombs, explode them with intimidating effect and arrogantly display our naval strength in the face of the whole world?"

BERNARD M. BARUCH

Shortly before President Truman went before Congress to ask for military aid to Greece and Turkey in March 1947, J. Robert Oppenheimer spoke with Dean Acheson in the State Department. The Under Secretary showed him a copy of the "Truman Doctrine" speech and explained how the situation had changed. Oppenheimer could see that Acheson, too, had changed. "He wanted me to be quite clear that we were entering an adversary relationship with the Soviet, and whatever we did in the atomic talks we should bear that in mind."[53]

EIGHT ☆☆

Dean Acheson and the "Holy Pretense"

"If people are unreasonable," wrote an anonymous British Puritan in the seventeenth century, "then must the Prince bow for a time and bring them to his purpose by some craft or by some holy pretense."[1] Like those seventeenth-century Puritans who suddenly found themselves in power at the end of the English civil war—when all society around them seemed imperiled—Dean Acheson's convictions about revolution and social order led him to "bow for a time," and to use reasons of state, policy, or the "holy pretense" to secure men to his high purpose. The real issue, wrote Louis Halle, one of Acheson's associates in the State Department at the time of the Truman Doctrine, was the balance of power: "As in 1917, as in 1941, it was still not possible to tell the American people what the real issue was."[2] Halle's effort to put the Cold War into a "realistic" mold might do justice to Machiavelli, but not to the convictions of Dean Acheson.

The son of a clergyman, Acheson came to intellectual maturity in the World War I era. He proclaimed himself a Wilsonian "liberal." Like the President he emulated, Acheson's "liberalism" was coldly rational and austere, built upon the edifice of Anglo-Saxon legal precedent. Both Wilson and Acheson were completely dependent upon this structure for their political thought, which told them that their country must play the key role "in the realignment of power which the crumbling of empires and emergence of new forces necessitated."[3]

Acheson first came into the federal government in the early New Deal period, but left within months when FDR's unorthodox gold policies foretold a more adventurist kind of liberalism. Unlike Will Clayton, however, he never joined the Liberty League or left the Democratic party; when war again touched America, he accepted the post of Assistant Secretary of State for Economic Affairs just in time to confront the most unorthodox capitalist of them all, Lord Keynes, in a sharp encounter over British imperial preferences. Acheson solemnly warned Keynes that Great Britain could not accept Lend-Lease aid and then revert to closed-empire policies after the war. That would curtail America's share of world trade, he declared, and the American people simply would not stand for it.[4]

"We cannot go through another 10 years like the 10 years at the end of the twenties and the beginning of the thirties," Acheson advised Congress in 1944, "without having the most far-reaching consequences upon our economic and social system. . . . So far as I know, no group which has studied the problem, and there have been many, as you know, has ever believed that our domestic markets could absorb our entire production under our present system."[5] Postwar British trade policies were therefore of immense consequence to American institutions. In a radio broadcast with Assistant Secretary of State Archibald MacLeish on August 4, 1945, Acheson explained, "Our whole foreign policy has been reoriented, reimplemented. It's not simply the [United Nations] charter, but the whole pattern of cooperation that has emerged—Bretton Woods, the reciprocal trade act, and the others—that will really make it possible to deal with some of the causes of wars and depressions." Like Will Clayton, Cordell Hull, Harry Hopkins, and others in both the Roosevelt and Truman administrations, Acheson was convinced that economic nationalism anywhere was not only economically disastrous but deeply wrong. "Most of the peoples of the world turned to measures of economic nationalism," he said in describing the prewar period, "which simply aggravated the evil and did a great deal, incidentally, to bring on the present war."[6]

"Are not all of those countries [in Europe] . . . confronted with more than a possibility, with a rather strong possibility, of one or two more revolutions and counterrevolutions before they will achieve what might be called a stable system of government?" Senator Eugene Millikin once asked Acheson.

"Well, I wouldn't want to limit that danger to those particular countries," Acheson replied. "I should think that we might look with some apprehension upon the whole state of the world. . . . Certainly that is a danger if we are not able to work out some sensible international economic arrangements."[7]

Acheson demonstrated his views even more graphically in describing Great Britain as the lung of international trade: if we contract this lung we will soon have "a pulmonary disease." "It cannot breathe so well. It collapses. The stimulating effect on the health of the rest of the world is missing." The British loan should not be regarded as a commercial transaction at all. "We are interested not primarily in lending money to keep good relations with the British, but in *an economic system which is the very basis of our life*—the system of free, individual enterprise. We are interested tremendously in maintaining that way of life in all of the world which depends upon it. It is important in international trade that the people should be able to buy and sell and produce in the most profitable way to themselves. That is the heart of everything we have."[8]

Acheson had Wilson's gift of being able to lift the struggle up out of the dust and sweat of the arena into the realm of the spirit, where life became a "pilgrimage from birth to death through a battleground between good and evil." "The individual," Acheson once wrote, "makes the pilgrimage to choose what is good and reject what is evil, to transcend appetites and achieve the aspirations of the spirit."[9] Yet, as he pointed out on another occasion, the many facets of a problem that confronted the policy-maker seldom could "be separated in the intellectual equivalent of a cream separator."[10] In August 1946 he told the Associated Harvard Clubs in Boston that the continued moral, military, and economic power of the United States was essential to organizing the peace and to hastening recovery in other countries "along lines which are essential to our own system."[11] Acheson put all these ideas together during testimony on the bill to aid Greece and Turkey. "What the President was talking about," he began,

> and I think what we are trying to do in one part of the world by his bill, is to assist people to live the kind of life and have the kind of institutions which they wish to have. We are talking particularly about free institutions, countries which have that system, a system in which we believe. In this particular case they are under pressure which may force them to give that up. And in that situation they ask for our help. *We are willing to help people who believe the way we do, to continue to live the way they want to live.*[12]

By the time of the Korean War, Acheson was blaming the "distant and shadowy figures in the Kremlin" for practically everything that had gone wrong since World War II. Frustration and intense bitterness were natural in this struggle against evil, he wrote to a man whose son was stationed in Korea:

> This agony of spirit, so understandable and right, makes it hard to believe that so monstrous an evil can exist in a world based upon infinite mercy and justice.
>
> But the fact is that it does exist. The fact is that it twists and tortures all our lives. And, I believe, to each of us in this case, as in so many others, the great thing is not what happens to us but how we bear what happens to us.[13]

Upon this rock Acheson built a final justification for the American Cold War position. "It has been hard for us to convince ourselves that human nature is not pretty much the same the world over," he told the Advertising Council in 1950. "The only way to deal with the Soviet Union, we have found from hard experience, is to create situations of strength."[14] There was very little to discuss with the Soviets when their very existence twisted and tortured "all our lives." As Acheson said in 1957, "It is my conviction that the only agreements which are possible now would be disadvantageous to us and would not diminish the dangers of nuclear war." Whatever way the so-called balance of power leaned after 1947, Acheson's views remained firm and unchanging through the Cold War, "peaceful coexistence," the Cuban missile crisis, and "realist" revisionism of the origins of the Cold War.

In Cold War histories, the Truman Doctrine speech of March 12, 1947, is generally regarded as the main turning point, though there is a great difference of opinion about how the signposts at that juncture should be read. Truman gave his own opinions on that matter in a special interview with members of the American Society of Newspaper Editors, shortly after he had gone before Congress to ask for substantial economic and military aid for Greece and Turkey. "There has been a great deal of speculation," he began, "as to the why and wherefore, and how it came about—to quote one paper that I saw, 'so suddenly.' It didn't come about so suddenly. . . . Back about the 25th of April, if I remember correctly, in 1945," Truman continued, Foreign Minister Molotov had called at the White House before going on to the United Nations organization conference. "He stated categorically what he expected to get out of San Francisco. And I told him, categorically, what he was going to get. And he made the statement when he went out of here that he had never been talked to in that manner by anybody before in his life. It did him good."[15]

After summarizing world events in the time between Molotov's visit and his own recent message, Truman concluded briskly:

> And finally, when Great Britain came to the point where she could no longer maintain the situation in Greece and Turkey, I called in the Foreign Relations Committee of the House and the Senate, and the leaders of both parties in the House and the Senate, and laid the facts before them. . . . And that is how the situation developed. It wasn't a sudden proposition that happened in 5 minutes. It had been developing ever since the Germans surrendered. And it finally got to the point where we had to state our case to the world.[16]

Truman's recitation failed to note Dean Acheson's singular performance during that White House conference with congressional leaders, though the President later gave Acheson full credit for his achievements as Secretary of State. "History I am sure," he wrote in his *Memoirs*, "will list Dean Acheson among the truly great Secretaries of State our nation has had."[17] Endowed, as Truman said, with a "keen mind, cool temper, and broad vision," the Under Secretary (at the time of the Greek crisis) was indeed a master logician, who, once his premise was granted, could run circles around an adversary. If the premise of a total Bolshevik challenge to Western civilization was not self-evident in 1947, Acheson's vivid analyses at the White House meeting preceding the Truman Doctrine Message, and his brilliant performances before congressional committees in the weeks that followed, very nearly established the threat permanently. His exposition of the "Mr. X" theme before the House Foreign Affairs Committee in 1948 was a fine example of all these abilities. "I think two things must be clear," Acheson began,

> to those who have considered Soviet policy over the past three decades. The first is that the Soviet Union accepts with complete realism a strong and stable situation and adjusts its policy accordingly. The other is that the Soviet Union, with equal realism, accepts the opportunities offered by weak and unstable situations whether they result from defeat and occupation or from the exhaustion of an ally. It was the weakness of Iran and Greece which led to pressure upon those countries. It was the crisis of western Europe which led to internal Communist pressure in Italy and France, where the Communist parties attempted to capitalize on the difficulties of the people in an effort to overthrow the governments. Such efforts will continue until there is internal stability.

Having made the different Iranian and Greek situations quite indistinguishable by invoking the "containment" theme, Acheson could develop that theme into a complete theory of the current troubles in Western Europe: "This leads to weakness and continual change of governments, unemployment, and the break-up of employer-employee relations, the collapse of the financial system, and the immediate disappearance of that large middle class upon which has been founded the stability of western Europe."[18]

Long before the Truman Doctrine speech in 1947, these views had consolidated into Acheson's world outlook. The change that came over the Under Secretary following that speech consisted first in putting together the total nature of the challenge—primarily the link-up of the Soviet Union and world revolution—

then in making use of the holy pretense to combat it. Once put together properly, this new view held sway without further conscious effort. The essential fact of the European situation, Acheson advised the House Foreign Affairs Committee in 1948, was that those nations could not have sound internal economic systems without large-scale foreign trade. Shut off from Eastern European trade, they would have to look elsewhere to maintain their present social and economic organization, especially to Southeast Asia where, under the stimulus of the Marshall Plan, it was to be hoped a large part of Europe's exports would go. Otherwise European nations would suffer internal revolutions from which minority governments would emerge and turn inevitably to the only alternative: "the closed economic system which now extends from Poland to the Pacific." "The Communist area cannot solve the problem," Acheson concluded, "but it can promise some amelioration of it. The result may well be, as it has already been with some of the countries of eastern Europe, the inclusion of still further areas within the Russian system and the extension of Russian domination still further westward."[19]

Acheson had developed a double-domino theory: Russia pushed outward until confronted with sufficient force to halt the progression of dominoes falling westward, while the Western countries themselves had to be held up so that they would not fall to the east. By this somewhat confusing metaphor, it was possible to convince a Congressman that almost any result would follow logically. The Greek case is a good example: In 1947 Acheson admitted to one congressional committee that "many persons" honestly supported the "communist-led" forces opposing the present Greek government. A year later such distinctions were unnecessary. "The [Greek] civil war was *instigated* and aided by people from the outside," Acheson affirmed uncritically, then promptly agreed with a demonstrably erroneous statement from a committee member that less than 1 per cent of the people supported the attacks upon the government in Athens.[20]

Although there had been no specific outside military threat to Greece in 1947, such statements, by making it seem there had indeed been a serious threat, prepared the people for the next step in the Cold War. The whole process amounted to almost total disregard for the realities of the situation. However, Russian probes in the Mediterranean since 1945 did help Acheson to make his presentation of Greek turmoil look like a total crumbling of defenses before the barbarian onslaught from the East. Churchill, who had first offered that interpretation of Greek events, used the Truman Doctrine message to chide his American critics in a letter to the editor of the *New York Times*: "On Greek affairs in 1944–45 I seemed to find myself out of step. But today it seems I was pursuing the exact policy which, little more than two years later, the United States has adopted with strong conviction. This is to me a very intense satisfaction."[21] If no longer so simplistic in Acheson's explications, Churchill's defense was still basically self-serving for both Great Britain and the United States, albeit for somewhat different reasons.

The Greek struggle against British imperialism appealed to Americans in 1944–1945, but only when the Cold War developed did they support—ironically—the "imperialists." Although Roosevelt had never really accepted the arrangement as final, Greece had been assigned to Great Britain during the 1944 Churchill-Stalin discussion of the Balkans. Turkey had not been discussed that day, but the heart of the "Eastern Question" had always been control of the Dardanelles. From March 1947 on, the United States became responsible for "containing" Russian expansion in this area. To stop there, however, is to put much too negative a connotation on American policy in the Eastern Mediterranean after World War II. Truman's repeated efforts to push American influence into the Danube area, as well as to secure an "open-door" regime in the Turkish Straits, provided the frustrated President with more than enough evidence on which to base a new doctrine. American interest in securing equal access to other Middle Eastern countries went back much earlier than either the London Foreign Ministers' Conference or Potsdam. John C. Campbell's able review of *The United States in World Affairs, 1945–1947,* generalized this theme aptly:

> We wished to develop the Middle East's resources and to increase our trade in friendly competition with Great Britain, loosening if we could the ties of the sterling bloc. Some called it a policy of "underwriting the British Empire." But that empire was itself in

> the process of drastic change and partial liquidation. There were signs that, by force of events, American policy might be developed along the more imaginative lines suggested by Dean [James] Landis as "a substitute for empire under the superstructure of San Francisco." The result would be about the same. Both the United States and Great Britain favored the organization of the Near and Middle East within the "western" political and economic orbit, without denying independence to its peoples. They wished to strengthen its weak spots and particularly to hold up Soviet expansion on its northern rim, in Turkey and Iran.[22]

Since the first decade of the twentieth century, Great Britain and Russia had divided Iran between them. While American economic and political interest in the country had also blossomed, it did not get the chance to crack this diumvirate until 1942 when American troops moved into the country to insure that the Persian Gulf supply route to the Soviet Union remained open. In 1943 American diplomats slipped into Iranian economics and politics via this military route; then the United States took a big leap forward into Iranian affairs by insisting upon the Teheran Declaration in 1943. The declaration pledged the Big Three to respect Iranian political and economic independence after the war.

One of the State Department's special advisers to the Shah's government was Arthur C. Millspaugh, who developed (at Roosevelt's specific request) an expansive program for implementing the Teheran Declaration by a twenty-year economic aid program —a New Deal for Iran. While Roosevelt was "rather thrilled with the idea of using Iran as an example of what we could do by an unselfish American policy," he quickly concluded it was a task for younger men.[23] One younger man in the State Department, Herbert Hoover, Jr., picked up the task and turned it over to an American oil company seeking a large concession in Iran; Hoover thus restored the initiative to private enterprise, a move faithful to his father's tradition. Millspaugh, himself deeply interested in expanding American interests, was shocked at the way this matter was handled: "It is surprising that our government should have launched such a combustible enterprise in an unstable area in the midst of war. It is equally surprising that in view of our devotion to three-power cooperation and to the principle of equal access to raw materials we should have applied for the concession with no understanding with the Soviet Union and none of any practical value, unless we had a secret one, with Great Britain."[24]

The ruling Shah was especially pleased at this evidence of long-term American interest in his country while it was still occupied by British and Soviet troops. When, however, these latter powers demanded a share in any new oil concessions, he was not so well satisfied. His Ambassador told the State Department that the Shah had responded by postponing all talk of concessions until after the war, when foreign troops had been removed according to the Declaration on Iran. "Iran should be of special interest to Americans after the war," added the Ambassador. "All other countries in that part of the world were affiliated with British or French interests, while Iran was free of such affiliations, and his country was furthermore in an important position *as a back door to Russia*."[25]

When they learned about the American oil policy, the Soviets had demanded a concession over most of northern Iran, and protested the Shah's decision to postpone talks both in Teheran and in Washington. Discussion between the United States and the Soviet Union was put off until Yalta. At a brief preliminary meeting with British leaders at Malta, Eden and Stettinius agreed that they had a "grievance against the Russians" in that their oil companies had proceeded quite far by the time the negotiations were arrested "by the ham-handed procedure of the Russians in demanding a concession in the north which raised political issues."[26]

The two foreign ministers decided to ask Molotov at Yalta to agree not to press the matter until foreign troops had been withdrawn, a time when, as the Ambassador from Iran had pointed out, his country would be free of any forced affiliations. Molotov was plainly angered by this move, but finally suggested that the Big Three leave the matter to take its own course. "The situation was not acute at the present time."[27]

Although excluded from Anglo-American oil diplomacy in the Middle East, the Russians had far more than a simple economic interest in Iran. Thus they responded to the Anglo-American policy with an effort to detach Azerbaijan from Iran and turn it into a satellite. Yet what is often forgotten about this struggle is that it took place in the midst of a general American movement into the Middle East, one which brooked no opposition from the Soviets, Britain, or France. General Charles de Gaulle's special representative in Washington once questioned the specifics of American interference in France's established policies in Syria and Lebanon. An officer in the Near Eastern Division of the State Department recorded the question and his answer for Department files:

> During this discussion, M. Lacoste made some "personal" observations on the American "open-door" policy. He said that at the turn of the century, when this policy was defined, the United States was only one of a number of powers in the world of relatively equal size and strength. However, we had now become so colossal that if the open-door policy were followed, the others would be unable to compete with us. Consequently, M. Lacoste implied, other Governments would have to seek exclusive areas and advantages.
>
> Mr. [Paul] Alling vigorously disagreed with this analysis, emphasizing the decreasing size and the increasing interdependence of the whole world. He pointed out that equality of opportunity was high on our list of war aims and that we had no intention of fighting this war and then abandoning our objectives.[28]

In discussions with several Middle Eastern ambassadors and leaders, State Department representatives repeatedly stressed the need for free and direct access for American civil aviation and radiotelephone and telegraphy circuits, so that messages back and forth would not have to pass through other capitals. This was the first step toward implementing the open door policy. After several such conversations, Will Clayton warned Truman that the British opposed American commercial aviation in the Middle East, and were taking action to prevent the use of dollar exchange in the sterling bloc countries for the purchase of American aircraft. Truman promised to take up these questions with Churchill at Potsdam. It was precisely this kind of problem which Clayton had so much on his mind later, in September, when he began negotiations on the British loan; it was also this kind of problem which Acheson had earlier had in mind when he met with Keynes in the summer of 1941.[29]

The situation in Iran, meanwhile, had become acute by the fall of 1945, when the Shah's army tried to reoccupy provinces evaculated by the Soviets, who were now cheering on local communists in Azerbaijan. Byrnes and Bevin both pressed Stalin on this question at the Moscow Foreign Ministers' Conference. In reply, Russian leaders charged that American and British troops had not withdrawn from Greece and Indonesia, alleged that the Iranian government was unfriendly to the Soviet Union, and finally insisted that it was necessary to protect the nearby Baku oil fields from saboteurs.

At a private meeting with Stalin, Byrnes gave notice that if the issue came before the first meeting of the General Assembly, the United States would have to support Iran. Stalin claimed there was one thing wrong with the 1943 Declaration on Iran: it contained no statement of Teheran's obligations to each of the Big Three. Byrnes recalled that Stalin then concluded more amicably: "We will do nothing to make you blush." That proved not to be the case.[30]

The official record of this conversation, besides being more complete, varies on key points from the Secretary's memory. Stalin said, according to the record, that the people in Teheran were desperately looking around for support in making a case against the Soviet Union. "He concluded by saying that no one had any need to blush if this question was raised in the Assembly." This was quite a different statement, of course, from a supposed promise that the Russians would do nothing to make Byrnes blush.

Even the Secretary's memory of what he told Stalin would be the American position in the General Assembly on the Iranian question was put in doubt by the 1967 publication of the Moscow Conference records. Byrnes indicated he had told Stalin that, according to the facts as we knew them, "and in view of our solemn pledge, we would be forced to support the position of Iran." But the records do not indicate that the American position had been made so clear to the Kremlin.[31]

Byrnes may have been trying to toughen his record, or he simply may have interpreted Stalin's statements differently. But once the United States took a strong position in the General Assembly, it was certainly necessary to play down any ambiguities in the record for the American public. Put another way: public diplomacy meant no diplomacy; thus there should be nothing in the record to suggest that compromise had been contemplated by either side.

On January 19, 1946, the Iranian delegate to the London meeting of the General Assembly formally complained of Russian interference in the internal affairs of his country. After several days of debate the Security Council called upon the Soviet Union and Iran to settle the matter by direct negotiations between them. Meanwhile, in Teheran the Big Three ambassadors paid a visit to Premier Ghavam-es-Sultaneh to give him "friendly advice" on how to handle the situation.

The negotiations failed, however, and in March the question was back before the United Nations. In new bilateral negotiations the Russians pledged to remove their troops in five to six weeks. But the terms they agreed to were not exactly what Washington had hoped for in encouraging the Iranians to bring the question before the U.N. The Soviets demanded the creation of a joint Russian-Iranian oil company to exploit potential resources in the northern provinces, and assurances of a good deal of local autonomy for Azerbaijan.

Even if the details were not yet put in their proper places, Byrnes was immensely pleased at this apparent evidence that public diplomacy could bring quick results. At the first of the several Foreign Ministers' meetings in Paris, Molotov complained bitterly to Byrnes about the anti-Soviet campaign launched by Iran and given support in the U.N. by Great Britain and the United States. In reply the Secretary soberly recalled his "statements" to Stalin in December. "Because the dinner opened on this note of discord," Byrnes wrote, "it is not surprising that our later discussions of the treaties, and the United States' proposals about Germany and Austria, met with little success."[32]

Though he fails to speak further about these risks of public diplomacy, the Secretary's offhand recognition that the atmosphere created did not make for serious discussion of German and Austrian problems is one of the frankest statements in *Speaking*

Frankly. After the Russians finally evacuated northern Iran, American influence in the Iranian parliament blocked the ratification of the Russian oil concession, and American advisers were at the head of the troops the Shah sent into Azerbaijan.[33]

Far from justifying the Truman Doctrine, the Iranian episode revealed that it was possible to extend American interests even to the doorstep of the Soviet Union without effective challenge. "The U.S.S.R.'s recognition of this fact," said *Business Week*, "accounts for Moscow's aggressive diplomacy in northern Iran, for the bitter Soviet demands that British troops get out of Greece, and for feverish Russian diplomatic activity in Egypt, Syria, Iraq and Iran."[34] By 1953 America also had almost completely replaced British influence in Iran, and had a 40 per cent cut of the old Anglo-Iranian oil holdings.

What then of the supposed strategic threat to the Dardanelles? After the Truman-Stalin collision at Potsdam over the American waterways proposal, the Big Three left Berlin having agreed only to a public statement that the Montreux Convention should be revised, and that each of the three powers would begin direct negotiations with Ankara to see how the revisions could be facilitated. On November 2, 1945, Washington revived its proposal for internationalization of the Dardanelles in a message to Ankara suggesting an international conference to discuss the plan.

The British, however, still showed little interest in any significant revision of the old Convention. Labourite speakers filled Parliament with sonorous perorations, hardly different even in tone from past Tory rhetoric on the "Eastern Question." "We have been willing, equally with our predecessors, to consider the revision of the Montreux Convention," Foreign Minister Bevin declared on June 4, 1946. "What we are anxious to avoid, and I emphasize this, is to do anything, or agree to anything, which will undermine the real independence of Turkey, or convert her into a mere satellite state."[35]

Moscow repeated its original demands for joint control in a long note to the Turks on August 7, 1946. At that point, Acting Secretary of State Dean Acheson took his first serious initiative in Middle Eastern affairs, calling a meeting of the State-War-Navy Coordinating Committee and the Joint Chiefs of Staff to consider the serious situation created by the Russian note. He opened the meeting by emphasizing the gravity of the matter. It was clear, so far as he was concerned, that the Russians were trying to take over the straits and would eventually establish naval and air beachheads there if they succeeded. The problem, then, was whether the United States could—or would—stand with the Turks to defend the gates into the Mediterranean.

If so, a note should be sent to the Russians, gentle in tone but absolutely firm in purpose. There was general agreement around the table that the Acting Secretary's proposal was the only way to meet the threat. Several days after this secret meeting, James Reston wrote in the *New York Times* that Acheson was in fact developing "a foreign policy," one which would demonstrate to Moscow that the United States did not intend to repeat the political mistakes it had made after World War I. Acheson was convinced, Reston said, that the emerging disputes called for a long-term commitment to internationalism. The Acting Secretary was "aware of the dangers involved in the policy of intervention . . . but [felt] that the dangers of intervention [were] less than the dangers of non-intervention."[36]

Put in the context of Russia's withdrawal from Iran, its abandonment of prior claims to trustee rights over a former Italian colony in Africa, and other signs of retreat in the Mediterranean, Reston's analysis deserves serious attention as an alternate way of explaining the foreign policy then being developed by the Acting Secretary of State. It was indeed based on a long-term commitment to internationalism and intervention. The State Department's August 19 note to Moscow warned that any attack on the straits by an aggressor would justify the Security Council in taking action. Truman backed up the message by sending the aircraft carrier *Franklin D. Roosevelt*, four cruisers, and a destroyer flotilla to the eastern Mediterranean to join the battleship *Missouri*, stationed there since April. Navy Secretary Forrestal announced that these vessels would be placed on permanent station in the Mediterranean—the first such act since Jefferson's day. Ankara promptly rejected the Soviet proposal, and once again the Russian threat melted away.

Dean Acheson's August 19 note was potentially embarrassing

to the State Department, should any later critic of the Truman Doctrine have brought it up at those congressional hearings. It was made public in the State Department *Bulletin* at the time, but later ignored. The note read: "It is observed that the note of the Soviet Government contains no reference to the United Nations. The position of the Government of the United States is that the regime of the Straits should be brought into appropriate relationship with the United Nations and should function in a manner entirely consistent with the principles and aims of the United Nations."[37] But in 1947 the administration paid no heed to its own advice that the U.N. should underwrite Big Three policies. Instead it pushed forward with unilateral military aid, justifying it in ways that actually weakened the U.N.

The increasingly obsolete mainstay of Western influence was still British military and economic aid, but this finally gave way on Friday afternoon, February 21, 1947, when the British Embassy asked for an appointment with Secretary of State Marshall. The Secretary had left his office, so it was decided to postpone the meeting until Monday. In the meantime, the First Secretary might bring over the documents so that preparations could be made over the weekend. Later that afternoon, therefore, the British handed two notes to Loy Henderson, director of the Office of Near Eastern Affairs. In Greece, said the first note, the economic situation was near collapse. That country needed between $240 and $280 million in financial aid in the next few months. London would be unable to offer further assistance after March 31. The second note on Turkey simply stated that Britain could not underwrite the modernization of the Turkish army. "Reading the messages," Henderson and his associates realized "that Great Britain had within the hour handed the job of world leadership, with all its burdens and all its glory, to the United States."[38]

The following Thursday, Marshall and Acheson met with congressional leaders in the White House. The conference did not begin well:

> Things were going very badly indeed, and Acheson was greatly disturbed. Leaning over to Secretary Marshall, who sat beside him, Acheson asked in a low voice, "Is this a private fight or can

anyone get into it?" Whereupon Marshall addressed the President and suggested that Acheson had something to say.[39]

For the next ten to fifteen minutes the Under Secretary spoke as a fervent advocate of the American mission in a suddenly bipolarized world, a last Athens or Rome against the greatest and most dangerous Sparta or Carthage. The defense of Western civilization, even the sacred place of its birth, had been left up to the United States. In a world where one of the two great powers was aggressive and expanding, the protection of countries threatened by Soviet aggression *or* communist subversion was not pulling chestnuts out of the fire for anyone—it was the protection of freedom itself. Once the Russians succeeded in gaining control of the eastern Mediterranean, the possibilities for further penetration into Asia and Africa became almost limitless. And in Western Europe the psychological impact on countries like Italy and France, with their large communist minorities, would be devastating, if not conclusive.

"When [Acheson] finished," an aide noted, "a profound silence ensued that lasted perhaps ten seconds." It was broken by Senator Vandenberg, who said he had been greatly impressed, even shaken by what he had heard. But, he added, if the President wanted to get any results, he would have to "scare hell out of the country." Leaving the White House, Acheson held an off-the-record press conference with correspondents who regularly covered the State Department. Giving them the sense of the British notes, he carefully explained the situation in the same terms he had used hours earlier. The first "scare" had been well placed. The next day formal work began on details of the program to be recommended to Congress and the President's speech which would sound the tocsin.

Joseph M. Jones was assigned the task of drafting the original working paper for the President's message. A few days earlier, he had himself previewed the British notes, and what they would imply for the United States, in a letter to Senator William Benton:

> There are many signs that the world is approaching this year the greatest crisis since the turn in the tide of the war in November, 1942. It is primarily an economic crisis centered in Britain and

Empire, France, Greece and China. . . . If these areas are allowed to spiral downwards into economic anarchy, then at best they will drop out of the United States orbit and try an independent nationalistic policy; at worst they will swing into the Russian orbit. We will then face the world alone. What will be the cost in dollars and cents of our armaments and of our economic isolation? I do not see how we could possibly avoid a depression far greater than that of 1929–1932 and crushing taxes to pay for the direct commitments we would be forced to make around the world.[40]

In the *New York Times* of March 2, 1947, Hanson Baldwin sounded a more ideological theme taken directly from Acheson's briefings. The United States, Baldwin said, "far more than any single factor, is the key to the destiny of tomorrow; we alone may be able to avert the decline of Western civilization, and a reversion to nihilism and the Dark Ages."

A week before the President went before Congress, he spoke on foreign economic policy at Baylor University. His remarks began with the statement that world peace and freedom were all bound up in the problem of reestablishing world trade. The three goals were inseparable: "The grave lessons of the past have proved it. . . . We are the giant of the economic world. Whether we like it or not, the future pattern of economic relations depends upon us. The world is waiting and watching to see what we shall do. The choice is ours. We can lead the nations to economic peace or we can plunge them into economic war."

There was one thing, the President continued, that Americans valued more than peace:

> It is freedom. Freedom of worship—freedom of speech—freedom of enterprise. . . . Throughout history, freedom of worship and freedom of speech have been most frequently enjoyed in those societies that have accorded a considerable measure of freedom to individual enterprise. . . . So our devotion to freedom of enterprise, in the United States, has deeper roots than a desire to protect the profits of ownership. *It is part and parcel of what we call American.*

The trade pattern least conducive to freedom of enterprise was the one in which decisions were made solely or principally by governments. ". . . If this trend is not reversed, the Government of the United States will be under pressure . . . to fight for markets and raw materials. And if the Government were to yield to this pressure, it would shortly find itself in the business of allocating foreign goods among importers and foreign markets among exporters, and telling every trader what he could buy or sell. . . . It is not the American way."[41]

Truman's White House advisers wanted to continue the Baylor themes in the message on Greece and Turkey. "If, by default," one draft stated, "we permit free enterprise to disappear in the other nations of the world, the very existence of our own economy and our own democracy will be threatened."[42] Acheson raised objections to all such specifics. He had been insisting that the matter ought to be phrased in general and ideological terms—totalitarianism versus freedom. Acheson therefore deleted another White House reference to American interest in the natural resources of the Middle East. Truman later put it in his memoirs, speaking of Russia's threat to Iran as one which endangered Western economies and the "raw material balance of the world." Acheson explained to Clark Clifford that even the reference to the trend away from free enterprise would adversely affect current relations with Great Britain, and give certain elements who were upset by the British loan another shot at the administration.[43]

Truman's message drew hard and fast ideological lines around the world. By constant references to free and unfree peoples, democratic and totalitarian governments, the President led Congress to his key paragraph: "I believe that it must [Truman had changed the State Department's "should" to "must"] be the policy of the United States to support free peoples who are resisting attempted subjugation by armed minorities or by outside pressure." Elsewhere in the speech Truman referred to the United Nations, but in such a way as to make it clear the United States had assumed the burden of defining how the status quo might be changed: "The world is not static, and the status quo is not sacred. But we cannot allow changes in the status quo in violation of the Charter of the United Nations by such methods as coercion, or by such subterfuges as political infiltration. In helping free and independent nations to maintain their freedom, the

United States will be giving effect to the principles of the Charter of the United Nations."

Even friends of the administration were troubled by the speech and the answers they received to their questionings. Overt Soviet military moves in the Mediterranean had virtually come to an end, yet the Truman Doctrine sounded a call to arms. "It was something like the feeling on the day of Munich," said Paul Smith, the *San Francisco Chronicle*'s editor and a close friend of Secretary Forrestal. "The man in the street began thinking about the taste of brackish water in canteens, and the mud of foxholes, and the smell of the dead, and all those reminders of the recently finished war, and wondering . . ." In answer to Smith's editorials and private questions, Forrestal answered that America had to keep the Mediterranean a free highway for "this economy of ours. . . . These raw materials have to come over the sea and a good many have to go through the Mediterranean."[44] Although Smith eventually supported the Greek-Turkish aid bill, his concern about the way Truman pictured the struggle was shared by a good many others. In his newspaper he warned the administration that some would want to build the Truman Doctrine higher and higher around Russia until it was "so stifling that war would explode inevitably as the one means of breaking the stranglehold. That eventuality . . . is one of the alternative avenues down which the new policy could lead us."[45]

Another newsman, Howard K. Smith, was in Moscow covering the Foreign Ministers' Conference of March–April 1947. As a direct result of the President's dramatic appearance before Congress, he wrote, the whole atmosphere changed, not only in Moscow itself but all through Eastern Europe, where the last representatives of non-Communist parties were soon driven from the governments of Hungary and Bulgaria.[46] Administration spokesmen denied then and later that the message's timing had anything to do with the Moscow meeting. On the other hand, they almost universally believed that Stalin was playing for time on the assumption that capitalism would fail in the West. Acheson told David Lilienthal that he never once believed the Politburo would deliberately provoke a war with the United States, "unless they are absolutely out of their minds." Instead the Politburo would work to achieve its ends through internal subversion. Indeed, the only thing that had so far held the Communists back in France was a fear that they could not control a civil war if de Gaulle were to rally the forces of French nationalism.[47]

Acheson's policy of building "situations of strength" began with the Truman Doctrine and continued into the next decade with the Korean War. He knew full well that such a quest was unlikely ever to produce a clear military advantage over the Soviet Union. He had said as much in his September 1945 memorandum to Truman on atomic energy. In 1949, however, he became a vigorous advocate of the hydrogen bomb on the grounds that not developing it would lead to an "erosion" of American power and force negotiations between East and West on unfavorable terms. The search for a perfect negotiating position is, of course, the most unreal of all diplomatic postures—and the most suitable to the holy pretense. With the Truman Doctrine the United States had declared to the world that it would decide when changes in the status quo violated the U.N. Charter, when revolutions were strictly an internal affair, and when they were fomented from abroad by coercion, subterfuge, or political infiltration.

"It is not unfair to Acheson," wrote political scientist Coral Bell in *Negotiation from Strength* (1963), "to see in his attitude . . . a hint of the free-thinking clergyman, with his own reservations about the pearly gates, feeling it psychologically proper nevertheless to inspire the Sunday-school class to virtue with the prospect of ultimate bliss crowning a period of meritorious endeavour." Whether as puritan divine or free-thinking clergyman, Acheson's Sunday school was the Congress of the United States, which held yet a few backsliders. Moreover, General Eisenhower had recently made a statement to thirty-five members of Congress that Greece and Turkey were not of strategic importance to the United States, and could not be held in time of crisis.[48]

Support to Greece thus posed a particularly difficult problem when Acheson appeared before the House Committee to defend Truman's request. Representative Jacob Javits suggested that there ought to be some way to exact commitments from Athens for serious political reforms. Acheson insisted first that the 1946 Greek election had been a fair one, then explained that the

United States was not helping any specific party to maintain power. It only sought to aid a duly elected government operating under a legitimate constitution. Javits suspected that the Greek constitution was about as effective under the party in power as the American Constitution had been under the Bourbon redeemers in Mississippi. Acheson's concern for constitutional processes was supported by a dark vision of the alternative:

> Those people will continue to be there until constitutionally they are removed. If we allow Greece to go to pieces, then you are quite right, you probably will have a commissar in charge of the place in short order.

Javits resented Acheson's attempts to set aside his original question by "scare" tactics, and he remonstrated politely, but quite forcefully, that the Under Secretary was not answering his question:

> Mr. Secretary, is not that explanation just a little bit—and I am not using this term invidiously at all—but just to get us clear, is it not a little pat, because we know very well that not less than 20 percent of the people in Greece failed to participate in the last election on political grounds.

Nor would Javits concede the administration's argument that the partisans were inspired and directed from Bulgaria and Yugoslavia. Shouldn't we consider a new election as one of the key ways to pacify the country? he asked. Acheson's reply was too nicely diplomatic to suit Javits and other dissenters, especially at a hearing where administration witnesses had been imploring Congress to accept full political responsibility for an area previously dominated by European nations: "Whether or not any advisers we would have there would advise the Greek Government to hold elections, I cannot possibly say."

Javits simply refused to be put off. Had the Greek government been "advised" to offer the rebels amnesty, he queried? That had been done, said the Under Secretary, "and it has been offered."

"But it has not been coupled with any prospect of a new election?" Javits continued. No, Acheson said, "and I see no particular reason why it should be."

"Realistically, is it not a fact, Mr. Secretary, what we ask the

Greek Government to do will go a very long way toward getting them to do it, especially under these circumstances?"

"I should think our advice would be taken seriously, yes."

"To say the least . . ."[49]

So the exchange ended, without satisfying Javits on any count. As for the Turkish government, the administration made no serious attempt to picture it as democratic; and it was quite evident in the hearings that, as one witness put it, when "the new dish was being prepared for American consumption, Turkey was slipped into the oven with Greece because that seemed to be the surest way to cook a tough bird."[50]

But Representative Helen Gahagan Douglas asked Acheson why the United States had not insisted that Turkey take its complaint directly to the U.N., instead of appealing for American military aid against Soviet encroachments. The Under Secretary replied a bit patronizingly: "My judgment would be that that would not be a productive course." Even so, said Mrs. Douglas, "we would have gained much. . . . We could then act on the unilateral plan that we now have under consideration, but we would have first explored the possibility of settling the problem through the international machinery which we helped set up. If we do not do so are we not culpable morally before the world?"

Acheson's reply was a study in holy hair-splitting: "I should not say so. I really think we ought not to use this word 'unilateral' quite as freely as some of us do. Unilateral means something that one country does. What we are now talking about here is responding to a request of another country. That at least involves two countries."[51]

Conservative Senator Harry Byrd was not convinced. On April 22 on the floor of the Senate he charged that after sixteen days had elapsed, and after Congress had been called upon to provide the funds for the Greek-Turkish problem, our representative to the world organization had done nothing more than give notice to that body of American intentions. Byrd roundly lambasted the Russians for the next several minutes, but finally called for a showdown on these issues within the United Nations. In conclusion he raised two key questions: "If our unilateral action in arming other nations is provocative of war, upon what ally can we depend? If we act independently and arm nations to oppose communism, can we assume that Russia will not follow our lead and establish a counterpolicy?"[52]

Such charges were serious enough to force bipartisan leaders to attempt to plaster over the "colossal blunder," as Senator Vandenberg called it, of ignoring the United Nations. He offered an amendment to the bill which provided that when the U.N. felt capable of taking over the work in Greece and Turkey, or of terminating it, the United States would accept a majority vote to that effect in either the Security Council or the General Assembly. Subtle as his mind was, Acheson had not thought of that one. A Russian veto could have blocked an attempt to initiate action in the U.N., but Vandenberg's amendment would have also made it impossible for the Soviets to step in after the plan was going full steam. And it looked good to the American public as well.

The bill called for $400 million to Greece and Turkey. Sixty-two per cent of the money was designated for military aid. This was the main reason why the program could not be sold through the United Nations in the first place. "I was shocked at the impression given by the President and by Assistant Secretary of State [Willard] Thorp, and by Mr. [Henry] Villard," said an anti-administration witness, left-liberal economist Broadus Mitchell, "that this was primarily to go for feeding people. The hunger, the illness, in Greece particularly, was dwelt upon—the need for restoring the economy of that wartorn country. Then, we are told by Assistant Secretary of State Clayton, in charge of economic affairs, of all people, that almost two-thirds of the amount of $400,000,000 is to go for war purposes."[53]

Approval of the Greek-Turkish aid plan by Congress, even after all these questionings and revelations, significantly reduced congressional control of foreign affairs. Through a blend of puritan dogma and Yankee pragmatism, Americans justified even their own self-deception in the cause of anti-communism. In this atmosphere liberalism became almost pure relativism, conservatism chauvinism: Joseph Alsop soon sounded like Fulton Lewis, and vice versa.

Having scared hell out of the American people, and a good many Western European leaders as well, the administration tried to channel its response to the Soviet threat into more positive directions. The militance had been necessary, argued some who justified Truman's speech, in order to call attention to the seriousness of the threat. Acheson had already initiated studies which ultimately led to the Marshall Plan for European economic recovery.[54] He then explained why it was necessary to enlist the support of all special interest groups in Congress behind the Marshall Plan.

"We had at that time a tremendous export surplus," Acheson recalled for Jonathan Daniels on one occasion, "as we still do, but there was then very little likelihood of the recipient nations being able to fill the dollar gap. It was also clear that if our exports did not continue, the political consequences in the battle of resistance against the spread of Communism in Europe would be lost."[55] But should the United States fail to meet this challenge, Secretary Marshall said, there would inevitably be other consequences for the nation. "It would impose incalculable burdens upon this country and force serious readjustments in our traditional way of life. One of our important freedoms—freedom of choice in both domestic and foreign affairs—would be drastically curtailed."[56]

Marshall's speech at Harvard on June 5, 1947, offered European leaders significant American economic aid if they would work together to restore the institutions of the old order on an inter-European basis. But they had to come up with a plan which would promise substantial recovery within a reasonable number of years, yet stay within a cost figure which Congress would approve. Several officers in the State Department besides Under Secretary Acheson had contributed to the speech, but George Frost Kennan supplied the answer to the $64 Question: What about the Soviet Union?

Marshall was naturally concerned that if Eastern Europe and the Soviet Union were invited to participate, Congress would then refuse to supply the necessary money. On the other hand, if these nations were automatically excluded at the start, how would the rest of Europe react? Kennan's advice was to "play it straight." He had opposed the Truman Doctrine speech, and in fact had opposed any aid to Turkey as an unnecessary risk. When asked about the Marshall Plan, he was even more emphatic that the United States should not define the area that would receive American aid. Following the Marxist maxim, "From each according to his ability, to each according to his need," Kennan remarked, the Russians could be invited to share in the burdens as well as the benefits of a common recovery program. One could almost be certain that the Russians would refuse, for this would force them to forgo a chance to exploit Western weaknesses.[57]

In proposing this plan, American leaders were aware, then, that it would complete the division of Europe, whether or not the initiative belonged to the United States. But if Greece and Turkey "and the the other countries should adopt closed economies," Will Clayton warned Congress, "you can imagine the effect that it would have on our foreign trade . . . it is important that we do everything we can to retain those export markets."[58] The deterioration of the European economy would force those countries to adopt state controls, Acheson told another House committee in 1948. Their domestic economies would then have to be severely regulated, and ultimately the American system of free enterprise would be endangered.

In this view the specific moved quickly to the general: the Truman Doctrine became the Marshall Plan, the Anglo-American loan agreement became a general effort to stabilize currencies in all Europe. The eagerness with which the British Labour government reached for American aid and encouraged the French to do the same demonstrated that the 1946 loan had served its political purpose: it had "contained" British socialism, even if it had not met an immediate economic success.

Acting upon Marshall's suggestion, British and French leaders constituted themselves into a "steering committee" and called a preliminary conference for Paris. They were chagrined when Moscow not only accepted an invitation to attend the meetings but sent eighty-nine experts with Foreign Minister Molotov. Bevin and Bidault glowered at the Russians through six days of acrimonious debate over Molotov's proposal that each nation prepare a shopping list, a proposal which cut directly against Marshall's warning that any plan should provide for an overall European balance sheet. When no one wanted to compromise, Molotov shooed his eighty-nine assistants back to the Paris airport and departed, hurling charges that the American plan would subvert Europe's national economies—a fine ironic prophecy from a Bolshevik commissar to Europe's capitalist leaders.

But Molotov had had a second reason for attending the Paris meeting: Russian concern over the German question. The Truman Doctrine had been announced just as the Moscow Conference of Foreign Ministers began discussions of that question. Since it had forestalled serious consideration of the problem there, the Kremlin had seen the Paris meeting as an opportunity to press the Big Three. Throughout the six days he was in Paris, Molotov insisted that Germany could be considered only by the Foreign Ministers. Proposals at Paris to study the ways German resources might be integrated into the European recovery project, Molotov charged, ignored prior reparations claims by those countries which had suffered from German aggression. These remained unsatisfied, he said, and yet it was now proposed to use German resources for quite different purposes.[59]

After the Russians left, the presence of Czech and Polish representatives at Paris soon proved embarrassing to both sides. The Czechs had even agreed to attend a second conference sometime in the future to work out details of the economic plan. This desire for Western aid was widely hailed by Anglo-French sources as a break with Moscow. Two days later, however, Foreign Minister Jan Masaryk announced that Prague had reversed its position. Both Washington and Moscow made sure that other grey areas between East and West disappeared. Throughout June and July, for example, the State Department agitated the Eastern European question regularly in its *Bulletin.* Coalition cabinets in France and Italy were reorganized in May and June, excluding the left parties, especially any Communist ministers.

In Prague during the summer of 1947, Czech leaders were trapped between American rhetoric and foreign bayonets. James Warburg personally witnessed their agony with a sense of foreboding about the future that grew day by day. Conversations with Jan Masaryk and the American Ambassador, Laurence Steinhardt, convinced him that it was wrong to write off Czechoslovakia —and with it any last chance to avoid the Cold War. Returning home, Warburg pleaded with State Department officials to grant Prague credits for cotton purchases. But his private memos to the new Under Secretary of State, Robert Lovett, were politely disregarded. Either the Department had simply abandoned Czechoslovakia, or it was afraid of the effect such a credit would have on congressional attitudes toward the Marshall Plan, or both. "The gist of my reportage was that, if an Iron Curtain had been drawn around Czechoslovakia, it had been drawn by us—not by the Soviet Union."[60]

Even as the meetings in Paris continued, Acheson returned to Truman Doctrine rhetoric in a commencement speech at Wesleyan University. The *New York Times* characterized it as a vehement denunciation of Russian foreign policy, one filled with assertions that the Soviets had unilaterally abrogated the Yalta agreements and were primarily responsible for turmoil in the Middle and Far East. Acheson also referred to the Truman Doctrine as a natural outgrowth of the Monroe Doctrine—an increasingly common practice—and combined all this with a none-too-subtle suggestion of a more active policy in Eastern Europe:

> We can do, and are doing, many things. We can expose for all to see the shams and frauds behind which peoples are deprived of their liberty by little groups supported by foreign power. The methods have not changed basically since the days of Maximilian in Mexico, merely improved in organization and brutality and propaganda techniques. But they dislike exposure, and it remains to be seen whether they can survive much longer than Maximilian did the withdrawal of the foreign bayonets.[61]

In 1947, then, Acheson preferred a bipolar world. The dynamic of the Truman Doctrine helped him to cite historical precedents for the creation of a useful past. A decade later he expanded this usable past into one that explained everything in a series of lectures titled "Power and Diplomacy."

On the one side there was the United States, reluctant leader of the free world, "primarily interested in . . . [its] own absorbing and immensely profitable affairs, and only secondarily interested in the doings and business of distant peoples." Opposed to the free world was the Soviet Union, "a revolutionary society, repudiating the most fundamental postulates of the established order, and [caught] . . . in the grip of an ideology which imbues it with unquestioning confidence in its superiority and its destined progression to triumph and dominion."[62]

Almost everything that followed in Acheson's lectures flowed directly from these assumptions. With those of the historical main stream of the 1950's, they formed the consensus on America's entrance into world politics: the country had been forced into the arena by external explosions in Havana Harbor in 1898 (possibly in combination with an internal psychological spasm or two); but always it pulled against the forces of history, seeking some simpler life. Acheson and the "realist" diplomatic historians could agree on that, even if some of them differed with him on how to meet the Soviet challenge. Insistence upon seeing the Soviet Union as the instigator of turmoil and revolution everywhere was the main pretense of the whole ritual. By 1957, ironically, Soviet military power at last matched that pretension.

In 1949 Acheson agreed fully with the decision to go ahead with the construction of a hydrogen bomb. Indeed, he apparently had a large part in making the decision. He was never convinced that possession of the hydrogen bomb would enable the United States to dictate its own terms, but he feared any "erosion of power" which might lead to inescapable pressures for negotiation. The erosion he had in mind was psychological; so long as there seemed to be an alternative to negotiations in building situations of strength, there was no need to risk disengagement or any other neutralization of Central Europe as a prerequisite for ending the Cold War.

"I found it difficult," said George F. Kennan in 1954 in explaining his opposition to the hydrogen bomb decision, because "we would come to think of our security as embraced solely in the mathematics of whatever power of destruction we could evolve, and we would forget our security lies still very largely in our ability to address ourselves to the positive and constructive problems of world affairs, to create confidence in other people."[63] The mathematics of destruction soon brought to the fore a different kind of diplomatic history, often written by a new sort of political thinker—the mathematician turned political scientist, complete with a new vocabulary to span the intellectual gap. This was, of course, part of the inevitable fallout of atomic diplomacy, and in the end it finally destroyed the diplomatic process itself.

The Marshall Plan was advanced behind the ideological armor plate Acheson showed to key congressional leaders on February 27, 1947. The blinding reflections off its polished surface prevented the possibility of distinguishing between the details of communism in the Soviet Union and in the People's Democracies in Eastern Europe; around the peripheral edges of the glare, all things looked equally dark. Only a few American leaders claimed these differences were significant, and they were soon undercut by the Czechoslovakian *coup d'état* in 1948.

Kennan's deep fears about the imbalance in America's response to the Soviet challenge after 1947 were also confirmed in the creation of the North Atlantic Treaty Organization. It appeared to its proponents, however, as the only way to build Germany's will to resist Russian provocations at Berlin, and the only way other European countries would accept German reintegration into the political and military community of Western Europe.[64]

"There is no question in my mind whatever," Secretary of State Marshall testified in November 1947, "that the German economy is the heart of Europe, and if we do not coordinate that in connection with the rest of Europe, certainly western Europe, we would be in difficulties for an interminable procession of years until there had been a readjustment of the economic processes that have been developed through several hundred years."

In Germany itself, Russian and American proconsuls executed some decisions and initiated others which brought the Cold War to its first critical confrontation, one that was sparked, in an immediate sense, by the American Military Government's currency reform under the direction of General Lucius D. Clay.

NINE ☆☆

Lucius D. Clay: American Decisions in Germany

Franklin Roosevelt's death unmasked the reality behind the Unconditional Surrender declaration adopted at Casablanca, revealing the absence of any clear-cut presidential policy on postwar Germany. Even that famous statement itself had been intended primarily for the Kremlin, to assure the Soviets that there would be no separate peace in the West, rather than to prescribe a postwar German policy. At the Teheran Conference, Roosevelt had put forward vague suggestions for dividing Germany into several small states; but then at Yalta, when Stalin asked that they settle the German question, FDR had slipped off into a variety of obfuscations and reminiscences about his student days in the Germany of "forty years ago."

The only document which had survived the bitter 1944 debate within Roosevelt's Cabinet over what to do about Germany was the much-amended Joint Chiefs of Staff Memorandum No. 1067. Since the reparations issue dominated American-Russian relations in Germany immediately after the war, the language of No. 1067 concerning reparations is of some interest. It instructed the American military governor: "No action will be taken in execution of the reparations program or otherwise which would tend to support basic living conditions in Germany or in your zone on a higher level than that existing in any of the neighboring United

Nations." Much of the American debate, and then the Russian-American debate, centered on the problem of interpreting No. 1067—or, as some insisted, changing it altogether.

On one side of the argument was Secretary of the Treasury Morgenthau, who wanted to deny the American commander any leeway to *re*-centralize Germany, even for the sake of providing large reparations to the victors.[1] Morgenthau had almost persuaded Roosevelt to this position at the time of the 1944 Quebec Conference with the British. Using the President's angry dissatisfaction with an Army paper on postwar Germany as his opening, Morgenthau enlarged his views into a plan for deindustrializing Germany—and redistributing its prewar foreign markets. When Prime Minister Churchill first heard the "plan" he objected violently, but two factors led him to change his mind. First, FDR and Morgenthau were insistent about it; second, he had come to Quebec anxious to discuss transitional financial arrangements between Britain and the United States, and Morgenthau offered to throw in a $6 billion credit. On that basis, Churchill thought Morgenthau's plan might be a bargain. Besides, he could count on the reality of European conditions to modify American "idealism."

At Yalta, therefore, Churchill was pleased by Roosevelt's unwillingness to go through with his Teheran plan for dividing Germany into small states. That discussion had ended weakly with Big Three instructions to the Foreign Ministers to report on "the best method for the study of plans to dismember Germany."[2] Churchill was alarmed, on the other hand, at FDR's willingness to take a figure of $20 billion as a basis for the discussion of German reparations with the Russians. Moscow, according to this decision, was to receive one-half and the Western powers were to divide the remaining sum.

Though this figure of $20 billion was later associated with the "Morgenthau Plan," no one could have been unhappier about it than the Secretary of the Treasury. He knew that unless German industry were rebuilt to make possible major extractions from current production, $20 billion was a pipedream. Morgenthau recognized Russian postwar economic needs, but he hoped to satisfy them like those of the British—with a multi-billion-dollar credit. Roosevelt's disinclination to talk with Stalin about American aid, even after Molotov specifically linked the two issues in conversations with Secretary of State Stettinius, probably made it inevitable, Morgenthau thought, that the Russians would demand their full measure of reparations. Indeed, the Yalta protocol specifically mentioned extractions from current production as one of three main sources for German reparations. If that decision were carried out, it meant the abandonment of anything like the Morgenthau Plan, including JCS 1067.

Morgenthau's opponents were equally upset by the Yalta protocol. In the first place, as Morgenthau suspected, many of them *were* concerned about the bolshevization of Germany, or of allowing Germany to work out its own long-deferred revolution. But they also feared a new nationalism which, though it might resist Soviet incursions, could be turned against the West once again. They were interested in reintegrating Germany into the world economy just as soon as possible, and in such a way as to minimize the threat of German nationalism. They feared that the President's "generosity" in promising huge reparations presaged a return to the patchwork financing of the 1920's, when private and public loans blew up in the debacle of the Great Depression. Thus the stimulus toward integrating Germany into the American-led world system originated much earlier than the 1947 economic crisis which produced the Truman Doctrine and the Marshall Plan. And it did not grow out of Soviet-American disagreements. As Secretary of War Stimson wrote the President after first hearing about the Morgenthau Plan: "Sound thinking teaches that prosperity in one part of the world helps to create prosperity in other parts of the world. It also teaches that poverty in one part of the world usually induces poverty in other parts. Enforced poverty is even worse, for it destroys the spirit not only of the victim but debases the victor. It would be just such a crime as the Germans themselves hoped to perpetuate upon their victims—it would be a crime against civilization itself."[3]

After Yalta a second issue appeared, one that had been lurking in the background since the Nazi-Soviet Pact—since Munich, in fact. Anglo-American negotiators in Berne had begun secret talks with SS General Karl Wolff concerning a surrender of all German forces in northern Italy. The Soviets therefore suspected the Western Allies of seeking a separate peace. Roosevelt's responses to Stalin's bitter messages on this subject did little to ease the situation, in large part, it is now apparent, because the President was in fact not fully informed about OSS maneuvers. Stalin's argument was not that the field commanders should refuse to accept a local surrender, but that the Western Allies had gone ahead with a plan which, if carried out, would permit the transfer of even more German divisions to face the Russians in the East.

"The Germans have 147 divisions on the Eastern Front," Stalin cabled Roosevelt on April 7, 1945. "They could safely withdraw from 15 to 20 divisions from the Eastern Front to aid their forces on the Western Front. Yet they have not done so, nor are they doing so." Instead, they were fighting for obscure places in Czechoslovakia which, Stalin asserted, they needed "just as much as a dead man needs a poultice. . . . You will admit that this behaviour on the part of the Germans is more than strange and unaccountable."[4] The actual casualty figures supported Stalin's complaint about German resistance in the East, even if they did not support his conjecture about the situation in Berne. In the ten days between April 11 and 20, 1945, 577 Germans died on the Western Front, and 7,587 perished in the East. 1,151 were wounded in the West, 35,414 in the East. But perhaps of even greater interest, 268,229 Germans were listed as missing in the West, but only 25,823 in the East.[5]

From Moscow, the Berne negotiations seemed intended to open the Western Front for an Anglo-American drive on Berlin. On April 1, 1945, Stalin summoned two of his marshals, G. K. Zhukov and I. S. Konev, to the Kremlin, where he read them a "telegram" which stated that the Anglo-American command was at that moment preparing such a thrust. "Well," said Stalin, "who is going to take Berlin, we or the Allies?"[6] Even though the Russian dictator had that same day informed Eisenhower that he regarded Berlin as strategically unimportant, this conference in the Kremlin signalled the beginning of the final all-out Russian offensive in the East: Stalin would beat the Western armies to the heart of the dying Third Reich. He was therefore furious when the surrender was signed first not in Berlin, where his soldiers had raised Soviet banners, but in Reims, where the Russians were represented by only an insignificant artillery general.[7]

Byrnes had taken his former assistant in the office of War Mobilization and Reconversion, General Lucius D. Clay, to see Roosevelt at the end of March. Having himself declined the President's offer of the High Commissionership, Byrnes suggested that Clay be named Deputy Military Governor of Germany under General Eisenhower. Both Byrnes and Clay were disturbed by the lack of firm guidelines for the treatment of Germany. "Instead of letting Clay speak," Byrnes recalled, FDR "began to talk rapidly and without rest, saying he had learned about Clay's experience as an army engineer building a large dam in Texas and suggesting that he consider the possibility of building a great power development in Central Europe."[8] Roosevelt died two weeks later, never realizing that Clay would help to build a different kind of great-power development in Europe. Ambassador Robert K. Murphy, Clay's political "commissar" after Eisenhower left Europe, wrote in his memoirs that the "Byrnes-Clay partnership not only changed the American conception of the German occupation, but affected the whole pattern of European events."[9] It is more accurate to say that this partnership clarified German policy, so that imperfect plans could be brought into line with overall American policy.

In a letter describing his initial activities and organizational plans to Assistant Secretary of War John J. McCloy, General Clay warned that Washington must rethink its position on the destruction of German war potential: the war had in fact destroyed it already. What industry was left was needed for even a very low standard of living. Hasty reparations removals could "make it impossible to bring order back to Germany."[10] Clay was also thinking of the impact of reparations upon all Europe's economic recovery. "Clay and I were convinced that the rehabilitation of the Ruhr was vital to our best interests," General Eisenhower was to write in *Crusade in Europe*. For American occupation officials, it was not simply a question of whether huge reparations *could* be extracted, but whether they *should* be extracted at the expense of re-establishing Germany's economy. A few officials protested this reasoning, but they were in a minority even in second-echelon posts. Clay also believed that any reparations policy depended upon successful four-power control in Germany. The Russians did not want war, Clay told Secretary Forrestal in 1946; he thought it would be possible to get along with them. But what if the Russians believed the world revolution was still on? Forrestal protested. "[Clay] admitted that that must necessarily condition what he had to say."[11]

Clay's estimate of total German destruction was soon revised downward by General John Hilldring in congressional testimony in the summer of 1945. In Cologne, Hilldring said, first reports of the destruction of the Ford plant had proved erroneous when "closer inspection revealed that falling walls and roof had buried the heavy machinery with layers of bricks and mortar which had in fact served to protect the equipment against the weather." Within a short time the plant was producing five hundred trucks a month. It was also estimated that I. G. Farben installations could be brought back to 90 per cent capacity within three months if the necessary input of raw materials was released by the Allies.[12] To a great extent, then, early rehabilitation of the Ruhr depended primarily upon policy decisions—especially reparations decisions.

Clay awaited the Potsdam Conference with considerable apprehension that Big Three agreements on reparations would make it impossible to integrate Germany into American policy. This fear was shared by his aides, Ambassador Averell Harriman and Truman's chief representative to the Allied Reparations Commission, Edwin Pauley. Pauley had been sparring with Soviet negotiators for some time, trying not to make a single definite commitment. At the San Francisco Conference he had queried Molotov closely about Soviet removals from Eastern Germany—suggesting pointedly that there ought to be some kind of accounting of these goods before any further settlements were reached. A few days after this conversation, Washington instructed the American chargé in Moscow, George F. Kennan, to invite Russian reparations negotiators to accompany their British and American counterparts on an inspection tour of German industrial areas before the Allied Reparations Commission began work in Moscow according to its Yalta directive.[13]

Kennan misinterpreted Washington's policy. Thinking it was seriously intended to implement a careful study of all the factors involved, he protested the instruction as a waste of time in a message to Ambassador Harriman, then in Washington helping to make the policy. "In the end," said Kennan's cable, "it will come down to a simple horse trade. How much are we going to make available to the Russians from our zones, and what price are we going to demand for it?" Harriman replied with a short lecture on the virtues of postponement: "The principal point is that Mr. Pauley's instructions are very firm and while *we may not reach any agreement* I have no fears about us giving in."[14]

The chief Russian reparations negotiator, Ivan Maisky, was perturbed by Washington's attitude on a whole series of questions related to German obligations and warned Kennan in general terms about the dangers of further dalliance. "If this delay continue[s]," said Maisky, "a number of countries interested in receiving reparations from Germany [will] take unilateral action to get what they [can]." Maisky was one of the few high-ranking Russian diplomats identified with a consistent "pro-Western" policy, but his plea that such unilateral seizures would be "highly undersirable" did not make the impression it might have had there not been so many complicated tangles to the overall reparations question.[15] Since mid-April Churchill had been urging Truman to keep troops stationed in advanced positions in the Russian-designated zone of Germany in order to exert diplomatic leverage. The Russians had countered by stating that four-power control in Berlin could not begin until proper zonal occupations were completed. At one point Churchill even went so far as to propose holding the line until "the whole question of the future relations of the two governments with the Soviet Government in Europe generally had been discussed *and settled*. . . ."[16]

Meanwhile Hitler's successor, Grand Admiral Karl Dönitz, had been trying to exploit the widening cracks in the Grand Alliance to preserve a remnant of the Third Reich. "In these critical days," began a Berlin radio broadcast on April 28, 1945, "the Führer has taken the major decision that, whatever else happens, the available strength of the Reich shall be concentrated on the attempt to prevent the Bolshevik flood from rolling westwards. This is not merely a German but a European decision. . . . It is indeed a ghastly and obscene irony that the men who are defending the Western world against the mighty hordes from hither Asia should be stabbed in the back by the Western democracies."[17]

A few days later, however, German officers were dispatched to the Russian command post outside Berlin with a similar mission, to negotiate a partial surrender in the East. "You can imagine the disintegration and political disorder in their ranks," Marshal Vasily I. Chuikov told his comrades, "for Goebbels to turn to us!"[18] On May 7, 1945, Dönitz delivered a farewell address to the Nazi officer corps, charging them to work with Anglo-American forces in "hopes of later retrieving our land from the Russians."[19] And he boasted to his captors that he had organized a radio campaign which had persuaded more than a million Germans, including the ablest scientists and technicians, to flee to the West.[20]

Stalin was no doubt chagrined at this powerful evidence that Russian rule would be resisted—perhaps with encouragement from the West. On May 9, 1945, he therefore issued a victory proclamation to the German people: "The Soviet Union is celebrating victory, although it does not intend to dismember or destroy Germany." So ended the dismemberment question, and by unilateral decision—albeit one that was more than acceptable to Great Britain and the United States. Nevertheless, it was a bad omen. Even as Stalin's message was being broadcast, Russian dismantling teams were busy reducing German factories for shipment eastward, while Russian political reassembling teams were equally busy organizing Communist party machinery in the Soviet zone. Their first tactic was to be a German land reform program which had been worked out in the Soviet Union during the war. In July one of its chief architects, a German Communist of long standing, was flown into Berlin with instructions to begin this second phase of political reassembly. The Russians assumed that the main stronghold for neo-Nazism in postwar Germany would be the agricultural areas, those parts of the German economy least directly affected by the war—and its lessons of destruction and defeat. The Germans will recover, Stalin told Yugoslav Communists, "and very quickly." "That is a highly developed industrial country with an extremely qualified and numerous working class and technical intelligentsia. Give them twelve to fifteen years and they'll be on their feet again . . . and then we'll have another go at it." [21]

At least initially, the Russian-sponsored land reform represented an effort to reduce the possibility of such resurgence, not a plan to introduce communist collectives. The Soviets redistributed Junker estates in Prussia to small farmers and to refugees coming into East Germany from the areas lost to Poland. "A new class was to be created," wrote J. P. Nettl, "whose existence and prosperity would replace the previous pattern of agricultural life. Clearly the existence of this new class was closely tied up with that of the regime in Eastern Germany. Irrespective of party politics the new agricultural proprietors as a body would support whatever Government protected them against the possibility of a return to the old owners." By 1950, 200,000 new farm owners had been created out of the holdings of the previous owners, and though they purchased and marketed goods through state monopolies, it was clear that Marxist ideology was at best ancillary to the aim of using land reform and local communists to achieve whatever degree of "people's democracy" best suited Russian national interests.[22] That was also the prime factor, it is now apparent, in the Russian desire to move Poland westward several hundred miles: it made any regime in Warsaw dependent upon Russian good will to protect its new frontiers against resurgent German nationalism.

United States interests, on the other hand, centered in the desire to build a world order politically and economically oriented toward American capitalism. JCS 1067, a presidential adviser told Lucius Clay after Roosevelt's death, "was assembled by economic idiots! It makes no sense to forbid the most skilled workers in Europe from producing as much as they can for a continent desperately short of everything." This divergence of interests in Germany, as Maisky said, could produce unilateral acts on both sides. Although there were plenty of grounds for complaint that the Russians had been carting away German resources, such actions had begun on both sides even as the war ended. Special intelligence officers, operating with advance units of the American Army, sought out German physicists and rocket experts to prevent them from falling into Russian hands. On June 14, 1945, Secretary of the Interior Harold Ickes informed Truman that northwest Europe would be desperately short of coal once the cold weather began. Truman responded by directing Eisenhower to make available 25 million tons of West German coal for export over the next nine months. The President sent Moscow an "information copy" of the directive, as he put it, "to avoid delay."[23]

Pauley went to Moscow prepared to insist that because of Russian "looting," the Yalta protocol on reparations would have to be changed. He insisted flatly that there would be no reparations out of current production until the Germans could export enough to pay for essential imports. He topped it all, however, with a statement that the United States could no longer commit itself to *any* total reparations figure.[24]

"I want to make it clear that not only the Russians have sinned," Stalin told the others at Potsdam, handing them a report from General Zhukov which estimated that more than eleven thousand railroad cars had been removed from West Germany by British and American authorities. If so, Truman responded, it had not been authorized; he would have General Eisenhower look into it at once. The American delegation made no further comment on the Zhukov report at Potsdam, but a separate memorandum drafted by Pauley's aides admitted that the Russian paper was "probably largely correct." It insisted only that the equipment described by Zhukov was not needed for peacetime uses, "whereas the Russian removals observed, such as agricultural equipment, sewing machines and textile machines, are certainly not war potentials."

The term "war potentials," like that other Potsdam phrase, "essential imports," was incapable of close definition. Both symbolized larger ambiguities in the Potsdam agreement which finally emerged. Secretary of State Byrnes had opened the discussion of German reparations by asking—"not in any attitude of hostility"—if it was true that the Russians had taken large quantities of equipment and material out of Germany. Surprisingly, Molotov admitted the removals and immediately offered to subtract $300 million from Soviet claims as payment. Byrnes responded by asking if Molotov seriously contended that $300 million would cover the removals. Almost at once, Molotov agreed to deduct $1 billion, "and thus dispose of the question." Later he offered to deduct still another billion dollars provided Russia received a fixed amount of industrial equipment from the Ruhr—"say two billion."

Byrnes had never intended to debate the point; what he was after was a totally new solution. Rejecting each of the Russian bids, the Secretary of State proposed instead that each power take reparations from its own occupation zone. He was willing to make available from the Ruhr and other parts of the Western zones not $2 billion in reparations but 25 per cent of the plants which might eventually be declared eligible for reparations. The total dollar figure could not be determined until there was agreement on what level of industry would be permitted to the Germans. Obviously, the lower the level, the more plants would become surplus to the needs of the Germany peacetime economy. The American proposal, therefore, had a built-in incentive for the Russians to demand a low standard of living for the Germans, especially when it was coupled with Byrnes's proposed amendment to the Yalta agreement on reparations from current production: "The proceeds of exports from current production and stocks shall be available in the first place for payment . . . [of essential] imports."

Before final agreement on the German standard of living, Byrnes proposed that the United States ship some plants as an advance payment against the final reparations figure. Ten per cent of all plants designated for shipment to the Russian zone were to be sent without any compensation from the East, but 15 per cent were to be in return for Russian food and coal shipments. All plants were to be dismantled and shipped within two years, while the raw materials were to be shipped in lots over the next five years. (This became important later when the United States justified suspension of reparations deliveries in May 1946 in part because the Russians had supposedly broken their promise concerning shipment of raw materials.) Stalin and Molotov accepted these terms only when Byrnes informed the latter, on July 31, 1945, that he and the President were leaving Potsdam the next day—whether or not the issue had been resolved.[25]

Molotov had seen the implications in the American proposal at the outset of their discussions eight days before:

> MR. MOLOTOV: said that would not the Secretary's suggestion mean that each country would have a free hand in their own zone and would act entirely independently of the others?
>
> THE SECRETARY: said that was true in substance.[26]

From an American point of view the Byrnes "ultimatum" had three distinct advantages over Yalta. First, it eliminated reference to any total figure and tied reparations to a four-power level-of-industry agreement; second, it virtually eliminated the possibility that the Russians would get any reparations from current production in the West (and under later Anglo-American interpretations, perhaps even from the East if it could be managed); and third, it forced the Russians to continue "looting" East Germany if they expected to get anything like $10 billion. Samuel Lubell grasped these points when he wrote in 1946: "The extent to which the handling of reparations . . . produced the effects of an economic iron curtain splitting Europe in two is not generally appreciated."[27]

Relieved that what he considered the worst features of the Yalta agreement had been eliminated at Potsdam, General Clay seemed confident that new four-power agreements could be negotiated on the basis of the Potsdam protocol. "We are finally moving on quadri-partite control," he wrote privately in August, "and I am still an optimist with respect to its possibility of success. I have found our Russian colleagues, while fully realistic, desirous of a co-ordinated and co-operative treatment of Germany. They know what they *want* and it is always easy to do business with those who do know their own desires. I think that we, too, know our objectives now, and that with patience and understanding much can be accomplished."[28]

No sooner had he finished that letter, however, than the French began obstructing the Allied Control Council, making it difficult, then impossible to carry out the Potsdam agreements on the creation of centralized economic agencies. Though the French had been granted a seat on the Control Council and the Reparations Commission, they continued to challenge the validity of all Big Three agreements on Germany. This challenge was particularly embarrassing to the Anglo-American representatives, who had demanded that Paris be given an equal role in Germany. Moscow suspected that France was being allowed to block the Potsdam agreements with the connivance of Britain and the United States, but Clay was just as put off by French behavior as were the Soviets. Not only was France uncooperative in the Control Council, but General de Gaulle had set about incorporating the French zone into metropolitan France. On top of that, he was publicly demanding amputation of the Saar and an equal share in the Ruhr. De Gaulle's determination to flout all Big Three agreements was the first indication that the Potsdam "ultimatum" might boomerang—that it might produce zonal boundaries within West Germany which would thwart stated American purposes. It was this development that Clay had not anticipated when he wrote that things were finally getting moving.

France was running its zone at a huge deficit—the highest in all three Western zones. French soldiers and officers lived better in occupied Germany than they had before the war at home; and it was all charged off to the Germans as occupation costs. Great Britain's economic policies in Germany threatened to produce the same result through slow disintegration. The Labour government was theoretically committed to socializing its own economy, but its military representatives in occupied Germany seemed determined to implement a relatively conservative economic policy there. Suspended between two economic policies, and American disapproval of "socialism" in any Western zone, London proved unable to carry out either. The result was that Ruhr factories and coal mines failed to produce at anywhere near prewar levels. In 1945 Ruhr output was 25 per cent of prewar level, in 1946 only 40 per cent, in 1947 50 per cent, and in 1948 still only 60 per cent.[29]

The American Military Government developed a series of official reasons for this poor performance, including the specious argument that Russian removals had drained the Western zones.[30]

But American officials soon lost patience with Anglo-French obstructionism and difficulties which undercut, for example, Clay's efforts to restore Germany to the world economy in the fall of 1945 by introducing the dollar trade system into the American zone.

The desire to introduce the dollar system was the first in a series of plans to stabilize German currency which continued for the next three years and culminated in the 1948 currency reform, which the Russians met with the Berlin Blockade. This long-range policy put big-power agreement on reparations in a second priority below German reintegration. "To the east of the line," explained Lewis H. Brown, chairman of the board of Johns-Manville, and one of those commissioned by Clay at various times to report to the American people on the situation in Germany, "the iron fist of the police state enforces the planned-economy concepts of Russia. To the west of the line, there is 'Schachtism,' control, and bureaucracy, but the philosophy of private enterprise is not yet without honor and there is still hope for its restoration."[31]

As this situation became clear to the American Military Government in Germany, Clay's chief aide, General William H. Draper, Jr., a former Wall Street investment lawyer who had been put in charge of the economics division of the American occupation, including decartelization, slowed down the deindustrialization program. Both Clay and Draper were determined to leave a liberal safety margin in the American zone should four-power economic cooperation break down completely. Clay's objectives were underscored in the American Military Government's first "level-of-industry" report completed on September 10, 1945, in Berlin. At Potsdam it had been agreed that a German "level-of-industry" would be determined, but it had not been stipulated whether that estimate was to constitute a maximum or minimum standard.

Draper's Industry Division, for example, interpreted the Potsdam agreement and the "intent of American policy to be to incite and encourage the German people to contribute to the welfare of Europe by holding out to them the promise that they will be permitted to raise their own standards indefinitely, so long as they help their neighbors up to the same level."[32] It was this interpretation which went into the interim "level-of-industry" report that Berlin sent to Washington for approval. It stated: "The conclusion cannot be avoided that the conflict between an extreme degree of industrial disarmament spread over a number of key industries and the goal of maintaining a minimum German standard of living according to the assumed formula while providing for the costs of occupying forces seems insoluble under conditions such as those brought about by losses of territory."[33]

This report touched off the first serious Soviet-American disagreement in the Allied Control Council, and its impact was twofold: it justified American reluctance to ship reparations until a fuller accounting was available in the East, and it implied once again that the Russians would have to choose between the Polish-German frontier they had imposed and reparations from the Western zones. Even before the interim report had been completed, the Soviets had proposed speeding things up in the Reparations Commission by allowing Soviet participation in determining reparations properties in the West. The State Department had responded to this proposal by insisting that Russia would first have to agree to treat Germany as an economic unit for reparations. "This means that Soviet removals of industrial capital equipment from Eastern Zone must be based on plan arrived at among four powers, which will treat each zone as part of a unified Germany after reparation removals to subsist without external assistance." Otherwise, the Western zones would make their own computations.[34]

But as Clay had recently said, the Russians were and had been perfectly prepared to go ahead with German economic centralization—it was the French who were holding up four-power agreement on this point. The Soviet Foreign Office replied to the State Department by offering to allow inspection of the Soviet zone by Western officials, but it refused to accept responsibility for a single four-power plan for reparations collections. To this end, it cited the Potsdam agreement as support: "The Berlin Conference not only did not contemplate the drawing up of such a four-zone plan (it accepted the principle proposed by the American delegation of collection of reparations by zones—an Eastern Zone and Western Zones), but established one procedure of reparations collections in the Eastern Zone and another in the Western Zones."[35] This had been done, the Russian note concluded, because all parties at Potsdam had recognized that most of Germany's industry was to be found in the West.

While the Potsdam Protocol bore out the Soviet contention that the amount and character of reparations to be made available from the West "shall be made by the Control Council," it also said that these reparations would be subject to final approval by the zone commander. But at the London Foreign Ministers' Conference, the Russians served notice that since the Potsdam agreement on reparations still had not been fulfilled, they were justified in returning to earlier positions—in this case, a demand that the Ruhr be internationalized. The beginnings of a Franco-Soviet alliance on this question raised very serious problems indeed for American policy.

Meanwhile, Robert Murphy, Clay's political adviser, wrote the State Department:

> It is gradually being realized by officials here that any wholesale transfer of German plants to liberated areas will greatly disturb production generally for several years and is likely to drag down living standards for all concerned. In other words, it is becoming clearer that extreme, ill-considered de-industrialization of Germany may well have the effect of creating and extending chaos in Europe.[36]

Murphy's statement of the German situation, the impasse at the London Foreign Ministers' Conference, and the continuing failure of Western economic policy in Germany, all called for a review of policy directives. In November Clay and Murphy were therefore called to Washington for consultations with the War and State departments. Clay reported that the French had declared they would hold up the creation of centralized agencies for Germany until their proposals for internationalization of the Ruhr and the Rhineland had been decided. It was impossible, Clay said, for his experts in Berlin to reach any decision on how to calculate the peacetime level of industry (and therefore what would be available for reparations) without a clear decision on all these matters. Had the State Department applied any diplomatic pressure on the French to cooperate? he asked.

The answer was no. Then, said Clay, the Soviets could not be expected to agree to central agencies either. To Clay's insistence that the French must be dealt with first, the Department replied that the Soviets had not demonstrated any intention to carry out the political and economic principles of the Potsdam agreements. And their behavior in Germany—press control, support of favored political parties, unilateral land reform, and nationalization—were cited as indications of very ominous developments in the future. Somewhat annoyed by these statements, Clay argued that the French had done some of the same things, as indeed had all the zonal commanders. Despite Clay's arguments, State Department officials remained cool toward efforts to press the French at that moment. They agreed with Clay, however, that it was necessary to restate American reparations policy. The statement released at the conclusion of the consultations on December 11, 1945, produced a significant change within Big Four relationships.[37] American reparations goals, it said, aimed at a "balanced economic position," and did not seek "to eliminate or weaken German industries of a peaceful character, in which Germany has produced effectively for world markets."[38] Although surrounding paragraphs were much the same as in previous policy declarations, the statement that Germany should be allowed to resume production for "world markets" raised new questions, especially as there was still no four-power agreement on what level of industry was to be permitted that country. If German industries were to produce effectively for world markets, didn't that mean increasing support industries, iron and steel? "Serious repercussions were inevitable," wrote two American reparations experts. "The Russians would not take this lying down."[39] They would not accept a unilateral decision to raise the level of industry and reduce the number of plants available for reparations.

Once again, however, the unanticipated happened. The Russians said they were prepared to talk about raising the German level of industry—provided the Western powers first agreed to large-scale reparations from current production. Moscow had evidently had some second thoughts about its economic policy in Germany. Those who originally favored immediate dismantling had persuaded Stalin with two arguments: the need to make certain Germany would not rise again to dominate Central Europe (at least until Russia had recovered fully), and the lack of alternative sources to rehabilitate the Soviet economy. When these removals did not meet either expectation, opposition elements, led by Anastas Mikoyan, gained a chance to offer counter-proposals. Mikoyan's group could even cite, ironically, the recent American reparations declaration to discount the likelihood that there would ever be very many plants made available from the West under any circumstances. But Soviet-owned corporations in East Germany, Mikoyan asserted, could produce both for reparations and for German consumption.

Having received a green light in Moscow, Mikoyan hurried to Germany. "Remember," he told Russian aides there, "that economics determines politics. Speaking metaphorically, you are Soviet colonists. If it should happen that our government decides to withdraw its troops from Germany, you will be left there to face a bitter struggle with capitalist competitors. Remember that the most important thing is the solvency of the enterprise, its profits!"[40] In 1946 more than three thousand industrial properties, comprising nearly 30 per cent of East Germany's industrial output, were converted into state-owned businesses.[41]

Mikoyan's triumph in the corridors of Soviet power had powerful repercussions in the West, especially within the inner circles of the American Military Government. The new Soviet policy seemed to Clay to be directed toward converting East Germany into a launching site for all-German communism. How else to explain Soviet proposals for all-German political parties, constant "leftist" agitation, and now the renewed demand for large-scale reparations from current production? The more sensitive Clay became to every hint of Soviet-inspired subversion, the more vigorously he opposed any form of socialism in the West. This made his political tasks more difficult, for in many instances the Social Democrats were in a majority in his zone. Efforts to contain socialism exposed the American Military Government to all the left political parties in Germany, from the Social Democrats to the Russian-sponsored Socialist Unity party, a 1946 fusion of Eastern zone Communists and Social Democrats. In Germany, perhaps even more than in other West European countries, opposition to Russia became at once opposition to socialism.

The predominant American view held that it was worth the risk, however, as Germany was the "spark plug" of the whole European economy. This attitude was well expressed in an exchange between Alfred P. Sloan, chairman of the board of General Motors, and Bernard Baruch, one of the few who still held to the general idea expressed in the defunct "Morgenthau Plan." It began on October 31, 1945, when Sloan asked Baruch if he still believed Germany's foreign markets should be redistributed to other nations. When Baruch replied testily that he never said anything he did not believe, Sloan lectured him on GM's outlook on international trade and the world economy. To eliminate production in any area, said Sloan, let alone in that nation which had been the "spark plug" of the whole European economy, would lower living standards everywhere. "In my small way I continually advocate Americans exporting their capital and knowhow to develop countries otherwise backward in relation to the United States in industrial production. . . . And I have always been of the belief and conviction . . . that that is the real attack on the problem." General Motors, he concluded, had already spent over $600 million getting ready to supply the pent-up demands of American consumers. The German "question," that is, German industrial recovery, would affect that demand, if not right away, then all the more ultimately.

"We were, and still are, facing Germany's war potentiality," protested Baruch. It was still impossible to divorce that nation's potential industrial contribution from this terrible political reality. That was why he had long advocated building up other nations to replace "those production and distribution centers called Germany . . ." Norway, Denmark, Belgium, France, Italy, Greece, and others were all more suitable outlets for American capital.

Sloan's final reply was sent on November 30. The Potsdam agreements on Germany were a dismal failure, he argued. It was clear that to carry them out the United States would have to feed Germany. Conclusion after conclusion followed, each more worrisome than the one before, until Sloan reached the classic post–World War II justification for any and all policies: a continuance of the present situation in Germany would cause a tragic retreat into isolationism.

> Now I recognize that if the production facilities formerly in Germany were eliminated it is bound to stimulate, in degree, the business opportunities of adjacent countries including England and incidentally ourselves. But I want to point out to you—and I say this from intimate experience . . .—the other countries that you mention are just not comparable with Germany in their efficiency, their ability to work, and all the other things that form the foundation stones of an industrial development and production on the basis of efficiency. So far as we in General Motors are concerned, we were glad to have been able to operate in Germany, prewar, and it was frequently passed on to us by the German Economic Ministry that we had contributed much to the expansion of industry in Germany and to the advancement of their technological position in the areas in which we were operating.
>
> But, on the other hand, when it comes to operating in some of the countries that you mention on the second page of your letter, we would not be at all interested. For instance:—There is nothing that could convince us in General Motors that it was either sound or desirable or worthwhile to undertake an operation of any consequence in a country like France.[42]

If a split with Russia was now unavoidable—as a result of Moscow's desire to go back to the Yalta agreement—it was crucial to manage it so that the British and French fell in step with American policy.[43] The output of the Soviet plants in East Germany, Clay observed, were "proving an important contribution to a disrupted economy." In April 1946 the United States demanded that all German exports be pooled to pay for "essential exports." As might have been expected, this proposal met "with objection after objection" from the Russians.

"Actually there has been little removal of reparations in the western zones," Clay admitted privately, "and yet their economy is not on as substantial a basis as it is in the Soviet zone, where the removals have been heavy. The reason for this is quite simple. The Soviet zone is self-contained. The western zones are not self-contained, and the existence of artificial boundaries and restrictions has retarded economic recovery until almost complete economic collapse threatens."[44] Despite this admission, the American Military Government publicly declared that the Russian removals were the cause of the crisis in the West. American officials also insisted that the Russians had broken their promise to deliver raw materials. In May 1946 Clay suspended all reparations deliveries to the East on his own initiative, ostensibly to force the Russians to acquiesce in the higher level-of-industry agreement, but actually so that Washington could reconsider the whole German question.

Clay now insisted that the Russians agree to pool exports from all zones to pay for essential imports, even before four-power agreement on the future of the German economy. To the Russians this was a clear repudiation of the United States' Potsdam promise to ship reparations *before* such agreement. And it demanded access to the output of the Soviet zone, leaving little or nothing for the Mikoyan plan. Meanwhile, nothing was being done to correct British and French occupation policies, especially their practice of underpricing exports (which even Clay had denounced as disguised reparations) and their charging off excessive military expenditures to German funds. Even if the Russians agreed to pool exports, could Clay guarantee a four-power agreement? For as long as the pooling existed, it would drain the Eastern Zone—and the situation Clay complained of would be reversed with a vengeance.[45]

Most Americans regarded Russian reaction to Clay's order as typically unreasonable, especially as it seemed part of a whole series of actions and reactions which increased Russian-American tensions. In February Byrnes had sent the British and Russians copies of the proposed security treaty over Germany which he had first mentioned at London the previous fall and later urged upon Stalin informally at the Moscow Conference. Foreign Minister Molotov had informed Byrnes just before the April session of the Paris Conference of Foreign Ministers that he had some objections to the American draft.

In Paris the Russian surprised Byrnes by declaring that the treaty draft appeared to postpone German disarmament until after the occupation period. So the Secretary of State suggested a quadripartite inspection to insure that demilitarization was in fact carried out. Byrnes's account of this confrontation does not, however, mention General Clay's insistence that if such an inspection were to be useful it must include "the use of German industrial production for war purposes." This gambit effectively stymied the Russians, because they knew very well (as they themselves had argued) that production for war purposes and for peaceful purposes was often difficult to separate.

Consequently, such a public inspection would give General Clay an opportunity to demonstrate for the press in all the Western countries that he had been right in charging that the Russians were exporting "excessive amounts" from industrial facilities, and also right, therefore, in demanding "concurrent" efforts toward pooling all German exports in exchange for further reparations shipments. Backed into this position, the Russians would only agree to an inspection to see if all German soldiers had been demobilized.[46] The War Department had already arranged a German tour for leading editors and newspapermen in April 1946. According to one of Clay's assistants, the tour would be a marvelous opportunity to show them that without centralized agencies the American zone would "become a large WPA project for the United States."[47]

Less than a month after he had halted reparations deliveries, Clay proposed merging the Western zones. If some agreement could not be reached soon, he warned his superiors in Washington, "we face a deteriorating German economy which will create a political unrest favorable to the development of communism in Germany."[48] Since Clay had also convinced the press on this point, the principal obstacle was now the French demand for the Saar and a share of the Ruhr. Following the London Conference the previous fall, Russo-French agreement on that point had grown into a wedge which split every attempt to break down zonal barriers in the West. On July 10 Molotov delivered a speech on Germany's future which handed to Byrnes the hammer he was looking for to knock out that wedge. Attacking all plans that called for the "agrarianization" of Germany—an attack in line with the new Soviet policy of building up state corporations—Molotov then promised wide-scale development of peaceful industries. "I realized at once the strength of this appeal," Byrnes recalled. The West needed a comprehensive and effective answer. Two days later Byrnes and Bevin announced their intention to merge the British and American zones. Bevin also implied that the Ruhr would soon be turning out a strong list of exportable commodities. But this statement raised other problems, particularly among those who had reason to fear an industrialized Germany; and it presumed the French had been brought into line, which they hadn't at this point. Finally, Byrnes wanted to deliver a speech that would embarrass the Russians and make it impossible for them to talk one way to the Germans and another way to the Poles, to whom they had promised security in exchange for their eastern lands.

Clay encouraged Byrnes to develop and blend these concerns into a major address at a meeting of American occupation officials in Stuttgart. In the audience too would be local German officials who needed American encouragement against the Russian and socialist ideological offensive. International radio coverage was planned, and news reporters had been tipped that Byrnes would make an important speech. Two decisions in Germany must be reached at once, Byrnes began: to move ahead on an all-German political administration, and to find a final settlement on postwar German territorial boundaries. Austria should be free and independent, while France's right to the Saar could not be denied. As for Silesia and other eastern territories, however, these had only been transferred to Polish administrative authority by Soviet action before Potsdam. There was nothing in that conference's protocol which committed the other Allies to any settlement beyond the general agreement that Warsaw should receive compensation in the West for land lost to the Russians in the East. The German-Polish boundary could not be fixed until the final peace negotiations.

The revelation to a local German audience and an international radio audience that the German eastern boundary had not been fixed exposed the most sensitive nerve in Russian-American relations in Europe. It is not so well understood that the Stuttgart speech also dealt with French obstructionism. As Murphy wrote later, "After studying the problem from every angle, Byrnes's advisers came up with an adroit scheme." After conceding the Saar, the Secretary would endeavor to cast serious doubt upon the finality of the cessions to Poland. By conceding the Saar, Byrnes made additional French demands seem greedy; by re-arguing the Eastern border, Byrnes created separate interests for France and Russia, or so he hoped, at any rate. The speech forced Molotov to release a memorandum he had sent to Warsaw admitting that the boundary had not been finally fixed, but asserting that this was only a formality, as the Western powers had already acquiesced in the decision to remove the populations from these areas.[49]

But there was more to the speech than refencing, diplomatic or otherwise. Byrnes had insisted that the four powers must now get on with the problem of an all-German political administration. His suggestion for the composition of this new all-German government would have confirmed the political process that had already taken place in the American zone:

> It is the view of the American Government that the provisional government . . . should be a German national council composed of democratically responsible minister-presidents or other chief officials of the several states or provinces which have been established in each of the four zones.

This council was to have been charged with the preparation of a new German constitution. It could be expected that with a 3 to 1 majority on the council, the constitution would satisfy most Western goals.

Former Under Secretary of State Sumner Welles anticipated Russian objections in his own sharp criticisms of the Stuttgart speech in the *New York Herald Tribune*. Byrnes's speech demonstrated more clearly than ever, Welles argued, the disastrous results brought on by the policy of postponement. "In a panic effort to circumvent Russia, whose increasing influence in Germany our own lack of foresight alone made possible, we have declared our intention of rebuilding a unified and strong Germany, under a central government. Such a Germany can once more bring ruin to the rest of the world."[50]

Behind the furor, American policy-makers quickly moved to

insure economic recovery in the American and British zones—now called, Orwell-like, "Bizonia." "If we delay," Allen Dulles admonished the 1946 National Foreign Trade Convention, "I rather fear we will play into the hands of those who favor a different kind of economy than our own. . . . Obviously failure by the Western powers to make the free economy system work in Germany is a strong argument for communism." Conversely, a free-enterprise system working "in Germany" would be a powerful argument for capitalism everywhere in Europe.

Clay moved in a variety of ways to prevent the infection of Bizonia with socialism. He permitted the government in Hesse to include an article in its constitution providing for socialization of industry only after it had been submitted to a separate referendum. When 71 per cent of the voters approved the article anyway, Clay decided that while it would remain in the constitution, its operation would be suspended "for the time being."[51] The issue in Bizonia was made more difficult because, at least in theory, the Social Democrats were supported by the British Labour government. When the two zones were merged, a German executive economic committee was created on which the Social Democrats gained a majority and promptly pushed for state ownership of all major industries. Acting under his own impulses and Washington's orders, Clay enlisted the collaboration of his colleagues in the British Military Government to block this development. The bizonal administration was reorganized so that an economic council, on which the Christian Democrats (headed by Dr. Ludwig Erhard) held the majority, became responsible for such decisions.[52]

Although the French had still not been brought around by the end of 1946, their arguments and appeals had been effectively nullified. This did not mean that American policy-makers looked on Germany as securely tied into the American system. Far from it. The question was, Reinhold Niebuhr wrote in the *Nation*, "Will Germany Go Communist?" "We have learned the necessity of strategically resisting Russian penetration into Western Europe. But unless we support our political policy with an adequate economic policy, Soviet ideology will cross over our strategic barrier."[53]

The Moscow Foreign Ministers' Conference of March–April 1947 opened at a time when American policy-makers still were not sure they had acted soon enough to save Germany—or the rest of Europe. The sessions had no sooner begun than President Truman went before Congress to alert the nation to immediate dangers in Greece and Turkey and the general peril. While the speech had direct repercussions in the conference, the Foreign Ministers probably would have deadlocked on Germany in any event. The delegates from the Western powers believed that Stalin thought he had a pat hand.

In part this belief stemmed from the fact that the Soviets had not responded in expected fashion to the Stuttgart speech. On October 28 Stalin granted an interview to Hugh Baillie, president of the United Press, in which he indicated that he too thought it was possible to go ahead immediately with German unification, politically as well as economically. And Foreign Minister Molotov opened the Moscow conference with concrete proposals for unifying trade unions and political parties in all four zones. He questioned whether the Western powers had really carried out de-Nazification policies, but said the Soviet Union was prepared also to talk about raising the level-of-industry agreement for Germany and integrating German exports into the European economy. Of course, the Russians still insisted upon reparations out of current production, and resurrected the figure of $10 billion to be extracted over a twenty-year period.

The Russian delegation then presented a detailed plan for a provisional German democratic constitution which could be quickly put into operation by the Allied Control Commission. This document envisioned a German parliament with two chambers, the formation of national political parties, the secret ballot, local self-government on the same principles, and practically all the freedoms guaranteed in the American Bill of Rights! The next day Secretary Marshall's bipartisan adviser, John Foster Dulles, wrote to Senator Vandenberg that the Russians were for German unity because they felt that under the present circumstances it would give them all the country—and, for that matter, probably all the continent soon after. According to the American Ambassador to Moscow, Walter Bedell Smith, the American delegation was prepared to accept continued separation of Germany rather than acquiesce in any plan that would eventually serve Soviet purposes.[54]

While the American delegates seemed overly suspicious of their own Bill of Rights, they had received a memorandum prepared in the State Department on Communist power in the German trade union movement which confirmed all their worst fears: "Growing Communist control in the huge German trade union movement is a fact the importance of which can scarcely be overestimated. The recent Ruhr strikes, which are probably going to be repeated, are only an indication of what power such control gives the Communists and their Soviet masters." What made the situation so difficult, however, was that the majorities in the trade unions were not Communists but Social Democrats, who were pushing for what they called a co-determination policy: "This is probably the most important and universal demand of German trade unions today." Co-determination was another way of saying that the Social Democrats, like British Labour, wanted the socialization of major industries, or at least an equal voice in how they should be run. This had been the key issue in the recent strikes; and it was a perfect one for the Communists to exploit with great hopes of success. Vigorous countermeasures had to be taken at once, including all-out aid to the noncommunist trade unions. Even more important, under no circumstances could the Russian proposal for all-German unions be accepted until it was certain that these unions would remain democratic—in other words, capitalist oriented.[55]

In what Hannah Arendt's preface calls the most important political book about postwar Germany, German philosopher Karl Jaspers has criticized sharply the Adenauer-shaped regime which emerged out of the ashes of Nazism, but he cautions that Germany still owes the man a great debt for saving it from communism: "You could not read a Social Democratic platform in those days without cold shudders running down your spine, without the feeling that a united Germany recognized by Stalin might undergo something like the rape of Czechoslovakia."[56] While Jaspers specified the Social Democratic party, the Socialist Unity party in the Russian zone had in fact made a more definite statement that, while it aimed at socialism by democratic means, it would "resort to revolutionary means if the capitalist class departs from the basis of democracy."[57]

Dulles and a minority group within the American delegation at Moscow wanted to meet the Russian challenge with a counter-offer: neutralization of the Ruhr under four-power management and mutual withdrawal from the rest of Germany, East and West, by all foreign troops. Dulles apparently believed that Ruhr resources could thus be used by all of Europe, any future German menace eliminated at once, and the United States could then begin rebuilding Western Europe through France. Murphy and Clay were adamantly opposed, and the debate-within-a-debate raged all through the conference. Like Sloan, Clay argued that France was unstable, and that under this plan the Russians would not evacuate their zone, only expand into the Ruhr. "We had created a political vacuum in Central Europe," Clay insisted, and "unless we could restore some sort of economic opportunity to the German people, there was nothing we could do to prevent Communism from taking over. Therefore, we had the problem of rebuilding Germany."[58]

Clay and Murphy won the battle of the position papers at Moscow, but they knew it had been a close one, saved only by Russian recalcitrance on all issues. This was the first big-power conference for Secretary Marshall, who wanted to test every possibility of agreement, short of accepting the Russian centralization plan. He suggested in reply to Molotov's proposals that the United States might be willing to agree to some reparations out of current production when the level of industry was raised, but only to replace those that would be lost from the West because of new requirements established for German production, and only if the Russians agreed to earlier American proposals for pooling exports.

The Secretary of State then submitted a plan for a German government based on strong federal principles. The United States, he added, wanted no central German government which could be taken over at some future date by a determined minority. When Molotov argued in reply that the German people should have some say in the kind of government they were going to have,

Ernest Bevin snapped that he would not have European security decided by a plebiscite in Germany.

The Russians opposed the Anglo-American political proposal because such a scheme was most easily converted (or reconverted perhaps) into separatist states in East and West, a fear already partially realized so far as they were concerned in Bizonia's very existence. On this issue, each side was negotiating more out of fear than from strength or weakness. The Americans had a right to be concerned when the Russians put forward a plan for a united Germany; the old worry about an alliance between Russia and Germany was still in their minds. The Russians, on the other hand, naturally were uneasy about a government that could easily fragment and regroup under Western guidance and inspiration.

One material result of the Moscow Conference was a fatal weakening of the Franco-Russian entente. Any mention of a strong German central government always stirred deep fears in the French delegation. Nor did Georges Bidault's private conversations with Stalin ease his mind, despite the latter's expression of continued interest in internationalization of the Ruhr. As Bidault confided to American leaders, a communist government in Germany would demand tight control over the Ruhr anyway, so the issue might become academic unless France conceded somewhat to the Anglo-American position. Paris could not change its public stance all at once, however, because of the strength of the French Communist party. If any additional evidence of the communist "international conspiracy" were necessary to the American delegation, Bidault's remark certainly supplied it.

After the Moscow Conference, General Clay invited several groups—economic writers and policy-makers—to visit Bizonia and report to the American people on what they observed. Earlier reports favoring stepped-up American aid had been filed by former President Hoover—whose view was that America should sign a peace treaty with a West German republic and then help it to stand on its own—and by Averell Harriman's special committee on European economic problems. But Clay wanted to bring these reports up to date. The Moscow Conference, Clay's briefing officers told the visitors, proved that the Russians would do all they could to obstruct German recovery.

Actually the Russian demand for $10 billion could have stimulated German production, since the Soviets wished to extract it from current production. This could have been accomplished, of course, only under a centralized political and economic system. "We did not want Germany quickly rebuilt as a great, modern industrial machine," John Foster Dulles explained on an American radio broadcast after the conference. But what he really meant, as he wrote to Senator Vandenberg, was that the present zonal system provided a shield against communist penetration of the West. As for reconstruction in Bizonia, it was full speed ahead. "It is too late," wrote Joseph Ridder, editor of the *New York Journal of Commerce*. "It is too late . . . to wait longer to rectify the economic situation in the British and American zones." Then, in a letter to Navy Secretary Forrestal, he added privately: " I came away convinced that we have got to put at least five billion dollars a year for five years into this situation if we do not want the Russians to take over all of Europe, certainly the whole continent, possibly the Scandinavian countries and possibly also England."[59] Ridder's comments were hardly original after Marshall's famous commencement speech at Harvard, but they were especially welcome in Washington.

Fortune's editors had an effective variation on the same theme which cleverly turned inside out all the phrases about "plans" for Germany: "In the case of Germany, the flow of private investment into the Rhine Valley is the only way of accomplishing that 'internationalization' of the powerhouse of Europe about which the planners are always talking. Here is the key not only to taking Europe off the American taxpayer's shoulders, but to much more."[60]

United States Steel Export Company's George Wolf, for another example, thought such aid to Germany was the key to the success of the Marshall Plan and ultimately, therefore, to the survival of free enterprise in the United States. "Men of the Trade, Industry and Commerce of the world must be called upon to undertake the task, but not as deputies of governments, but rather as pioneers willing and eager to accept the challenge of restoring order, productivity, self-respect and happiness to a desponding world, harassed, thwarted and demoralized by enforced idleness resultant from smothering governmental barriers."[61]

But the fullest *Report on Germany* filed that summer by a returning visitor from Clay's headquarters was that of Lewis H. Brown of Johns-Manville. Brown began by reviewing the European war in a way which minimized Russian contributions to the Allied victory over Germany and thus justified all that he was to say in his conclusions. America's position at Potsdam had been hampered not by the military results of the war, he continued, but by unnecessary promises to Stalin. Moreover, since Roosevelt's death and Churchill's retirement, no one could effectively dispute Stalin's claim to so-called "secret agreements."

As the Russian-American split widened into full-scale Cold War, few were willing to correct Brown's distorted view of the immediate past: "The combination of the failure to get Germany on her feet, the retardance of recovery in Europe, and the threat to Britain's dollar position is threatening to curtail exports from America. As a consequence we may be faced with a depression." Made up of one-fifth scare tactics and four-fifths genuine concern for the American international economic system, Brown's "report" claimed that de-Nazification was a total failure. Anglo-Saxon democratic beliefs could not be stuffed down sore German throats. American policy had not produced the right kind of German leadership, only a bad economic cold. "And it is high time we face the facts. It produces political leaders who ask the wishes of the people and function as their elected representatives in a democratic assembly. But the German masses do not want to be asked, they want to be told. They don't want to be represented. They want to be directed." In Germany the truly effective leader has his mouth to the people's ear. "He doesn't whisper, he yells like a drill sergeant." It was unfortunate that Germans had this kind of mentality, but now they were beginning to associate their hunger and misery with the democracy we were trying to build for them. "That way gives a Communist dictator his chance."[62]

Brown's arguments were crudely put, even objectionable, but his conclusion was on the minds of most of those who had answered Clay's invitation to come have a look. For the first time in quite a while, Clay began to be optimistic about the outcome of the "German question." One obvious reason was that the American press and public were responding in the right way. In October 1947 Washington asked Clay if he needed any further directives on socialization. Clay said he needed none because he had interpreted his instructions to mean there must be political and economic stability in Germany before the German people could be expected to express their views freely. "Time is on our side," he continued. "If we can thus defer the issue while free enterprise continues to operate and economic improvement results, it may never become an issue before the German people."[63]

In July and August 1947, the new rulers of Bizonia had unilaterally raised the level-of-industry in their zones, jumping the Ruhr steel quota from 5.8 to 10.7 million tons per year. On August 29, 1947, Generals Clay and Brian Robertson informed the Russians that as a result of these decisions the number of properties eligible for reparations would have to be reduced significantly. The Russian representative on the Allied Control Council, Marshal Sokolovsky, immediately charged that the Americans and the British had turned their backs on the Potsdam agreements. Clay merely replied that the record was clear: the Americans had tried to get economic unity for more than two and a half years. The invitation to join Bizonia (on Anglo-American terms, of course) was still open.

Against the backdrop of rising tensions in Germany itself, the Big Four Foreign Ministers made one final try at the problem in London during November and December 1947. At one of the early sessions, Molotov brought forward a statement attributed to the deputy British commander in Germany to the effect that the London meeting was no more than a *pro forma* exercise to prepare the way for the creation of a West German republic. Although Secretary Marshall vehemently denied the accusation, there was some fire behind the smoke. Now in full agreement with Clay and Murphy, John Foster Dulles advised Marshall that the Foreign Ministers' debates had to be related to the question of Germany's expected functions within the European Recovery Program (the Marshall Plan). The present meeting should be used to get immediate four-power decisions on key issues, such as currency reform and German self-government, and "if this fails to create a moral basis for interim decisions on less than a four-power basis."

Each side presented its old arguments at the Council sessions, then promptly released the speeches to the press, an indication that "White Papers" were being readied even as the debates continued.

The United States considered that the establishment of a German government was a paramount necessity, said Marshall. Then he reviewed his nation's policies in that regard since the Stuttgart speech. At the same time he made it more difficult for the Russians to agree to any American proposal for a provisional German government by setting forth the strongest position yet on the Polish-German boundary, including that thrown out at Stuttgart the year before. Marshall's statement was read into the conference record with pointed references to the Atlantic Charter, the usual non-negotiating phrases which marked open diplomacy:

> In seeking to create a democratic and peaceful German state the Council should avoid any decision which would deny hope to the moderate forces in Germany, and, by violating the principles of the Atlantic Charter, would fail to win approval in the court of enlightened world opinion. In considering cessions of territory to Poland, provision should be made for insuring that key industrial resources in such territories be made available to the European economy, including Poland and Germany.[64]

At the fourteenth plenary session, Marshall made it plain that the United States would never accept the Rusian demand for reparations from current production as the price for German unity. He insisted that much of the German economy was already being operated for the Russian account, and the situation had to be corrected before all of Europe was dragged down by Germany.

Marshall then asked for an accounting within three days of what the Russians had already taken out of their area. Molotov slashed back that he would be ready to make such a statement provided Britain and France would state how much timber and coal they had sold out of Germany, and at what price, and how much enterprise in the Western zones had been purchased by British and American capitalists. He also added another condition: the Soviet delegation would make such an accounting only in connection with a final reparations settlement.[65]

The London meeting came to an end in a flurry of accusations, without an agreement to meet again. Anticipating this outcome, General Clay had already ordered a new currency prepared as part of a general monetary reform in Bizonia. After the last session of the conference, Secretary Marshall told Clay to make one more attempt at currency reform in Germany on a four-power basis, then go ahead with the bizonal measures. On December 17, 1947, hearings began in Washington on H.R. 4579, Representative Christian Herter's bill to help foreign countries reform their currencies and bring about economic stabilization, so as to encourage American private investment. Clay's "boss," Army Secretary Kenneth C. Royall, testified that German currency reform was a key prerequisite "if incentives to work and produce are to be restored."[66]

After the breakdown of Big Four negotiations over Germany in early 1948, the pace of events quickened and began rumbling ominously across the face of Europe. The British moved first. In January they informed Washington that they planned to approach France and the Benelux countries with a proposal to undertake the formation of a "Western Union," with political and military connotations as well as economic content. Actual talks were under way by mid-March, with strong American encouragement. Next came the Russian-fomented Czech *coup d'état*. And General Clay's March 5, 1948, cable: For many months, he said, logic had persuaded him that war with Russia was unlikely, at least for ten years. But within the last few weeks, "I have felt a subtle change in Soviet atitude which I cannot define but which now gives me a feeling that it may come with dramatic suddenness." Washington overreacted, George F. Kennan asserted recently, "in the most deplorable way," and a real war scare ensued. In Berlin, Marshal Sokolvsky turned on his heel and walked out of an Allied Control Council meeting on March 20, after having been refused information on trizonal meetings held in London over the previous two months.

Soviet traffic obstructions against the Western sectors of Berlin began on March 31 and reached the point of total blockade on June 24, the day after the Western powers introduced a currency reform into the trizonal area—and their sectors of Berlin. "If we withdraw," Clay warned Washington as the obstructions began, "our position in Europe is threatened. If America does not understand this now, does not know that the issue is cast, then it never will and communism will run rampant." Although Clay had earlier warned his superiors that the introduction of a currency reform might mean that force would have to be resisted, he always insisted that the reform itself was not the cause of the Berlin Blockade. In fact he was right; but he left out of this statement his conviction that the reform *was* necessary to the economic rejuvenation of the Western zones if they were to be integrated into the European Recovery Program. After reparations, the matter of integration had become the heart of the Russian-American conflict over Germany.

Clay and Murphy recommended at one point that the blockade be smashed by sending an armored column across the Autobahn straight into Berlin. On this tactic they were overruled, though Clay continued to think that the column would have gotten through without a war. Instead, on August 2, 1948, Washington's request for East-West talks on the Berlin crisis was answered by a Soviet invitation to send representatives to Stalin's Kremlin office. Leaning back in his chair and lighting a cigarette, the Soviet Premier looked directly at Ambassador Walter Bedell Smith and smilingly asked, "Would you like to settle the matter tonight?" Stalin then proposed that the Russian mark be used in Berlin (in a later conference he agreed to four-power controls over its issuance), that all transport restrictions be removed by both sides, and that the insistent wish of the Soviet government to defer trizonal unification be recorded in the new agreement. At a subsequent meeting Molotov, in a draft communiqué, added the statement that "consideration" had been given to the Soviet "wish," and that the three Western powers had "stated" they did not propose to go ahead with the formation of a West German government. The three Western ambassadors regarded Molotov's draft as an attempt to go beyond the immediate currency question and to maneuver them into accepting Stalin's contention that unilateral currency reform had invalidated all Big Four agreements on access to Berlin. The American position, of course, was that the Western powers had earned that right solely by conquest.

On August 23 another meeting was held in Stalin's office to try to resolve the differences that had developed over the wording of the communiqué. Stalin persisted in attempting to have some statement included about the Western powers' plan to go ahead with the formation of a new government for the trizonal area. Since late 1946, Clay and his aides had been stressing the "economic magnet" thesis, as John Gimbel put it, which postulated that once economic recovery had been achieved in the West, the Eastern Zone (and perhaps all Eastern Europe) would be pulled out from under Soviet control. Thus General Hilldring testified in 1947: "If we succeed in the program we have instituted now in western Germany, it will require all our partners in Germany, including the Soviets, to carry out their agreement arrived at Potsdam."[67]

At a meeting in September with Secretary Marshall, Ambassador Smith, and several other American officials, Clay suggested that the Berlin crisis could be turned to great advantage as a symbol of "all of those who wanted freedom, and especially to offer hope and courage to the eastern European countries." From an American point of view, the Berlin Blockade promoted harmony in the West, though the French continued to lag. It also gave the West an ideological spearhead in Eastern Europe; the more repressive the Russians became in attempting to blunt that danger, the more they would reduce the political momentum left in German communism. Only Ambassador Smith had his doubts about this ideological counteroffensive, suggesting that in the long run Berlin would prove a liability. Clay rejected this at once: "Berlin had become a symbol of the firmness of the free countries of the world to retreat no further in the face of Communist expansion." Clay's brilliant improvisation of the airlift gave his words the added authority of one who had proved that he could "get the job done." In effect, the blockade resolved the German question.

"The West will make Western Germany their own," Stalin told East European communists, "and we shall turn Eastern Germany into our own state."[68] Marshall Plan aid to West Germany was channeled—at Clay's insistence— through the American Military Government. Ruhr "agreements" were negotiated which gave the United States a veto over allocations from that area to the rest of Europe, during the period that Washington remained responsible for economic and financial aid to Germany. In 1948, of course, that was a long-term expectation. The French, Clay candidly informed Washington, "say that there are evidences of a tendency to make Germany the strongest economic power in Europe and the center of the continental economy. Unquestionably this comes about from the present upturn in the German economy which has made its recovery real and no longer academic." In any event, Britain and France receded into the shadow of American policy. As Clay explained to Baruch, the United States recognized the various fears of Germany's neighbors. "However, their traditional and well justified fear of German aggression sometimes blinds them to the immediate and overshadowing menace of the Red Army externally and planned revolution internally."[69] But whichever shadow overfell the British and French, the only revolution which occurred in West Germany was an American counterrevolution—against the policy of postponement, against French obstructionism, against German Social Democracy, and, finally, against European radicalism.

American leaders felt fully justified in this action because, as James Forrestal said, "socialism . . . in the long run, in my opinion, will wind up as communism because it can't do the job."[70] In addition, as Forrestal had written Senator Homer Ferguson in May 1945, the Bolsheviks had the initial advantage "of having a clear-cut line of economic philosophy, amounting almost to a religion, in which they believe is the only solution to the government of men." And "to ignore the existence of seventy-five or eighty millions of vigorous people [in Germany] or to assume that they will not join with Russia if no other outlet is afforded them I think is closing our eyes to reality."[71]

Forrestal soon found in George Frost Kennan an intellectually superior Foreign Service officer who could not only explain this phenomenon in philosophic and practical terms, but who could also provide the talisman the nation needed to combat this evil. Years later Kennan would look back on this period and his writings with puzzlement and concern at what he saw.

TEN ☆☆

James V. Forrestal and George F. Kennan: Will the Real "Mr. X" Please Stand Up?

Sometime in May 1944 the new Secretary of the Navy James V. Forrestal exclaimed to a friend, "My God . . . you and I and Bill Bullitt are the only ones around the President who know the Russian leaders for what they are."[1] Forrestal thought his doubts about the "Grand Alliance" set him apart from most of official Washington. Preoccupied with his own fears about the shape of postwar politics at home and abroad, he mistook the public rhetoric of the Office of War Information for the private views of Roosevelt's advisers. While he was "around" Roosevelt occasionally, Forrestal was not part of the President's inner circle. Most of that circle hoped for good relations with the Soviets after the war; nonetheless, they realized more than Forrestal imagined the contradictions in the Grand Alliance.

Bullitt, of course, was even more isolated from the decision-makers by this time, and could seek to influence American foreign policy only through his magazine writings. Another man separated both by distance and influence from Washington policy-making was Bullitt's former aide in Moscow, George Frost Kennan, now once again in the Soviet capital as chargé d'affaires. Kennan shared Bullitt's and Forrestal's deep foreboding about Washington's "concessions" to entice the Russians into the United Nations.

As Bullitt had written in his 1943 memorandum: what America should have done was to secure iron-clad agreements from Russia and Great Britain before the invasion, not after the Soviets were already established in Eastern Europe. Bullitt had drafted his memorandum while he and Forrestal were both in second-level positions in the Navy Department. The memorandum and their discussions about it had made a deep impression on Forrestal, who wrote Bullitt on the first anniversary of D-Day, June 6, 1945, that "the turn of events" made it even more pertinent to the current situation. Forrestal later made the failure to heed Bullitt's suggestions the central thought in a brief outline for a book on international affairs, in which he traced America's difficulties back to the period before the second front: "Development of the pattern of Russian action. The failure of FDR to (possibly largely due to Hull's inertia) foresee the Russian objectives. Russia could have been dealt with in 1943 before the landing in Normandy."[2]

This view fitted Forrestal's preoccupations and habits of mind more than it described Roosevelt's and Hull's failures. Contemptuous of theoreticians, intellectual "meddlers," and social planners who criticized capitalism, Forrestal nonetheless chose the most ideological and theological among alternative explanations of Russian attitudes and motivations. A conservative Democrat who had been called to Washington after a spectacular rise to power and fortune on Wall Street, he was extremely uncomfortable around "New Dealers." Even more than other conservatives, Forrestal thought world capitalism was under seige, and throughout the war he kept large files on individuals, organizations, and publications he suspected of being under communist influence.[3] The Navy Secretary believed that the New Dealers rejoiced at Labour's victory in the British elections of July 1945 because it represented what they wanted to see happen in America, and because now they could promote socialism throughout the world directly by underwriting a Labour government with American tax dollars. Forrestal even tried to obtain a confession to that scheme by setting a trap for Harry Hopkins just before the British elections. On June 30, 1945, he had dinner with Hopkins, who had recently returned from Moscow after several pre-Potsdam conversations with Stalin. When Hopkins tried to explain the Russian position on Poland, and his own misgivings about the future of Soviet-American relations, Forrestal interjected that the real problem was whether the United States had to deal with a national entity or with the Third International's original objectives—world revolution under the banner of the Red Army. Hopkins passed over that question with the comment that he doubted that anyone could really answer Forrestal's speculation—a comment which implied that the concrete situation was far more important.

Forrestal wanted to press the ideological question, however, and suggested that ideology was so deeply imbedded in Soviet policy that the Russians probably could not answer his question themselves. He went on to suggest that it might be a good thing if the Left were to win a few political victories in England and France so that conservatives and middle-of-the-roaders would be spared blame for postwar difficulties. Concerned about the drift in the conversation, Hopkins remarked carefully that the world was indeed swinging leftward; it would be unsafe to try to step in and arrest that movement now. England, for example, must inevitably go socialist. At this admission, Forrestal became excited, revealing that his comment about political victories for the "Left" had been simply a gambit to draw Hopkins out. How could a small island nation, a trading nation for centuries, go socialist without finally ending up communist? Forrestal demanded. The United States or the Soviet Union might be able to bring off socialism because they had sufficient agricultural and raw materials resources for near self-containment. But not Great Britain, whose resources could support only about fifteen million people. Of all nations in the industrial brotherhood, Forrestal claimed, England had to remain capitalist.

"Harry obviously did not want to pursue this conversation too far," Forrestal insisted in his diary, "because, I suspect, he did not want to be driven to the position that he was advocating either revolution or Communism for this country."[4]

According to Forrestal, Hopkins knew that Great Britain could go socialist only if the United States was willing to give its full blessing and economic support to a Labour government. Since

Hopkins obviously favored such a course, ergo he also favored socialism for the United States! A more likely interpretation of Hopkins' retreat, however, was that he recognized Forrestal's deep emotional concern about this issue, and had no wish to engage a Cabinet member in pointless debate. He was not advocating revolution or communism in the United States—nor anywhere else, for that matter—except in the Navy Secretary's imaginings. Hopkins' warning about the leftward swing of world politics had been meant only to discourage the idea that the Soviet Union was behind that swing, and to plead for a cooler assessment of postwar conflicts with Moscow.

Convinced he had forced a damning admission from Hopkins, Forrestal was little inclined to heed such warnings or to re-examine his own position. During Cabinet debates on atomic policy the following September, Forrestal argued that it would be dangerous to enter into atomic control agreements with the Russians because, like the Japanese, they were essentially "oriental" in their thinking. Such value judgments were also at the heart of his profound conviction that East-West disputes, now Russian-American conflicts, were basically ideological. His deepest worry was that the President and his advisers did not grasp these facts, that they did not understand the United States was grappling for its soul with a spiritual power working its temporal will through the Red Army. In this state of anxiety, Forrestal kept searching for the one complete document, the one perfect explanation of the sources of Soviet conduct. The quest was complicated by his narrow view of men like Harry Hopkins who argued a more pragmatic version of Russian-American conflicts, and his own failure to distinguish between the expanding power of the Soviet Union and indigenous radicalism. In a letter to Raymond Moley on February 13, 1946, for example, Forrestal claimed there was altogether too much veneration of imported theories in American universities. This posture had begun, he said, with the acceptance of German philosophy in the nineteenth century. Karl Marx was the spiritual descendant of Fichte, Kant, and Hegel. (But in a discarded draft of this letter, he had referred to Marx as a direct spiritual heir of Genghis Khan.[5]) Forrestal's emotional obsession was a parody of the old fear that European radicalism would finally terrorize the world as a German head on a Russian peasant. Forrestal made it out as a German head on a Mongol warrior.

As parody on parody, Forrestal's demeanor resembled Ichabod Crane's terrified flight in Sleepy Hollow—were it not for the fact that these views soon were not considered unusual at all. In a letter to Walter Lippmann, Forrestal insisted that the fundamental question was whether the United States had to deal with a nation or a religion—but he added that religion, after all, was merely the practical extension of philosophy.[6]

For a time he was drawn to Reinhold Niebuhr's Christian neo-orthodoxy and the way the theologian applied it to the current world situation. Both Niebuhr's repudiation of all theories of man save that thought by the early Church fathers and his attack on purely scientific politics struck a responsive chord in Forrestal. Hitler's triumph, Forrestal wrote to a Catholic clergyman, had been the product of three movements: German idealistic philosophy, the categorical imperative, and the false hopes placed upon pure reason. "A lot of admittedly brainy men believe that governments, history, science and business can be rationalized into a state of perfection," he said in 1947. "Their ideals all come out of the same hat whether it is one worn by a German, a Russian or a Stafford Cripps!"[7]

Having ruled out all theorists of radical social change as charlatans of roughly equal talents and the forebears of tyrannical despots, Forrestal returned again and again to the pragmatic evolution of the American social-economic-fiscal system, which, he wrote Moley, had produced the major contribution to man's welfare in the twentieth century—the creation of the managerial class. Despite the admiration of some of the nation's thinkers for foreign ideology, he added, American capitalism was still the chief prop for the rest of the world. "Our present position in the world," he suggested to the dean of the Harvard Graduate School, "is that we are trying to provide the catalyst for recovery against almost insuperable difficulties in the way of inertia and the disposition to try new schemes of social and political organization which, tried after the last war, produced Hitler and Stalin."[8]

The economic problem was an international problem because the United States could not act dictatorially if it were to fall into depression; yet such a depression was inevitable unless world order was re-established, which meant above all else restoration of commerce, business, and international trade. Like many other policy-makers, Forrestal urged that Germany and Japan be brought back into an American-led world economy just as soon as possible. "Financial support," he said in a memorandum to President Truman on March 6, 1947 (the day of the President's Baylor speech),

> should be provided for local enterprises in those countries where a struggling economy needs a helping hand—but the furnishing of such support should in every case be handled by competent American personnel, in order to assure that the money goes into *productive* enterprises that are of direct use both to the country involved and to world trade. (Wherever possible, *private capital* in this country should render the necessary financial assistance—for this is essentially a business task, in which government's greatest contribution is the creation of favorable conditions under which business can work.)[9]

It would have to be made plain to the British, for example, who were operating their economy on the $3.75 billion credit from the United States, that they could not introduce socialism into their zone of Germany. Forrestal had championed General Clay's anti-socialist policies in Bizonia in Cabinet discussions; in 1948 he called the Cabinet's attention to "the real need" to appoint ambassadors with business experience "who would vigorously and continuously push the interests of American business." Wherever the Navy showed the flag, he assured a New York banker, it did all it could to advance legitimate American interests, including American business. When he repeated some of his sentiments on German affairs to Thomas Lamont, J. P. Morgan and Company's most experienced international banker and unofficial State Department adviser for many years, Forrestal received a warning against interfering in other nations' internal affairs. The key problem, Lamont countered, was to get these national economies producing, then they would be independent of all foreign influence. If one were really interested in preserving Western civilization against bolshevism, the selection of the right antidote was critical.[10]

Forrestal did not agree at all. Like former President Hoover, he insisted that foreign aid be used only to bolster capitalist economies. "You will gather that I am an advocate of business, and so I am," he wrote on another occasion. "Mr. Calvin Coolidge was ridiculed for saying some years ago, 'The chief business of the United States is business,' but that is a fact. Our whole economy and the increases we have made in living standards flow, in my opinion, largely from the energies of the businessman."[11]

As Arnold Rogow noted in his study of Forrestal's personality and career, the British political theorists of the left held a terrible fascination for Forrestal, especially Harold Laski, who was almost an obsession with him. The only intellectuals he excepted from opprobrium were those he relied on for theoretical analyses of Russian behavior. "The practical people are going to have a hell of a time getting the world out of receivership," he wrote the American Ambassador in Poland, "and when the miracles are not produced the crackpots may demand another chance in which to really finish the job. At that time it will be of greatest importance that the Democratic Party speak for the liberals, but not for the revolutionaries."[12]

By June 1946 Forrestal had found George Kennan, whose views on Soviet behavior, according to the editors of his published diaries, provided the "whole truth" about Russia that Forrestal had been seeking since the end of the war. In another year Kennan would himself become famous as the "secret" author of an anonymous article by "Mr. X" in the July 1947 *Foreign Affairs*—"The Sources of Soviet Conduct." In fact, the "X" article was a retitled copy of a paper, "Psychological Background of Soviet Foreign Policy," which Kennan had originally privately submitted to Forrestal on January 31, 1947. "I . . . crossed out my own name in the signature of the article," Kennan noted later, "replaced it with an 'X' to assure anonymity, sent it on to Mr. [Hamilton Fish] Armstrong, and thought no more about it."[13]

This anonymity disappeared almost at once, and the article Kennan thought no more about propelled him to the front rank of Cold War policy-makers. Even before it appeared in print, Kennan had been named to head Secretary Marshall's new State Department Policy Planning Staff. He moved to that position from the National War College, where he had been serving as Deputy for Foreign Affairs. Both appointments owed much to Forrestal's personal intervention. Never close to Roosevelt or to Truman, he sought to bolster his advice to those Presidents by seeing to it that views congenial to his reached the most important private decision-makers of American foreign policy.

Forrestal's attention had first been drawn to Kennan's analyses of Soviet behavior when he read an eight-thousand-word cable the chargé sent to Washington on February 22, 1946, ostensibly in reply to the Treasury Department's plea for detailed information on Moscow's refusal to join the International Monetary Fund and the World Bank. "The occasion," Kennan commented afterward, "to be sure, was a trivial one, but the implications of the query were not. It was no good trying to brush the question off with a couple of routine sentences describing Soviet views on such things as world banks and international monetary funds. It would not do to give them just a fragment of the truth. Here was a case where nothing but the whole truth would do. They had asked for it. Now, by God, they would have it."[14]

When Forrestal asked his aides to find out more about the author of this cable, Naval Intelligence reported that the chargé was responsible for most of the excellent telegrams now emanating from the Moscow Embassy. Kennan had long been an exponent of the "realistic" approach to the Soviet problem, the report continued, but during Harriman's tenure his attempts to formulate a firm policy had been discouraged by his superior, who had "derived considerable amusement from Kennan's earnestness in the matter."[15] This judgment on Harriman, as Forrestal well knew, was simply wrong, but that was unimportant compared to the other information in the report. The Navy Secretary made the telegram required reading for several hundred top officers in the armed services. He then had Kennan recalled from Moscow for duty at the new National War College, which itself owed much to Forrestal's deep interest in furthering the study of geopolitics and strategy. He subsequently was a frequent visitor to Kennan's lectures at the College.

Before going into the results of the Forrestal-Kennan "collaboration," the "X" article itself, a few words are needed on the terms "realistic" and "realist." While Naval Intelligence may have been the first to define Kennan's efforts as "realistic," since that time the term has been commonly used to describe a point of view on foreign policy. The simplest way to define "realism" might be to say that it was a reaction against the Wilsonian-Rooseveltian "idealism," particularly as expressed in "one world-ism." The realists rejected much of the so-called traditional American approach to foreign policy in favor of European power-oriented approaches because America's excessive concern with moralism had resulted in a baleful neglect of the national interest and quixotic crusades to right the world's wrongs.

In Kennan's case, however, as in many others, this definition is not enough. Almost paradoxically, the realists of the early Cold War period became especially involved in an "idealism" of a different sort, one, however, that was surprisingly "Wilsonian" as well. "What was disturbing about the new realists of the forties and fifties," asserts intellectual historian Christopher Lasch, "was their willingness prematurely to commit themselves to a view of American society in which the United States appeared unambiguously as the leader of the 'free world' and the only alternative, for all its faults, to Soviet 'despotism.' "[16]

The Forrestal-Kennan collaboration is fascinating for other reasons as well. Forrestal's conservatism came from his station in American life; Kennan, like Henry James, was almost completely alienated from that society. He returned from the American Embassy in Moscow in the 1930's, but the experience "only emphasized the degree of my estrangement." Like James he never grappled with the facts of American life, nor confronted the political-economic issues Forrestal faced daily. Kennan sought to evade the physical consequences of the "X" article almost at once, as James sought to avoid the physical in his fiction. For example, Kennan excluded military aid for Turkey; but Forrestal found in Kennan's writings precisely the justification he had been seeking to extend American naval power throughout the Mediterranean.

In Kennan's later writings it became clear that he always preferred a spheres-of-influence approach to the Soviet Union—albeit one heavily larded with moral condemnation of what the Russians were doing in their sphere—to the universalism of some of his "realist" colleagues in the State Department. Though Kennan was and is a consistent critic of the American world-view, the "X" article was used by Dean Acheson and others to justify the "holy pretense," and to exclude moral considerations when dealing with the barbarians. Therein, of course, lies much of the fascination with the article and its author, a fascination now shared by Kennan himself, as he reveals in his *Memoirs*.

Kennan's views on dealing with the Soviets had received a final shaping from Ambassador Bullitt during his first tour of duty in the new American Embassy in Moscow. Having spent several years training to be a Russian expert after graduating from Princeton, he had been rewarded with this assignment. In Moscow Kennan fully shared Bullitt's conviction that the United States should adopt a hard line, though he was much less confident than the Ambassador that any quick results could be expected. But the mere recommendation of a hard line, Kennan asserts in his *Memoirs,* caused Bullitt to be sidetracked by the President: Roosevelt wanted a different orientation. Here and later Kennan ignores all factors except the nature of the Soviet government and Roosevelt's supposed naiveté. In this case, the orientation of America's Russian policy in the 1930's was not only anti-Russian, it was anti-intervention in Europe. Bullitt was left alone with no instructions beyond his original orders on the war debts question—a question that quickly became minor as Europe fell under the shadow of Nazi Germany. Roosevelt's perplexing half-gestures toward collective security have been described by Kennan himself in his incisive comment that the idea "of trying to enlist Soviet strength in a cause for which we were unwilling to develop and mobilize our own seemed to me particularly dangerous."[17]

During the spring of 1936, when a deeply pessimistic Bullitt left Moscow for Paris, Kennan prepared a special report on Soviet attitudes entitled, "The War Problem of the Soviet Union." It began—as Bullitt now began his reports on the Soviet Union—with a description of the Kremlin's hostility toward all noncommunist governments; the Politburo regarded peaceful relations with such countries as only necessary breathing spaces. Russia's "stupendous" militarization program subsumed even the collectivization of the peasants and the Five-Year Plans. Stalin was willing to enter into pacts with noncommunist nations, but only to make sure the next war would be fought between them, not between the communist world and the capitalist world. Above all else, he wished to prevent a peaceful settlement among the Western European powers.

Bullitt carried this same message for Western Europe to Paris, from whence he relayed it to Washington. As we have seen, he encouraged Roosevelt to turn "a very deaf ear" to the songs of those sirens who urged American involvement in European political affairs. Bullitt's "isolationist" or "appeasement" period lasted from that time until the German invasion of Czechoslovakia in 1939. During that three-year period, Kennan was skeptical of the supposed German threat to Russia: "There was, I believed, little reason to suppose that a Russian government determined to tend strictly to its own business would find itself 'subjected to any immediate danger of aggression in the west.' *But the Soviet government did not answer to that description.*"[18]

Approximately a decade before Forrestal began his search for the answer to the question, Was the Soviet Union a traditional nation-state?, Kennan had concluded that it could not be considered a state determined to mind its own business, and thus, by implication, not a traditional European state. Yet this was precisely the period when the Soviet Union had all but abandoned the cause of world revolution. Whether or not the country was serious about a political alliance against Germany, and whether, having entered into such an alliance, it would have lived up to such, must remain unknown because no political leader in the West ever put Russian intentions to the test. It is certainly ahistorical, however, to regard Russian security fears in this period as baseless paranoia or the result of the Third International's unjustified meddling.

When Germany attacked the Soviet Union in June 1941, Kennan and Bullitt both warned Washington against following Churchill's example of giving moral support as well as military aid to the Russians. It was obvious, Kennan said in a letter to Loy Henderson of the State Department, that Russian involvement in the struggle had nothing to do with the "principles underlying the Allied cause." This letter, Kennan states in his *Memoirs,* embodied the essence of his disagreement with administration policy, a disagreement which continued until the official pendulum swung back from "left to right" and brought it close to his "own outlook in the years 1946 to 1948, only to carry it away once more in the other direction, with the oversimplified and highly militarized view of the Russian problem that came to prevail after 1949."[19]

Kennan has argued at some length and with great persuasiveness in his *Memoirs* that the "X" article was elevated into a doctrine, the "containment" doctrine through a deep misunderstanding. Taking all the blame upon himself, Kennan declares that there were serious deficiencies in the article's language. He now sees that he failed to make clear, for example, that he was not talking about military containment of a military threat, but political containment of a political threat.

But if that is so, as Kennan himself now points out, there remains something of a mystery about the article's reference to the need for confronting the Russians with unalterable counterforce *"at every point where they show signs of encroaching upon the interests of a peaceful world"* (Kennan's own emphasis in his *Memoirs*).[20] Kennan suggests that part of the answer is that he failed to make it absolutely clear that he was referring only to the five key regions of the world—the United States, Great Britain, the industrial areas of Germany, the Soviet Union, and Japan—"where the sinews of modern military strength could be produced in quantity."

The explanation still leaves the reader somewhat perplexed, however, because surely the region served by the Truman Doctrine, Greece and Turkey, was logistically vital to the "sinews of modern military strength," as were the oil-rich lands in neighboring Middle Eastern countries. Moreover, Kennan himself added a whole geographical area, India, as a potential key region at a 1949 State Department round-table discussion on America's future in Asia. The author of the "X" article had not limited himself geographically to five regions in 1947, because, given his interpretation of Soviet behavior, he simply could not do so. But it took others, like Dean Acheson, to make this point clear, to strip away "X" 's illusions. In 1950 the new Secretary of State had supposedly defined Korea as lying outside the American defense perimeter; but when the North Koreans invaded the South that June, he was immediately convinced that America must intervene because he had by then accepted the "containment" view (and made it his own) that the "distant and shadowy figures in the Kremlin" were responsible for nearly all the world's ills. Misunderstood or misplaced geography is not the answer to Kennan's self-questionings.

Another serious deficiency, Kennan asserts, was his failure to discuss Soviet power *in terms of* its involvement in Eastern Europe, and the likelihood that it could not permanently hold this great area in complete subjugation. "To this day, I am not sure of the reason for this omission," Kennan writes. "It had something to do, I suspect, with what I felt to be Mr. Forrestal's needs at the time when I prepared the original paper for him."[21] This statement certainly opens up the question of the article's authorship and the dominant will in the collaboration—at least in the form in which it had such an influence on the policy-making elite. Kennan further notes that the first hint of the official origin of the "X" article came in a *New York Times* column written by Arthur Krock, who had seen it "when it was no more than a private paper lying around in Mr. Forrestal's office."[22]

Kennan offers his readers a real insight into two pieces of the puzzle with these statements: first, he suggests that the article was tailored especially to "Mr. Forrestal's needs," and, second, he calls our attention to Forrestal's key role in both distributing the article and supplying covering letters or conversational glosses to the author's words. For example, it originally reached the State Department from Forrestal's office; the Navy Secretary also had it reproduced and sent out to public and private leaders not only in Washington but across the country. These covering letters had much to do with the way the paper was received, as the recipient was told in advance what to expect from it. Forrestal received the final draft on January 31, 1947; on February 11 he sent a copy to an old friend in New York, Clarence Dillon, noting that "Nothing about Russia can be understood without also understanding the implacable and unchanging direction of Lenin's religion-philosophy."[23]

A few weeks later he informed another friend that Secretary of State Marshall had the equipment in terms of orderliness of mind and overall mental capacity to deal with world events, which seemed to be moving with the same speed as they had in 1940. But Marshall lacked economic understanding and an awareness of the nature of communist philosophy. "However, he learns fast."[24] So Forrestal "sent" Kennan to Marshall to head his Policy Planning Staff, and to tutor him in his weak areas.

Others, like Henry Cabot Lodge, Jr., were asked to the Pentagon to have lunch with Kennan. From a top executive at General Motors who had been sent Kennan's paper came a request for permission to run off additional copies for supervisory personnel.[25] When the editor of *Foreign Affairs* asked Kennan for something in writing along the lines of a talk he had given at the Council on Foreign Relations, Forrestal readily assured Kennan that he had no objection to publishing the paper. It was then submitted to the State Department's Committee on Unofficial Publication for approval.

Kennan remarks that this committee pondered the article at leisure, found nothing in it "particularly remarkable or dangerous from the government's standpoint," and granted permission for its publication. Louis Halle, in *The Cold War as History,* suggests a different interpretation, one which conflicts with Kennan's reticent account of the committee's action. A career Foreign Service officer, at that time soon to be a member of the Policy Planning Staff, Halle voiced the views of an insider who worked in the Department's higher levels. Halle notes the nice twist of fate which offered Kennan a prominent role in carrying out his own recommendations from the "X" article. "Since this article represented *the newly formulated position of the United States Government,* it would have been self-defeating to put it forward simply as the thought of one man, even if the discipline of the career service had not limited the public expression of personal views by its members."[26]

Kennan filled this fateful role but a short time—barely past the first scene, in fact. The "X" article and the containment policy it described were taken over by other principals who were more sure of their roles and less concerned with the nuances and skills of the international drama. Some of the most important players went on to write their own versions of the policy. Halle, for example, wrote on the theme *Civilization and Foreign Policy*. Employing a far cruder reading of Karl Marx's writings than that advanced by even some so-called vulgar Marxists, Halle concluded that the Soviet Union's challenge to Western civilization was not the challenge of heretics but the threat of soulless animals herded into marauding bands. "It is mass man, having no existence as a self-contained individual, but only as a statistical component. . . . A vision which merely identified men with the beasts of the field, obliterating all distinction, would hardly move them to distinguish themselves by building a civilization at all."[27] Halle blurred any distinctions between the Marxist vision of a classless society and the Stalinist reality in Soviet Russia. He also presumed that Stalin was bent on making over the world in that horrifying image—a profoundly erroneous estimate of Russian motives. Halle's phrasing of the "containment" doctrine did an injustice to Kennan's more subtle formulations, but not to his central thesis.

The "X" article acted as a powerful magnet on loose fragments of an ideology and shaped them into a pattern which was easily understood by men like Forrestal. These ideas were then transmitted to policy-makers generally, and ultimately into action. The State Department committee apparently viewed the "X" signature as a perfect symbol for the new policy formulation; symbols often become as important as substance in doctrinal matters.

"If, then, I was the author in 1947 of a 'doctrine' of containment," Kennan admits, "it was a doctrine that lost much of its rationale with the death of Stalin and with the development of the Soviet-Chinese conflict."[28] Like the effort to limit his responsibility for containment geographically, Kennan's desire to halt it chronologically was only a quiet voice raised against Cold War crusaders on the march to provide that unanswerable force he had once called for. In the months after he completed his *Memoirs*, Kennan's wish for an end to containment conflicted with his outrage upon the Soviet invasion of Czechoslovakia, causing him to reassert the impossibility of détente. "I have never understood this talk about détente," Kennan told a newspaper reporter in August 1968. The United States should send 100,000 troops to West Germany immediately, he said, and inform the Russians that they would not be removed until Czechoslovakia was evacuated. "Although speaking in scholarly terms," the *New York Times* report of September 22, 1968, concluded, "Mr. Kennan did not conceal his emotions when he discussed the Soviet-led invasion of Czechoslovakia." In this interview, as in the "X" article, it is not easy to tell where Kennan's moral censure of the Soviet system and its conspiratorial diplomacy leave off, and where his "realistic" views of American foreign policy begin.

"In writing the X-article," Kennan says in his *Memoirs,* "I had in mind a long series of what seemed to me to be concessions, that we had made, during the course of the war and just after it, to Russian expansionist tendencies—concessions made in the hope and belief that they would promote collaboration between our government and the Soviet government in the postwar period." Perceiving that others now saw the failure of this policy, Kennan argues that he was concerned that Americans not jump to the panicky conclusion that war between the two super-powers was inevitable.[29] Like Bullitt and Forrestal, he was dismayed by Roosevelt's faith in personal diplomacy; and he saw the proposed United Nations as a product of the longstanding American dream of projecting onto the world at large its national consensus and belief in juridical settlements of international disputes.

In George Frost Kennan the Presbyterian elder wrestled with the Bismarckian geopolitician: that struggle produced the "X" article. The moralist was on top when Kennan spoke of disassociating America from the Soviet Union on the occasion of the Warsaw uprising in August 1944, when Stalin refused to permit the Western Allies to come to the aid of the Polish underground against the Nazis. The impact upon Americans in the Soviet Union cannot be gauged from this distance, but in Kennan's case it produced a revulsion at American complicity in Russia's dark undertakings not only in Poland but in other countries. American and British signatures on the Russian-dictated armistice agreements for Rumania and Hungary were black marks on the West's cause, and they made a mockery of the Atlantic Charter and all the rest of it: "We in the West had a perfect right to divest ourselves of responsibility for further Soviet military operations conducted in the spirit of, and with the implications of, the Soviet denial of support for the Warsaw uprising."[30]

But as another "realist," William Hardy McNeill, once suggested, the morality in Polish-Russian relations was never so one-sided as all that. The uprising in Warsaw, he wrote, had all the elements of Greek tragedy about it. But how could Kennan define the Western reaction to that grim occurrence as a "concession" to Soviet expansionist tendencies? Certainly it was not a military concession, for Kennan himself assumed that the United States could not have effectively challenged the Soviets in Eastern Europe without risking an unacceptable confrontation with the Red Army. To disassociate the West from Russia publicly while the war against Germany was still going on—and another war yet to be finished in Asia—would have been a quixotic gesture. It would not have helped the Poles, and could have made their condition even worse. Russian suspicions of a separate peace in the West, followed by an Allied effort to drive to the East, could have produced an even more frantic effort on Stalin's part to secure Eastern Europe. Such a policy would have permitted moralism to dominate national interest with a vengeance.

Kennan's use of the term "concessions" may be interpreted differently, however: as pretenses carried out in Washington so that the American people would remain unaware of the cracks in Soviet-American relations. The chief "concession" to the Russians, and to the dream of the United Nations, then, came as a result of FDR's pretense to the American people—or so it would seem from this viewpoint. Roosevelt's second-front diplomacy, to his own great chagrin, did not change Russian policy or ameliorate the contradictions in the Grand Alliance. FDR tried to avoid Wilson's mistakes, but his reliance on Wilson's methods discouraged Kennan and a great many others. Remembering Wilson's failure at Paris, Roosevelt pretended there were no "secret treaties" this time to mar the plan for a new League of Nations. Even so, it is still not clear, as Kennan insisted at the time and later, that a public disavowal would have improved the Eastern European situation, then or after the war. The cost of a pure conscience is often highest for the one being rescued, especially in international relations.

To reach Kennan's conclusion, one must be convinced that Roosevelt's policy, and the one followed by Byrnes through 1946, posed no restraints at all on Soviet actions. We have already agreed that second-front diplomacy brought no fundamental strategic changes, but that is not the same as saying that it could not have, or that Americans did not believe that ultimately it could have. A disavowal in August 1944 would have immediately foreclosed any possibility of working with and strengthening noncommunist elements in Eastern Europe after the war. Kennan's proposal, like Wilson's at Versailles, would have isolated the Soviet Union to stew in its own juices. But Kennan's superiors in Washington remembered Herbert Hoover's far from naive use of food relief in Rumania and Hungary after the First World War, to roll back the Soviet threat. Soviet reactions to the American-sponsored United Nations Relief and Rehabilitation Agency (UNRRA) demonstrated that the Soviets remembered, too. Molotov's eagerness for compromise at London in September 1945, the free elections in Hungary that fall, and the abandonment of Yugoslav comrades in the Trieste debate, all encouraged Washington to think that more concessions could be forced from the Soviets. In some ways the situation was almost the reverse from what Kennan has described as "concessions" *to* the Russians.

Kennan says the gulf between himself and Washington reached its widest point in 1945 when, after Roosevelt's death, the new President sent Harry Hopkins to talk with Stalin about Poland and Soviet-American relations in general. While Kennan did not expect to be consulted on these problems, to his amazement Truman's special emissary was most interested in his opinions. So Kennan told Hopkins exactly what he thought: the United States should accept no share of the responsibility for what the Russians intended to do in Poland. The chargé recalled their conversation in his *Memoirs*:

> "Then you think it's just sin," he said, "and we should be agin it."
>
> "That's just about right," I replied.
>
> "I respect your opinion," he said, sadly. "But I am not at liberty to accept it."[31]

Kennan possibly misinterpreted Hopkins's feelings as much as Forrestal did a few weeks later; but even if Hopkins was acting under orders odious to himself, ones forced on him by men who clung to false notions about communist ideology and Stalinist Russia, neither he nor Kennan was free to act without considering the larger historical situation. As Kennan points out in *Russia and the West Under Lenin and Stalin* (1961), the basic Western internal moral failure to deal with the fascist and Nazi threat had resulted by 1939 in the unhappy situation where those nations could defeat Hitler and his allies only with Russian aid. And as it turned out, of course (though Kennan does not mention it), the Soviet Union bore the brunt of German firepower for three years while the West defended its interests in the Far East and the Mediterranean. Kennan complained that Great Britain and the United States behaved as if they "owed" a second front to Moscow, and that some of the concessions made to the Russians stemmed from false guilt feelings. In fact, American leaders were chagrined that the second front had not been opened sooner for other reasons—either because they distrusted British machinations or because they worried where Anglo-American armies would meet the Soviets in Europe. But whatever did worry Americans about the tardiness of the second front, the objective fact was that the United States had opened it too late to prevent a strong westward advance by the Russians.[32] Nor did it help the predicament Kennan and Hopkins found themselves in over Poland continually to bemoan that fact or just to be "agin" it as sinful. Perhaps, therefore, Hopkins was sad because others would very probably take such a principled stand on Poland, and the Grand Alliance would fail in its peacemaking efforts. It may have been unrealistic to assume that the Grand Alliance could make a secure peace; surely it was naive to think that Soviet ideology determined its foreign policy in Poland and Eastern Europe without testing that belief.

In any event, Kennan's position was as theoretical as Bullitt's 1943 plan to strike eastward through the Mediterranean at Japan and renegotiate American entrance into the European war from "strength." To deal with the historical situation, and to try to alter it, is one thing; to ignore it in favor of principle, quite obviously, is not "realistic" in any meaningful sense of the word.

Much of what Kennan wrote in 1947 had been in his mind

since the 1930's. With Russia's great victory over Germany in May 1945, Kennan foresaw no Kremlin attempt to advance communism in the West through the mechanized units of the Red Army. Instead, he said in a cable to the State Department, it was possible that Communist parties in Western countries would take advantage of Soviet-American conflicts to further their own cause. "Behind Russia's stubborn expansion," he wrote,

> lies only the age-old sense of insecurity of a sedentary people reared on an exposed plain in the neighborhood of fierce nomadic peoples. Will this urge, now become a permanent feature of Russian psychology, provide the basis for a successful expansion of Russia into new areas of east and west? And if initially successful, will it know where to stop? Will it not be inexorably carried forward, by its very nature, in a struggle to reach the whole—to attain complete mastery of the shores of the Atlantic and the Pacific?

Since the Soviets regarded conflict as inevitable, they counted on a masochistic element in American policy to increase communist power in Europe: "They observe with gratification that in this way a great people can be led, like an ever-hopeful suitor, to perform one act of ingratiation after the other without ever reaching the goal which would satisfy its ardor and allay its generosity."

> Should the western world, contrary to all normal expectations, muster up the political manliness to deny to Russia either moral or material support for the consolidation of Russian power throughout eastern and central Europe, Russia would probably not be able to maintain its hold successfully for any length of time over all the territory over which it has today staked a claim. In this case, the lines would have to be withdrawn somewhat. But if this occurred, the nuisance value of Soviet power in the western countries and in the world at large would be exploited to the full. The agents of Soviet power might have to abandon certain districts where they now hold sway; but they would, to use Trotski's vivid phrase, "slam the door so that all Europe would shake." Every difficulty that could conceivably be created for the western democracies by communist parties and communist claques would be used in this baring of the fangs; and the world would have cause to remember Molotov's warning at San Francisco that if the conference did not

> give Russia peace and security on her own terms, she would seek and find it elsewhere.
>
> But no one in Moscow believes that the western world, once confronted with the life-size wolf of Soviet displeasure standing at the door and threatening to blow the house in, would be able to stand firm. And it is on this disbelief that Soviet global policy is based.[33]

Kennan's images were never as subtle as his arguments; even in 1945 he introduced his arguments in favor of a policy of containment and patience with visions of Soviet power inexorably moving toward America's Atlantic and Pacific shores. Moreover, he badly misread the political atmosphere in Washington if he thought that Truman intended to play the role of Russia's ever-hopeful suitor. Such images only promoted the very oversimplification of the Russian problem that Kennan deplored in retrospect in his *Memoirs.* "My recollection," Louis Halle has recently said, "remains that the predominant worry in Washington, as the war approached its end, was over the deadly struggle to contain the Soviet Union that could already be foreseen."[34]

The "X" article had come to be written as a result of Forrestal's request that Kennan comment on another paper, Edward F. Willett's "Dialectical Materialism and Russian Objectives." Willett, a former Smith College professor then in the Navy Department, had been asked by Forrestal to do this paper in an attempt to answer "the" question. Willett's paper was far more ambiguous and ideologically oriented than anything Kennan had ever produced. The key sentence was: "We have to deal on the one hand with the seeming *certainty* of war if Marxian Communism prevails, and on the other hand with the *possibility* of avoiding war if Communism does not prevail."[35]

To Willett's all-encompassing statement that war was a certainty if communism "prevailed" (whatever that actually meant), Kennan replied that he had no doubts about America's ability to "contain" the Russians—provided its people managed themselves reasonably well. But he did not agree with Willett's somewhat optimistic assertion that an improvement in living standards in the capitalist countries would automatically negate the internal communist threat. This assertion struck at the very core of Kennan's personal and public philosophy; his reply to it goes a long way toward explaining much of the remaining "mystery" about the "X" article. The Soviet system—as well as the Nazi system—had risen not from the corruptions of man's institutions, but from the deeper corruptions of man himself. Once established, Kennan said, such systems brought out the full capacities for evil within man. Thus, while it was a reasonable conclusion that without Stalin the purges of the 1930's would not have taken place, the final result was not the work of Stalin's personality alone, but of his personality and will as they functioned through a political system dedicated to shutting out the nobler impulses of man. In general, Kennan said, communism seemed to be strongest in nations such as Czechoslovakia and France, where the living standard and degree of cultural advancement were highest, weakest in nations such as Portugal. He doubted whether those members, even of the American labor movement, who served as conscious or unconscious "vehicles for Communist influence" were suffering any material hardships. Communism reflected more subtle and profound maladies than material suffering.

Soviet leaders, Kennan maintained, were no longer committed to improving the living standards of the Russian people. Perhaps they had been so committed at the height of the revolution; now, however, they were concerned with maintaining only a minimum standard so that the people could work efficiently to increase the military-industrial potential of the regime. For communist leaders, power was the main thing. Fortunately there was little evidence that these leaders could extend their power over any area greater than that which they already controlled. Russia simply did not have either the manpower or skill to dominate any greater area—at least unaided.[36]

While Kennan's analyses blended logic and conviction, the mixture varied considerably from paper to paper. Logic predominated in his efforts to describe Stalinist foreign policy tactics—their basic realism and reliance upon Western weaknesses and mistakes; profound conviction filled his pessimistic descriptions of human behavior.[37] In this respect, his response to Willett's paper was especially complex. He wanted, on the one hand, to discourage the notion of the inevitability of war; on the other hand, he was equally anxious to sound a warning against the liberal fallacy that improvement in man's material well-being would bring a solution of his basic problems.

Highly impressed with this critique of Willett's paper, Forrestal asked Kennan to rewrite it along the lines of his suggestions. Kennan replied that because it was difficult to fit oneself into another's attitudes, he would prefer to submit a completely original paper. Thus his approach to the "X" article had three sources: his life-long convictions about human nature; a career-long belief that America had made too many concessions to the Soviets (and others) in the vain hope that a League of Nations would restrain man's inherent traits; and a more recent vexation, widely shared in official Washington, at Henry Wallace's plea for greater "trust" in Soviet-American relations.

Kennan interpreted Wallace's criticisms of the "get-tough" policy as a foolish desire to continue Rooseveltian personal diplomacy and, at Yale University, on October 1, 1946, indirectly criticized him in a lecture on the dangers of misunderstanding Soviet motives and policy. Unhappily, Kennan began, such bids for "trust" in international relations all too often had great appeal "to the Rotarian heart." But the Russian challenge demanded something more from Americans than "a few propitiatory offerings fearfully and hastily tossed in the path of the advancing opposition." It was important to disabuse ourselves completely of such feelings by employing the most dispassionate arguments and logic. Here again, however, Kennan's overreaction to Rooseveltian foreign policy led him to draw militant images for instructional purposes rather than describe the reality of Soviet capabilities. He was chasing Roosevelt's ghost in Henry Wallace.

Kennan went on to say that Wallace apparently thought—as had many vain people before him—that the "golden touch of his particular personality and the warmth of his sympathy for the cause of Russian Communism would modify to some important degree the actions of the Soviet Government." Such a false notion could only be the product of complete ignorance of the conduct of international relations (let alone relations with the Soviets). Wallace was simply flying in the face of the most basic realities of the Russian situation and insulting the ideological firmness of men who had followed the sternest of doctrines, "followed it through extreme danger, through extreme hardship, and through the sacrifice of every other value known to human life." These men would not thank Wallace for slighting their integrity as Marxists, though they might contemptuously take advantage of him.

Some listeners, Kennan said, might find this analysis too ideological. "Never forget that ideology is the only positive feature in a regime which has otherwise brought little but harshness, cruelty and physical misery to the human beings who have fallen within the range of its influence." Ideology was the figleaf of Soviet respectability. Tear it away and all that was left was the last in a series of rulers "who have driven a great people from one military ordeal to another throughout the course of centuries in order to assure the security of their own oppressive regimes."

The destruction of Russia's two great enemies, Germany and Japan, had confronted these men with the horrible possibility that they might be forced to live in a friendly world. "Is it any wonder that they rose up as a body to deny that this precariousness had passed?" The Russians had only themselves to fear and only their backwardness to blame for their insecurity. Appeasement of these fears would not dispel Soviet ideology and could lead only down a path to which there was "no end short of the capitulation of the United States as a great power in the world and as the guardian of its own security."

> We can contribute only by a long-term policy of firmness, patience and understanding, designed to keep the Russians confronted with superior strength at every juncture where they might otherwise be inclined to encroach upon the vital interests of a stable and peaceful world, but to do this in so friendly and unprovocative a manner that its basic purposes will not be subject to misinterpretation.[38]

The ratio between logic and conviction was changing, and the imagery had hardened; almost completely bypassed were the specific events which had led to the beginnings of Cold War or to the split in the Truman Cabinet which had produced Wallace's Madison Square Garden speech. It was all psychology and ideology. In this mood Kennan wrote what eventually became the "X" article for Secretary Forrestal.

Among other interruptions as he set to work was a request for a conference from two of Bernard Baruch's aides in the United States delegation to the U.N. Atomic Energy Commission. A meeting was arranged for November 8, 1946. The aides outlined their strategy for bringing the Baruch Plan to a vote before the end of the year, despite the likelihood of the Russians' refusing it. While Kennan approved, he felt the plan should not be regarded as a final step by either side, only an interim position. The Politburo was undoubtedly waiting to see what the United States would do if the Kremlin did not sign up. The proper response after the vote, therefore, was for the United States to begin a series of moves designed to convince the Russians of its serious intent—and of the consequences should they choose to continue their present course. Such moves might include military staff conversations with the British and Canadians, the construction of a new bombproof general staff headquarters somewhere in a remote region, and so forth. "He firmly believes," Baruch's aides reported, "we must keep a constant and firm pressure on the Russians. We must show no sign of weakening whatever in the position we have taken." Despite pessimism, they added, Kennan thought it might ultimately be possible to reach a satisfactory agreement with the Russians on atomic energy controls.[39]

As in the Yale lecture on Wallace's Rotarian-like errors, Kennan placed his real emphasis on American behavior in meeting the Soviet challenge, not on the reality of that challenge itself. In formulating his containment policy, however, it was difficult for him to maintain any balance between reason and principle or political and military tactics. There was simply *no* clear delineation between such internal elements—just as real geographical limitations and boundaries break down when policy is applied. Containment could not be restricted to the five "key" regions, to political tactics, or to nondoctrinaire applications. Argument from moral conviction, especially in the new atomic age, guaranteed the absolutist character of the competition, while discussion of the techniques of this new struggle reciprocally reinforced this absolutism.

The first sentence of the "X" article, completed a few months later, went a long way to justify such a conclusion. Perhaps the nature of Forrestal's specific assignment had been just enough to tip Kennan's balance in favor of principle and military imagery: "The political personality of Soviet power, as we know it today, is the product of ideology and circumstances: ideology inherited by the present Soviet leaders from the movement in which they had their political origin, and circumstances *of the power* which they now have exercised for nearly three decades in Russia." Those circumstances, let us note, were not of Russia's international position in those three decades, but of the power which the Soviet leaders had exercised at home. It was a crucial definition and a crucial distinction. It made Kennan the original popularizer of the so-called "domestic change" thesis as well as the containment thesis. Its supporters have regarded diplomatic adjustment with the Soviets difficult if not impossible until there has been a "domestic change" inside Russia.[40] The persistence of this theme in Kennan's writings even after he had abandoned containment in favor of "disengagement" further illustrates how difficult it was for him to separate his moral judgments from policy recommendations, at least so others could adopt a "realistic" policy. "Can men who can neither eradicate nor deny nor explain the blood that disfigures their own hands be fit leaders of a great country and a great empire today?" he wrote in a 1968 book-review article.[41]

In the "X" article, however, unlike the Yale lecture, Kennan did not insist upon a simple "power" explanation of Soviet behavior, one which had no aim except the perpetuation of cruel rulers. He stressed that the original Bolshevik leaders had not sought absolutism for its own sake; they had believed that they alone knew what was good for society and that they alone would bring it about once their power was absolute. Until that time, however, the happiness and well-being of the Russian people remained far down on the list of operational priorities. The one outstanding characteristic of the Soviet regime was that this process of political consolidation had never been completed according to its satisfaction. The men in the Kremlin had been absorbed with the struggle to make absolute the power they had seized in November 1917. As early as 1924 Stalin had justified retaining the organs of suppression on the grounds that capitalists had encircled the Soviet Union.

Kennan gave no indication in the "X" article that he considered the Stalin-Trotsky struggle after Lenin's death relevant to these problems, nor, more important, did he distinguish between the implications of Stalin's favoring socialism in one country and Trotsky's insistence upon permanent revolution. As for Russian emphasis on the foreign menace, Kennan argued that it was not founded in the realities of international politics, but in the need for explaining the continued dictatorship at home. The foreign menace was a fiction canonized in Soviet philosophy by the excesses committed in its name. It had become anchored in Soviet thought by bonds much greater than those of mere ideology.

But Kennan did not mention America's part in the 1918–1920 intervention against the new Soviet regime, or Western efforts to keep Russia quarantined politically and morally throughout the following decade. As for collective security in the 1930's, Kennan said, there could never have been a time when Moscow regarded its relations with capitalist nations as based upon any mutual interest. Instead, Soviet motives remained implacable behind the changing face of its diplomacy. Whenever that face changed expression, however slight the movement, there would always be foolish Americans eager to rush in and claim that Russian goals had changed—even to take credit for bringing about these marvelous alterations. With this final shot at World War II diplomacy, Kennan moved on to his most famous image, that of the whole Soviet governmental machine moving inexorably along a prescribed path, "like a persistent toy automobile wound up and headed in a given direction, stopping only when it meets with some unanswerable force." But the United States, he concluded, had the power to increase enormously the strains under which Soviet power must operate, and to force upon the Kremlin a far greater degree of moderation and circumspection that it had had to observe in recent years—"and in this way to promote tendencies which must eventually find their outlet in either the break-up or the gradual mellowing of Soviet power. For no mystical, Messianic movement—and particularly not that of the Kremlin—can face frustration indefinitely without eventually adjusting itself in one way or another to the logic of that state of affairs."[42]

The "X" article "soon became the center of a veritable whirlpool of publicity," Kennan said with remembered feelings of alarm in his *Memoirs*. Both *Life* and the *Reader's Digest* printed long excerpts from it, and the single word "containment" was used as a concise description of American foreign policy—even by those who had never read the "book." John Foster Dulles boldly sought to hang on it all the faults of the Truman administration's foreign policy in the plank he wrote for the 1952 Republican platform: "We shall again make liberty into a beacon light of hope that will penetrate the dark places. It will mark the end of the negative, futile and immoral policy of 'containment' which abandons countless human beings to a despotism and godless terrorism, which in turn enables the rulers to forge the captives into a weapon of our destruction."

When the chance came to intervene for "liberty" in the 1956 Hungarian revolution, even Dulles preferred to stay in the dark with containment rather than risk a nuclear confrontation with Moscow. By that time, Kennan had shifted to a new formulation, "disengagement." With the success of the Marshall Plan seemingly assured, Kennan had begun the search for a way to allow the Soviet Union to disengage itself from its military presence in Eastern and Central Europe. The explosion of the Russian atomic bomb in September 1949 speeded this thought process. But Secretary Acheson was not yet ready to negotiate. So long as there was the possibility of a major technological breakthrough, the Cold War might yet be won. At least one could hold out that hope a while longer. Of course, after hydrogen bombs came intercontinental ballistic missiles, and then a series of imagined "gaps."

This search for a perfect negotiating position, as Kennan realized, denied the desirability or even the possibility of significant diplomatic adjustments, including disengagement. But his new prophecy was not wanted in the temple built to containment, and the founder of the faith was driven from its walls as a "mystic" heretic.[43]

The highly ideological formulation of the containment thesis foretold such a result. Kennan was himself alarmed when he read Walter Lippmann's perceptive critique of the "X" article and the Truman Doctrine. In a series of daily newspaper columns, later published as *The Cold War: A Study in U.S. Foreign Policy,* Lippmann set about wrecking the containment thesis from its ideological underpinnings to its tactical prescriptions for checking the Soviets. Soviet foreign policy was the same as Russian foreign policy under Peter the Great, Lippmann countered. Ideologies might come and go, but Russian national interests (like those of the British Empire) were eternal. Containment gave an opponent shorter logistical lines of communication; it saddled the U.S. with unreliable allies to hold the line; it meant, in sum, trying to police the world. While Kennan had in fact taken many of Lippmann's positions in the intra-administration debates on the Truman Doctrine and the Marshall Plan, in the "X" article he was preoccupied with the irony of man's nature and destiny as he perceived it in the grotesque and misshapen figure of Stalinist "Marxism." Kennan and his later followers all too often dispensed with any historical analysis except that which sustained their particular ironic view.

No consensus has yet emerged among scholars on the role that ideology played in Soviet foreign policy in the Stalinist era. Because the Russians are not likely to open their archives to Marxist searchers, let alone to anyone else, the nature of the evidence is not going to be very much different in ten or perhaps even in fifty years. "It is clear," writes Marshall Shulman, a former aide to Acheson, in a striking reappraisal of Stalin's foreign policy, "that fundamental differences in the perception of the situation were involved." Russian efforts in 1946 to define their sphere of influence in Eastern Europe may have given the impression that Soviet actions were baldly expansionist. Soviet probes in the Mediterranean, Shulman contends, awakened the West to a realization that until power relationships were defined afresh in both areas, there could be no stabilizing of Soviet-American relations. But the nature of the American response in the Truman Doctrine appeared to confirm, on the other hand, Soviet expectations of capitalist hostility, and stimulated a far greater Soviet militancy against the Marshall Plan as a threat to its hegemony. This response took several forms, but a key one was the effort to turn the French and Italian Communist parties into lines of forceful resistance against their national governments.[44]

By late 1948, Shulman asserts, "it had become apparent that Soviet misreading of events and miscalculations had resulted in a trend massively adverse to Soviet interests. Yugoslavia had been estranged, the Western zones of Germany were on the way toward unification, the militancy of French and Italian Communists had only served to contribute to the further cohesion and mobilization of the Western alliance. In the following years, the Soviet leadership sought to undo these consequences by intermittent gestures toward a reduction in the atmosphere of tension."[45]

Shulman's analysis explicitly refutes both the notion that ideology or the urge to power determined Soviet policy, and the later amendment to that thesis—that Stalin's paranoia was largely responsible for Russian actions in international affairs. The belief that Soviet policy in Eastern Europe was only the prelude to further expansion, perhaps following internal breakdowns in the West, came easily to those who by instinct and definition of national interest distrusted a spheres-of-influence approach to world peace. As Kennan now belatedly recognizes, the "X" article did not enlighten those who shared this belief. It only excited them.

If, as now seems reasonable given Kennan's explanations in his *Memoirs* and his penetrating critiques of the liberal world-view in *American Foreign Policy, 1900–1950,* he had set out only to instruct American policy-makers, not to start a crusade, he did himself and his purposes a grave disservice in the "X" article. Always standing behind "Mr. X" was Forrestal, the man who had given him the time and opportunity to perform a special function for the American policy-making community. A profoundly moral man whose revulsion at the excesses and inhumanities carried out in the name of social justice overrode nearly all his other feelings and ultimately led him into equally profound disagreement with his nation's foreign policies in the 1960's, Kennan watched with increasing dismay as the "X" article assumed the attributes and separate life of an anonymous spokesman for American foreign policy, one whose pen sounded the call to arms in the early morning of the Cold War.

ELEVEN ☆☆

The Cold War in History

Early books on the origins of the Cold War were little more than annotated collective memoirs of Americans who participated in that transition period. The historian's facts and conclusions had already been chosen for him before he began. Scholars personally involved in the Cold War devoted themselves to producing "White Papers" on Russian violations of their agreements with the West. The object was to see how big a list of these misdeeds one could put together. If the President said that the Soviet Union had violated forty-seven pacts and treaties, the State Department scurried around to draw up a list to conform to the accusation, and Cold War historians all too often came following after.

The major critique of American diplomacy that emerged in later years claimed that it had erred principally in trying "to be nice" to other countries. American policy-makers had foolishly expected to convert them to the democratic way of life. Around this proposition rallied a variety of disillusioned liberals and scholars, who, if they would not directly criticize Roosevelt's conduct of Russian-American relations, were prepared to do so obliquely in treatises stressing the "balance of power," the "realities of American foreign policy," and similar tough-minded efforts to avoid assessing FDR's noble but futile efforts at personal diplomacy. These writers produced a body of literature on past foibles, and on occasion uncovered fresh insights into America's view of its place in the world. But the framework they established for the study of American foreign relations was ahistorical and abstract. How, for example, could one ignore history in trying to understand the development of the Soviet-American conflict? Their answers were often as simplistic as the interpretations they criticized. It was a critique suited to a "presumably mortal antagonism" between "two rigidly hostile blocs." Its proponents argued that twenty years of Cold War were better for all mankind than two hours of nuclear holocaust, and that "realist" policies were in fact the only way to avoid war.

The argument that the Cold War itself could have been avoided was put forward in greatest detail by Denna Frank Fleming in *The Cold War and Its Origins* (1961), a massive two-volume work which began the assault on Harry Truman as the instigator of the conflict between East and West. Fleming's study had three main features: Above all, President Truman had dramatically reversed FDR's foreign policy in the days after his untimely death. Whether from inexperience and insecurity or shortsightedness and stubbornness, or some other reason, Truman broke with Roosevelt's postwar plan as early as April 23, 1945, when he ordered Russian Foreign Minister Molotov to toe the line on Poland or face the loss of American economic aid in the transition period. Fleming's assertion presumes, of course, that FDR had a consistent policy toward the Soviet Union, or, at least, had finally settled upon one at the recent Yalta Conference. Ironically, it was a similar presumption by George Kennan which led him to overcorrect the errors of Roosevelt's diplomacy in his cables to the State Department and his writings for Forrestal. While Kennan found FDR's attitude toward the Russians deplorable, the "revisionists" following Fleming applaud it. As we have seen, the position is difficult to uphold from either point of view, whether one talks about economic aid to the Soviets or more general questions.

A second feature of Fleming's book was its emphasis upon certain crucial events and the responses of both sides. Each salvo fired from Moscow or Washington was recorded to demonstrate that the Soviet Union was most often simply reacting to external events, rather than engaging in a rude, unprovoked assault upon American positions. The result sometimes made it appear that the

Russians weren't really there, Fleming's critics complained. Sympathizers answered that America was at the pinnacle of its power, so the initiative and direction did come from the West in most instances. Russian policy appeared more sinister than it was because of the existence of large Communist parties in the West; despite Stalin's basic disregard for the goal of world revolution, these parties still professed loyalty to Moscow.

The third major characteristic of Fleming's work was its lack of emphasis upon ideology and political economy: Russia was acting in self-defense, America was on the offensive. Fleming saw Roosevelt as an exception to the normal laws of political economy, which revisionist historians see operating upon other American Presidents. A parallel development on the "orthodox" side of the argument was Arthur M. Schlesinger, Jr.'s October 1967 *Foreign Affairs* article. He argued there that "A revisionist fallacy has been to treat Stalin as just another Realpolitik statesman, as Second World War revisionists see Hitler as just another Stresemann or Bismarck. But the record makes it clear that in the end nothing could satisfy Stalin's paranoia. His own associates failed. Why does anyone suppose that any conceivable American policy would have succeeded?"[1] If Marxism could be suspended by Stalin, no one could control the man's illness. Whether the orthodox historians made an exception of Stalin, or the revisionists an exception of Roosevelt, the result in either case was essentially a devil theory of the Cold War.

Fleming's book did not attempt a political analysis of the origins of the Cold War but rested its case with a personalized and emotional defense of Wilsonian "internationalism." "Both Roosevelt and Hull," Fleming declared,

> had been filled with a mighty resolve that this time the peace should not be frittered away and lost, that there should be no resurgence of self-defeating isolationism, no re-entry into the old, old treadmill of rival alliances, armaments race, mounting tension and war. This time it should be different. They both willed it and had faith that the fatal cycle could be avoided. They both knew that preserving good relations with Russia was the factor upon which all their hopes depended and they meant to achieve a solid working agreement with the U.S.S.R. in a new league of nations.[2]

But then Roosevelt died. "There are some who think the Cold War did not begin until around 1947," Fleming explains, "but it is clear . . . that President Truman was ready to begin it before he had been in office two weeks. The years of labor by Roosevelt and Hull to build a basis of understanding with the Soviet leaders which would last through the peace making were cancelled out on April 23, 1945."

In indicting Truman for his repudiation of Wilsonian "internationalism," Fleming shapes his case to support the old "internationalist" thesis of twentieth-century American diplomacy—that it has been a constant struggle between selfdefeating "isolationism" and "internationalism." He is simply unable to offer significant criticisms of those he feels are true "internationalists," men like Secretary Hull, whom he elevates to a position nearly co-equal to Roosevelt on the assumption that the Secretary of State sought to cooperate with the Soviet Union in a new league of nations.

Those who wrote after Fleming wisely did not attempt to duplicate this feat. Hull's attitudes and policies toward the Kremlin from 1933 through 1944 reveal an ambivalent attitude not at all suited to Fleming's hypothesis. Hull's doubts about the wisdom of the 1933 recognition policy were still not fully resolved by 1943, when he told British Foreign Minister Anthony Eden that it would be difficult to prevail upon the American people to aid the Soviet Union after the war—unless, of course, the Russians showed more interest in cooperating with traditional American economic liberalism. Perhaps amused by this statement, Eden remarked laconically that, after all, the Russians *had* been destroying Germans. Hull's answer was a classic statement of traditional American objections to European diplomacy. "We all know this, of course," he replied without a pause. "But the people who are dissatisfied with the failure of Russia to show any interest or concern about future joint efforts to promote peace and economic rehabilitation based on liberal commercial policies find that nothing would be gained thereby except that Russia and Great Britain will have succeeded in eliminating Germany."[3] In the end, Fleming's book fragments American liberalism unrealistically. Surely America's opposition to spheres of influence and economic and political blocs was close to the heart of its quarrel with Russian policy in Eastern Europe in 1945, just as close, in fact, as it had been when Washington opposed German and Japanese plans in the 1930's. "The San Francisco Charter," wrote the long-time liberal editor of the *Nation,* Oswald Garrison Villard, to former Secretary Hull on August 2, 1945, "is promising in its possibilities, but I think you will agree with me that it will fail to achieve its end if economic nationalism is not done away with and every barrier to freedom of trade removed."[4] Freedom political and economic were indivisible.

David Horowitz, author of *Free World Colossus,* acknowledges a strong debt to Fleming but shies away from a defense of "internationalism." He sees Roosevelt more simply as an exceptionalist who kept men like Hull, Forrestal, and Leahy under control. According to Horowitz, Truman's April 23 dressing-down of Molotov made it clear that "the Russian policy of the new administration was predicated on a very different set of assumptions." In the introduction to a British paperback edition of his book, Horowitz modifies this thesis somewhat toward the view that American foreign policy has been basically consistent and continuous in this century; then, however, he swings back to his earlier position. "That there was indeed a change in U.S. policy in the spring of 1945, as this study maintains, is not, I think, open to serious question any longer." To help establish this point he adds to this edition a quotation from the British historian A. J. P. Taylor: "The detailed records . . . destroy the accepted legend completely. They show perhaps almost too emphatically that the Cold War was deliberately started by Truman and his advisers."[5]

Gar Alperovitz, in his dramatic *Atomic Diplomacy,* begins with a similar assertion: "It is now evident, that far from following his predecessor's policy of cooperation, shortly after taking office Truman launched a powerful foreign policy initiative aimed at reducing or eliminating Soviet influence from Europe." At this point, however, Alperovitz introduces the atomic bomb as the crucial new element in Truman's change of policy, *the* element which made it possible for American leaders to reassert their influence even in Eastern Europe. In Alperovitz's words, "I believe new evidence proves not only that the atomic bomb influenced diplomacy, but that it determined much of Truman's shift to a tough policy aimed at forcing Soviet acquiescence to American plans for Eastern and Central Europe."[6]

In a later article in the *New York Review of Books,* Alperovitz zeroes in on the "forgotten man of Cold War history," Truman's closest foreign policy adviser in the fateful two months after Roosevelt's death, James F. Byrnes. His, Alperovitz says, was the quiet, persistent voice urging a change in the late President's policy. While not abandoning his original thesis, Alperovitz, in his search for the decision to use the bomb, gives greater recognition to the role played by key individuals.[7]

The central difficulty with Alperovitz's "atomic diplomacy" thesis, in either form, is that by beginning the book after Roosevelt's death he asks questions that pertain only to immediate decisions, not to larger issues. It is historically unfair to Truman to make him responsible for his predecessor's conduct of wartime diplomacy, including the decision to delay formulating a policy toward the Soviets on the atomic bomb. Even the period Alperovitz has isolated for detailed inspection, the weeks leading up to and including the Potsdam Conference, do not demonstrate how American possession or expected possession of the bomb changed Washington's position on any main issues. Truman's arrogant boasts about the bomb after Potsdam and Hiroshima notwithstanding, it cannot be demonstrated that the bomb "determined much of Truman's shift to a tough policy." And the debate over Alperovitz's book has further narrowed the subject into confusing exchanges over the meaning of "atomic diplomacy."

Professor Schlesinger's rebuttal article in *Foreign Affairs* attacks the revisionist idea that Truman broke sharply with FDR's Russian policy: "While the idea that Truman reversed Roosevelt's policy is tempting dramatically, it is a myth." But then he substitutes an equally questionable hypothesis: that Roosevelt had changed his own mind earlier! Citing the evidence of an observer present in the White House when Roosevelt received a cable on the European situation in late March 1945, Schlesinger insists it was the President who became disillusioned with the Russians and initiated a firm policy: "He read it [the cable] and became quite angry. He banged his fists on the arms of his wheelchair and said,

'Averell is right; we can't do business with Stalin. He has broken every one of the promises he made at Yalta.' "[8]

While the reader is not told what promises Roosevelt was complaining about, one can presume he meant Poland; if that is the case, however, Roosevelt's angry outburst was not translated into policy. As late as March 29, 1945, the President was still playing for time and pressuring Churchill not to bring the issue to a head. Clearly unable to focus on any problem for long periods, Roosevelt had reached a high point of ambiguity. But while he was indeed anxious about the impending end of the war—and all that it would mean—there does not seem to be any clear-cut instance of Roosevelt deciding that he could not do business with Stalin. Both FDR and Truman had a primary concern to establish a new international order.

On the other hand, Schlesinger in this article gives significant attention for the first time to the issue previously ignored by the orthodox defenders of America's position at the outset of the Cold War: the historical weight of America's traditional foreign policy. By tradition and inclination, Schlesinger points out, the United States has been opposed to "spheres of influence." "The tradition of American thought in these matters was universalist—i.e. Wilsonian." President Roosevelt was at times ready to depart from this view, but whenever he came too close to such a break, there were always enough true Wilsonians around to pull him back. Schlesinger to the contrary, there was nothing in Roosevelt's public behavior—especially in his report to Congress on the Yalta Conference—to indicate that he had abandoned that universalism so far as relations with the Soviets are concerned. Liberal critics during the war were basically anti-imperial, not anti-communist, so they often chastised Roosevelt for not being "tough" enough with the British. The effort to boost the Soviet Union as Western-style social democracy, in handouts from the Office of War Information during the war, helped to create a false image of Russian-American relations, and of what could be expected from the Kremlin after the war. No one was more embarrassed than the liberals when the Russians became a "problem."

The refusal to recognize Roosevelt's ambiguity probably delayed serious reappraisals of his foreign policy for too long; continued blindness to it produces a devil theory of the Cold War by those revisionists who follow Fleming's lead. This refusal also helps to explain why American liberals so readily accepted the orthodox view of the Cold War. Only a few American leaders—of widely different political views—advocated a "spheres of influence" peace. They did so, Schlesinger adds, for one of three reasons: from the belief that the United States, which had always demanded a free hand in Latin America, should not have been unreasonable about Russian policies in Eastern Europe; from despair at the possibility of influencing Eastern European events in the first place; or, finally, from the altogether different conviction that any attempt to interfere in Eastern Europe would preclude postwar economic or social cooperation with Moscow. Those who advocated a "spheres of influence" peace for the first two reasons were largely conservative "realists" whose critique quickly shifted to the excessive idealism and moralism, as they saw it, of American diplomacy. Those who advocated the last reason were best represented by former Vice-President and Commerce Secretary Henry A. Wallace.

In his *Foreign Affairs* article, Schlesinger says that Wallace set forth the spheres-of-influence case "with trenchancy in the famous Madison Square Garden speech of September 1946 which led to his dismissal by President Truman." In 1948, however, Schlesinger wrote *The Vital Center* in an attempt to round up stray liberals from Wallace's Progressive Party, that camp of Maypole revelers who had cavorted in unseemly fashion with Left heretics and communists at emotion-filled political rallies—and threatened Truman's chances in the 1948 election. In this book Schlesinger "proved" the Kremlin's sole responsibility for the Cold War by introducing its readers—as Schlesinger had hoped, mostly members of the liberal community—to an April 1945 article by the French communist "Frère Jacques" Duclos. Schlesinger asserted that Duclos's article was actually a Moscow announcement "by the Comintern official formerly responsible for the western Communist parties that the period of anti-fascist collaboration was over."[9] Stalin was once again firing communist agents into the West in hopes of starting a world revolution. Thus the Cold War resulted when the West defended itself against this ideological attack.

When Schlesinger boldly repeated this assertion in attacking 1960's revisionism, Gar Alperovitz countered it by charging that the real significance of the Duclos article had been very nearly the opposite: it should have been interpreted to mean that European communists had abandoned violent revolutionary action in favor of legal participation in elected bourgeois governments. Communist cooperation in Italy after 1943 and the first postwar French government, and their abandonment of obstructionist tactics elsewhere, were proof enough of Stalin's conservatism to anyone who approached the issue unemotionally.[10]

Aside from Stalin's intentions toward Western Europe, however, the point overlooked by both Schlesinger and Alperovitz is that American reaction to a resumption of communist political activity, even of an apparently legitimate nature, was sure to concern those American leaders who had entered the transition period at the end of the war worried about the leftward impetus of world politics and the "radicalization" of labor. This, at any rate, was the conclusion drawn by *Business Week's* editors about the Duclos article; they warned readers that communists already nearly controlled the electrical workers' unions, the East Coast maritime unions, and the West Coast longshoremen's unions.[11]

Whatever Jacques Duclos said in France, or did not say, the fact was that the movement led by the American Congress of Industrial Organizations toward a World Federation of Trade Unions—it actually came into being in 1945—troubled American economic leaders. For the first time, a large segment of American labor was interested in working actively in an "International" linking American labor unions with British and Russian organizations.[12] Duclos's article was simply one more sign that the class struggle which had submerged during the war was about to be renewed through legal means. While American corporate leaders misread the CIO's intentions, the WFTU did adopt more radical resolutions than American unions had in the depression—and there was no denying that it *was* an "International."

The WFTU episode was a minor incident; but it serves to suggest the edgy mood of American society in 1945, when Duclos's article was written, and it helps to explain a much larger occurrence: the Wallace affair. Henry Wallace was fired by Truman shortly after his Madison Square Garden speech; in the bitter aftermath hardly anyone recalled the link between Wallace's domestic views and his foreign policy ideas which alarmed policy-makers on all levels of public and private responsibility. Wallace's appointment as Secretary of Commerce had focused many of the tensions developing about domestic postwar policies (of which the CIO's participation in the WFTU was only a minor worry) on one man. That Schlesinger's response to Wallace changed so radically tells us something very important about the atmosphere in America from the war's end through 1948. Nearly all the "realists," to take a different example, are much more positive about the present need to respect spheres of influence than they were during the early years of the Cold War. Compared with Soviet activities in Eastern Europe after the war, Russia's 1968 intervention in Czechoslovakia received an almost nonchalant response in the American press; nor was this only the result of having lived with an ugly situation for so long that one more scar made little difference. Halle's *Cold War as History,* Olympian in its detachment, pictures the Cold War as a struggle between two scorpions in a bottle, each trying to maximize its power—an image as different in mood from his *Civilization and Foreign Policy* as Kennan's *Memoirs* are from the "X" article.

Wallace's controversial appointment in 1945 also made it clear that the postwar atmosphere offered no easy distinction between combatting the Soviet Union and the "left" in general. At home most American leaders were concerned about the likelihood of a popular demand for a super New Deal to ward off domestic depression. In such an event, they feared, a coalition of New Deal liberals, supported by various vote-supplying blocs including radical labor elements, would gain the upper hand in the transition period. A postwar popular front of this nature would set a direction for government policies which could not easily be reversed.

While Wallace had been kept off the 1944 presidential ticket for just this reason, his persistence in affirming that he was a production-oriented Commerce Secretary, affirmations which he always wrapped in "one-world" rhetoric, did little to calm fears of a new New Deal. Wallace had been associated (ironically) with the economics of scarcity as Agriculture Secretary in the first New Deal; now he displayed equally great enthusiasm for production men like Henry J. Kaiser who had been given such a boost by war and government subsidies. In both instances, the key to Wallace's attitudes was his advocacy of government intervention and regulation, whether for scarcity or production. In the postwar economic debate within Truman's Cabinet, he was isolated both for these views and his views on the Soviet Union. The Fair Deal frowned on liberal experimentation.

In addition to his attacks on American monopolists and conservative corporation leaders, Wallace insisted that the United States could do a profitable business with Russia. In fact, it was essential to his plan that Americans *be able* to do so. "The American businessman of tomorrow," he said, would understand that "the new frontier extends from Minneapolis . . . all the way to Central Asia." This was the main point in his Madison Square Garden speech. After comparing the "get-tough" policy with schoolyard bullying, Wallace said that whether we liked it or not, "The Russians will try to socialize their sphere of influence just as we try to democratize our sphere of influence." By contrasting and polarizing socialism and democracy—not socialism and capitalism—Wallace had for all intents and purposes conceded the central ideological argument of Truman's foreign policy. Later in the speech, however, he confused the issue badly: "We cannot permit the door to be closed against our trade in Eastern Europe any more than we can in China. But at the same time we have to recognize that the Balkans are closer to Russia than to us—and that Russia cannot permit either England or the United States to dominate the politics of that area."[13]

No wonder Secretary of State Byrnes complained bitterly that Wallace was muddying the waters of postwar American foreign policy. In the first place, one did not talk about American spheres of influence, even by implication. But what Wallace's critics could not understand was how he hoped to keep the door open in Eastern Europe or prevent social revolution in China or Western Europe without first containing the "threat"—no matter what guise it appeared in: Russian, Russian Communist, or communist. Thus this speech confused the American public at a crucial time, when conceptual changes had still not been adequately formulated (as in the "X" article), and when it was still hard to find the right questions to elicit the proper responses in public opinion polls.

Louis Halle's recollection of the Wallace episode illustrates this atmosphere perfectly. Halle was among those most responsible for the ideological purity of Washington's Cold War policy: "The tragedy of those who adhered to the obsolete concepts is most notably exemplified by Mr. Henry Wallace . . . whose long and distinguished career now ended in a sort of public disgrace." Wallace's disregard for the key role played by words in conceptual change produced nothing but consternation in the public's understanding of the situation. Up to 1945 such terms as "peace-loving" and "aggressor" had specific meaning; after 1945 they could not again be used properly until the overall situation had been redefined under the rubric of "containment."[14]

Halle does not go far enough in this remarkable statement. Kennan now insists that containment was directed against the political threat, yet his old friend and colleague among the "Kremlinologists," Charles Bohlen, when called upon to testify as Ambassador-designate to the Soviet Union, said just as affirmatively: "I think it is only strictly applicable in the military sense, meaning that we had not adopted a policy of armed aggression ourselves."[15] Of course, Kennan cannot be made responsible for what others said containment was—that is not the point. Under the rubric of containment, the North Korean attack on the South had to be seen as directed from Moscow.[16] "The Communist attack against South Korea," writes Marshall Shulman, "instead of being interpreted primarily in the local context of developments in Asia, came to be understood in the West, and I believe wrongly, as an indication of heightened Soviet militancy generally, which might also manifest itself by overt aggression in Europe and elsewhere."[17]

Without offering any real explanation, Schlesinger, too, now suggests that regrettable developments unfolded from the containment policy. "One might wish," he concludes the 1967 article, "America had preserved the poise and proportion of the first years of the Cold War and had not in time succumbed to its own forms of self-righteousness." It would be interesting to know how Schlesinger would date that process: at what point did America begin to lose its "poise and proportion"? Or if, as seems more likely, this development was inherent in the containment policy, does that policy in turn suggest the need for a different interpretation of the origins of the Cold War?

Each time containment has been invoked, from the Truman Doctrine to the present, it has been in connection with a military confrontation, and each succeeding time it has become more remote from any Russian military threat to the West. (The Cuban missile crisis is not an exception to this rule, for it was America's isolation of Fidel Castro and its attempt to overturn his government that led him to ask for Russian missiles.) Seen through the prism of American illusions about the peace, the postwar era brought American leaders face to face with their traditional goals, their nightmare-like memories of the depression, their newfound economic power, and the reality of a profound challenge seemingly centered in the Soviet Union. As relations grew tense, attacks upon the United States in the Russian press and the Marxist rhetoric of Molotov and his aides confirmed this view, no matter how conservative Stalin's policies actually were.

Among those who had a good claim to authorship of the containment policy was John Foster Dulles, whose lengthy article, "Thoughts on Soviet Foreign Policy: And What to Do About It," appeared in *Life* a year before the "X" article. "The makers of Soviet foreign policy," Dulles began, "take seriously the fact that the world is 'one world' and that peace *is* 'indivisible.' " War and revolution, he said, were part of the same struggle to the Soviets. "Soviet foreign policy is carried out in a rigid, mechanistic and uncompromising way. The policy, both strategic and tactical, is made in and directed from Moscow, in considerable part by men who are personally ignorant of foreign conditions and foreign people and who map out moves on the basis of what, from the Soviet standpoint, seems logical. To them it is like playing a game of chess, the world being the chess board."

Dulles maintained that Russian foreign policy was based on dividing the world into three zones: (1) An Inner Zone made up of the Soviet Union and its territorial acquisitions. (2) A Middle Zone of areas not quite ripe for inclusion in the Soviet

Union, but amenable to Soviet influence by virtue of the presence of Red Army troops. Serious efforts were then under way to extend this Middle Zone to Greece, Iran, and Turkey. (3) An Outer Zone comprising the balance of the world. In this last zone, Russian agents agitated against Western European economic and political unity, encouraged violent independence movements in colonial nations, promoted civil war in Spain, took advantage of Anglo-American mistakes in Italy to encourage disorder, wooed nationalist leaders in the Arab world, and agitated serious economic conditions in Latin America.* Even in the United States the Kremlin's agents were developing "the recently organized World Federation of Trade Unions as a mechanism for exerting worldwide political influence." "The national labor unions which are constituents of the W.F.T.U. represent, in the main, the left wing of labor (in the U.S. it is the C.I.O.), and the Communists and Communist sympathizers among them exert concerted influence along lines favored by the Soviet Union."[18]

Dulles' was the most all-encompassing statement of the problem since Bullitt's 1918 "XYZ" memorandum; beside it, Kennan's "X" article seemed merely a *Reader's Digest* condensation—albeit a most famous document in the end simply because it reduced the issue to one word: containment.

American reaction to Dulles' "Inner Zone" was largely conditioned by political conditions in Stalinist Russia, both real and fancied, and by concern about the extension of such an abhorrent system. But if the most elementary forms of justice were disregarded in the Inner Zone, that was not the case in the Middle Zone in the first years of the Cold War. As James Warburg pointed

*Ambassador Averell Harriman had sent Washington an outline for Dulles' interpretation as early as April 6, 1945:

> We have recognized for many months that the Soviets have three lines of foreign policy. (1) Overall collaboration with us and the British in a World Security Organization; (2) The creation of a unilateral security ring through domination of their states; and (3) The penetration of other countries through exploitation of democratic processes on the part of Communist controlled parties with strong Soviet backing to create a political atmosphere favorable to Soviet policies. [*FR, 1945,* V, 821–824.]

out, an East German election in this period was at least comparable to a primary in Mississippi. The transition to "People's Democracies" followed different patterns and even different definitions in Eastern Europe. In the Middle Zone, moreover, the early years of the Cold War saw a genuine interaction of Russian-American policies.

The election of a Labour government in July 1945 in the Outer Zone was a far more serious challenge to American leaders, and on three distinct levels, each of which illustrates the need for a larger historical perspective on the Cold War. To Forrestal and many others, that election appeared as the beginning of a movement toward radical socialism, perhaps communism, in Great Britain—and by example in Western Europe as well. Second, Labour had theoretically committed its zone of occupied Germany to socialism. The kind of socialism that might emerge there, especially if all-German political parties and labor unions were permitted, was a constant source of American concern from 1945 to the Berlin blockade in 1948. A third dark possibility raised by Labour's victory was that Great Britain might choose to close the sterling bloc, modernize its industry through nationalization and utilization of the empire's resources, and thus set in play a movement toward worldwide neo-mercantilism.

Dulles' definition of the world as it appeared to Moscow makes it possible to ask, In which zone did the Cold War begin? The answer from Washington was, of course, in all three zones. And so the Russians might well be behind every adverse development everywhere.

On February 9, 1946, Stalin announced a new Five-Year Plan in an "election" speech. The sacrifices he was now asking for, he contended, were justified by an analysis of world conditions he had received from "our Marxists," who believed that the examples of World Wars I and II taught that the unevenness of national development in the capitalist world inevitably led to internal conflict, then to the "splitting of the capitalist world into two hostile camps and war between them." There was no intimation in Stalin's speech that the Soviet Union felt it had to revolutionize the world to forestall this development, no threat to initiate a conflict with the capitalists. But Americans of usually calm demeanor, such as Justice William O. Douglas, thought they saw in it "The Declaration of World War III." Others believed it was a more peaceful invitation to backward and underdeveloped nations to emulate the Soviets and industrialize their lands without going through a capitalist stage of development. But to almost all Americans, Stalin's warning of war in the capitalist world had especially sinister overtones, particularly with Russian troops in Eastern Europe and Germany.

In the immediate postwar period, while his troops were stationed in Eastern Europe, almost anything Stalin said became suspect. In a speech at the Princeton Bicentennial celebration on October 14, 1946, Isaiah Bowman, despite the fact he was sharply attacking Russian behavior since the end of the war, admitted that Soviet policies could easily be misinterpreted because of inherent suspicions of Stalin.

> The Soviet government, never sure of the extent of our military power or our occupation policies or the date and circumstances of our withdrawal from European affairs . . . acted in a forethoughtful, if possibly shortsighted way. It signed individual treaties with Great Britain (July 22, 1941), Czechoslovakia (July 18, 1941), and France (December 10, 1944), for mutual military control of a revengeful and defeated Germany. The Charter of the United Nations was a later development. The Soviet leaders have consistently held that control of Germany is a first plain duty while an evolving world organization *may* in time develop strength for the task of enemy and world control, or it may not.

In 1947 Stalin granted Harold Stassen a nonpropagandistic interview which both completed Bowman's point and appraised America's basic advantages in world politics—advantages which, Stalin said, no other nation could really equal:

> Things are not bad in the United States. America is protected by two oceans. In the north there is a weak country, Canada, and to the south a weak country, Mexico, and so you need not be afraid of them. After the War of Independence, the United States did not have another war for sixty years and that was a great help to the rapid development of the United States of America. America's population is made up of such people as fled from monarchy and tyranny and kings and landed aristocracy, and that was also a

great help, and that is why America developed in leaps and bounds.[19]

To the Soviets, American foreign policy after the war had been spearheaded by a military view of the world. All physical points of contact were military: Austria, Korea, Germany, Venezia Giulia, Iran, Japan, China, and Manchuria. Despite the demobilization of ground forces, the 1947 American military budget was the largest in peacetime history, $7,091,000,000. Thus, from the dropping of the atomic bomb on Hiroshima through the race for the hydrogen bomb and the development of ICBM's, there was relentless pressure on the Soviet Union to match American weapons development. Russia could not assume that America would use its technological and scientific advantages only for purely defensive purposes. Undoubtedly such pressures produced a general hardening of attitudes on both sides.

To argue, however, that American Cold War policy or Soviet policy was simply part of an action-reaction syndrome in which one side or the other was totally justified, or for which neither side was responsible (as former Cold Warriors now argue), oversimplifies matters. Responsibility for the *way* in which the Cold War developed, at least, belongs more to the United States. At the end of the war it had much greater opportunity and far more options to influence the course of events than the Soviet Union, whose situation in victory was worse in some ways than that of the defeated countries. That being the case, there were at least three issues which, if they had been decided differently, *might* have spared the world the worst moments of the Cold War. These were:

(1) The way in which the question of economic aid for the Soviet Union was handled. It was foolish to believe, as Truman and his aides seemed to, that the economic lever could have been used to force drastic changes in Russia's East European policy. Harriman's anxiety to disabuse Soviet Foreign Minister Molotov of the idea that America needed Russian economic outlets led him to urge Roosevelt and Truman to make such aid contingent upon Russian good behavior—*before* such issues as German dismemberment and reparations had been settled, *before* peace treaties had been agreed upon with the former satellite countries, and

before it was clear what policy the United States would follow in the United Nations.

(2) The failure to offer the Soviets the guarantee of a German disarmament and security treaty in early 1945. It was Senator Arthur Vandenberg who forced this issue into the open in January 1945; when nothing was done about it, however, he discounted his own advice and, at San Francisco, pressed ahead with "majoritarian" diplomacy. *Life* magazine also stated frankly that only after having made such a treaty with Russia would the United States have the right to challenge and reopen to postwar review Anglo-Russian political and boundary settlements.

(3) The decision to pursue the Baruch Plan in the United Nations rather than Stimson's proposal to approach the Soviets directly on the matter of controlling atomic energy. It is unlikely that the Russian response would have been different in any event; but the way in which the United States presented the Baruch Plan offered no inducements to the Soviets to subscribe to it. All it really did was free Americans of any uneasy feelings about going ahead with the arms race. The result of the U.N. "vote" on the plan made it less likely, for example, that the United States would make any significant new offer at the time when, having stabilized Western Europe, it decided to go ahead with the hydrogen bomb.

The principal purpose of this book has been to inquire into the reasons why these seeming advantages did not produce greater flexibility in American foreign policy; and to suggest why American policy-makers acted as they did, what ideas about and perceptions of their situation controlled their actions, what visions dominated their thoughts about the future as they built the image of American postwar foreign policy. Upon his return from a European tour in the summer of 1947, Eugene Meyer, publisher of the *Washington Post* and head of the new International Bank for Reconstruction and Development, addressed the District of Columbia Bankers' Association on this very issue. He told them:

> I hope that I took with me this time a minimum of prejudices. But I admit that I carried one conception and came back with it intact—indeed strengthened. That was the idea of America's having succeeded to the world power which once was Britain's. . . .
>
> This was an idea which I found—but only after my return—had

> been brought out in a most interesting way in a book just published, or rather republished. It is by Brooks Adams, brother of Henry Adams. Marquis Childs has written a long introduction to it, which he calls "Evaluation." I want to commend the volume to your attention. The book is called *America's Economic Supremacy.*

The rediscovery of Brooks Adams by American leaders, and the "evaluation" of his early twentieth-century writings by Childs and others, was one indication that those leaders had completed the reconception and reorientation of American foreign policy. Adams had predicted that the ultimate struggle would be between the United States and Russia, and not simply as two nations but as two powerful conglomerates of economic power; the most efficient would prevail. "Brooks Adams . . ." George Kennan agreed in 1950, "probably came closer than any American of his day to a sort of intellectual premonition of what the future had in store for us."

Adams' geopolitical predictions appealed to State Department realists like Kennan who would isolate the Soviets and break down their empire through the steady pressure of "containment," and those who would force the issue with "liberation." But Adams had not figured on revolution and social upheaval in Europe and America in the 1930's. At the end of the war these facts combined with the awesome new power of the atom to prepare the American consciousness for the illusions of the Cold War.

Against the fear of revolution, the United States erected a barricade built upon the Bretton Woods system and anchored by the British loan. Economic opportunity in Eastern Europe was not essential to American capitalists, but an open world was—especially after twelve years of depression and war. The world could not be divided without being closed to someone, so it had better not be divided. Washington turned a deaf ear to the Soviet complaint that the United States enjoyed its own "sphere of influence" in Latin America and the Pacific. Americans were willing to admit only that they had inherited world leadership from Great Britain, and that meant responsibility for world capitalism. United States policies were thus a legitimate defense of this moral and economic leadership, against the onslaught of an alien system centered in Moscow.

The Cold War ended American history, as distinct from world history, and became the central event in a unique perception of the universe. The illusion was shattered only when other peoples asserted a claim to determine their share of world history.

NOTES

Abbreviations Used in the Notes

Baruch MSS	The Papers of Bernard M. Baruch, Princeton University Library, Princeton, New Jersey.
Bullitt-House MSS	The Papers of William C. Bullitt in the Edward M. House Papers, Sterling Library, Yale University, New Haven, Connecticut.
CWP	Department of State, *United States Relations with China.* Washington, 1949 (China White Paper).
Winston S. Churchill, *The Second World War*	Six Volumes, Boston, 1948–1953.
Dodd MSS	The Papers of William E. Dodd, Library of Congress, Washington, D.C.
Dulles MSS	The Papers of John Foster Dulles, Princeton University Library, Princeton, New Jersey.
FAQ	*Foreign Affairs Quarterly.*
FR	Department of State, *Foreign Relations of the United States,* Washington, volume date.
FR, Potsdam	Department of State, *Foreign Relations of the United States: Conference of Berlin* (Potsdam), 2 vols., Washington, 1960.
FR, Teheran	Department of State, *Foreign Relations of the United States: The Conferences at Cairo and Teheran,* Washington, 1961.
FR, Yalta	Department of State, *Foreign Relations of the United States: The Conferences at Malta and Yalta, 1945,* Washington, 1953.

Abbreviations in Notes

FRSU	Department of State, *Foreign Relations of the United States: The Soviet Union, 1933–1939.* Washington, 1952.
Forrestal Diaries	Walter Millis, ed., *The Forrestal Diaries,* New York, 1951.
Forrestal MSS	The Papers of James V. Forrestal, Princeton University Library, Princeton, New Jersey.
Grew MSS	The Papers of Joseph Clark Grew, Houghton Library, Harvard University, Cambridge, Massachusetts.
Lane MSS	The Papers of Arthur Bliss Lane, Sterling Library, Yale University, New Haven, Connecticut.
Moffat MSS	The Papers of J. Pierrepont Moffat, Houghton Library, Harvard University, Cambridge, Massachusetts.
Moore MSS	The Papers of R. Walton Moore, Franklin D. Roosevelt Library, Hyde Park, New York.
NA	National Archives of the United States, Washington, D.C.
NFTC	Annual Report of the Convention of the National Foreign Trade Council.
Roosevelt MSS	The Papers of Franklin D. Roosevelt, Hyde Park, New York.
Stalin Corr.	*Correspondence between the Chairman of the Council of Ministers of the USSR and the Presidents of the USA and the Prime Ministers of Great Britain During the Great Patriotic War of 1941–1945,* Moscow, 1957.
SDB	*State Department Bulletin.*
Stimson MSS	The Papers of Henry L. Stimson, Sterling Library, New Haven, Connecticut.
HST: *Public Papers*	Office of Foreign Relations, National Archives, *Public Papers of the Presidents of the United States, Harry S. Truman,* Washington, volume date.
Vandenberg Papers	Arthur H. Vandenberg, Jr., ed., *The Private Papers of Senator Arthur H. Vandenberg,* Boston, 1952.
Villard MSS	The Papers of Oswald Garrison Villard, Houghton Library, Harvard University, Cambridge, Massachusetts.
White MSS	The Papers of Harry Dexter White, Princeton University Library, Princeton, New Jersey.

Notes to Chapter One

Chapter One. *Wiliam S. Bullitt: Thomas Jefferson in Moscow*

1. Bullitt to FDR, December 5, 1941: Roosevelt MSS, PPF 1124. See also Bullitt to FDR, July 1, 1941, Roosevelt MSS, *PPF* 1124, and Ivan Maisky, *Memoirs of a Soviet Ambassador,* London, 1967, pp. 200-202.
2. Memorandum of a Conversation with the British Ambassador, August 20, 1920, The Papers of Norman H. Davis, Library of Congress, Washington, D.C.
3. Hull to John G. Winant, December 5, 1941, *FR, 1941,* I, 19. See also Hull to Chargé Thurston, December 15, 1941, *ibid.,* p. 196.
4. "Memorandum for Mr. Phillips," June 14, 1918, Bullitt-House MSS.
5. "Statement by Alfred W. Klieforth, Regional Economist on Russia of the Foreign Trade Adviser's Office, of the Department of State, Before the Foreign Relations Committee of the House of Representatives," February 11, 1921, NA 661.001/21.
6. New York, 1920, pp. 10–11, 38–40.
7. Bullitt to House, September 3, 1932, Bullitt-House MSS.
8. Walter F. George to FDR, September 9, 1933, Roosevelt MSS, OF 220-A. For general background on these problems, see Memorandum by William Phillips, undated [July 27, 1933], Roosevelt MSS, PSF 18; Donald Bishop, *The Roosevelt-Litvinov Agreements: The American View,* Syracuse, N.Y., 1965, pp. 160–161; Robert Paul Browder, *The Origins of Soviet-American Diplomacy,* Princeton, 1953, pp. 62–65; and *Review of Reviews and World's Week,* XLVIII (May 1933), 817.
9. Diary Entries, December 9, 1933, and January 22, 1934, of Ambassador William E. Dodd, in William E. Dodd, Jr., and Martha Dodd, eds., *Ambassador Dodd's Diary, 1933–1939,* New York, 1941, pp. 62, 74. A copy of Bullitt's speech is in NA 711.61/471.
10. The complexities of this matter can be traced in part to discussions between administration officials and the business community before diplomatic recognition. See W. Irving Shuman, Treasury Department, to Marvin H. McIntyre, Secretary to the President, August 12, 1933, Roosevelt MSS, OF 220-A. See also Cordell Hull to Frank C. Walker, October 29, 1933, in Bishop, *Roosevelt-Litvinov Agreements,* p. 8, and Robert F. Kelley to William Phillips, September 25, 1933, *FRSU,* p. 14.
11. See William Appleman Williams, *American-Russian Relations, 1781–1947,* New York, 1952, pp. 240–245; Bishop, *Roosevelt-Litvinov Agreements*; and Browder, *Origins of Soviet-American Diplomacy.*
12. *FRSU,* p. 60. The episode is also recounted in Beatrice Farnsworth, *William C. Bullitt and the Soviet Union,* Bloomington, Ind., 1967, p. 119.
13. FDR to Hull, February 16, 1934, Roosevelt MSS, PSF 18.
14. State Department "Draft," marked "Approved by the President," Feb-

ruary 11, 1934, Roosevelt MSS, PSF 18. The negotiations can be followed in *FRSU,* pp. 55ff.

15. Browder, *Origins of Soviet-American Diplomacy,* Chap. 8; Moore to Bullitt, March 19, 1934, Moore MSS.
16. Bullitt to Hull, March 15, 1934, and Hull to Bullitt, March 17, 1934, *FRSU,* pp. 66–67.
17. FDR to Bullitt, May 9, 1934, Roosevelt MSS, PSF 18.
18. Bullitt to FDR, July 23, 1937, Roosevelt MSS, PPF 1124.
19. Bullitt to Moore, March 29, 1934, Moore MSS; Bullitt to FDR, April 13, 1934, Roosevelt MSS, PSF 18.
20. Bullitt to FDR, August 5, 1934, Roosevelt MSS, PSF 18; Bullitt to R. Walton Moore, September 8, 1934, Moore MSS.
21. Bullitt to Hull, March 21, 1934; Bullitt to Hull, April 22, 1934; Bullitt to FDR, September 8, 1934, Roosevelt MSS, PSF 18.
22. FDR to Bullitt, May 14, 1934, Roosevelt MSS, PSF 18.
23. Bullitt to FDR, April 13, 1934, Roosevelt MSS, PSF 18. See also Bullitt to FDR, February 5, 1934, Roosevelt MSS, PSF Japan.
24. Bullitt to Hull, Despatch 188, October 2, 1934, "Personal Observations of Ambassador William C. Bullitt on Conditions in the Soviet Union," Roosevelt MSS, PSF 18.
25. Browder, *Origins of Soviet-American Diplomacy,* pp. 209–210, is the standard interpretation of U.S. reactions to the 1935 Moscow Congress; dissenting opinions are found in Jane D. Ickes, ed., *The Secret Diary of Harold Ickes: The First Thousand Days,* New York, 1954, p. 428, and Williams, *American-Russian Relations,* pp. 240–241; quotation is from Bullitt to FDR, August 3, 1935, Roosevelt MSS, PSF 18.
26. Bullitt to Hull, April 20, 1936, *FRSU,* pp. 291–296. See also Bullitt to Hull, July 19, 1935, and August 21, 1935, *ibid.,* pp. 224–227, 244–248.
27. Farnsworth, *Bullitt and the Soviet Union,* pp. 153–154.
28. Bullitt to FDR, May 1, 1935, Roosevelt MSS, PSF 18; Bullitt to Hull, November 23, 1935, NA 711.61/577.
29. Bullitt to FDR, May 1, 1935, Roosevelt MSS, PSF 18.
30. Dodd to R. Walton Moore, December 1, 1935, Dodd MSS, and Diary Entry, December 15, 1935. The Diary of Henry Morgenthau, Jr., Franklin D. Roosevelt Library, Hyde Park, N.Y. See also Bullitt to Moore, March 30, 1936, Moore MSS.
31. *Ambassador Dodd's Diary,* pp. 277–278.
32. Bullitt to Moore, November 29, 1936, Moore MSS.
33. Bullitt to Hull, May 18, 1936, The Papers of Cordell Hull, Library of Congress, Washington, D.C.
34. Bullitt to Hull, "Personal for the President," May 22, 1938, NA 760F.62/280, and Bullitt to FDR, June 13, 1938, Roosevelt MSS, PSF 18.
35. Bullitt to FDR, February 22, 1939, Roosevelt MSS, PSF 5.

36. Nancy Harvison Hooker, ed., *The Moffat Papers,* Cambridge, Mass., 1956, pp. 213, 231–232, 295; Ivan Maisky, *Who Helped Hitler?*, London, 1964, p. 122.
37. Bullitt to FDR, July 1, 1941, Roosevelt MSS, PPF 1124.
38. National Association of Manufacturers, *Can We Avoid a Postwar Depression?*, New York, 1941.
39. All quotations are from *The American Century* as published in book form, New York, 1941, *passim.*
40. *New York Herald Tribune,* March 7, 1939, clipping from the Diary of Henry Morgenthau, Jr., Franklin D. Roosevelt Library, Hyde Park, N.Y.

CHAPTER TWO. *Franklin D. Roosevelt: The Perils of Second-Front Diplomacy*

1. Stimson to FDR, March 27, 1942, Roosevelt MSS, PSF.
2. Diary Entries, March 2, 3, 4, 1942, Moffat MSS.
3. Bullitt, "How We Won the War and Lost the Peace," *Life,* XXV (August 30, 1948), 82–97.
4. FDR to Stalin, received April 12, 1942, *Stalin Corr.,* II, 22–23.
5. Harriman to FDR, September 30, 1941, quotation from Norman D. Bernstein and Francis L. Lowenheim, "Aid to Russia: The First Year," in Harold Stein, ed., *American Civil-Military Decisions,* Birmingham, Ala., 1963, p. 119. On other aspects of this decision, see *ibid.,* pp. 102, 150–151, and Raymond H. Dawson, *The Decision to Aid Russia, 1941: Foreign Policy and Domestic Politics,* Chapel Hill, 1959, especially pp. 62–65.
6. FDR to Churchill, July 14, 1941, *FR, 1941,* I, 342. See also "Memorandum of a Conversation," August 9, 1941, *ibid.,* pp. 345–354, and Bullitt to FDR, July 1, 1941, Roosevelt MSS, PPF 1124.
7. Martin F. Herz, *Beginnings of the Cold War,* Bloomington, Ind., 1966, pp. vii–viii. Herz may not have been the first to note this reservation, but he was the first to point out that the reservation did not appear in any American documentation on the issue, even though the State Department is usually scrupulous in such matters. Intentional or not, this was similar again to the way the United States treated responses to its Open Door notes on China at the turn of the century.
8. As William Hardy McNeill, *America, Britain and Russia: Their Cooperation and Conflict, 1941–1946,* New York, 1953, p. 19, puts it: "As representative of a nation whose power was clearly on the increase, [FDR] . . . could look to the future of the world without too anxious a concern for the special interests of the United States. American power could be trusted to look after American interests, as it were, automatically."
9. Stalin to Churchill, November 8, 1941, *Stalin Corr.,* I, 33–34; Maisky, *Memoirs of a Soviet Ambassador,* pp. 200–202.

10. Maisky, *Memoirs of a Soviet Ambassador,* p. 218; John G. Winant to Hull, January 10, 1942, and January 19, 1942; Hull to FDR, February 4, 1942, *FR, 1942,* III, 491–492, 494–503, 504–512. See also William L. Neumann, *After Victory: Churchill, Roosevelt, Stalin and the Making of the Peace,* New York, 1967, Chap. 3.
11. Churchill to Eden, January 8, 1942, in Churchill, *The Second World War,* III, 696.
12. Lord Moran, *Churchill: The Struggle for Survival, 1940–1965,* Boston, 1967, p. 34.
13. Churchill's realism was pronounced indeed in the period he called "The Hinge of Fate"; when the tide turned, however, he took much stronger positions. But following the quotation cited here, the Prime Minister added: "This was the basis on which Russia acceded to the Charter, and I expect that a severe process of liquidating hostile elements in the Baltic States, etc., was employed by the Russians when they took these regions at the beginning of the war." Churchill to FDR, March 7, 1942, in Churchill, *The Second World War,* IV, 327–328; Dean Albertson, *Roosevelt's Farmer,* New York, 1961, pp. 267–268; "Memorandum of a Conversation," February 18, 1942, *FR, 1942,* III, 512–514.
14. Maisky, *Memoirs of a Soviet Ambassador,* pp. 261–268.
15. FDR to Churchill, April 3, 1942, in Churchill, *The Second World War,* IV, 314.
16. Robert Sherwood, *Roosevelt and Hopkins: An Intimate History,* rev. ed., New York, 1950, p. 573.
17. Churchill, *The Second World War,* III, 444.
18. *Ibid.,* IV, 485.
19. Robert Murphy, *Diplomat Among Warriors,* New York, 1964, pp. 167–168. See also Maisky, *Memoirs of a Soviet Ambassador,* pp. 251, 282, 304, and an especially suggestive essay, John Bagguley, "The World War and the Cold War," in David Horowitz, ed., *Containment and Revolution,* Boston, 1967, pp. 76–124. I am grateful to William L. Neumann for calling my attention to the important article by Maurice Matloff, "The 90-Division Gamble," in Kent Roberts Greenfield, ed., *Command Decisions,* Washington, 1960. Matloff concludes that the gamble in favor of small ground forces was undertaken in order to "provide for a global coalition war without unduly straining the war economy and standards of living of the American people," and that it had (among others) two profound results: it relied on Russian manpower to hold and fight the Germans, and it stimulated even greater efforts to make air power the principal American weapon. This last, of course, had postwar implications for the drive to establish an independent Air Force. Quite obviously, then, there were internal tensions in American military and political planning as well as in Anglo-American disputes.

20. Bullitt to FDR, May 12, 1943, Roosevelt MSS, PSF 1.
21. Sherwood, *Roosevelt and Hopkins,* p. 714.
22. Anthony Eden, *The Reckoning,* Boston, 1965, pp. 430–432, 482; Herbert Feis, *Churchill, Roosevelt, Stalin: The War They Waged and the Peace They Sought,* Princeton, 1957, pp. 174–175.
23. "Memorandum to the President," March 18, 1945, Baruch MSS. Churchill, wrote Baruch, "was anxious to know what would happen when Germany was beaten. I told him we would then pass into the economic phases of the transition period, looking towards peace, that the democracies of the world, particularly America, would be the greatest source of aid to Russia, and that England and America were the only sources to which they could look for the things that Russia would need."
24. *Ibid.*
25. Edgar Snow, *Journey to the Beginning,* New York, 1958, pp. 343–344; Robert I. Gannon, *The Cardinal Spellman Story,* New York, 1962, pp. 222–224.
26. Stimson to FDR, August 10, 1943, Stimson MSS.
27. "Notes of the President's Meeting with the Joint Chiefs of Staff," November 19, 1943, *FR, Teheran,* pp. 248–261.
28. Feis, *Churchill, Roosevelt, Stalin,* pp. 174–175.
29. Harriman to Harry Hopkins, February 13, 1944, *FR, 1944,* IV, 1052–1053.
30. Harry L. Coles and Albert K. Weinberg, *Soldiers Become Governors,* Washington, 1964, pp. 446–447.
31. *Ibid.,* pp. 448–449.
32. *Ibid.*
33. "The World from Rome," *Life,* XVII (September 4, 1944), 94–109. See also his "The Future of France," *Life,* XVII (August 14, 1944), 74ff.
34. Barbara Ward, "Europe Debates Nationalization," *FAQ,* XXV (July 1946), 44–58. Miss Ward's point was not simply that the "Left" had moved to the forefront of the political scene, but that the extreme right and the left met on the question of national planning. "As in all political struggles, the issue was not clear cut. The fascists did not reject 'the organizing power of the state.' The Nazis in Germany created in such enterprises as the *Hermann Goering Werke* the largest nationalized undertakings in Europe. What the Fascists rejected was not so much the technical implications of Socialism as its political and moral content." In Bullitt's original definition, the basis of a temporary alliance between the "x's" and the "z's." Hence, America's great concern about the future.
35. McNeill, *America, Britain and Russia,* pp. 417–418, 468. FDR to Stalin, received October 5, 1944, Stalin Corr., II, 162–163.
36. Churchill, *The Second World War,* VI, 226–228.

37. *Ibid.,* Chap. 18. See Howard K. Smith, *The State of Europe,* New York, 1949, p. 234, for the way in which the American liberal press reacted to British action, and L. S. Stavrianos, *Greece: American Dilemma and Opportunity,* Chicago, 1952, for the fullest statement of American complicity by critical dissenters.
38. Churchill, *The Second World War,* VI, 289.
39. Churchill to Baruch, January 13, 1945, Baruch MSS.
40. Diary Entries, week of 17–23 December, 1944, *FR, Yalta,* pp. 435–436.
41. "Battle for Postwar Unity," *Business Week,* February 3, 1945, p. 16.
42. Diary Entry, October 23, 1944, Stimson MSS.
43. Morgenthau to FDR, January 1, 1945, *FR, Yalta,* pp. 309–310.
44. "Will America Back Out?," *Nation,* CLX (January 13, 1945), 42–43 (emphasis added).
45. Will Clayton to Stettinius, January 20, 1945, and Clayton to Harriman, January 26, 1945, *FR, Yalta,* pp. 318–319, 321–322.
46. Stettinius to FDR, January 18, 1945, and Leo Pasvolsky to Stettinius, January 23, 1945, *ibid.,* pp. 97–101.
47. Arthur Bliss Lane, *I Saw Poland Betrayed,* Indianapolis, 1948, pp. 66–67.
48. Arthur H. Vandenberg, Jr., ed., *The Private Papers of Senator Vandenberg,* Boston, 1952, pp. 140–144.
49. *Ibid.*
50. Stimson to Stettinius, January 23, 1945, *FR, 1945,* I, 23–27.
51. The editorial continued: "After Vandenberg had finished, Senator Connally tried to poohpooh the whole thing, asking for blanket trust in the President . . . . But for average citizens Senator Vandenberg's forthright proposal swept away months of accumulated confusion and doubt." Editorial, *Life,* XXII (January 23, 1945), 26.
52. "We don't seem to have gotten along very well . . . with our suggestions to the President. . . . I also had a telegram from Stettinius about my suggestion as to the Dumbarton Oaks and the interim organization. The cable was rather cryptic and Stettinius said that he had shown the message to the President and would be glad to explain the matter satisfactorily to me but from that I gathered that the President was not with me." Diary Entries, February 12, 22, 1945, Stimson MSS.
53. Despite efforts to explain Roosevelt's attitude toward the Declaration of Liberated Europe, several problems remain unresolved. When it came up at Malta at an Anglo-American Foreign Ministers' Conference, Stettinius noted: "The President had indeed some misgivings that its adoption might prejudice the prospects of the World Organization which was the question of paramount importance." This sentence may be read to mean: (1) FDR did not want to challenge the Russian sphere of influence if it meant upsetting the chances for postwar cooperation; (2) FDR was more worried that the proposed machinery would derogate from the overall authority of the UN, or (3) FDR

was simply ambiguous on this as on other issues. Three days later, Roosevelt told his advisers that he preferred "periodic meetings" between the Big Three Foreign Ministers to the creation of a formal commission. Alger Hiss's cryptic notes later that same day of a Byrnes meeting with the American delegation support the second interpretation of FDR's motivations, but not conclusively: "Mr. B doesn't like indep. auth. of U.S. Commissioner. Would prefer decl. with auth. to *Ambassadors* to act as specified in protocol. Ambs. are appointed with consent of Pres. & are under control of Sec. Mr. B. fears any agency would perpetuate itself. Redraft as mere decl.—ad hoc commission for any country." See *FR, Yalta,* pp. 503, 566, 570.

54. Minutes of the Sixth Plenary Meeting, February 9, 1945, *ibid.,* pp. 844–850.
55. William D. Leahy, *I Was There,* New York, 1950, p. 314.
56. 992nd Press Conference, in Samuel I. Rosenman, ed., *The Public Papers and Addresses of Franklin D. Roosevelt,* 13 vols., New York, 1938–1950, 1944–1945 vol., pp. 562–563.
57. "Dumbarton Oaks and San Francisco," *Fortune* supplement, May 1945, p. 7. Another powerful publisher, James H. McGraw of McGraw-Hill, also commented editorially on the dilemma in *Business Week* for January 6, 1945, in "What Does America Want?" "Our one bargaining weakness stems from the fact that other nations, by contrast feeble in potential power, know what they want and are able to mobilize all their strength to achieve it" (pp. 94–95).
58. *Mr. Citizen,* New York, 1960, p. 165.
59. Allen W. Dulles to John Foster Dulles, February 6, 1945, Dulles MSS; Allen Dulles, *The Secret Surrender,* New York, 1966, pp. 147, 161, 164–165.

CHAPTER THREE. *Harry S. Truman: From San Francisco to Potsdam*

1. Joseph C. Grew to John M. Coffee, June 30, 1945, *SDB,* XIII (July 8, 1945), 49–52.
2. Coffee to Grew, May 18, 1945, Grew MSS.
3. Harry S. Truman, *Memoirs,* II: *Years of Trial and Hope,* New York, 1965 ed., 61.
4. Diary Entries, April 26, 30, 1945, Stimson MSS.
5. Truman, *Memoirs,* I: *Year of Decisions,* New York, 1965 ed., 454-455.
6. "Fortune Survey," *Fortune,* XXXII (January 1945), 260ff., and *ibid.* (September 1945), 233.
7. "Does Russia Want Credit?," *Fortune,* XXXII (July 1945), 110.
8. Fletcher Knebel and Charles W. Bailey II, *No High Ground,* New York, 1960, pp. 2–3.
9. Cabell Phillips, *The Truman Presidency,* New York, 1965, p. 79.

10. Harriman to Stettinius, January 6, 1945, *FR, Yalta,* pp. 313–314.
11. Truman, *Memoirs,* I, 85–87.
12. "Memorandum of a Conversation with the President," March 2, 1945, Franklin Roosevelt Memorial Foundation Papers, Franklin D. Roosevelt Library, Hyde Park, N.Y. Also in Grew MSS.
13. *Time,* April 30, 1945, p. 19; News Conference, April 17, 1945, HST: *Public Papers,* 1945, pp. 8–15.
14. "Memorandum of a Conversation by Mr. Charles Bohlen," April 20, 1945, *FR, 1945,* V, 231–233.
15. *Ibid.*
16. "Memorandum of a Conversation by Mr. Charles Bohlen," April 23, 1945, *ibid.,* pp. 256–258; Truman, *Memoirs,* I, 93–99; Diary Entry, April 23, 1945, Stimson MSS.
17. Truman, *Memoirs,* I, 93–99.
18. "Minutes of the Sixteenth Meeting of the United States Delegation . . . ," April 25, 1945, *FR, 1945,* I, 386–402.
19. Diary Entry, April 24, 1945, *Vandenberg Papers,* pp. 175–176.
20. Harriman to Stettinius, December 28, 1944, *FR, Yalta,* pp. 64–66; Truman, *Memoirs,* I, 388–389.
21. Bohlen Minutes, Third Plenary Session, February 6, 1945, *FR, Yalta,* pp. 660–671.
22. *SDB,* XII (April 29, 1945), 796–798.
23. *Aide Memoire,* March 9, 1945, *FR, 1945,* I, 113–114.
24. Diary Entry, April 27, 1945, *Vandenberg Papers,* p. 181.
25. *New York Herald Tribune,* May 1, 1945.
26. *Ibid.,* April 30, 1945.
27. See Vera Micheles Dean, "The San Francisco Conference," *Foreign Policy Reports,* XXI (July 15, 1945), 110–125.
28. Vandenberg to Stettinius, May 5, 1945, Dulles MSS. See also *Vandenberg Papers,* pp. 188–189.
29. "Memorandum of a Conversation with John J. McCloy," May 8, 1945, Stimson MSS.
30. The terms of the trusteeship are given in *SDB,* XV (November 17, 1946), 889–890; although the UN trusteeship system was designed to bring peoples forward to full nationhood, the U.S. refused to even speak of the Pacific islands on those terms. The American delegate to the Trusteeship Council, Francis Sayre, made this plain in response to a Soviet proposal for adding the words "or independence" to the American plan for "self-government." Sayre said, "The United States feels that it must record its opposition not to the principle of independence, to which no people could be more consecrated than the United States, but to the thought that it could possibly be achieved within any foreseeable future in this case." Sayre, "Dependent Peoples," Denver, 1947, pp. 14–15. Truman was blunter in this exchange with newsmen on those bases America "needed":

QUESTION: And those that we need—
THE PRESIDENT: We will keep.
QUESTION: We will annex, sir?
THE PRESIDENT: We will keep.
QUESTION: Forever.
THE PRESIDENT: That depends. As long as we need them. (HST: *Public Papers,* 1946, pp. 19–23.)

31. Press Conference, May 23, 1945, HST: *Public Papers,* 1945, pp. 65–69.
32. Editorial, "Shall America Help Russia Rebuild?," *Nation,* CLX (May 26, 1945), 588–589.
33. Dulles to Stettinius, May 24, 1945, Dulles MSS.
34. Truman, *Memoirs,* I, 343.
35. *FR, 1945,* I, 1432.
36. Diary Entries, May 13, 15, 1945, Stimson MSS.
37. U.S. Senate, Subcommittee on Banking and Currency, *Hearings: Full Employment Act of 1945,* 79th Cong., 1st sess., Washington, 1945, pp. 2–3.
38. *Ibid.,* p. 658.
39. *Ibid.,* p. 182. I have reversed the last two sentences in this quotation.
40. *Business Week,* January 27, 1945, p. 51.
41. Wallace, "Transform Liberal Words into Concrete Action," *Vital Speeches,* XI (February 15, 1945), 273–275.
42. John M. Hancock to Baruch, January 26, 1945, enclosing a copy of the speech, Baruch MSS.
43. Undated Memorandum, 1945, in Baruch MSS; see also Hoover to Stimson, May 15, 1945, Stimson MSS.
44. "Britain's New Government," *Vital Speeches,* XI (August 15, 1945), 649–650. See also Eric Goldman, *The Crucial Decade,* New York, 1960, p. 8. Goldman notes *Business Week's* observation that "The Labour victory . . . brought worried reconsideration of the general strength of 'New Deal' forces in and outside Britain."
45. "The Great Transition," *Fortune* XXXI (January 1945), 142–144.
46. Baruch to Gore, November 9, 1945, Baruch MSS. See also Claude Pepper to Baruch, June 23, 1945, Baruch MSS.
47. Baruch to Wright Patman, July 9, 1945, Baruch MSS.
48. Truman, *Memoirs,* I, 263.
49. "U.S. Stake in Soviet Sphere," *Business Week* (June 9, 1945), 117–118.
50. Press Conference, June 13, 1945, HST: *Public Papers,* 1945, pp. 118–127; Minutes of the Fifth Plenary Session, July 21, 1945, *FR, Potsdam,* II, 209.
51. Truman, *Memoirs,* I, 391.
52. Murphy, *Diplomat Among Warriors,* pp. 278–279.
53. Byrnes, *Speaking Frankly,* New York, 1947, p. 75.
54. *FR, Potsdam,* I, 256–264.

55. *Ibid.*
56. Thompson Minutes, First Plenary Session, July 17, 1945, *ibid.*, II, 52–59; Thompson Minutes, First Meeting of the Foreign Ministers, July 18, 1945, *ibid.*, pp. 66–76, 611–613.
57. "Memorandum," July 19, 1945, *ibid.*, pp. 645–646.
58. Department of State Minutes, Seventh Plenary Session, July 23, 1945, *ibid.*, pp. 299–312.
59. *Ibid.*
60. Truman, *Memoirs,* I, 415.
61. *FR, Potsdam,* II, 654.
62. Thompson Minutes, Eighth Plenary Session, July 24, 1945, *ibid.*, pp. 357–368.
63. Murphy, *Diplomat Among Warriors,* pp. 278–279.
64. Thompson Minutes, Twelth Plenary Session, August 1, 1945, *FR, Potsdam,* II, 565–578.
65. Truman, *Memoirs,* I, 455.
66. Diary Entry, July 17, 1945, Stimson MSS.
67. See Herbert Feis, *Between War and Peace: The Potsdam Conference,* Princeton, 1960, pp. 173–174.
68. *Ibid.* p. 177.
69. *Ibid.*
70. *Ibid.*, p. 178.
71. From an excerpt published in the *New York Times,* March 2, 1969.
72. HST: *Public Papers,* 1945, pp. 203–214.
73. Almost completely ignored by Truman were the conditions in Eastern Europe which made it "inevitable" that the USSR should make it a sphere of influence. During the German occupation, wrote Margaret Dewar, these economies were completely directed toward the war potential of Germany. "The collapse of Germany created an economic and political vacuum in the Eastern European area. . . . The countries concerned were in varying stages of economic dislocation, with industries and transport systems practically at a standstill, currencies enormously inflated, and agriculture severely hit by droughts in the years immediately following the war. All this made the resumption of foreign trade, particularly with the Western countries, very difficult." *Soviet Trade with Eastern Europe,* London, 1951, pp. 1–2.

CHAPTER FOUR. *James F. Byrnes: Collective Security Through Public Diplomacy*

1. FDR to Byrnes, June 10, 1944, and Byrnes to FDR, September 13, 1944, Roosevelt MSS, PSF 50.
2. Byrnes, *Speaking Frankly,* p. 18.

3. Burton K. Wheeler to Oswald Garrison Villard, February 21, 1945, Villard MSS.
4. Byrnes, *Speaking Frankly,* pp. 102–105; George F. Kennan, *Memoirs, 1925–1950,* Boston, 1967, p. 287.
5. Bohlen Minutes, Tripartite Dinner Meeting, February 4, 1945, *FR, Yalta,* p. 589.
6. U.S. Senate, Committee on Foreign Relations, *Hearings: Treaties of Peace with Italy, Rumania, Bulgaria, and Hungary,* 80th Cong., 1st sess., Washington, 1947, p. 29.
7. Byrnes, *All in One Lifetime,* New York, 1958, pp. 309–310.
8. Harriman to Grew, June 28, 1945, *FR, Potsdam,* I, 727–728.
9. Grew to Arthur Bliss Lane, July 12, 1945, *ibid.,* pp. 788–789; see also Lane, *I Saw Poland Betrayed,* pp. 142–146, 226–227.
10. Byrnes, *Speaking Frankly,* pp. 102–105.
11. Ethridge and C. E. Black, "Negotiating on the Balkans," in Raymond Dennett and Joseph E. Johnson, eds., *Negotiating with the Russians,* Boston, 1951, p. 181.
12. Byrnes, *All in One Lifetime,* pp. 283–284; Leo Szilard, "Personal History," University of Chicago, *Roundtable* (1949), pp. 14–15.
13. Leo Szilard, "Reminiscences," ed. by Gertrud Weiss Szilard and Kathleen R. Winsor, in Donald Fleming and Bernard Bailyn, eds., *Perspectives in American History,* II, Cambridge, Mass., 1968, 128.
14. Diary Entry, September 4, 1945, Stimson MSS.
15. "Memorandum by the Soviet Delegation . . . ," September 12, 1945, *FR, 1945,* II, 150.
16. Record of the First Meeting . . . ," September 11, 1945, *ibid.,* pp. 114–115; "Memorandum by Mr. Cavendish Cannon . . . ," September 14, 1945, *ibid.,* pp. 182–185.
17. Burton Y. Berry to Byrnes, September 16, 1945, Dulles MSS.
18. "Memorandum of a Conversation," September 19, 1945, *FR, 1945,* II, 243–247.
19. Text of Molotov Press Conference, September 20, 1945, in Dulles MSS.
20. Byrnes, *Speaking Frankly,* p. 102.
21. "Memorandum by the United States Delegation," September 19, 1945, *FR, 1945,* II, 263; "Memorandum of a Conversaion," September 20, 1945, *ibid.,* pp. 268–269. See also McNeill, *America, Britain* and *Russia,* pp. 724–725.
22. "John Foster Dulles Comment on Reservation re Groza Government," undated [October 13], 1945, Dulles MSS.
23. "Memorandum of a Conversation," September 20, 1945, *FR, 1945,* II, 268–269.
24. Truman to Grew, June 9, 1945, *FR, Potsdam,* I, 163, 191.
25. Quoted in Gar Alperovitz, *Atomic Diplomacy,* New York, 1964, p. 173.

26. Byrnes, *Speaking Frankly,* pp. 102–105.
27. Vera M. Dean, "U.S. Policy in Europe," *Foreign Policy Reports,* XXI (January 15, 1946), 281–295.
28. Unsigned Memorandum, August 8, 1945, Dulles MSS.
29. Byrnes, *Speaking Frankly,* pp. 94–95.
30. Harriman to Byrnes, September 28, 1945, Dulles MSS.
31. October 15, 1945, p. 21.
32. From a note pinned to printed copy of Dulles' radio broadcast address of October 6, 1945, Dulles MSS.
33. *New York Herald Tribune,* November 7, 1945. Molotov added significantly, "A number of European countries have carried out such fundamental social reforms as the abolition of the obsolete system of landed estates, turning the land over to needy peasants." The implications for capitalism in those countries was clear.
34. Ethridge and Black, "Negotiating on the Balkans," p. 172.
35. Elbridge Durbrow to Arthur Bliss Lane, November 29, 1945, Lane MSS.
36. "Memorandum of a Conversation," October 24, 1945, *FR, 1945,* II, 568–569.
37. "United States Delegation Minutes, First Formal Session . . . ," December 16, 1945, *ibid.,* pp. 610–621.
38. Byrnes, *Speaking Frankly,* pp. 115–120; "Memorandum of Conversation," December 23, 1945, *FR, 1945,* II, 750–758.
39. Byrnes, *Speaking Frankly,* pp. 171–172.
40. Acheson to Byrnes, December 20, 1945, *FR, 1945,* II, 707–708; Byrnes to Acheson, December 22, 1945, *ibid.,* p. 725.
41. Press Conference, January 8, 1946, HST: *Public Papers,* 1946, pp. 9–13; portions of the "letter" were first published in William Hillman, *Mr. President,* New York, 1952, pp. 21–22; the full text was then published by Truman in his *Memoirs,* I, 604–606.
42. "America's Position on World Problems," *Vital Speeches,* XII (March 15, 1946), 326–329. See also *Vandenberg Papers,* pp. 249–250.
43. Tris Coffin, "Truman's Second Guess," *Nation,* CLXIII (September 28, 1946), 342–344.
44. Lippmann's comments are reprinted in Norman Graebner, ed., *Ideas and Diplomacy,* New York, 1964, pp. 705–710.
45. Byrnes, *Speaking Frankly,* p. 129.
46. V. M. Molotov, *Problems of Foreign Policy: Speeches and Statements,* Moscow, 1949, p. 42.
47. *Vandenberg Papers,* p. 263; *SDB,* XV (August 4, 1946), 207–208.
48. *New York Times,* March 14, 1946.
49. "Gloom in Paris," *Nation,* CLXII (May 18, 1946), 588–589.
50. *Ibid.*
51. McNeill, *America, Britain* and *Russia,* p. 694.
52. Byrnes, *Speaking Frankly,* p. 130; Molotov, *Problems,* pp. 37–38.

53. Text in *SDB,* XV (August 4, 1946), 262–263.
54. Byrnes, *Speaking Frankly,* pp. 144–145.
55. *Vandenberg Papers,* pp. 298–299; *SDB,* XV (October 20, 1946), 712–713.
56. Molotov, *Problems,* pp. 214–215.
57. Charles E. Bohlen, "Third Session of the Council of Foreign Ministers," *SDB,* XVI (February 2, 1947), 183–186.
58. Senate Foreign Relations Committee, *Peace Treaties . . . ,* pp. 9–10, 28–29.
59. *Ibid.*

CHAPTER FIVE. *Will Clayton, the British Loan, and the Political Economy of Cold War*

1. Diary Entry, February 2, 1940, Moffat MSS.
2. "Memorandum by the Assistant Secretary of State," July 28, 1941, *FR, 1941,* III, 10–12; Keynes to Acheson, July 29, 1941, *ibid.,* pp. 16–17.
3. Elliott Roosevelt, *As He Saw It,* New York, 1946, pp. 35–36.
4. This background material is based primarily on three sources: Ellen Clayton Garwood, *Will Clayton: A Short Biography,* Austin, Tex., 1958; "Cotton Colussus," *Business Week* (April 14, 1945), pp. 18–19; "Will Clayton's Cotton, I," *Fortune,* XXXII (November 1945), 138–146.
5. The exchange is explained in greater detail in Lloyd C. Gardner, *Economic Aspects of New Deal Diplomacy,* Madison, Wisc., 1964, pp. 262–264.
6. *Ibid.*
7. Gabriel Kolko, *The Politics of War: The World and United States Foreign Policy, 1943–1945,* New York, 1968, pp. 256, 294.
8. *Ibid.*
9. Cited in Richard N. Gardner, *Sterling Dollar Diplomacy,* Oxford, 1956, p. 197.
10. These two paragraphs are a summary of Chap. 13 of Gardner, *Economic Aspects.*
11. "The Bretton Woods Proposals," undated memorandum, Roosevelt MSS, OF 5544.
12. Raymond F. Mikesell, "Negotiating at Bretton Woods," in Dennett and Johnson, eds., *Negotiating with the Russians,* pp. 103–109; Ernest F. Penrose, *Economic Planning for the Peace,* Princeton, 1953.
13. Balogh, "Political Economy of the Cold War," in T. E. M. McKittrick and Kenneth Younger, eds., *Fabian International Essays,* New York, 1957, pp. 41–77.
14. *New York Times,* March 11, 1945, p. 33.

15. *Ibid.*, March 21, 1945, p. 12.
16. *SDB,* XII (April 29, 1945), 826–831; *SDB,* XII (May 20, 1945), 942–946.
17. *Ibid.* (April 22, 1945), pp. 760–762. See also Dean Acheson, "The Interest of the American Businessman in International Trade," *Vital Speeches,* XI (February 15, 1945), 263–265; *SDB,* XII (May 27, 1945), 979–982.
18. Clement Attlee, *Twilight of Empire,* New York, 1962, p. 134.
19. "Memorandum for the Secretary of State," September 3, 1945, Forrestal MSS. Also Forrestal to Byrnes, December 7, 1945, Forrestal MSS.
20. R. H. Brand to Baruch, November 23, 1945, Baruch MSS.
21. Baruch to Churchill, November 30, 1945, Baruch MSS.
22. Clayton to Baruch, December 16, 1946, Baruch MSS.
23. Gardner, *Sterling Dollar Diplomacy,* Chap. 11; *SDB,* XIII (December 9, 1945), 913: Klaus E. Knorr, "The American Trade Proposals," in *Yale Institute of International Studies Memos,* No. 19 (October 28, 1946), pp. 3–7; L. S. Amery, *The Washington Loan Agreements,* London, 1946.
24. William D. Pawley to FDR, October 15, 1944, Roosevelt MSS, OF 48-H; see also "Memorandum of a Luncheon Meeting," November 17, 1943, White MSS; Henry Grady to FDR, August 5, 1942, Roosevelt MSS, OF 48-H; "Memorandum of a Conversation with Anthony Eden," May 16, 1945, Grew MSS.
25. Clayton to Forrestal, May 14, 1946, Forrestal MSS.
26. Quotation is from p. 55 of *Foreign Commerce Weekly,* XX (July 21, 1945), but the whole issue is filled with various kinds of statistical analyses of the Indian market.
27. *NFTC,* 1946, pp. 244ff.
28. Eugene Varga, "Anglo-American Rivalry and Partnership: A Marxist View," *FAQ,* XXV (July 1947), 583-595.
29. Press Conference, December 7, 1945, HST: *Public Papers,* 1945, pp. 524–529.
30. Eleanor Roosevelt to Truman, November 20, 1945; Truman to Eleanor Roosevelt, November 26, 1945, Baruch MSS.
31. Clayton to Forrestal, May 10, 1946, Forrestal MSS.
32. Press Conference, February 21, 1946, HST: *Public Papers,* 1946, pp. 127–131.
33. *New York Herald Tribune,* March 3, 1946. On the whole development of this question, see Herbert Feis, "Political Aspects of Foreign Loans," in *FAQ,* XXIII (July 1945), 609–619, and McNeill, *America, Britain and Russia,* pp. 687-691.
34. U.S. House of Representatives, Committee on Banking and Currency, *Hearings: Anglo-American Financial Agreement,* 79th Cong., 2nd sess., Washington, 1946, pp. 219–221, *passim.*

35. U.S. Senate, Committee on Banking and Currency, *Hearings: Anglo-American Financial Agreement,* 79th Cong., 2nd sess., Washington, 1946, pp. 174–175; Clayton, "Memorandum for Mr. Baruch," April 26, 1946, Baruch MSS.
36. Diary Entry, December 19, 1945, *Vandenberg Papers,* pp. 230–231.
37. Gardner, *Sterling Dollar Diplomacy,* p. 251.
38. Herbert Feis, "The Conflict over Trade Ideologies," *FAQ,* XXV (January 1947), 217–228. See also Feis, "Keynes in Retrospect," *ibid.,* XXIX (July 1951), 564–577.
39. November 30, 1946, pp. 95–96. See also *New York Times,* August 31, September 5, 1946.
40. *SDB,* XIV (February 24, 1946), 273–276.
41. Gardner, *Sterling Dollar Diplomacy,* p. 337.
42. *Ibid.,* p. 339. See also Diary Entry, February 25, 1947, *Forrestal Diaries,* p. 246.
43. U.S. Senate, Foreign Relations Committee, *Hearings: Interim Aid for Europe,* 80th Cong., 1st sess., Washington, 1947, p. 238.
44. *New York Times,* December 19, 1947, p. 2.
45. U.S. Senate, Foreign Relations Committee, *Hearings: North Atlantic Treaty,* 81st Cong., 1st sess., Washington, 1949, p. 381.
46. *Ibid.,* p. 405.
47. "American Liberals and British Labor," *Nation,* CLXII (June 8, 1946), 683–684.
48. J.-J. Servan-Schreiber, *The American Challenge,* trans. by Ronald Steel, New York, 1968, p. 17.
49. *Ibid.,* p. 11.
50. New York, 1946, p. 121.
51. Bullitt to Louis Wehle, March 23, 1948, The Papers of Louis Wehle, Franklin D. Roosevelt Library, Hyde Park, N.Y.

CHAPTER SIX. *George C. Marshall: Traditional Policy in Post-Traditional China*

1. Quoted by Tang Tsou, *America's Failure in China, 1941–1950,* Chicago, 1963, p. 35.
2. "Memorandum of Conversation . . . ," March 14, 1944, *FR, 1944,* VI, 216–218; John F. Melby, *The Mandate of Heaven: Record of a Civil War, China 1945–1949,* Toronto, 1968, p. 16. Melby specifically identified Stanley K. Hornbeck as the culprit, but whether or not it was in fact Hornbeck, it seems fair to say that this characterization was not foisted upon Americans by the international communist conspiracy.
3. Wallace to FDR, July 10, 1944, *FR, 1944,* VI, 240–244.

4. Truman, *Memoirs,* II, 61–62.
5. Albert C. Wedemeyer, *Wedemeyer Reports!,* New York, 1958, pp. 345ff.
6. American Embassy at Chungking to State Department, July 17, 1943, reprinted in U.S. Senate, Judiciary Committee, *Morgenthau Diary* (China), 2 vols., 89th Cong., 1st sess., Washington, 1965, II, 901–903.
7. American Embassy to State Department, December 9, 1943, *ibid.,* pp. 920–922.
8. "Memorandum of Conversation . . . ," October 4, 1944, *FR, 1944,* VI, 260–264; Gardner, *Economic Aspects of New Deal Diplomacy,* p. 250.
9. "Summary Notes of Conversations Between Vice President Henry A. Wallace and President Chiang Kai-shek, June 21–24, 1944," *CWP,* pp. 550–551.
10. Stimson to Truman, July 16, 1945, *FR, Potsdam,* II, 631. Of Truman's advisers at Potsdam, Stimson was the most vociferous in calling Truman's attention to the traditional American policy toward China, and in pointing up the importance of the atomic bomb in this regard. See also "Notes for Diary, July 15–24, 1945," Stimson MSS.
11. *The Great Globe Itself,* p. 148.
12. The letter is quoted in Don Lohbeck, *Patrick J. Hurley,* Chicago, 1956, p. 427.
13. Herbert Feis, *The China Tangle,* New York, 1965 ed., p. 419; Robert Ferrell, *George C. Marshall as Secretary of State, 1947–1949,* New York, 1966, pp. 27–28.
14. Feis, *China Tangle,* p. 419.
15. Diary Entry, July 8, 1946, *Forrestal Diaries,* pp. 174–175.
16. *CWP,* p. 308.
17. H. Maurer, "The Tyrannous Decade," *Fortune,* XXXVII (February 1948), 113–119.
18. U.S. Senate, Subcommittee of the Committee on the Judiciary, *Hearings: Institute of Pacific Relations,* 82nd Cong., 1st sess., Washington, 1951, pp. 1713–1714.
19. *Fifty Years in China,* New York, 1954, pp. 182–183.
20. Andrew Roth, "Cross-Fire in Korea," *Nation,* CLXII (February 23, 1946), 220–223.
21. Anthony Kubek, *How the Far East Was Lost,* Chicago, 1963, p. xiv.
22. *NFTC,* 1948, p. 172.
23. Robert C. North, *Moscow and Chinese Communists,* Stanford, Calif., pp. 222–223.
24. George H. Blakeslee, "The Far Eastern Commission," in Dennett and Johnson, eds., *Negotiating with the Russians,* pp. 122–123.
25. "Memorandum of Conversation . . . ," December 23, 1945, *FR, 1945,* II, 750–758.

26. Davies, *Foreign and Other Affairs,* New York, 1966, pp. 134–135.
27. Diary Entry, March 8, 1947, Melby, *Mandate of Heaven,* pp. 194–195.
28. Chiang Kai-shek, *Soviet Russia in China: A Summing Up at Seventy,* New York, 1957, pp. 146–150.
29. Interview, January 22, 1969.
30. Chiang, *Soviet Russia in China,* pp. 148–150.
31. Press Conference, January 31, 1946, HST: *Public Papers,* 1946, pp. 102–105.
32. Interview, January 22, 1969.
33. O. Edmund Clubb, *Twentieth-Century China,* New York, 1964, pp. 267–268.
34. Melby, *Mandate of Heaven,* p. 90.
35. Mao Tse-tung, *Selected Works,* 4 vols., Peking, 1961, IV, 159.
36. *CWP,* pp. 652–654.
37. *New York Times,* June 29, 1946; Chiang, *Soviet Russia in China,* pp. 150–151.
38. Melby, *Mandate of Heaven,* p. 161.
39. *Ibid.,* pp. 160–161; Diary Entry, December 7, 1946, Diary of Leighton Stuart.
40. Senate Judiciary Subcommittee, *Institute of Pacific Relations,* pp. 2257–2260.
41. HST: *Public Papers,* 1946, p. 348.
42. *Forrestal Diaries,* pp. 180; Forrestal to Marshall, February 27, 1947, Forrestal MSS.
43. Senate Judiciary Subcommittee, *Institute of Pacific Relations,* p. 1309.
44. Melby, *Mandate of Heaven,* pp. 227–228.
45. Reprinted in Franz Schurmann and Orville Schell, *The China Reader: Republican China,* New York, 1967, pp. 340–357.
46. Forrestal to MacArthur, April 20, 1946, Forrestal MSS; *Forrestal Diaries,* p. 341.
47. *CWP,* pp. 828–829.
48. *Ibid.,* pp. 870–871.
49. Press Conference, March 11, 1948, HST: *Public Papers,* 1948, pp. 178–181.
50. David E. Lilienthal, *The Journals of David Lilienthal,* 3 vols., New York, 1964, II, 525.
51. *Ibid.,* pp. 345–346.
52. John K. Fairbank, *et al., The Next Step in Asia,* Cambridge, Mass., 1949.
53. Senate Judiciary Subcommittee, *Institute of Pacific Relations,* pp. 1551–1682.
54. U.S. Senate, Foreign Relations Committee, *Hearings: Japanese Peace Treaty and Other Treaties Relating to Security in the Pacific,* 82nd Cong., 2nd sess., Washington, 1952, p. 12.

55. Marshall to Baruch, August 21, 1946, Baruch MSS.

CHAPTER SEVEN. *Bernard M. Baruch: Atoms for Peace*

1. Alperovitz, *Atomic Diplomacy,* p. 173.
2. Knebel and Bailey, *No High Ground,* pp. 1–2.
3. Quoted in Gardner, *Economic Aspects of New Deal Diplomacy,* p. 292.
4. Leahy to Baruch, June 11, 1946, Baruch MSS.
5. Fred Searls, Jr., to Byrnes, October 24, 1946, Baruch MSS.
6. "International Control of Atomic Energy," *FAQ,* XVI (January 1948), 239–252; U.S. Atomic Energy Commission, *In the Matter of J. Robert Oppenheimer, Transcript of Hearing Before Personnel Security Board,* Washington, 1954, p. 38.
7. McNeill, *America, Britain and Russia,* pp. 198-199. McNeill's usual insight ran short here.
8. Leslie R. Groves, *Now It Can Be Told: The Story of the Manhattan Project,* New York, 1962, p. 132; Diary Entry, December 27, 1942, Stimson MSS.
9. Alice Kimball Smith, *A Peril and a Hope: The Scientists' Movement in America, 1945–1947,* Chicago, 1965, pp. 7–10.
10. Richard G. Hewlett and Oscar Anderson, Jr., *A History of the United States Atomic Energy Commission,* I: *The New World,* University Park, Pa., 1962, 329–331.
11. Diary Entry, December 31, 1944, Stimson MSS.
12. Diary Entries, February 15, March 15, 1945, Stimson MSS; Hewlett and Anderson, *The New World,* p. 338.
13. Hewlitt and Anderson, *The New World,* p. 344; Groves, *Now It Can Be Told,* pp. 234–243; *FR, 1945,* II, 1–25.
14. Diary Entries, May 13, 14, 15, 1945, Stimson MSS.
15. Truman, *Memoirs,* I, 104–105; Hewlett and Anderson, *The New World,* p. 354; Szilard, "Reminiscences," p. 126.
16. Truman, *Memoirs,* I, 104–105. See also Louis Morton, "The Decision to Use the Atomic Bomb," *FAQ,* XXXV (January 1957), 334–353.
17. Diary Entry, June 6, 1945, Stimson MSS.
18. Atomic Energy Commission, *Oppenheimer,* pp. 32–34.
19. Szilard, "Reminiscences," pp. 128–129.
20. Morton, "Decision to Use the Atomic Bomb," pp. 334–353.
21. "Memorandum of a Talk with HST," June 6, 1945, Stimson MSS; also "Notes at Potsdam," Stimson MSS, and Diary Entry, June 24, 1945, Stimson MSS.
22. The memorandum has been printed in several places; my background notes come from the Stimson Diary from August 12 to September 12, 1945, Stimson MSS.
23. *New York Times,* September 22, 1945; Patterson to HST, September

26, 1945; Acheson to HST, September 25, 1945, *FR, 1945,* II, 48–50, 54–55.

24. Attlee to Truman, September 25, 1945, cited in Attlee, *Twilight of Empire,* pp. 97–101.
25. *SDB,* XIII (October 7, 1945), 514; Truman, *Memoirs,* I, 585–587; Press Conference, October 8, 1945, HST: *Public Papers,* 1945, pp. 381–388.
26. *FR, 1945,* II, 55–57.
27. "Minutes of a Meeting . . . ," October 16, 1945, *ibid.,* pp. 59–61.
28. *SDB,* XIII (November 18, 1945), 783ff; *New York Herald Tribune,* November 16, 1945.
29. Kerr to Bevin, December 3, 1945, *FR, 1945,* II, 82–84.
30. Byrnes, *All in One Lifetime,* pp. 336–338.
31. Hewlett and Anderson, *The New World,* p. 548; Lilienthal, *Journals,* II, 30.
32. See R. W. Albright to Baruch, March 14, 1950, Baruch MSS.
33. Secretary of State's Committee on Atomic Energy, *A Report on the International Control of Atomic Energy,* Washington, 1946, pp. 13–14.
34. "Atomic Pie in the Sky," *Nation,* CLXII (April 6, 1946), 390–391; "Notes on Bernard M. Baruch," undated, 1949, Baruch MSS.
35. Baruch MSS.
36. John M. Hancock Notes of Meeting, April 4, 1946, Baruch MSS.
37. John M. Hancock Notes of Meeting, May 8, 1946, Baruch MSS.
38. Lilienthal, *Journals,* II, 51; "Memorandum . . . , June 1, 1946, *Baruch* MSS.
39. Lilienthal, *Journals,* II, 49.
40. "BMB Memorandum of Meeting on June 7, 1946, with the President and J. F. Byrnes," Baruch MSS.
41. Hewlett and Anderson, *The New World,* p. 584.
42. Baruch to Truman, July 2, 1946; Truman to Baruch, July 10, 1946, Baruch MSS.
43. Adam B. Ulam, *Expansion and Coexistence: The History of Soviet Foreign Policy, 1917–1967,* New York, 1968, pp. 415–416.
44. 'Excerpts from Telephone Conversation Between Hon. James Forrestal . . . and Mr. Walter Lippmann," November 29, 1946, Forrestal MSS; Lilienthal, *Journals,* II, 70.
45. Tris Coffin, "In the Light of Bikini," *Nation,* CLXIII (October 5, 1946), 370–371.
46. *SDB,* XV (August 4, 1946), 209–210.
47. *Vandenberg Papers,* p. 291.
48. "Excerpts from Telephone Conversation Between Hon. James Forrestal and Mr. Walter Lippmann," November 29, 1946, Forrestal MSS.
49. "Memorandum for the President," September 17, 1946, Baruch MSS; "Telephone Conversation with H.S.T.," October 28, 1946, Baruch MSS.
50. Byrnes, *All in One Lifetime,* pp. 385–386.

51. Transcript of Speech at National War College, December 5, 1946, Baruch MSS.
52. Lilienthal, *Journals,* II, 123; Baruch to Conant, December 24, 1946, Baruch MSS.
53. Atomic Energy Commission, *Oppenheimer,* p. 41.

CHAPTER EIGHT. *Dean Acheson and the "Holy Pretense"*

1. See George L. Mosse, *The Holy Pretense,* Oxford, England, 1957.
2. Louis Halle, *The Cold War as History,* New York, 1967, *passim.*
3. Dean Acheson, *A Democrat Looks at His Party,* New York, 1967, p. 91.
4. Gardner, *Economic Aspects of New Deal Diplomacy,* p. 277.
5. U.S. Senate, Special Committee on Post-War Economic Policy and Planning, *Economic Problems of the Transition Period,* 78th Cong., 2nd sess., and 79th Cong., 1st sess., Washington, 1945, p. 1082.
6. *SDB,* XIII (August 5, 1945), 181-188.
7. U.S. House of Representatives, Committee on Banking and Currency, *Hearings: Bretton Woods Agreements Act,* 79th Cong., 1st sess., Washington, 1945, p. 48.
8. Senate Banking and Currency Committee, *Anglo-American Financial Agreement,* p. 313.
9. Acheson, *A Democrat,* p. 159.
10. Noted in Walter LaFeber, *America, Russia, and the Cold War, 1945–1966,* New York, 1968, p. 102.
11. *Vital Speeches,* XII (August 1, 1946), 633–635.
12. U.S. House of Representatives, Committee on Foreign Affairs, *Hearings: Assistance to Greece and Turkey,* 80th Cong., 1st sess., Washington, 1947, p. 43.
13. Reprinted in McGeorge Bundy, ed., *The Pattern of Responsibility,* Boston, 1952, pp. 298–299.
14. *Ibid.,* pp. 427–428.
15. "Remarks at a Meeting with the American Society of Newspaper Editors," April 17, 1947, HST: *Public Papers,* 1947, pp. 207-210.
16. *Ibid.*
17. Truman, *Memoirs,* II, 429.
18. U.S. House of Representatives, *Hearings: United States Foreign Policy for a Post-war Recovery Program,* 80th Cong., 1st and 2nd sess., Washington, 1948, pp. 696–697.
19. House Foreign Affairs Committtee, *Post-War Recovery Program,* pp. 695–696.
20. *Ibid.,* pp. 734–735.
21. *New York Times,* April 12, 1947.

22. New York, 1948, pp. 99–100.
23. FDR to Mrs. L. Stuyvesant Chandler, January 12, 1944, Roosevelt MSS, OF 4678; see also Edward R. Stettinius, *Roosevelt and the Russians,* New York, 1949, pp. 180–181.
24. Millspaugh, *Americans in Persia,* New York, 1947, p. 233.
25. "Memorandum of a Conversation," January 31, 1945, Grew MSS.
26. "Minutes of Foreign Ministers' Meeting," February 1, 1945, *FR, Yalta,* p. 501.
27. "Minutes of Foreign Ministers' Meeting," February 8, 1945, *ibid.,* pp. 739–740.
28. "Memorandum of a Conversation," March 10, 1945, Grew MSS.
29. "Memorandum of a Conversation with the President . . . ," May 28, 1945; "Memorandum of a Conversation with Nuri Pasha . . . ," May 29, 1945, Grew MSS; and "Memorandum of a Conversation with the President . . . ," June 5, 1945, Grew MSS.
30. Byrnes, *Speaking Frankly,* pp. 118–119; Byrnes, *All in One Lifetime,* pp. 333–334.
31. "Memorandum of a Conversation . . . ," December 23, 1945, *FR, 1945,* II, 750–751.
32. Byrnes, *Speaking Frankly,* pp. 126–127.
33. Library of Congress, Legislative Reference Service, "Middle East Oil in United States Foreign Policy," by Halford L. Haskins, PAB 89, Washington, 1950, p. 60; J. C. Hurewitz, *Middle-East Dilemmas,* New York, 1953, p. 29.
34. October 5, 1946, pp. 111–112.
35. *SDB,* XVI (January 26, 1947), 143–151, 167, provides an excellent summary of the diplomatic exchanges up to that point.
36. Joseph M. Jones, *The Fifteen Weeks,* New York, 1964 ed., p. 62; *New York Times,* September 3, 1946.
37. *SDB,* XV (September 1, 1946), 420–422. See also Millis, *Forrestal Diaries,* p. 211.
38. *SDB,* XVI (January 5, 1947), 29; *SDB,* XVI (February 23, 1947), 341; Jones, *Fifteen Weeks,* pp. 6–7.
39. Jones, *Fifteen Weeks,* pp. 138–142.
40. Jones to William Benton, February 26, 1947, cited in Henry W. Berger, "A Conservative Critique of Containment," in David Horowitz, ed., *Containment and Revolution,* Boston, 1967, pp. 125–139.
41. "Address on Foreign Economic Policy . . . ," March 6, 1947, HST: *Public Papers,* 1947, pp. 167–172.
42. "Draft," March 10, 1947, Clark M. Clifford Papers, cited in Barton J. Bernstein, "American Foreign Policy and the Origins of the Cold War," unpublished MS.
43. Jones, *Fifteen Weeks,* pp. 155–157.
44. Forrestal to Paul Smith, March 19, 1947, Forrestal MSS.

45. *San Francisco Chronicle,* March 13, 15, 1947.
46. Howard K. Smith, *The State of Europe,* New York, 1949, pp. 89–90.
47. Lilienthal, *Journals,* II, 215.
48. Pp. 18–19, 45–49; Forrestal to Admiral Chester Nimitz, April 12, 1947, Forrestal MSS.
49. House Foreign Affairs Committee, *Assistance to Greece and Turkey,* pp. 56–57.
50. Jones, *Fifteen Weeks,* p. 163.
51. House Foreign Affairs Committee, *Assistance to Greece and Turkey,* pp. 46–47.
52. *Congressional Record,* April 22, 1947, pp. 3888–3889.
53. U.S. Senate, Committee on Foreign Relations, *Hearings: Assistance to Greece and Turkey,* 80th Cong., 1st sess., Washington, 1947, p. 97; *Vandenberg Papers,* pp. 344–345.
54. Jones, *Fifteen Weeks,* pp. 274ff.
55. Jonathan Daniels, *The Man of Independence,* New York, 1950, p. 322.
56. U.S. Senate, Committee on Foreign Relations, *Hearings: Interim Aid for Europe,* 80th Cong., 1st sess., Washington, 1947, p. 12.
57. Jones, *Fifteen Weeks,* pp. 252–253; see also Harry B. Price, *The Marshall Plan and Its Meaning,* Ithaca, N.Y.; 1955, pp. 21-24, and in general for background material.
58. Senate, *Assistance to Greece and Turkey,* p. 81.
59. James Paul Warburg, *Germany, Key to Peace,* Cambridge, Mass., 1953, p. 45; Molotov, *Problems of Foreign Policy,* pp. 465–471.
60. Smith, *State of Europe,* p. 219; James Paul Warburg, *The Long Road Home: The Autobiography of a Maverick,* New York, 1964, p. 239.
61. Reprinted in Raymond Dennett and Robert Turner, *Documents on American Foreign Relations, 1947,* Princeton, 1949, pp. 11–13; *New York Times,* June 16, 1947.
62. Dean Acheson, *Power and Diplomacy,* Cambridge, Mass., 1958, p. 9.
63. Atomic Energy Commission, *Oppenheimer,* p. 367.
64. Senate, *Interim Aid,* p. 47.

CHAPTER NINE. *Lucius D. Clay: American Decisions in Germany*

1. Morgenthau's belief that those who thought in terms of a re-centralized Germany were seeking an anti-Bolshevik bulwark came more and more to dominate his view, although he himself was equally "conservative" when it came to the rest of Western Europe. "The more I think on this problem, and the more I hear and read discussion of it, the clearer it seems to me that the real motive of most of those who oppose a weak Germany is not any actual disagreement. . . . It is simply an expression of fear of Russia and communism." Cited in

Paul Y. Hammond, "Directives for the Occupation of Germany," in Stein, *Civil-Military Decisions,* pp. 405–406.

2. Bohlen Minutes, Second Plenary Meeting, February 5, 1945, *FR, Yalta,* pp. 622–623. See also pp. 624–633.
3. "Memorandum for the President," September 15, 1944, Stimson MSS.
4. Stalin Corr., II, 208–210.
5. These figures are from Seweryn Bialer, ed., *Stalin and His Generals,* New York, 1969, p. 621.
6. Quoted in Bialer, *Stalin and His Generals,* pp. 516–517.
7. *Ibid.,* pp. 557–559.
8. Byrnes, *All in One Lifetime,* p. 273; Murphy, *Diplomat Among Warriors,* pp. 247–248; Lucius D. Clay, *Decision in Germany,* New York, 1950, p. 5. Clay's recollection of the incident suggests that the President in his last days could bring himself only to think about the broadest kinds of issues, after the likely political conflicts had been settled and a clear field established for American policy. "He believed that a huge hydroelectric power development serving several of the European countries—a sort of international TVA—was essential to economic rehabilitation and would lead to better co-operation among the participating countries."
9. Diplomat Among Warriors, p. 251.
10. John Gimbel, *The American Occupation of Germany: Politics and the Military, 1945–1949,* Stanford, Calif., 1968, p. 6.
11. Memorandum, July 16, 1946, Forrestal MSS.
12. U.S. Senate, Subcommittee of Committee on Military Affairs, *Hearings: Elimination of German Resources for War,* 79th Cong., 1st sess., Washington, 1946, p. 621; see also p. 1026.
13. General background on this question can be found in *FR, 1945,* III, 1186ff. On this specific point, see "Memorandum . . . ," May 7, 1945, and Grew to Kennan, May 13, 1945, *ibid.,* pp. 1208–1211.
14. Kennan to Harriman, May 14, 1945; Harriman to Kennan, May 20, 1945, *ibid.,* pp. 1212–1213.
15. Kennan to Secretary of State, May 14, 1945, *ibid.,* pp. 1213–1215.
16. British Embassy to State Department, May 28, 1945, *ibid.,* p. 313.
17. Cited in Lionel Kochan, *The Struggle for Germany, 1914–1945,* New York, 1967 ed., p. 127.
18. Bialer, *Stalin and His Generals,* p. 549.
19. J. W. Wheeler-Bennett, *The Nemesis of Power: The German Army in Politics, 1918–1945,* New York, 1961, pp. 698–699.
20. Murphy, *Diplomat Among Warriors,* p. 243.
21. John L. Snell, *Wartime Origins of the East-West Dilemma over Germany,* New Orleans, 1959, pp. 227–228; Manuel Gottlieb, *The German Peace Settlement and the Berlin Crisis,* New York, 1960, pp. 72–73; J. P. Nettl, *The Eastern Zone and Soviet Policy in Germany,*

1945–1950, New York, 1951, pp. 25, 85, 86; Milovan Djilas, *Conversations with Stalin,* trans. by Michael B. Petrovitch, New York, 1962, p. 114.
22. Nettl, *Eastern Zone,* pp. 85–86.
23. Gimbel, *American Occupation of Germany,* p. 9.
24. "Summary of Procedure of Allied Commission on Reparations," undated, Summer 1945, in The Papers of Richard A. Scandrett, Cornell University, Ithaca, N.Y.
25. Byrnes, *Speaking Frankly,* pp. 83–85; Bohlen Minutes, Byrnes-Molotov Meeting, July 23, 1945; Bohlen Minutes, Byrnes-Molotov Meeting, July 27, 1945; Department of State Minutes, Eleventh Meeting of the Foreign Ministers, August 1, 1945, *FR, Potsdam,* II, 274–275, 450–451, 543–562.
26. See William Appleman Williams, *The Tragedy of American Diplomacy,* New York, 1962 rev. ed., pp. 250–251.
27. Quoted in Gottlieb, *German Peace Settlement,* p. 39.
28. Clay to Baruch, August 8, 1945, Baruch MSS.
29. See F. Roy Willis, *The French in Germany, 1945–1949,* Stanford, Calif., 1962, pp. 27–32; Byrnes, *Speaking Frankly,* p. 170; Gottlieb, *German Peace Settlement,* pp. 47–48, 78–79.
30. Gottlieb, *German Peace Settlement,* pp. 83–84.
31. Lewis H. Brown, *Report on Germany,* New York, 1947, p. 31.
32. Gimbel, *American Occupation of Germany,* p. 25.
33. Quoted in B. U. Ratchford and William D. Ross, *Berlin Reparations Assignment: Round One of the German Peace Settlement,* Chapel Hill, N.C., 1947, pp. 83, 89–92; see also Smith, *State of Europe,* p. 128.
34. Will Clayton to Harriman, September 6, 1945, *FR, 1945,* III, 1283–1284.
35. *Ibid.,* pp. 1294–1295.
36. Murphy to Secretary of State, September 30, 1945, *ibid.,* pp. 1320–1321.
37. Gimbel, *American Occupation of Germany,* p. 27.
38. Hammond, "Directives for Germany," pp. 440–441.
39. Ratchford and Ross, *Berlin Reparations Assignment,* pp. 174–176; Clay, *Decision in Germany,* pp. 108–109.
40. Robert Slusser, ed., *Soviet Economic Policy in Postwar Germany: A Collection of Papers by Former Soviet Officials,* New York, 1953, pp. 52–53.
41. Gottlieb, *German Peace Settlement,* pp. 60-61.
42. Sloan to Baruch, October 31, 1945; Baruch to Sloan, November 7, 1945; Sloan to Baruch, November 9, 1945; Baruch to Sloan, November 19, 1945; Sloan to Baruch, November 30, 1945, all in Baruch MSS.
43. See *New York Times,* December 6, 1945, pp. 1 and 5; Winifred Hadsel, "The Ruhr: Object of Allied Rivalries," *Foreign Policy Reports,*

XXII (September 15, 1946), 158-167; Gottlieb, *German Peace Settlement,* p. 68.

44. Clay to Baruch, April 22, 1946, Baruch MSS.
45. Clay, *Decision in Germany,* pp. 120–125. See also LaFeber, *America, Russia and the Cold War,* p. 32.
46. Clay, *Decision in Germany,* pp. 125–126; James Stuart Martin, *All Honorable Men,* Boston, 1950, p. 193; Byrnes, *Speaking Frankly,* pp. 174–175.
47. Gimbel, *American Occupation of Germany,* p. 55.
48. *Ibid.,* pp. 56–57.
49. Molotov, *Problems of Foreign Policy,* pp. 63–68; Nettl, *Eastern Zone,* p. 51; Warburg, *Germany: Bridge or Battleground,* New York, 1947, pp. 101ff; Byrnes, *Speaking Frankly,* pp. 179–187; Clay, *Decision in Germany,* pp. 78–79; Murphy, *Diplomat Among Warriors,* pp. 302–303.
50. *New York Herald Tribune,* September 11, 1946.
51. *NFTC,* 1946, p. 50; Gimbel, *American Occupation of Germany,* p. 117.
52. Smith, *State of Europe,* p. 110; Clay, *Decision in Germany,* pp. 329–330; also, *ibid.,* pp. 200–201.
53. CLXIII (October 5, 1946), 371–373.
54. Warburg, *Germany: Bridge or Battleground,* pp. 380–381; Walter Bedell Smith, *My Three Years in Moscow,* New York, 1950, p. 212; Statement by Molotov, "Provisional Political Organization of Germany," March 22, 1947, Dulles MSS; Dulles to Vandenberg, March 22, 1947, Dulles MSS.
55. Louis A. Wiesner, "The Present Status of the German Trade Unions," April 17, 1947, Dulles MSS.
56. Karl Jaspers, *The Future of Germany,* Chicago, 1967, p. 25.
57. April 21, 1946.
58. Interview with Lucius Clay, Dulles Oral History Project, Dulles MSS.
59. *New York Journal of Commerce,* June 17, 1947.
60. Editorial, "The United States in Europe," XXXVI (July 1947), 2–4.
61. George Wolf to Forrestal, July 7, 1947, Forrestal MSS.
62. Brown, *Report,* pp. 5–8, 15, 24–25, 38, 52–53.
63. Gimbel, *American Occupation of Germany,* p. 170.
64. Press Release, November 27, 1947, Dulles MSS.
65. Gottlieb, *German Peace Settlement,* p. 179.
66. House Foreign Affairs Committee, *Post-War Recovery Program,* p. 357.
67. Clay, *Decision in Germany,* pp. 211–213, 360–361; Smith, *My Three Years,* 245ff; Department of State, "The 'Berlin Crisis,' A Report on the Moscow Discussion," Washington, 1948; Gimbel, *American Occupation of Germany,* p. 113.
68. Djilas, *Conversations,* p. 153; Nettl, *Eastern Zone,* p. 306.
69. Clay to Baruch, March 2, 1948, Baruch MSS.

70. *Forrestal Diaries,* p. 57.
71. *Ibid.*

CHAPTER TEN. *James V. Forrestal and George F. Kennan: Will the Real "Mr. X" Please Stand Up?*

1. Quoted in Arnold A. Rogow, *James Forrestal: A Study of Personality, Politics and Policy,* New York, 1963, p. 331.
2. Forrestal to Bullitt, June 6, 1945; Forrestal to Cass Canfield, June 19, 1946, Forrestal MSS.
3. Rogow, *Forrestal,* pp. 108–113.
4. *Forrestal Diaries,* June 30, 1945, pp. 72–73; see also Rogow, *Forrestal,* pp. 144–145.
5. Forrestal to Moley, February 13, 1946, Forrestal MSS; the draft is noted by Rogow, *Forrestal,* p. 148.
6. Forrestal to Lippmann, January 7, 1946, Forrestal MSS.
7. Forrestal to Father Maurice Sheehy, June 7, 1946; Forrestal to William C. Patten, September 2, 1947, Forrestal MSS.
8. Forrestal to Donald K. Dowd, September 10, 1947, Forrestal MSS.
9. Rogow, *Forrestal,* pp. 335–337; *Forrestal Diaries,* March 3, 1947, pp. 247–248.
10. Lamont to Forrestal, June 6, 1947, Forrestal MSS.
11. Forrestal to Ernest Havermann, August 26, 1947, Forrestal MSS.
12. Forrestal to Stanton Griffis, October 31, 1947, Forrestal MSS.
13. Kennan, *Memoirs,* p. 355.
14. *Ibid.,* p. 293.
15. "Memorandum," February 26, 1946, Forrestal MSS; *Forrestal Diaries,* p. 136.
16. Lasch, *The New Radicalism in America,* New York, 1965, pp. 304–305.
17. Kennan, *Memoirs,* p. 57.
18. *Ibid.,* pp. 70–73, emphasis added.
19. *Ibid.,* pp. 133–134.
20. *Ibid.,* p. 359.
21. *Ibid.,* p. 358.
22. *Ibid.,* p. 356.
23. Forrestal to Clarence Dillon, February 11, 1947, Forrestal MSS.
24. Forrestal to Paul Smith, March 10, 1947, Forestall MSS.
25. Forrestal to Henry Cabot Lodge, May 27, 1947; O. E. Hunt to Forrestal, August 25, 1947, Forrestal MSS.
26. Halle, *Cold War as History,* p. 106.
27. Halle, *Civilization and Foreign Policy,* New York, 1955, p. 167.
28. Kennan, *Memoirs,* p. 367.
29. *Ibid.,* p. 365.

30. *Ibid.,* pp. 210-211.
31. *Ibid.,* pp. 212-213.
32. Pp. 312-313.
33. "Memorandum by the Counselor of Embassy in the Soviet Union," undated, 1945, *FR, 1945,* V, 853–860.
34. Halle, *Cold War as History,* p. 39.
35. Rogow, *Forrestal,* pp. 151–153.
36. Kennan to Forrestal, October 7, 1946, Forrestal MSS; on Stalin and the purges, see Kennan's review of Robert Conquest, *The Great Terror,* New York, 1968, in *New York Times Book Review,* October 27, 1968, pp. 2–3.
37. John T. Connor to Kennan, October 29, 1946; Kennan to Connor, October 30, 1946, Forrestal MSS.
38. Quotations from a copy of the lecture in Forrestal MSS.
39. Franklin A. Lindsay to Staff, November 12, 1946, Baruch MSS.
40. On domestic change thesis, see Coral Bell, *Negotiation from Strength,* especially Chap. 1.
41. *New York Times Book Review,* October 27, 1968, pp. 2–3.
42. Quotations from "The Sources of Soviet Conduct," in *American Diplomacy, 1900–1950,* Chicago, 1951, pp. 89–106.
43. Bell, *Negotiation from Strength,* p. 23.
44. *Stalin's Foreign Policy Reappraised,* Cambridge, Mass., 1963, pp. 13–17.
45. *Ibid.,* p. 29; quotation from Marshall D. Shulman, *Beyond the Cold War,* New Haven, Conn., 1966, pp. 8–9.

CHAPTER ELEVEN. *The Cold War in History*

1. "Origins of the Cold War," *FAQ,* XLVI (October 1967), 22–52.
2. *The Cold War and Its Origins,* 2 vols., New York, 1961, I, 265.
3. Cordell Hull, *The Memoirs of Cordell Hull,* 2 vols., New York, 1948, II, 1248.
4. Villard to Hull, August 2, 1945, Villard MSS.
5. New York, 1965, p. 31; *From Yalta to Vietnam,* London, 1967, pp. 19–21. Horowitz's new book, *Empire and Revolution,* New York, 1969, redirects the emphasis of readers of the *Free World Colussus* as follows: "The proposition that U.S. cold war containment policies can only be understood as policies of containing social revolution rather than national expansion is a central thesis of my book" (p. 53).
6. New York, 1964, p. 13.
7. "The Trump Card," *New York Review of Books,* VIII (June 15, 1967), 6–12.
8. Schlesinger, "Origins," pp. 22–52.
9. Boston, 1948, p. 94–95.

10. The argument is summed up concisely in Christopher Lasch's article, "The Cold War, Revisited and Pre-Visioned," *New York Times Magazine,* January 14, 1968.
11. "The Labor Angle," May 12, 1945, p. 98.
12. E. H. Carr, "Two Currents in World Labor," *FAQ,* XXV (October 1946), 732–781.
13. Wallace's speech can be found in Graebner, *Ideas and Diplomacy,* pp. 701-705.
14. *Cold War as History,* p. 103.
15. U.S. Senate, Committee on Foreign Relations, *Hearings: Nomination of Charles E. Bohlen to Be Ambassador to the Soviet Union,* 83rd Cong., 1st sess., Washington, 1953, p. 5, *passim.*
16. Kennan, *Memoirs,* p. 367.
17. *Beyond the Cold War,* p. 8.
18. "Thoughts on Soviet Foreign Policy, and What to Do About It," *Life,* XX (June 3 and 10, 1946), 112–118ff, 118–120ff.
19. Published in Raymond Dennett and Robert K. Turner, eds., *Documents on American Foreign Relations,* IX, Princeton, 1949, 616.

A NOTE ON SOURCES

"Something of the feel and taste of the late 1940's has slipped into oblivion," H. Stuart Hughes wrote in the August 1969 issue of *Commentary* in an article entitled, "The Second Year of the Cold War: A Memoir and an Anticipation." If past experience in the field of diplomatic history is a guide, the availability of archival records will not reclaim that feel and taste of which Hughes speaks. At present much cannot be done because of the lack of such documents. They will be sifted by historians in the years ahead as governments finally unlock their secrets, but the variety of interpretations probably will not diminish, only become more burdened with "evidence." Making do with the facts one can find now may be no more a distortion of the past than the process of documenting "secret" diplomacy, and often leads to insights and revelations as sure as those produced later.

All the same, one wishes the records were available—if only to test conclusions reached in his own research. Professor Hughes's article is particularly tantalizing in this regard. (It became available after this book was already in type.) Hughes notes that he was a second-level State Department official whose dissenting views "oscillated between weary resignation and occasional explosions of wrath at the obtuseness of the conventional judgments." He records that increasing Soviet pressure on the democratically elected government in Hungary in 1947 prompted him to write in a memorandum: "It was not the democratic character of the Hungarian government that brought down upon it the wrath of the Soviet Union. It was its foreign policy of cultivating the favor of the Western democracies, particularly the United States." Access to now-secret records will not change the broad outlines of such matters as these. My own interpretation of these events in Eastern Europe, as set forth in the chapter on Secretary of State James F. Byrnes, is similiar—in other words, in the context of postwar Europe, collective security and Byrnes's public diplomacy were incompatible. I reached this conclusion by reading Byrnes's *Speaking Frankly* (1947); the speeches and documents published in the *State Department Bulletin,* especially the note on Soviet exploitation of Hungarian resources published on August 4, 1946; and V. M. Molotov's dire warning to Hungarian and American officials that Eastern European questions such as Truman's plan for the Danube could not be settled bilaterally between those states and the United States in private negotiations, or multilaterally through majoritarian diplomacy at international peace conferences. Moltov set forth the Russian position quite clearly at the time, and it has been available since 1949 in *Problems of Foreign Policy*. Whatever secret plans the Kremlin had then or later, Molotov's statements did not conceal the Soviet view that semi-independent governments in Hungary and Bulgaria existed only at Russia's sufferance.

What seems so startling as we re-examine the first years of the Cold War as "history" is that American influence in Eastern Europe was not snuffed out all at once in 1945 by the presence of the Red Army. In fact, America's influence there was perhaps greater than it had ever been, and this encouraged some policy-makers to believe that much could be accomplished through moral condemnation, nonrecognition, and economic diplomacy. Certainly this is the view implied in Mark Ethridge and C. E. Black's "Negotiating in the Balkans," published with other papers in Raymond Dennett and Joseph E. Johnson, eds., *Negotiating with the Russians* (1951), and confirmed in the published records of the Potsdam Conference and the 1945 Foreign Ministers' meeting. As a dissenter to orthodox policies in 1947, Professor Hughes discounted the likelihood of success along this line of endeavor; as a dissenter to "revisionist" writings twenty years later, he discounts the seriousness of American efforts to get the Russians out of Eastern Europe. Whether or not the Truman Doctrine ended these efforts because of more pressing needs elsewhere, or merely saved them from the embarrassment of outright failure, Byrnes continued to believe that the attempt to keep Eastern

Europe open had been worthwhile and at least minimally successful. He so stated in his testimony before the Senate Foreign Relations Committee in early 1947, reprinted in *Treaties of Peace with Italy, Rumania, Bulgaria, and Hungary* (1947).

Issues in Eastern Europe, however, were part of a more general picture of chaos which had nothing to do with "spheres of influence," and which, it seems to me, is not explained by the neorealist interpretation. Gabriel Kolko's first of several projected volumes, *The Politics of War: The World and United States Foreign Policy, 1943–1945* (1968) poses such questions in their fullest statement. One can admire Kolko's achievement of 685 pages, yet disagree with the first sentence on the first page that the history of the politics of World War II can conveniently and legitimately begin with the year 1943. In fact, by that time Roosevelt's "second-front" diplomacy had already come a cropper and the process of illusion-making had begun. Though Kolko reaches for background in succeeding pages, a full appreciation of America's approach to the politics of World War II and its reactions to leftist movements in Europe cannot be gained without a reading of Martin Herz, *Beginnings of the Cold War* (1966); Margaret Dewar, *Soviet Trade with Eastern Europe* (1951); Barbara Ward, "Europe Debates Nationalization," in *Foreign Affairs,* July 1946; and Robert Divine, *Second Chance: The Triumph of Internationalism in America During World War II* (1967). Several other books could be suggested; the point is simply that these four place Soviet policies and Western reactions in both an immediate and a traditional framework. The outlook for an open world based on liberalism, capitalism, and individualism was directly imperiled, as Barbara Ward suggested, by the debate over nationalism from right and left.

As I have tried to suggest, this issue is the key to an understanding of Anglo-American relations during the war and the developing Cold War, and of the U.S. effort to contain the victory of the British Labour party in 1945. No book provides a more satisfactory introduction to this situation than Richard N. Gardner's *Sterling-Dollar Diplomacy* (revised edition, 1969). His excellent bibliography includes relevant publications and unpublished papers. Also of unusual value is correspondence between Will Clayton and Bernard Baruch, and between Baruch and congressional leaders, recently opened to scholars in the Baruch Papers. Baruch disagreed with the rationale behind the Anglo-American Loan Agreement of 1945. James V. Forrestal's deep anxiety about the Labour victory, on the other hand, led him to take a different position on that question, and to take strong ideological positions on other issues in pursuit of the spiritual truth of the Russian-American conflict. His diary notes, edited by Walter Millis and published in 1951 as *The Forrestal Diaries*, help to explain why Walter LaFeber has entitled his excellent survey of the Cold War era, *America, Russia, and the Cold War, 1945–1966* (1967). Readers of both books will quickly discover my indebtedness to Professor LaFeber.

The unavailability of archival material naturally leads to greater reliance upon personal memoirs; in a study of this nature there are special advantages even to that situation. Comparison of *Speaking Frankly* with Byrnes's later *All in One Lifetime* (1958) reveal several differences of emphasis and interpretation on atomic policy, and the first admission that the Russian application for an American loan had in fact been placed in the "lost" file. Robert Murphy's *Diplomat Among Warriors* (1964) and Joseph M. Jones's *The Fifteen Weeks* (1955) reconfirm the need to explore Anglo-American relations in order to understand the development of the Cold War, a point often missed by the orthodox and by certain "revisionists." David Lilienthal's *Journals* (1964) are indispensable to understanding the origins of the "Baruch Plan." Walter Bedell Smith's *My Three Years in Moscow* (1950) adds little to what can be found in other sources. General Lucius D. Clay's *Decision in Germany* (1950) and Arthur H. Vandenberg's *Private Papers* (1952), on the other hand, provide rich sources of material now unavailable elsewhere. George F. Kennan's *Memoirs, 1925–1950* (1967) are at the center of the final problem posed in this study. Of all memoirs of the early Cold War era, however, the most important are those of President Truman, published in 1955 and 1956. A comparison of his recollections with the printed records of the Potsdam Conference and the complete records of his public statements and news conferences (since published as one of the volumes in *Public Papers of the Presidents of the United States*) raises anew a great many questions about the early Cold war period. The President's proposal on European waterways is a principal case in point.

The *Public Papers* may never again be as important to the historian as they are for the Truman period. The records of Franklin D. Roosevelt's press conferences remain unpublished except for those in the Samuel I. Rosenman edition of *Public Papers and Addresses of Franklin D. Roosevelt* (13 vols., 1938–1950). And, beginning with Dwight D. Eisenhower's presidency in 1953, the press conference became more public. Television allowed less and less opportunity for indirect quotation, until the press conference became something different from what it had been. In the Truman years, the press conference retained its semi-anonymity and its spontaneity. These qualities were essential to the relationships established by the President with the correspondents; and to the historian interested today in seeing how the President's mind was working on crucial issues, they are equally important.

Another major source for this study has been a variety of congressional hearings. They are cited in the footnotes, hence I will comment only generally here about these documents. Congressional hearings are, of course, most useful when Congress is in a nasty mood or is at least skeptical of administration arguments. While bipartisanism on foreign policy during war and Cold War never quite shut off criticism nor destroyed the value of the congressional hearing, the search for meaning becomes less fruitful after the debate on the Truman Doctrine and the Marshall Plan. The reader must probe the testimony of government officials and ask himself the questions left unasked by the subdued Senators and Representatives. In the period covered by this book, this is usually not necessary. Late abdication by Congress of its responsibilities in the area of foreign policy was popularly thought of in the 1950's as a product of the complex nature of the situation, including the new missile technology. We now know that it was much more a result of Cold War hysteria. The testimony of Under Secretary of State Nicholas Katzenbach that congressional approval of the Gulf of Tonkin resolution amounted to a declaration of war exploded more than one technological myth in Congress, and woke up Senators who had been spellbound since the days of Dean Acheson.

Though I have by no means surveyed all periodicals and newspapers for the period 1941–1949, I was much impressed by what a systematic review of several of them revealed about the postwar atmosphere in the United States. What came through particularly clearly was that while the Soviets were indeed idealized in journals of all persuasions during the war, there was a good understanding among intellectuals and opinion-makers of the perils and paradoxes of World War II diplomacy. At the time of Senator Vandenberg's January 1945 speech, there was even some recognition of what would be required to save the Grand Alliance or America's traditional policy of opposition to spheres of influence from the politics of postponement. But after Potsdam a curious fatalism about the course of Russian-American relations set in, erasing such doubts. Even those "liberal" journals that joined the anti-communist crusade rather late exhibited this attitude. From the middle of the war on, most journals thought (with the President) that there must be some way to use America's economic power either to build bridges between East and West after the war, or, more pessimistically, to break down Anglo-Russian spheres of influence. It was the common assumption of the *Nation, Business Week, Fortune,* and even of H. Stuart Hughes as late as 1947 that this must be the answer. Yet no one ever found a way to do this. As the magazine writers and editors of 1946 and 1947 were aware—for example, Reinhold Niebuhr in the *Nation*—one had to be sure first not only of England, but of France, Italy, and Germany, especially Germany.

Secondary works appearing in the footnotes are those referred to by most authors who have studied the origins of the Cold War. Even the diligent Cold War historian can scarcely keep up with the appearance of new books on the subject. There are several important older studies which I have consulted but have not had occasion to cite. Among these are John Lukacs, *History of the Cold War* (1961); Richard J. Barnet, *Who Wants Disarmament?* (1960); Gaddis Smith, *American Diplomacy During the Second World War, 1941–1945* (1965); Norman Graebner, *Cold War Diplomacy* (1962); Philip Mosely, *The Kremlin in World Politics* (1960); and J. P. Morray, *From Yalta to Disarmament* (1961). Studies which do not pertain directly to the issues discussed but which have deeply influenced my own approach to general Russian-American questions include Edward H. Zabriskie, *American-Russian Relations in the Far East: A Study in Diplomacy and Power Politics, 1895–1914* (1946); Howard K. Beale, *Theodore Roosevelt and America's Rise to World Power* (1956); Arno Mayer, *Wilson vs. Lenin: Political Origins of the New Diplomacy* (1958) and *Politics and Diplomacy of Peacemaking* (1967); and Herbert Hoover, *The Ordeal of Woodrow Wilson* (1958). Lest the original achievements of William Appleman Williams in this field be in any way diminished by talk about the "Wisconsin School" of American diplomatic history, I wish to call the reader's attention to Christopher Lasch's "The Cold War, Revisited and Pre-visioned," *New York Times Magazine,* January 14, 1968, for an assessment of Williams' *American-Russian Relations, 1781–1947* (1952) and *The Tragedy of American Diplomacy* (1959). As H. Stuart Hughes notes, the years have vindicated those few independent minds who labored in the late 1940's and 1950's under the suspicion of being "soft on communism," quixotic, or even subversive. With Hughes, who only now feels sufficiently vindicated in his earlier dissent to conclude that the "cold war and the fate of the population under Soviet control were separable issues and that an emphasis on the one was of little help to the other," one can also refuse the notion that America's "anti-communism was evil or misguided all along the line." Certainly the illusions erected by American policy-makers after World War II cannot be reduced to such simplistic terms. The reasons why options seemed closed go beyond conspiracy or malevolence on either side.

INDEX

INDEX

A NOTE ON THE AUTHOR

Lloyd C. Gardner is Professor of History at Rutgers University. Born in Delaware, Ohio, he studied at Ohio Wesleyan University and the University of Wisconsin, and was a Woodrow Wilson Fellow. Mr. Gardner is the author of *Economic Aspects of New Deal Diplomacy* and editor of *A Different Frontier*. He lives in East Brunswick, New Jersey, with his wife Nancy and their three children.